ROMAN SOCIAL HISTORY

This book contains many of the sources that a student in Roman social history will need in a single handy volume.

Tim G. Parkin and Arthur J. Pomeroy have assembled here a wide range of ancient texts in their own translations, ranging from the essential to the little-known and previously unavailable, focusing on the late republic and the first two centuries AD. Arranged thematically, all sources are quick and easy to find, are preceded by a readable introduction, and are accompanied by notes that guide and advise the student. The authors also provide summaries of previous scholarship in the field with bibliographies that will open the reader to further resources.

Rather than concentrating on the elite, a tiny fraction of Roman society, Parkin and Pomeroy also include material on the Roman peasantry, workers, and slaves, and view it all through a modern sociological lens: it explains Roman society in terms of its power structures. Their notes incorporate demography and criminology among many other contemporary disciplines to build a complete picture of the 'sociology of ancient Rome'.

Topics include:

- Social class
- Family
- Education
- Economy
- Leisure and games.

Including maps, chronologies, and useful references on measures and currency, this book is the complete introductory resource for students of Roman social history, and presents with clarity and vividness a rich and diverse society.

Tim G. Parkin is Professor of Ancient History at the University of Manchester.

Arthur J. Pomeroy is Associate Professor of Classics at the Victoria University of Wellington, New Zealand.

ROMAN SOCIAL HISTORY

A sourcebook

Tim G. Parkin and
Arthur J. Pomeroy

Routledge
Taylor & Francis Group

LONDON AND NEW YORK

First published 2007
by Routledge
2 Park Square, Milton Park, Abingdon, Oxon OX14 4RN

Simultaneously published in the USA and Canada
by Routledge
270 Madison Avenue, New York, NY 10016

Reprinted 2008

Transferred to Digital Printing 2009

Routledge is an imprint of the Taylor & Francis Group, an informa business

© 2007 Tim G. Parkin and Arthur J. Pomeroy

Typeset in Sabon and Helvetica by
Florence Production Ltd, Stoodleigh, Devon
Printed and bound in Great Britain by
TJI Digital, Padstow, Cornwall

British Library Cataloguing in Publication Data
A catalogue record for this book is available from
the British Library

Library of Congress Cataloging in Publication Data
Roman social history: a sourcebook/edited by Tim Parkin and
Arthur J. Pomeroy.
p. cm.
Includes bibliographical references and index.
1. Social history – To 500. 2. Rome – History.
3. Rome – Social conditions. I. Parkin, Tim G.
II. Pomeroy, Arthur John, 1953–
HN10.R7R66 2007
937 – dc22
2007007663

ISBN10: 0–415–42674–X (hbk)
ISBN10: 0–415–42675–8 (pbk)
ISBN10: 0–203–96084–X (ebk)

ISBN13: 978–0–415–42674–9 (hbk)
ISBN13: 978–0–415–42675–6 (pbk)
ISBN13: 978–0–203–96084–4 (ebk)

CONTENTS

Chronology and Roman emperors   vii
Acknowledgements   viii
List of maps   ix

Introduction   1

1 Social classes   3

2 Demography   43

3 Family and household   72

4 Education   136

5 Slavery   154

6 Poverty   205

7 The economy   244

8 The legal system and courts   292

9 Leisure and games   328

   Appendix A: Life expectancy   354
   Appendix B: The Roman status hierarchy   357
   Appendix C: Greek and Roman weights, measures,
                and coinage   359

Index locorum   361
General index   369

CHRONOLOGY AND ROMAN EMPERORS

Most of the material presented comes from the period of the early and high empire (approximately the first two centuries AD). However, where material from an earlier period (particularly the late republican period – the last century BC) or later (up to the fourth century AD) can reasonably be considered to illustrate behaviour current in the early empire, this has also been included.

Roman emperors (first two centuries AD)

Augustus	27 BC–AD 14
Tiberius	14–37
Gaius	37–41
Claudius	41–54
Nero	54–68
Galba	68–9
Otho	69
Vitellius	69
Vespasian	69–79
Titus	79–81
Domitian	81–96
Nerva	96–8
Trajan	98–117
Hadrian	117–38
Antoninus Pius	138–61
Marcus Aurelius	161–80 (with Lucius Verus 161–9)
Commodus	180–92
Pertinax	193
Didius Julianus	193
Septimius Severus	193–211
Caracalla	198–217

ACKNOWLEDGEMENTS

This collection is based on materials collected by the authors to assist in the teaching of Roman social history in New Zealand and Australia over the last two decades. In particular, we wish to acknowledge the influence of our former teacher at Victoria University of Wellington, Alex Scobie. Alex's knowledge of the ancient world, particularly the world of folklore and the novel, and of the abuse of ancient models in the modern world has been a continuing inspiration to his students. Many of the readings in this collection were originally selected by Alex and we hope that their wider distribution will be a small tribute to his work.

The translations are the work of the authors, but obviously build on the work of numerous predecessors. Arthur Pomeroy would like to thank the PBRF fund of the School of Art History, Classics, and Religious Studies at Victoria University for enabling him to employ a student assistant as the project approached completion; the FHSS Research Committee for assistance for proofreading and indexing; and also Anneliese Parkin and Robert Knapp. Tim Parkin thanks Roslynne Bell, Jane Gardner, Siobhan O'Rourke and April Pudsey.

We would also like to thank our students in social history and Latin language classes as well as supervisees over the years for their constant probing and questions that have enabled us to revise and improve this material.

MAPS

1   The Roman empire in the age of Trajan   x

2   The city of Rome in the second century AD   xii
    (*see* Key, p. xiv)

3   Travel times in the Roman empire and limits of vine and
    olive cultivation   xv

4   Trade routes in the Roman world   xvi

Map 1 The Roman empire in the age of Trajan

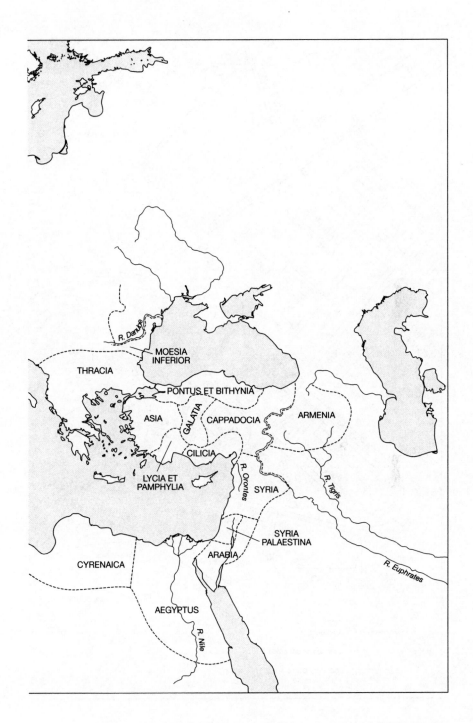

Source: From Martin Goodman, *The Roman World 44 BC–AD 180* (1997: 76–7).

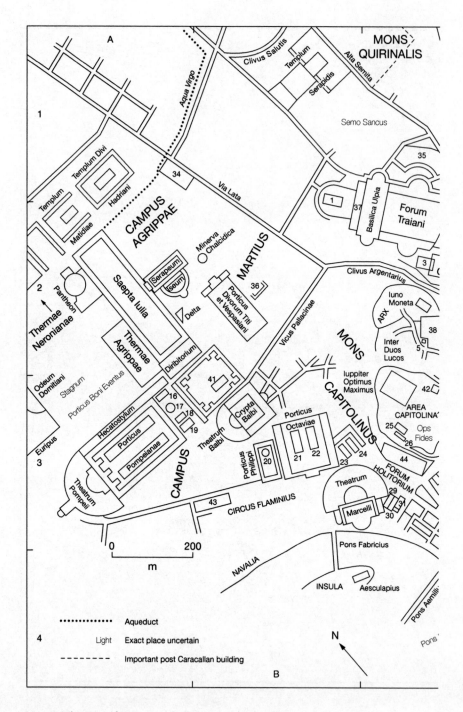

Map 2 The city of Rome in the second century AD

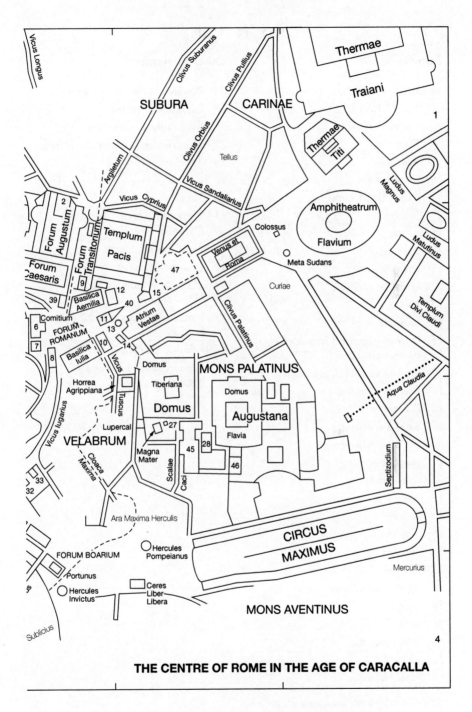

THE CENTRE OF ROME IN THE AGE OF CARACALLA

Source: From R.J.A. Talbert, *Atlas of Classical History* (1988: 121).

KEY TO MAP 2

Temples

1 Divus Traianus.
2 Mars Ultor.
3 Venus Genetrix.
4 Minerva.
5 Vediovis.
6 Concordia.
7 Divus Vespasianus.
8 Saturnus.
9 Ianus?
10 Castores.
11 Divus Iulius.
12 Divus Antoninus.
13 Vesta.
14 Iuturna.
15 Penates (the form indicated is post-Caracallan).
16 Iuturna or Iuno Curritis.
17 Fortuna Huiusce Diei.
18 Feronia.
19 Lares Permarini.
20 Hercules Musarum.
21 Iuppiter Stator.
22 Iuno Regina.
23 Apollo Sosianus.
24 Bellona.
25 Iuppiter Tonans.
26 Fortuna Primigenia.
27 Iuppiter Victor.
28 Apollo Palatinus.
29 Ianus.
30 Spes.
31 Iuno Sospita.
32 Fortuna.
33 Mater Matuta.

(Other temples are indicated by the name of the deity worshipped there.)

Other monuments

34 Porticus Vipsania or Minucia?
35 Markets of Trajan.
36 Unidentified porticus.
37 Libraries and column of Trajan.
38 Tabularium.
39 Curia.
40 Regia.
41 Porticus Minucia? Templum Nympharum?
42 Ara Gentis Iuliae?
43 Unidentified porticus.
44 Market-building of Forum Holitorium.
45 Houses of Augustus and his family.
46 Palatine Libraries.
47 Site of the later basilica of Maxentius.

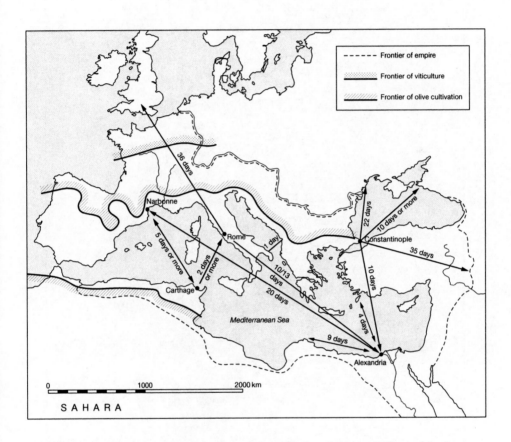

Map 3 Travel times in the Roman empire and limits of vine and olive cultivation
Source: From M. Maas, *Readings in Late Antiquity* (2000: xxvii).

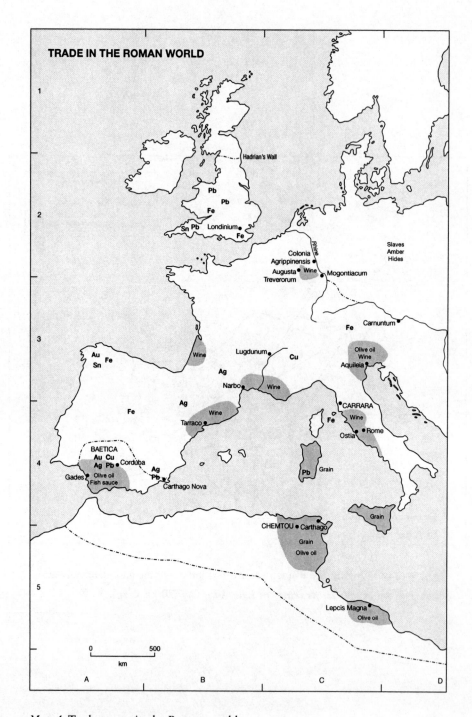

TRADE IN THE ROMAN WORLD

Map 4 Trade routes in the Roman world

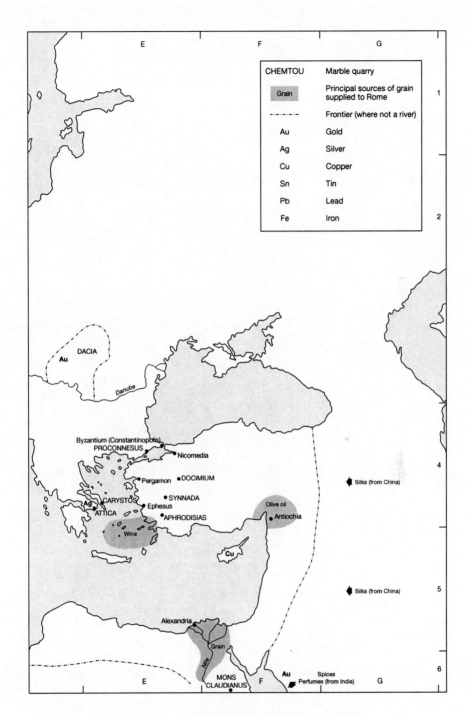

CHEMTOU	Marble quarry
Grain	Principal sources of grain supplied to Rome
–·–·–	Frontier (where not a river)
Au	Gold
Ag	Silver
Cu	Copper
Sn	Tin
Pb	Lead
Fe	Iron

DACIA
Au

Danube

Byzantium (Constantinopolis)
PROCONNESUS
Nicomedia

Pergamon ● DOCIMIUM

● SYNNADA
CARYSTOS
Ag Ephesus
ATTICA ●APHRODISIAS

Wine

Olive oil
● Antiochia

Cu

Silks (from China)

Silks (from China)

Alexandria

Grain

Nile

MONS
CLAUDIANUS

Au
Spices
Perfumes (from India)

Source: From R.J.A. Talbert, *Atlas of Classical History* (1988: 124–5).

xvii

INTRODUCTION

The last twenty years have seen a remarkable increase in interest in the investigation of the Roman world from a sociological viewpoint. While the daily habits of the Romans were once seen as of general interest (as witnessed by the popularity of Jérome Carcopino's *Daily Life in Ancient Rome* (1939, English translation 1940) and other similar studies), they were never treated in the same systematic fashion as Roman political and military events. Various factors have since led to a basic change in the examination of the Roman world: an interest in Roman economy and slavery, derived from the economic models of Marx and later German historians, such as Weber and Polanyi; a desire to recover the place of women and the family in Roman life, in part as the result of the rise of feminism; and a wish to outline the nature of population structures and their effects on life, which can now be attempted using more sophisticated modelling techniques derived from the social sciences.

To no small degree this also reflects changes in attitude to the ancient world during the twentieth century. The Roman world is no longer seen as an ideal to be emulated, but as one remarkably interesting human society among many. And just as sociological studies have revealed a wide range of shapes of family and various group behaviours in the modern world, so it is clear that there is no monolithic 'Roman' society. There were, of course, models recommended, especially by those in power (as, for instance, by the Emperor Augustus' marriage legislation). But Roman families in practice were as likely to differ from any norm as any modern family may vary from the 2.4 children with surviving mother and father nuclear unit that was once the model in the western world. The Roman world covers a huge geographical area around the Mediterranean and even within Italy there was considerable variation in practices according to place and status in society. Add the changes in custom that may have been gradual, but are substantial when centuries of Roman rule are taken into account, and it is clear that the diversity of the Roman empire may be its most salient feature.

For the investigation of Roman society, we have chosen as our starting point Peter Garnsey and Richard Saller's *The Roman Empire: Economy,*

1

Society and Culture (London, 1987). Work up to the mid-1980s is well summarised in this book and many of the trends in more recent work are signposted. The bibliographies that follow each chapter highlight the most important work on each topic since then.

Historical study is not, however, simply knowing what has been written on topics, but how those ideas were developed from ancient evidence. As a result, we have chosen to compile a sourcebook of material that illustrates important themes in the social history of the Roman empire of the first two centuries AD. There are other sourcebooks on aspects of Roman social history already available that are noted in our bibliographies, and material of varying value (from the very useful to the woefully mistaken) on the Internet. It is our hope that the wide selection that we present will be useful in popularising the field as a unified whole (rather than as separate studies of the Roman family or slavery or law, for instance) and that the range of material and its reliability will make this a valuable teaching resource. The translations are our own: it is hoped that this will give some consistency to the material and also help to bring out salient points in the selections.

The main source of information on the Roman world is its literary tradition, which has been preserved in much more substantial quantities than non-literary material such as papyri or inscriptions. But, because of its nature, literary evidence needs to be approached with care. It may display normative functions following the ideals of its upper-class producers or may portray deliberately abnormal events for excitement and the edification of the reader. To compensate for this, we have sought to offer less commonly cited evidence as well, including tables derived from inscriptional and archaeological material, and to give some guidance in our notes.

If there is a unifying theme for the wide range of material we present, it is our belief that Roman society is best explained in terms of its power structures. The Roman world was strongly hierarchical, with the balance of power clearly marked out not only in the relationship between master and slave, but also within families and even at public events such as the races and gladiatorial games. The Roman world shows both untrammelled capitalism and remarkable state intervention in the economy (e.g. in imperial monopolies). A great deal was spent on public buildings and display, but almost nothing on the impoverished – subsidies were as much for the benefit of the well off as they were for the needy. These paradoxes are, we hope, illustrated throughout this sourcebook.

1

SOCIAL CLASSES

An essential feature of the Roman world is the importance of hierarchies: as there was no strong governmental intervention in daily life, it was essential to fit in to a social group in order to gain assistance from one's peers and to facilitate patronage connections with those more powerful. The Roman senate and equestrian order were the most powerful groupings, and outside Rome the members of the upper classes, such as town councillors or even tribal chiefs, were assimilated to a similar status. These privileged few – probably less than 0.1 per cent of the population – dominated the vast majority beneath them. Yet all were subject to the power of the emperor. Traditionally, the Roman constitution was believed to be a mixture of the three main types (kingship, oligarchy, and democracy), avoiding the perils of each (**1.1**). In the empire, however, it is clear that rule by the best man (*optimus princeps*) dominated other sectors of the community. The imperial system of government served to protect the prestige of the higher ranked, both at Rome and in the provinces (**1.2**).

After the establishment of the principate by Augustus, the emperor (*princeps*) could be viewed as positioned somewhere between two poles: he could be viewed as a mediator, who ensured the stability of the empire but did not encroach on traditional rights (**1.3**); or as a Hellenistic monarch, assisted by courtiers, but with essentially autocratic powers, as can be shown by a personal oath of allegiance by subjects (**1.4**) and direct action by the sovereign to benefit his people (**1.5**). Certainly, the prospect of divinisation clearly indicated that the emperor was someone who surpassed all other mortals in his age (**1.6**). Associates of the emperor also flourished: there were informal groups of advisers who could be referred to as the ruler's 'friends' (*amici*) (**1.7**), while the female members of the emperor's family also gained reflected prestige and possible power (**1.8**).

The senate, traditionally the preserve of the male members of upper-class families who devoted their lives to public service and its rewards (**1.9**), now was expanded to include people from throughout Italy (**1.10**) and other areas of the empire who would support the ruler, undertake traditional administrative tasks, and offer advice on areas of their expertise (**1.11, 1.12**).

3

Barred from economic activity in the public sector (**1.13**), senators were in return rewarded with highly visible public privileges (**1.14, 1.15, 1.16**). Their public appearances were, however, regulated to ensure that there was no reduction in the dignity of the order (**1.17**). Their prestige extended also to other members of their families, including females (**1.18, 1.19**); imperial women were also required not to bring shame upon their status group (**1.20**). The power of the upper classes usually protected them against any attacks from those beneath their status, even if their inferiors tried to enlist the authority of the emperor on their side (**1.21**) or the collective opinion of provincial subjects (**1.22**). Indeed travel by such high-status persons might readily turn into an exemplary procession, illustrating the power and wealth of the persons making their way through the common crowd (**1.23**).

Associated with this group, but not bound to a life of state service and attendance at senatorial meetings, were the equestrians (*equites*). Originally derived from the group of wealthy non-senators who were privileged to guarantee the upkeep of a horse for state service (**1.24**), their obligations and rights were codified under the early emperors (**1.25, 1.26**) and the rank became a lower-level entry into the ruling class (**1.27**). The possibility of serving the emperor in postings outside those traditionally held by the senators also increased their status (**1.28, 1.29**). In a particularly interesting development, a female status title equivalent to *eques* was created in the second and third centuries AD (**1.30**).

Decurions, the councillors of Romanised towns (**1.28, 1.31, 1.32, 1.33**), and *bouleutai*, their Greek equivalents, performed administrative functions similar to those of senators and equestrians in their local areas. The regulations listing those who were eligible for selection as decurions also indicate the importance of fulfilment of military service, while revealing how some well-regarded professions might also lead to social embarrassment (**1.34**).

The group of public servants referred to as *apparitores*, the secretaries, heralds, and messengers who were listed on panels at Rome, gained prestige from their close association with power (**1.35, 1.36**), although many were only nominally available for public service and used their enrolment on the panels purely for social distinction. Some ex-slaves might even rise to become the patrons of their towns (**1.37**). Horace's depiction of Philippus' amusement at Vulteius' expense offers a striking depiction of the relations between the upper classes and the aspiring members of the populace, particularly the hopes of the latter to move into more reputable agricultural investments (**1.38**).

The rest of the free populace were viewed by their superiors as an amorphous mass who gained what little status they might possess from their relationship to the more powerful. Some within this group suffered from marked negative prestige, with resulting social disabilities. Cicero's well-known remarks on occupations and trade (**1.39**) illustrate this pattern

4

well, while suggesting that some at the upper echelons of the general populace might move up into a higher status category. The shrewd would hide their wealth in a veneer of respectability (1.40), while obvious get-rich-quick schemes might end disastrously (1.41). Funerary inscriptions suggest that many were not as successful as they may have wished to be (1.42), although some clearly prospered (1.43). Most urban dwellers would simply have got on with their lives, celebrating their trade as an indication of some continuity of employment (1.44, 1.45). Some engaged in fixed-term employment for regular wages, although this arrangement seems particularly suited to those employed in state monopolies, such as the mines throughout the empire (1.46). Ex-slaves (often working as tradespeople (1.47, 1.48)) and slaves, although superficially at the bottom of the status ladder, tended to draw their prestige from their masters and patrons, as is indicated in Chapter 5. The indigent sought whatever food and shelter they might obtain (for their lives, see Chapter 6). The predictions of the dream-interpreter Artemidorus suggest that there was a common concern about the preservation or improvement of status in all sections of the community (1.49).

Given the relatively undeveloped nature of the Roman economy, the majority of the populace would have been engaged in agriculture. While some would have been freeholders, it is likely that most would have been tenants (*coloni*) or similarly tied labourers, or agrarian slaves. Some may have achieved spectacular success and moved from dependent to dominating status, such as the North African example of the harvester from Mactar (1.50), but most would have left very little trace in either written or archaeological sources. On rare occasions, notice was taken, as when the imperial government intervened on behalf of its tenants in North Africa (1.51).

1.1 Cicero's defence of a mixed constitution and a warning against the perils of democracy, as adapted from Plato

In the late 50s BC, Cicero wrote a dialogue, based on Plato's *Republic* and with a historical setting of 129 BC, in which he sought to uphold what he saw as the traditional values of Roman society. In the following passages, Scipio Aemilianus is depicted as explaining that a society and its rules develop naturally, but that some forms of government fail to correspond to communal needs. In a properly organised community all have legal rights (*ius*) and the right to participate in decisions that affect the group as a whole, but there will need to be a hierarchical system of honour and office (*gradus dignitatis*). This corresponds approximately to the Roman governmental system of the republican period where the assembly of male citizens made decisions on legislation and matters of war and peace (the *Res Publica* is defined by Cicero as affairs affecting the general populace), but high offices were restricted to those of good birth (that is, to those from a senatorial background). In the first passage, rule of only one man or a few is rejected as leaving out the people, and rule of the people as undermining social structure. Cicero chooses what he considers to be the best historical examples of each type of rule: Cyrus the Great of Persia for kingship; Marseilles (a long-time Roman ally) for aristocracy; and Athens in the fifth century BC for democracy.

In the second passage, Scipio reminds his friend Laelius of Plato's description of the perils of democracy in his *Republic* (8.562d–563d: translated in modified form by Cicero): popular rule is portrayed as harmful to any sense of social order. The view that freedom in the community will also have effects within the family structure is one still commonly voiced in conservative circles today.

Cicero, *On the Republic* 1.43, 67

But under kingship the rest of the people are excessively deprived of legal rights and of participation in decision-making that affects all. And under the command of the top citizens, the masses can hardly participate in freedom, since they lack a share in power and decision-making. And when everything is controlled by the people, however justly and moderately, still that very equality is inequitable, since it has no levels of distinction. So, even if Cyrus the Persian was the most just and wise of kings, it seems to me that that organisation of the populace (this is, as I said before, its political organisation) should not be particularly sought after since this rule is by one man's wish and inclination. And although our allies from Marseilles are ruled perfectly justly by an elect of top men, still in the position of the populace there is something similar to slavery. If the Athenians at one time, after removing the Areopagus, did nothing except by popular laws and decrees, then, as they did not have clear-cut forms of distinction, the state had lost its political orderliness ...

Well then, this passage follows: 'Whoever obeys the leaders is hounded by the populace and called a voluntary slave. But they praise to the skies and heap offices of state on anyone in any magistracy who wants to be like the private citizens and on those private citizens who ensure that there is no difference between a magistrate and a private citizen. So, in a state of this type, everything has to be full of independence – even private households are free of all authority (and this evil extends even down to the animals). To cap it off, the result is that father fears his son, son ignores his father, and there is no sense of shame at all. They are all obviously free: there is no difference between citizen and foreigner. The teacher fears his pupils and butters them up, while the pupils scorn their teachers. The young take upon themselves the authority of age; the old sink down to the pastimes of the young to avoid being a hateful burden to them. The result is that slaves act quite like the free; that women enjoy the same rights as men. And in this picture of freedom even the dogs and horses, right down to the asses, go around so liberated that you have to make way for them on the street.

So from this limitless lack of control comes this upshot: the minds of the citizens become so flabby and finicky that, if the least power of restraint is applied, they get angry and can't bear it. As a result they also start to ignore the laws, so that they are truly without a master.'

1.2 How a governor should act with regard to status distinctions among the governed

By the start of the second century AD, there was no longer any thought of 'mixed government' at Rome. The emperor controlled policy and military force; beneath him, the senators acted as administrators in conjunction with the upper classes of the empire. Pliny the Younger here advises his friend Tiro (governor of Baetica (Spain) in 108) to act with due deference to the sensitivities of the locals, particularly those with influence. He should not disregard social hierarchies in a bid for popularity, nor act boorishly because he possesses absolute power.

Pliny, *Letters* 9.5

Pliny to Tiro.

I've been making inquiries. You are doing very well – keep it up! – in advancing the cause of justice that you are imposing on the provincials through plenty of courtesy. The greatest part of that is to draw in all the particularly worthy and to be liked by those beneath them in such a way as to hold the affection of their leaders at the same time. Many, while being afraid that they might give the impression of being too much concerned for the support of the powerful, gain a reputation for lack of manners and irritability. I know you're a long way from that mistake, but I cannot restrain myself from praising you, but with a warning to keep to the above method of preserving the differences between the ranks and statuses. If they are unclear, confused, or mixed up, there is nothing more unequal than this very equality.

1.3 The Good Emperor: Trajan in comparison with Domitian

In the latter part of AD 100, on the occasion of gaining a suffect consulship (after the previous consul had resigned and so a lesser honour, as the recipient's name would not appear as one of the two ordinary consuls used to identify each year), Pliny the Younger composed a speech thanking the emperor Trajan for his courteous rule, which respected the dignity of the senate and other classes. Throughout the speech, a negative comparison is made with the 'tyrant' emperor, Domitian, to emphasise that there is now freedom of speech that may be used in appropriate praise of the present ruler. Now a paternalistic description of the emperor is to replace the despotic portrayal of Trajan's predecessor.

Pliny, *Panegyric* 2, 3, 23, 59, 77

Indeed, I believe an effort should be made not only by the consul, but by all citizens to avoid saying anything about our emperor such as it might appear could have been said about any other ruler. So let the expressions depart and be gone which fear used to wring out of us; we are experiencing nothing like we used to in the past. We are not making public pronouncements about the emperor such as we did in the past, since in private we are not speaking the same words we used to speak. Let the change in times be noticeable in our speeches and from the very method of offering thanks let it be understood to whom it is being offered whenever it is offered. Let us nowhere offer flattery as to a god, as to a divinity – we are speaking not about a tyrant, but about a citizen, not about a master, but about a parent. And he excels and rises above us because he considers himself one of us and remembers that he is no less a man for all that he commands men. Let us recognise our blessings and show ourselves worthy of them in practice and continually consider whether we would offer greater obedience to emperors who enjoy the slavery of their citizens more than their freedom . . .

It is easy to offer thanks to one who deserves it, senators. For there is no danger that when I speak of affability, he thinks he is being accused of arrogance, when about economy, of extravagance, when about kindness, of resentment, when about self-restraint, of lust, when about industriousness, of laziness, when about bravery, of fear. I'm not even afraid that I might seem grateful or an ingrate according to whether I say too much or too little. For I have noticed that even the gods themselves are not so much pleased by the precision of the prayers of their worshippers as by their innocence and purity, and they think that the man who brings a clean and pure mind to their shrines is more gratifying than a man who has come with a rehearsed song . . .

Everyone was pleased that you greeted the senate with a kiss, just as you had been sent off with a kiss, that you marked out the leaders of the equestrian order by the honour of mentioning them by name without needing someone to remind you, that you – and this is such an honour – that when you greeted your clients you gave some indications of familiarity with them . . .

We have been taught that whoever has one virtue has them all. But we want to find out whether being a good consul and being a good emperor are now one and the same thing. Apart from the fact that it is hard to take on the two highest offices at the same time, there is also a considerable difference in the two: an emperor must be as much like a private citizen as possible, a consul as different as he can be . . .

The last part of the day would be given over to legal matters. What scrupulous concern for fairness, what respect for the law was shown there!

If someone approached him as emperor, he would reply that he was consul. He did not reduce the rights or the prestige of any magistracy; he even increased them, as he referred most cases to the praetors and called on their assistance as his colleagues, not because this was a popular measure and won the approval of the listeners, but because that was his opinion of the matter.

1.4 An oath of allegiance to the emperor

While 'good' emperors might conduct themselves as if the 'equals' of the senators at Rome, in the rest of the empire the ruler was king. Members of the army swore an oath of personal loyalty to the emperor every year. Other groups would swear allegiance to the imperial family when such a display was felt to be advantageous, particularly as part of the imperial cult. As the passage shows, this cult involved both Roman citizens in the provinces and locals wishing to display their links to Rome.

Inscriptiones Latinae Selectae 8781 (Paphlagonia)

In the third year after the twelfth consulate of the emperor Augustus, the son of the divine Caesar [3 BC], 6 March, at Gangra, in the marketplace: this oath was sworn by the Paphlagonians of the area and the Romans engaged in business among them.

I swear to Zeus, Earth, Sun, all the gods and goddesses, and to Augustus himself, that I will be loyal to Caesar Augustus, his children, and descendants all through my life, both in word, deed, and thought, holding as friends those they hold as friends and considering those as enemies whom they judge to be such, that with regard to things that concern them I will not be sparing of my body or my soul or life or children, but will face every peril with respect to things that affect them. If there is anything that I should recognise or hear as spoken, plotted, or done contrary to this, I will report this and be an enemy of the person speaking, plotting, or doing any of these things. Whomever they judge to be enemies, I will pursue and defend against them by land and sea with arms and steel. If I should do anything contrary to this oath or fail to follow up what I have sworn, I impose a curse on myself encompassing the destruction and total extinction of my body, soul, life, children, my entire family, and everything essential down to every successor and every descendant of mine, and may neither earth nor sea receive the bodies of my family and descendants nor bear fruit for them.

The same oath was sworn by all throughout the regions in the countryside at the temples to Augustus by the altars to Augustus. So did the Phazimonians inhabiting what is now called the New Town, all assembled at the temple of Augustus by the altar to Augustus.

1.5 Nero's Benefaction to the Greeks

While provincials displayed their loyalty to the Roman emperor, the emperor in turn might display his philanthropy to his subjects by civic building or grants. Perhaps the most striking example is that of Nero, whose displays of philhellenism included participation in Greek festivals and contests and the grant of immunity from taxation for Achaea, a gift that kept his reputation remarkably high in the East long after his overthrow at Rome.

The liberation of Greece was announced at Isthmia in November, AD 67 (Suetonius, *Nero* 24); it appears that the year of tribunician power below should be 14, just as the reference to designation of tribunician power is mistaken. The reference to Apollo Ptoios is to a cult of Apollo associated with Mount Ptoon in Boeotia. Note too the reference to a change of the geographical name Peloponnese: Nero appears to have renamed the 'island of Pelops' (*Pelopos–nesos*) as the 'island of Nero' (*Nerônos-nêsos*).

Inscriptiones Latinae Selectae 8794
(Acraephiae in Boeotia)

The emperor Caesar says:

'Wishing to repay your goodwill toward me and your piety, I have instructed the nobility of Greece from the province to assemble in as great a number as possible at Corinth on the 29th of November.'

When the crowds gathered at the assembly, he announced what is inscribed below:

'I am showing my gratitude by a gift that was unforeseen by you, men of Greece, though also hardly unexpected in the light of my grandeur, a gift so great that you have not been able to ask for it. All those inhabiting Achaea and what was until now the Peloponnese, are to receive a freedom free from taxes, which you did not all enjoy even in your most prosperous periods (when you were either slaves of outsiders or of one another). I wish that I were offering this gift when Greece was at its peak, so that more could enjoy my generosity. Hence I begrudge the passage of time for having eaten into the greatness of my generosity. Now, however, I am not being generous to you from pity, but from kindness, and I thank your gods whose continual goodwill to me I have experienced by land and sea, that they have allowed me to be so generous to you. For various generals have likewise given freedom to cities, but I, Nero, am giving it to the entire province.'

The chief priest of those who were Augusti when alive and of Claudius Nero Caesar Augustus, Epaminondas, son of Epaminondas, said:

'He has won approval from the senate and the people for this decree. Since the ruler of the whole world, Nero, the greatest emperor, designated for tribunician power for the thirteenth time, father of the fatherland, the new Helios shining on the Greeks, having announced his generosity to the Greeks, thanking and showing respect to our gods who always assist him in judgement and ensure his safety, the one and only emperor throughout the ages who has been the greatest lover of Greece, Nero-Zeus the Liberator, has given and made a present of the freedom that through all time has been born here and is native to the land but had previously been taken away from the Greeks, and since he has returned the country to the ancient state of self-rule and freedom, adding exemption from taxes to this great and unexpected gift, a boon that none of the previous emperors has given in entirety – because of all this, it has been resolved by the magistrates, the councils, and the populace to dedicate at the present time an altar to Zeus the Saviour, inscribing on it "To Zeus the Liberator, Nero, for all time", and in the temple of Apollo Ptoios that there be placed next to those of our ancestral gods statues of Nero Zeus the Liberator, and the divine Augusta _____ [either Octavia or Poppaea Sabina] (hence the erasure of the name in the inscription) so that, when these are completed, our city will also be seen to have fulfilled its duties of honour and piety to the household of the emperor Augustus Nero. The resolution will be inscribed on a stele in the marketplace by the temple of Zeus the Saviour and in the temple of Apollo Ptoios.'

1.6 The deification of emperors

From the death of Julius Caesar onwards, it was always possible for deceased leaders to be declared divine. Not all were so honoured (the 'bad' emperors, Tiberius, Nero, and Domitian were not), but where a dynasty survived having divine ancestors reflected well on the family. Such divinities would not intercede on behalf of their subjects, but they might be honoured with temples that would be sites of imperial cult. The prospect of divinisation was also part of the discourse surrounding the duties of good emperors; hence Pliny the Younger praises Trajan for deifying his adoptive father, the emperor Nerva.

Pliny, *Panegyric* 11

You honoured Nerva first with tears, as befits a son, then with temples, not in imitation of those who had done the same, but with other ideas in mind. Tiberius deified Augustus in order to introduce the charge of treason; Nero deified Claudius, but only to mock him; Titus deified Vespasian and Domitian, Titus, but that was so the first would appear to be the son of a god, the second to be a god's brother. But you installed your father in the stars not to frighten the citizens, not to ridicule the gods, not for your own prestige, but because you thought him a god.

1.7 The imperial court of Galba

As was the case with other Roman officials, the emperor lacked any large group of permanent assistants appointed to assist him in his governmental duties. Instead, he needed to rely on semi-official advisers – his 'friends' or courtiers. These individuals might offer good advice or be seen as taking advantage of their proximity to power to increase their own influence and wealth. Much depended on the personal strength of the emperor to control his officials – when there were weak emperors or ones at the close of their careers, the court would look to future imperial prospects, which in turn would tend to destabilise the government. In AD 69, the age of the emperor Galba encouraged a revolt of the German armies and the emperor's attempt to create a successor by adopting Piso only provoked a coup by his previous ally, Otho.

Tacitus, *Histories* 1.12

This event [the mutiny of the German frontier legions] hastened Galba's planning for an adoption, which he had often gone over personally and with those closest to him. Certainly there was no more common subject of gossip through the entire city during those months; first, because of the opportunity and pleasure in talking about such things, second, because of Galba's declining years. Few showed any judgement or love of the state, while many marked out this fellow or that in line with their fatuous hopes, according to whose friend or client they were, or to spite Titus Vinius – the more powerful he grew daily, the more hateful he became through this same occurrence. In fact the greed of his courtiers [*amici*], gaping open-mouthed when faced with such huge power, was increased by Galba's complicity, since, having a weak and naive emperor, they could commit their crimes with less fear and greater reward.

1.8 Trajan's wife and sister

The power of the emperor was reflected in those around him, not only his courtiers and household freedmen and slaves, but also his family. This included the female members of the imperial family, who might be portrayed as domineering (the two Agrippinas) or as appropriately modest, as Trajan's wife Plotina and sister Marciana are depicted by Pliny the Younger.

Pliny, *Panegyric* 83, 84

Your wife adds to your fame and glory. For who could be more respected or more traditional than her? If a wife had to be chosen for the pontifex maximus, wouldn't he choose her or someone similar (if there is anyone similar)? Look how she seeks nothing from your power except for her personal pleasure. How steadfastly she adores not your might, but you yourself. You are both the same as you were before and your good fortune has brought nothing extra to you both, except for each of you to start to realise how well each bears up under this good fortune. How modest she is in her attire, how restrained in her entourage, how courteous in her approach! . . .

Moreover, your sister knows how to be your sister. Your openness, your truthfulness, your transparency can be recognised in her. So, if anyone compared her with your wife, he would be left unsure whether being well raised or the fortune of good birth is more effective for living a good life . . . Both have the same character, because they both possess your character. From this derives a sense of restraint and also continual serenity – they will never run the risk of turning into private figures, because they have never ceased to be such. The senate had offered them the title of Augusta: they have doggedly avoided this, so long as you were to refuse the title of 'Father of the Fatherland'. Or else they judged that there was more gain in being spoken of as your wife and sister rather than as Augustas. But, whatever consideration persuaded them to such restraint, they are all the more worthy of being and being considered august [*augustae*] in our minds, because they are not called this.

1.9 A dedication from the time of Tiberius

Some senators might have careers that moved them around the empire in military and administrative capacities, while retaining their patronage in their hometowns. Thus Novellus Atticus is commemorated at Tivoli, although he died in southern France. Note that he is erroneously listed as one of the fifteen judges for deciding disputes, when the panel was actually ten; he is also listed as *praet(or) ad hast(am)*: the *hasta* (spear) was the symbol of the power of sale and hence of the centumviral court, as dealing with property and inheritance disputes.

Inscriptiones Latinae Selectae 950 (Tivoli, Italy)

To the memory of Torquatus Novellus Atticus, son of Publius, quindecemvir for deciding disputes, military tribune of the First Legion, tribune of a company, commander of the four legions [of Lower Germany] I, V, XX, XXI, quaestor, aedile, praetor of the centumviral court, curator of public buildings, legate for taking the census and military enrolment and proconsul in charge of the province of Narbonese Gaul – at the conclusion of this office, aged 44, he died at Forum Iulii [*Fréjus*].

1.10 Two dedications for the first Paelignian senator

In the empire, while the governing power of the senate was reduced, people from areas outside Rome who had previously been excluded from power gained opportunities of sharing in honours. This inscription from the first century AD reflects the successful political career of a local, celebrated in his home area, the hill country north east of Rome. It is possible that this is the Varius Geminus frequently mentioned as a declaimer by Seneca the Elder: such cultural pursuits are not normally commemorated on public dedications.

Inscriptiones Latinae Selectae 932 (Castelvecchio Subequo, central Italy) – Augustan and Tiberian periods

To Quintus Varius Geminus, son of Quintus, twice legate of the divine Augustus, proconsul, praetor, tribune of the plebs, quaestor, judge of the special court [*quaesitio*], prefect in charge of the grain supply, member of the board of ten for deciding disputes, curator for the preservation of sacred temples and public monuments. He was the first of all from Paelignium to become a senator and to hold these offices. The people of Superaequum have set this up at public expense, to their patron.

To Quintus Varius Geminus, son of Quintus, of the Sergian tribe, quaestor – dedicated by the Vecellan territory [*pagus Vecellanus*].

1.11 A dedication to Venus at Eryx

Although the main credit for military success was reserved for the emperor, some senators could still celebrate their victories in a limited manner. Early in the empire, under Tiberius, L. Apronius set up this inscription in Sicily to commemorate his efforts in AD 20 (Tacitus, *Annals* 3.21). On it he has dedicated: (1) his *toga praetexta* signifying his membership of the senatorial board of seven for public feasts; (2) his weapons from his successful military efforts; (3) a statue of his father; and (4) a statue of the emperor (jointly dedicated with his father). The dedication to Venus at Eryx recalls the theme of pietas and of inherited virtues celebrated in the Aeneas myth.

Inscriptiones Latinae Selectae 939 (Mt Eryx, Sicily)

L. Apronius Caesinus, member of the board of seven in charge of public feasts . . . gives and dedicates this to Venus of Eryx.

When this man sent by his father, the proconsul,
Fought successfully in Libya, the Moorish enemy fell
    before him.

The man who has dedicated to you this sword and the image
Of his father Apronius, was both son of a leader in war and a
    leader himself,
And he was victor also in a just war.
Because he laid down his praetexta and took it up again at the
    same time,
As a boy and as a member of the board of seven, a praetexta that
    his father had duly requested
And Caesar had granted, he leaves this robe behind for you, sacred
    goddess.
. . .

Apronius' son, greater in his deeds than in his reputation
Because he personally put the Gaetulian tribes to flight,
Has dedicated a statue of his dear father, as due reward to you,
Goddess, nurturing mother of the race of Aeneas,
And the arms that he bore: what great courage is revealed
By his shield, broken by blows! His sword is red with the enemy's
    blood,
Blunted by slaughter, and his spear completes the trophy,
Stabbed by which the wild-eyed barbarian fell.

Son and father have dedicated to you this image,
More venerable than any in the eyes of them both.
The matched efforts of them both have set up this statue of Caesar:
They vied in their devotion, but it was absolute in both of them.

Under the supervision of L. Apronius, son of Lucius . . .

1.12 Dedication to Tiberius Plautius Silvanus Aelianus

Tiberius Plautius Silvanus was probably a son of Aelius Lamia (consul AD 3),
adopted into the Plautius family. The following inscription shows a remarkable
career, with military successes in the Balkans under Nero, for which he was finally
rewarded by Vespasian.

Inscriptiones Latinae Selectae 986
(Tivoli, at the Mausoleum of the Plautii)

To Tiberius Plautius Silvanus Aelianus, son of Marcus, of the Aniensian
tribe; priest; companion of the cult of Augustus; member of the board of
three for the coining and minting of bronze, silver, and gold; quaestor of
Tiberius Caesar; legate of the Fifth Legion in Germany; City Prefect; legate
and companion of the emperor Claudius in Britain; consul; proconsul of
Asia; propraetorian governor of Moesia, into which he transferred more

15

than a 100,000 of those living across the Danube, with their wives, children, chiefs, and kings, to provide tribute. He suppressed an uprising of the Sarmatians in the west, although he had sent off a large part of his army for the expedition to Armenia. He brought across to the bank [of the Danube], which he was protecting, kings who were unknown or hostile to the Roman state so they could pay homage to the Roman standards; he sent back to the kings of the Bastarnae and the Rhoxolani their sons, to the king of the Dacians his brother, who had been captured or kidnapped by their enemies. He received hostages from a number of these. Through this he strengthened and extended the peacefulness of the province. He expelled the king of the Scythians from the Borysthenic Chersonese, having raised his siege. He was the first to assist the grain supply of the Roman people by a large amount of wheat from that province. When he was recalled from his governorship in Spain to become City Prefect, the senate honoured him with triumphal decorations during his Prefecture, on the petition of the emperor Vespasian, the words from whose speech are inscribed below:

'He governed Moesia so well that the honour of triumphal decorations ought not to have been put off until I dealt with it – except that the rank of City Prefect became more famous through the delay.'

The emperor Vespasian, consul for the second time [AD 70], has set this up during that same Prefecture.

1.13 Restrictions placed on senators

As members of the governing body of the Roman world, the senators were restricted in their activities. In some cases this was to avoid conflict of interest or excessive financial advantage (hence the restrictions on shipping and tax collecting); in other cases, participation in the activities of their social inferiors was seen as demeaning.

For conversion of amounts in **1.13c**: the minimum tonnage to give a shipowner tax immunity is 325 tonnes; this can be split among several ships, provided none is less than 65 tonnes burden.

(a) Livy, 21.63.3–4

Flaminius was also hated by the senators because of the singular law, which Q. Claudius had brought forward as tribune to oppose the senate and which only C. Flaminius among the senators had supported 'that no senator nor anyone whose father had been a senator should own a sea vessel which could hold more than 300 amphorae'. That was considered sufficient to bring the crop in from the estate, since all trade by senators was viewed as demeaning.

(b) Paul, *Sententiae*, Leiden fragment 2

Senators or their parents who still have legal power over them are prohibited from bidding for tax collection contracts, from possessing ships for financial gain, or from providing racehorses. That is punished under the law on extortion.

(c) *Digest* 50.5.3, Scaevola

Exemption from any public liturgy is granted on the grounds of shipping to those (1) who have built any single sea-going ship that holds at least 50,000 modii of grain, and offered it for the transport of the corn supply of the Roman people or (2) have built a number of ships, totalling over 50,000 modii, each holding not less than 10,000 modii, so long as these ships are in use or others are sailing in their place. Senators, however, cannot enjoy this exemption since they cannot even own a ship under the *lex Iulia* on extortion.

1.14 The privileges due to senators

Senators were required to have adequate wealth and housing to uphold the dignity of their position. In return, they enjoyed public privileges, such as prime seating at the games (**1.16**). As the debate below indicates, there could be a conflict between the ideal of not flaunting excessive wealth and the demands of public display and of reward for a career of public service (cf. **1.15**).

Tacitus, *Annals* 2.33

At the next meeting of the senate, long speeches were made against public extravagance by Q. Haterius, ex-consul, and Octavius Fronto, ex-praetor. A motion was put that gold vessels should not be manufactured for serving food and that men should not demean themselves by wearing silk clothing. Fronto got up and demanded a limit on silverware, furnishings, and slaves (it was still common for senators to propose whatever they thought was in the public interest when called on for their opinion). Asinius Gallus spoke at length in response. As the empire had increased, private wealth had grown too. This was not new, but had occurred with ancient customs. Money meant one thing to folk like Fabricius, another to the Scipios. Everything should be measured against the state: when it was impoverished, the homes of its citizens were small; but after it had reached this peak of magnificence, individuals were bettering themselves. In the case of slaves, silver, and things readied for household use, nothing could be considered excessive or modest except in comparison with the wealth of the owner. The wealth requirements for senators and equites differed, not because they were naturally distinct, but because, just as the former differed in place, rank, and esteem, so too they should differ in the things that are acquired for the repose of the mind and the health of the body. Unless, perhaps, anyone thought that the most prestigious should undergo more numerous duties and greater dangers, but should be deprived of the things that provide relaxation from these duties and dangers. This admission of his vices disguised by honourable words and the similar practices of his listeners resulted in ready agreement with Gallus.

1.15 Pliny objects to the senate's decision to censure Firminus

Hostilius Firminus was a senatorial adjutant to Marius Priscus, the ex-governor of Africa who was convicted of misgovernment of his province in AD 100. It was suggested that Firminus be expelled from the senate for his activities, but a motion to exclude him from promotion won the day. Here, as elsewhere, Pliny the Younger shows an upper-class disdain for an apparently democratic system of voting.

Pliny, *Letters* 2.12.2–3, 6

Acutius Nerva proposed that Firminus should not be considered when it came to the allotment of provinces. This proposal won the day as being milder, although in other respects it was harsher and more cruel. For what is more pitiable than to have to endure the toil and trouble when you have been excluded and set aside from a senator's honours? . . .

But that gained the votes of the majority. For the support for a motion is counted up, not measured. No other system is possible in a public meeting. There is nothing more inequitable in this method than the very equality used. For, although there is inequality in good sense, there is equality in voting rights.

1.16 Augustus sets aside seats in the theatre for senators and other status groups

Among the many efforts put in place by Augustus to strengthen traditional Roman values is his revival of the legislation that reserved the front-row seats for the senators and equestrians (the 'fourteen rows'). This allowed the display of the orders of society whenever public shows were presented.

Suetonius, *Augustus* 44.1

He changed the totally confused and disordered arrangement of seating and rearranged it, spurred on by the offence to a senator to whom no one had offered a seat at Puteoli when the theatre was packed for the most renowned of the games there. So a senatorial decree was passed: whenever a public show was put on anywhere, the first row of the seats should be reserved for the senators. At Rome, he prevented the representatives of both allied and free peoples from sitting in the orchestra, when he discovered that some of those sent were of freed status.

1.17 Senatorial decree of AD 19, setting restrictions on public appearances by those of senatorial or equestrian birth

This decree passed under Tiberius shows that attempts were made by members of the upper classes to escape restrictions on their conduct, particularly by incurring *infamia* (complete loss of status) through certain legal decisions. The senate acts to remove such loopholes by placing restrictions on anyone who had the right to privileged seating (see **1.16** above). At the same time, age restrictions are placed on those wanting to participate in demeaning professions (the games and the theatre), except for those seeking an escape from severe debt.

Tabula Larinas

[Passed at a meeting of the senate] on the Palatine, in the Portico of Apollo. Participating in the drafting were: Gaius Ateius Capito, son of Lucius, of the Aniensan tribe; Sextus Pompeius, son of Sextus . . . ; . . . Octavius Fronto, son of Gaius, of the Stellatine tribe; Marcus Asinius Mamilianus, son of Curtius, of the Aniensan tribe; Gaius Gavius Macer, son of Gaius, of the Poblilian tribe, quaestor; Aulus Didius Gallus, quaestor . . .

Marcus Silanus and Lucius Norbanus Balbus the consuls declared that they had produced a pamphlet (as they had been given that task) on the senatorial decrees applying to sons of senators or those who appear on stage or at the games contrary to the prestige of their order, and that youths were behaving contrary to the decrees of the senate, which had been passed in previous years on this matter, acting fraudulently to reduce the esteem of the senate. What would the senate wish to do about the matter?

They had decided about the matter: It was the resolution of the senate that no one should display on the stage or involve in a gladiatorial contract the son or daughter, grandson or granddaughter, great-grandson or great-granddaughter, nor anyone, male or female, who personally or whose father or maternal or paternal grandfather or brother ever had the right of viewing the games from the equestrian seats; nor should he engage them to hunt wild beasts in the arena or to win gladiatorial feathers or to take up the training sword or, if anyone should offer a similar service, to assist the effort; and that none of them should hire himself or herself out. And that for this reason there is more careful provision against the possibility that, in order to annul the previous decrees of the senate, for the sake of escaping

19

the power of their order when they had the right of sitting in the equestrian seats, they had accepted public ignominy or condemnation in a court decision involving loss of status and, after they had lost the right to sit in the equestrian seats, hired themselves out as gladiators or appeared on stage. If any of those specified above act contrary to the prestige of their order, they may not have a public funeral, unless they have already appeared on stage or contracted their services for the arena or are the sons or daughters of an actor or gladiator or gladiatorial trainer or a procurer.

And it was resolved that what was specified in the decree of the senate, passed when Manius Lepidus and Titus Statilius Taurus were consuls, be included: 'It should not be permitted to a free female younger than twenty years old or a free male younger than twenty-five to hire themselves out as gladiators or to contract out their services for the stage or for any other shameful purposes, except if any have been bound over to a creditor by the divine Augustus or by Tiberius Caesar and have been thrown by the creditor into chains – then, if they have made an agreement with the man who has thus imprisoned them that if he agreed to them hiring themselves out as gladiators or contracting their services for a price, the money should be paid over into his private account, it seems right for that arrangement to be preserved, unless they are any of those specified above.'

1.18 A senatorial wife as community patron

The prestige of senators also extended to the female members of their families who might hold religious offices or show personal generosity to their communities. In this case Aurelia Violentilla derives her standing from being the daughter of L. Marius Maximus Perpetuus Aurelianus, consul for the second time in AD 223, and from having been married to one consul and now having another as her husband.

Inscriptiones Latinae Selectae 1166 (Asculum)

To Maria Aurelia Violentilla, daughter of the ex-consul Perpetuus, woman of consular status, the wife of Q. Egnatius Proculus, the consul. The decurions and populace of Asculum have dedicated this because of her unique love for them.

1.19 The prestige of wives of senators

The prestige of women was generally derived from their husbands and, to a lesser degree, from their fathers and children (cf. 1.18 above). This could lead to uncertainty as to whether they enjoyed precedence over lesser males and about the status of women who remarried at a lower rank.

Digest 1.9.1, 1.9.12

Ulpian, in the sixty-second book, *On the Edict*. Certainly no one is in any doubt that a consular man has precedence over a consular woman. But one should consider whether a man of prefect status has precedence over a woman of consular status. I would think that he has precedence, because the male gender has greater prestige. Furthermore, we speak of the wives of ex-consuls as being women of consular status. Saturninus adds their mothers, but this has never been recorded nor ever accepted.

Ulpian, in the second book, *On Censuses*. Those who have previously been married to a man of consular status have usually made petition to the emperor, although it occurs infrequently in practice, that, although remarried to a husband of lower status, they might retain their consular prestige. I know that the emperor Antoninus so favoured his cousin Iulia Mammaea.

1.20 An attempt to avoid the laws on adultery by registration as a public prostitute (AD 19)

Just as the attempts were being made to avoid Augustus' legislation regarding those of senatorial birth appearing as entertainers (**1.17** above), so at least one attempt was made to avoid the Augustan legislation on adultery by lowering one's status, which was met by a severe response.

Tacitus, *Annals* 2.85

In the same year, women's lusts were checked by stern senatorial decrees and provision was made that no one whose grandfather, father, or husband had been a Roman *eques* should earn a living by prostitution. This was because Vistilia, from a praetorian family, had made a public declaration of her right to sexual promiscuity before the aediles. This custom had been established in the time of our ancestors, who thought there was sufficient punishment for the unchaste in the very admission of the crime. Titidius Labeo, Vistilia's husband, was called to account for why he had not asked for legal redress against a wife who was openly guilty of the charge of adultery. When he offered the excuse that the sixty days given for deliberation had not yet passed, it was considered sufficient to pass judgement on Vistilia alone: she was banished to the island of Seriphos.

1.21 The senate upholds its own prestige in the face of attacks using the reverence due to the imperial family

One of the effects of the possible divinisation of the emperor was to create confusion over the appropriate behaviour with regard to imperial statues or even coins. Under Tiberius there were numerous trials for lèse-majesté (*maiestas*), but the senate reacted vehemently when they felt outsiders were challenging their authority using reverence for the emperor as a shelter.

Tacitus, *Annals* 3.36

Next a matter was raised that was bubbling under the surface in the private gripes of many senators. The boldness of the worst types in society in stirring up insults and hostility against the respectable while grasping a statue of the emperor was increasing. Even freedmen and slaves, when without provocation they raised their voices and even their hands against their patrons and masters, had to be feared. So the senator Gaius Cestius made a speech indicating that the emperors were indeed equivalent to gods, but even the gods heard only just prayers; no one took refuge on the Capitoline or in any other temple in the city to use that assistance for criminal purposes. The law had been annulled and totally overthrown when Annia Rufilla, whom he had found guilty of fraud in a court case, was hurling insults and threats against him in the forum and at the steps of the senate house and he dare not take legal action because his path was blocked by a statue of the emperor placed in the way. Others spoke of similar problems and some muttered about even worse cases. They begged Drusus to make an example of retribution against her. Finally he had her summoned, passed sentence on her, and ordered that she be kept in the public prison.

1.22 The senate resolves not to allow provincials to pass judgement on the quality of senatorial governors

Another attempt to gain some hold over the Roman governors was to arrange votes of thanks to be sent to the senate. Such a system was open to abuse and soon incurred a response from the senate (AD 62).

Tacitus, *Annals* 15.20–22.1

Next Claudius Timarchus from Crete was arraigned as defendant. There were other charges, as happens with excessively powerful provincials who are encouraged by their inordinate wealth to insult those beneath them. But one utterance of his had gone so far as to offend the senate: he would regularly state that it lay within his power as to whether the governors in charge of Crete received a vote of thanks or not. Thrasea Paetus turned this opportunity to the public advantage: after he had expressed the opinion that the defendant should be banished from Crete, he added: 'Experience has shown, senators, that outstanding laws and noble precedents arise among the good from the sins of others. The lack of restraint from lawyers brought about the Cincian statute, the corruption of candidates brought about the Julian laws, and the greed of officials the Calpurnian legislation. Misdeed is prior in time to punishment and correction comes later than felony. So let us devise a plan that is worthy of Roman honesty and firmness to combat this recent arrogance of the provincials: the aim is to avoid stripping the provincials of any protection, but for us to rid ourselves of the belief that the judgement on any of us rests anywhere other than in the hands of the citizenry. Once upon a time, not only praetors and consuls but even private citizens were sent out to visit the provinces and report on what they thought about their compliance. The nations used to quake in expectation of the opinion of individuals. But now we humour foreigners and pay them court: just as votes of thanks are decided in accord with one person's wishes, so accusations are all the more readily agreed to. Let them make their decisions and let the chance to make a show of their power in this way remain with the provincials. But let fake praise, wrung out of them by entreaties, be checked just as their vindictiveness and viciousness has been. More crimes are committed in earning their gratitude than when we displease them. Indeed some virtues provoke their hatred, such as fixed resoluteness and a mind that is invincible in the face of flattery. So the beginnings of our terms in office are better, while their ends are worse since we are hunting up votes like candidates for office. If this were checked, the provinces would be governed more fairly and firmly. Just as greed has been constrained by the fear of a charge of peculation, so, if we outlaw the presentation of votes of thanks, self-interested behaviour will be reduced.'

This opinion was supported with great acclamation. But a resolution could not be passed as the consuls declared that the matter was not on the agenda. Later, with the emperor's agreement, they passed a resolution that no one should bring up before an assembly of the allies a resolution that a vote of thanks to praetorian or consular governors should be presented in the senate and that no one should undertake an embassy for that purpose.

1.23 The display of one's power through an entourage

In a society based on power, it was essential to publicly display this. Such spectacles could easily be satirised, yet might also help to avoid misunderstandings over comparative ranking.

Seneca, *Letters* 123.7

Nowadays everyone sets out on a journey with a squadron of Numidian horsemen riding in front, with a crowd of runners going on ahead. It's a disgrace if there is no one to push the on-comers out of the road, no one to show by a cloud of dust that there is a respectable fellow on his way. Nowadays everyone has mules to carry their crystal cups, their agate vases, and their silverware engraved by the hands of the greatest craftsmen. It's a disgrace if you only have packs that can safely be shaken up. Everyone transports their crowd of young slaves with their faces plastered in case the sun or the cold should hurt their tender skin. It's a disgrace to have any slave boy in your retinue whose face is perfectly fine without any ointment.

1.24 The parade of the equestrian horsemen

Next in rank to the senate were the Roman *equites*, or knights, originally associated with those who kept horses on behalf of the state. Augustus revived the habit of holding a procession of the horsemen, but sought to ensure that none would suffer social humiliation during the display from challenges or physical disability.

Suetonius, *Augustus* 38.3, 40.1–2

Augustus regularly inspected the squadrons of equites, bringing back the custom of a procession after a long period of disuse. But he would not allow anyone to be pulled out of the procession by a challenger as he paraded, which had previously happened, and he allowed those who were clearly aged or disabled to send their horse on ahead in their place and appear on foot to answer when summoned. Afterwards he gave an opportunity of returning their horses to those who were over thirty-five and did not want to keep them ... Since many equites, having had their wealth reduced by the civil war, did not dare to watch the games from the fourteen rows from fear of breaking the law about seating in the theatre, he declared that whoever personally had ever qualified to be an equestrian, or whose parents had qualified, were exempt from these provisions.

1.25 In AD 22, Tiberius regularises the wearing of rings as a sign of equestrian status

The growing prestige of the equestrian order led to more claimants to this status, when previously most equites had been younger members of senatorial families and their associates. Under Tiberius, the requirements of free birth for three generations, sufficient wealth, and a stainless reputation were instituted. Those who could claim to fulfil these conditions were registered and entitled to wear gold rings on their hands.

Pliny the Elder, *Natural History* 33.32

Finally in the ninth year of Tiberius' reign the equestrian order was unified and its shape fixed by the right to wear the [equestrian] rings – this was when Gaius Asinius Pollio and Gaius Antistius Vetus were consuls, in the 775th year from the foundation of the city. We are amazed at the almost ridiculous reason for this: Gaius Sulpicius Galba, seeking to gain a reputation in the eyes of the emperor while still a young man by bringing charges against the fast-food merchants, complained in the senate that the owners of these establishments were generally escaping being found guilty by claiming equestrian rank. For this reason it was decided that no one should have the right to wear [equestrian] rings unless he were of free birth, as had been his father and paternal grandfather, unless he had a property qualification of 400,000 sesterces, and could sit in the front fourteen rows under the Julian theatre law.

1.26 Vespasian defines the upper classes of Roman society

Under the Flavians, there were major reforms of the senatorial and equestrian orders to reward Italian and some provincial supporters of the regime. The result was a hastening in the process of changing a Roman ruling class to an Italian and in the background empire-wide body.

Suetonius, *Vespasian* 9.2

He cleaned up the highest ranks of society, which had been run down from the various massacres and polluted by a lack of concern over member-ship from long past. He made up their numbers by approved senators and equites, removing the most unworthy and adding the most respectable Italians and provincials. And to make it clear that the two orders differed not so much in their freedom of speech as in their prestige, he uttered this judgement with regard to a case of defamation involving a senator and an eques: one should not insult senators, but it was perfectly legal and proper to answer back to an insult delivered.

1.27 A joke address

Among the graffiti of Pompeii are various humorous records. The following stresses the social origin and standing of its subject and purports to offer a general address where he can be found.

Inscriptiones Latinae Selectae 1319 (Pompeii)

Gaius Hadius Ventrio [Pot-belly], knight, Roman-born; suburb: Among the Beets and Cabbages.

1.28 An equestrian career and gratitude for services to one's original municipality

In the empire, equestrians could follow a career of public service, as senators had always done. The following shows a military career followed by minor administrative tasks and governorships, rising to control of the grain supply and of Egypt.

Note the distinctive language to describe equestrians: Minicius is a *splendidissimus vir*, the title for a noble eques, whereas a senator would be *vir clarissimus*. In the council's motion it is noted that the emperor has granted a special right for outsiders living in Aquileia to undertake civic tasks just as the councillors do – hence Minicius can act as benefactor of his original town.

Inscriptiones Latinae Selectae 1374 (Aquileia, AD 105)

To Gaius Minicius Italus, son of Gaius, of the Velinan tribe; member of the board of four for judicial cases; commander of the Fifth Cohort of Gallic cavalry; commander of the First Cohort of Breucian cavalry who were Roman citizens; commander of the Second Cohort of Varcian cavalry; military tribune of the Sixth Legion, Victrix; cavalry commander of the First Wing of cavalry auxiliaries who were Roman citizens; honoured by the divine Vespasian with a gold crown and parade spear; procurator of the province of the Hellespont; procurator of the province of Asia, which, on the instructions of the emperor, he governed taking the place of the deceased proconsular governor; procurator of the provinces of Lyons and Aquitaine and Lactora too; prefect in charge of the grain supply; prefect of Egypt; priest of the divine Claudius; by decree of the decurions.

P. Tullius Max[..., ...], members of the board of four for judicial cases, approached the council on 29 May; [...] Proculus, C. Appuleius Celer, A. Iunius ..., Sex. Cossutius Secundus assisted in the drafting. After a speech had been made in honour of Gaius Minicius Italus, outstanding equestrian, because whatever influence or power he was able to acquire through the highest offices open to the equestrian rank, he turned it all to improving and enhancing his birthplace and did not consider himself after any appointment too prosperous to work on its behalf, they passed this motion in accord with their resolution about the matter:

'Since C. Minicius Italus ... has improved the standing of the place and since this is in addition known to all – that the most sacred emperor Trajan decreed on his request, that those living here, with whom we are generally on the same status level, may undertake duties along with us – and that through him we have gained greater generosity from the greatest emperor, it has been resolved by this order and considered in the interests of the state, that a bronze statue with a marble base be set up to him and that our decree be inscribed on the base, so that it may be more clearly attested that in responding to his acts of generosity and services we are unanimous in publicly praising him.'

Resolved. In the consulship of Titus Iulius Candidus, for the second time, and Gaius Antius Quadratus, for the second time.

1.29 Another equestrian career

Inscriptiones Latinae Selectae 1396 (Ankara)

Good fortune! To Lucius Didius Marinus, equestrian noble [v(ir) e(minentissimus)], procurator of our emperor of the province of Arabia; procurator of Galatia; procurator of the gladiatorial troupe of Gaul, Britain, Spain, Germany, and Raetia; procurator of Minucia; procurator for food supplies in Transpadane Istria and Liburnia; procurator of the taxes of the Roman people in the area beyond the Po; procurator of the gladiatorial troupe of Asia, Bithynia, Galatia, Cappadocia, Lycia, Pamphylia, Cilicia, Cyprus, Pontus, and Paphlagonia; tribune of the First Praetorian Cohort. Marianus, the freedman of our emperor, in charge of collecting the 5 per cent tax for manumission in Bithynia, Pontus, and Paphlagonia, his mentor, [has set this up].

1.30 A distinguished patroness

In the second and third centuries AD, in response to the demand for an equivalent status ranking for women, the term *femina stolata* appears as an equivalent of *vir eminentissimus*.

L'Année Epigraphique 1958 no. 177 (Tivoli)

To Marcia Ulpia Sossia Calligona, woman of equestrian standing, patroness of the young companions of Hercules.

1.31 The career of a successful grain merchant

Inscriptiones Latinae Selectae 6140 (Ostia, AD 222)

To M. Iunius Faustus, son of Marcus, of the Palatine tribe, recruited as a decurion, priest of the divine Titus, grain merchant, quaestor in charge of the treasury, priest of Rome and Augustus, patron of the corporation of agents for sea-going ships. The owners of ships trading throughout Africa, likewise of ships trading with Sardinia have set this up. The site has been donated at public expense by the decurions.

Dedicated 20 September, when Severus and Pompeianus were both consuls for the second time, under the supervision of P. Aufidius, [. . .], M. Clodius Fortunatianus Pudens, L. Tadius Felix, quinquennial magistrates for the fifteenth five-year term.

1.32 A decurion's generosity to his town

In the Roman towns of the empire, the wealthy (often people of local origin retiring after a successful career in the military or administration) were recruited into the councils. These decurions could ensure their status as benefactors by arranging for trusts that would finance gifts for the community, often set (as here) according to the standing of the beneficiary.

Inscriptiones Latinae Selectae 6271 (Ferentinum)

To Aulus Quinctilius Priscus, son of Aulus, of the Palatine tribe, member of the board of four with the power of aedile, member of the board of four for administering justice, member of the board of four elected every five years, recruited by a council decree, priest, and aide-de-camp [*praefectus fabrorum*]. In light of his outstanding generosity shown to his fellow towns-people, they have voted to place a statue of him in senatorial dress at public expense in the forum, wherever he himself desires.

He has accepted the honour, but rejected the offer to pay for it. He, in accord with a decree of the council, bought off the state the farms at Ceponia, Roia, and Mamia and the field at Exoscum for 70,000 sesterces and gave them back for the perpetual use of the state. From their rent of 4,200 sesterces each year, on 2 May each year on his birthday in perpetuity there should be given to townsfolk, inhabitants, and their legally married wives a pound of cake and a hemina of mead; and at a dinner for the decurions mead, cake, and a gratuity of 10 sesterces, the same to the children of the councillors; and to the six men entrusted with the cult of Augustus and those who would dine with them, cake, mead, and 8 sesterces; and at a larger dinner in my honour a sestertius for each man; and for the decoration of my statue and portrait busts, the state would in perpetuity spend 30 sesterces on the decision of the board of four, under the responsibility of the aediles. It is desirable that they should make a scattering of 30 modii of nuts to the children of the townsfolk without making distinction between free and slave, and a distribution of 6 draughts from jars of wine to the children of the councillors.

1.33 A family tragedy and pride in one's rank

This inscription not only records a father's feelings of loss at the death of a son on the verge of manhood, but also his own pride in achieving the highest office in his hometown (represented by wearing the *toga praetexta*, the garb of a magistrate).

Inscriptiones Latinae Selectae 6881
(Oppidum Novum, Algeria)

Traveller, as you pass pause for a little while
And read these words that you will not be able to refrain from
    repeating tearfully.

For here I lie placed in a coffin, a most unfortunate child, whose father was
a member of the board of two with the power of quaestor. I was not allowed
to see my father in his *toga praetexta* except for one day on the first of
January. Then I took to bed and on the twentieth day afterwards was handed
over for burial, having lived a life of 16 years, 10 months, 10 days. I left,
along with the light, a mourning mother together with a loving sister, a
brother, and my father.

C. Caelius Donatus, his father, constructed this for C. Caelius Sedatus, his
son, while in mourning.

1.34 Who are eligible to be decurions?

There are standard rules for the government of municipalities and Roman colonies
in the empire. Decurions must have served their military service or have gained
an exemption and not be currently involved in certain professions, the practice
of which might lessen the respect due to a town councillor. These include
undertaker, town crier, and *dissignator*, a term that generally refers to ushers, but
perhaps refers here especially to the ushers at funeral ceremonies.

Tabula Heracleensis (S. Italy) 89–97

If anyone will be less than 30 years old, he may not, in the next year following
1 January, seek, gain, or hold any post as a member of the board of two
or member of the board of four or any other magistracy in any municipality,
colony, or prefecture, unless he has undergone three years' service in the
cavalry in the legions or six years' service in the infantry in the legions, and
he must undertake this service in military camp or in a province for the
majority of each year, or for two six-monthly stints, which should together
count for a year's service (with the provision that this will be permitted to
count by law or plebiscite) unless he has an exemption from military service
by law, plebiscite, or by treaty terms, from which he does not need to undergo
military service against his will.

   And no one who will be a member of the profession of undertaker, master
of ceremonies, or town crier may, while he follows his profession, seek,
gain, or hold any post as a member of the board of two or member of the
board of four or any other magistracy in any municipality, colony, or
prefecture, nor be a senator, decurion, or conscript magistrate there or give
his opinion [in council].

If anyone listed above acts contrary to these regulations, he shall be liable to pay a fine of 50,000 sesterces to the populace and there shall be a right of action against his property for whoever wishes to bring it.

1.35 A senior secretary (*scriba*)

Apart from the classes of senators and equestrians, there was another registered group, the *apparitores*, originally lesser public servants, such as secretaries and ushers, which became an honour sought by those who could not aspire to higher offices.

Inscriptiones Latinae Selectae 1886
(Forum Clodii = Bracciano, Italy, AD 173)

To Publius Aelius Agathoclianus, son of Publius, of the Palatine tribe, praetor of the Laurentes Lavinates, senior tribunician secretary, one of the six senior secretaries attached to the quaestors, secretary of the curule aediles, member of the panel of the senior panel in charge of the sacred chickens, one of the three aides-de-camp, and supernumerary [*accensus velatus*]. The people of Forum Clodii, by a decree of their decurions, have dedicated this to their patron, because of his services and because he was the first to donate marble and columns for the public baths. In honour of this dedication he gave gratuities to each of the decurions individually.

Dedicated on 3 August, when Gnaeus Claudius Severus and Tiberius Claudius Pompeianus were both consuls for the second time.

1.36 A secretary puts on public entertainment

While providing games was normally restricted to the upper classes in the Roman world (especially those of the senatorial/decurion class), in smaller towns an *apparitor* could have enough status to perform this function.

Inscriptiones Latinae Selectae 1901
(Acquaspartae, Umbria)

——lius Clemens, the son of Titus, of the Pupinian tribe, one of the board of twenty-six secretaries, military tribune elected by the populace, one of the two men in charge of administering justice at Carsulae, put on six days of circus racing, six days of stage performances, and was the first to put on a gladiatorial show in his township.

1.37 A freedman as public benefactor

Even ex-slaves, if sufficiently wealthy and influential, might become public benefactors and be honoured by the community with a public burial and honorary
statue. Note that Philomusus' ex-slave Philippus was also sufficiently wealthy to
pay for this memorial.

Inscriptiones Latinae Selectae 6256 (Praeneste)

A site has been given for a public burial and statue in the forum of L.
Urvineius Philomusus, freedman of Lucius, the master of the guild of
freedmen, because in his will he granted free bathing for the populace for
three years and the combat of ten pairs of gladiators and a gold crown of
one pound weight for Fortuna Primigenia, and also games costing 200,000
sesterces over five days. Philippus his freedman set up this monument from
his own funds.

1.38 The happy auctioneer and herald

Horace's tale of the senator Philippus' joke at the expense of the auctioneer
Vulteius Mena offers useful details of Roman social relations. For instance, the
set of questions asked by Philippus' slave show the importance of identifying
class, family, and patron. Vulteius' life as an urban huckster is parodied, but the
view that the country offers a more respectable alternative to city life is also
shown to be highly dubious.

Horace, *Epistles* 1.7.46–97

Philippus was a sturdy, bold character, well known for his work in the
lawcourts. When he was returning from his duties at the eighth hour and,
now in his later years, grumbling that Carinae was too far away from the
forum, they say that he spotted a shaven-headed fellow in a barber's empty
shaded spot, leisurely cutting his nails with a pocket-knife. 'Demetrius' –
hereupon the slave readily picked up Philippus' orders – 'Go and ask, and
bring back the response, where his home is, what his status is, who is father
is, and who is his patron.' Off he went, returned, and told him: he was
called Vulteius Mena, the auctioneer; he was of little wealth, but blameless,
well known for rushing about the place, laying about, hunting things up
and using them, who took pleasure in his humble friends, a fixed abode,
the games, and the Campus Martius after a deal had been struck. 'I'd like
to learn from the man himself what you're saying. Tell him to come to
dinner.' Vulteius couldn't believe it, that's for sure, and silently wondered
to himself. To cut a long story short, he replied, 'Thanks all the same.' 'He
turned me down?' 'The rascal says no – he's either ignoring you or scared

31

of you.' Next morning Philippus surprised Vulteius selling cheap bits and pieces to the tunic-wearing rabble and got in his greeting first. He made his excuses to Philippus – his work and the chains of employment – for not coming to his house in the morning and, worst of all, that he hadn't seen him coming. 'Consider yourself forgiven, if you'll dine with me today.' 'Whatever you like.' 'So, come after the ninth hour. Now on your way, get hard at work at increasing your wealth.' The dinner took place, he spoke what he should and shouldn't, and at long last was sent home to bed. Then, when the fish was seen often swimming up to the hidden hook, appearing in the morning as a client and now established as a dinner companion, he told him to accompany him to his country estate outside town at the Latin festival. Driven along by ponies, Vulteius couldn't stop praising the Sabine fields and climate. Philippus saw this and laughed: ever on the lookout for a spot of relaxation and laughter from anywhere, giving him 7,000 sesterces and promising a loan of 7,000 more, he persuaded him into buying a farmlet. He bought it. Not to string you out with a long and winding tale more than necessary: he went from being a dude to being a yokel, barking on about furrows and unadulterated vineyards. He got his elms ready, got stuck into his studies, and spent ages in his love for profit. But when his sheep went from rustling, his goats from disease, his crop failed his expectations, his ox was killed off by the ploughing, he became fed up with his losses. He grabbed his nag in the middle of the night and set off for Philippus' house in a rage. As soon as Philippus saw him dirty and unshaven, he said, 'Vulteius, it looks to me that you are far too hard-working and keen.' 'Streuth, you could call me wretched, boss, if you wanted to give me a proper name. But, I beg and plead with you by your Genius, your right-hand, and your household gods, send me back to my previous life.' As soon as he saw how much more what he had given up was in comparison with what he was after, he hastily went back and took up again what he had left behind.

1.39 An upper-class definition of dishonourable and respectable trades

Cicero's negative judgement on small-time traders, but approval of larger-scale commerce, particularly when the profits are invested in land, has formed the basis for differing views of the Roman economy. For Finley (1985), it shows that the Romans were not used to investing for growth, but chose safe, if marginally productive, agricultural investments. By contrast, D'Arms (1981) has emphasised the role of senatorial families in fostering trade in the late republican and imperial periods. The debate continues: Erdkamp (2001).

Cicero, *On Duties* 1.150–1

This judgement is what we have more or less settled on about occupations and professions, as to which should be considered worthy of a free man and which low-class. First, those professions that meet with general hostility, such as those of customs collection and moneylending, fail to win approval. Next the trades of all men, who are available for hire and whose labour rather than skills are being paid for, are unworthy of a free man and are low-class. For in these trades the pay itself is a contract of enslavement. Also to be considered low-class are those who buy goods from retailers to sell immediately: they couldn't make a profit unless they lied to some degree, and there is nothing more shameful than misleading others. All craftsfolk engage in low-class skills, since a workshop has nothing respectable about it. Those skills are least deserving of approval that serve our pleasures, 'the fishmongers, butchers, cooks, poulterers, and fishermen', as Terence says [*Eunuch* 257]. Please add to this the perfumers, ballet dancers, and the whole cabaret set [*ludus talarius*: a low-status dance]. However, skills that involve considerable intelligence or aim at some particularly useful outcome, such as medicine, architecture, and the teaching of the arts, are respectable for those whose status they suit. Trading should be considered low-class if it is small-scale, but if it is large-scale and extensive, bringing in all sorts of things from everywhere and supplying many without misleading them, it is not to be particularly criticised. And if glutted – or better, satisfied – with its profits, trading turns from harbour to land and property (just as it has often come in from the high seas to harbour), it seems that it can rightly be praised. For of all things from which one can profit, nothing is better, nothing more productive, nothing sweeter, nothing more worthy of a man who is free, than farming.

1.40 How to be a successful businessman – without letting it show

More significant than trade was one's attitude towards it. Being overly concerned with such activities was depicted in the ancient world as banausic, but one escape route was to give the appearance of following traditional upper class interests, such as in literature.

Philostratus, *Lives of the Sophists* 2.21.2

[Proclus of Naucratis] received from Egypt incense, ivory, myrrh, papyrus, books, and all that sort of merchandise. He sold this on to those who deal with such products, but did not appear to be seeking profit, ungentlemanly, a lover of gain, nor to be hunting for revenue or for a return on his investment, but seemed to be devoted to antiquity.

1.41 Games put on for profit – a disgrace and a disaster

Tacitus' depiction of the Fidenae disaster once again contrasts the concept of public munificence with the profit motif. The reaction of the senate was to disqualify those beneath equestrian rank from putting on such displays.

Tacitus, *Annals* 4.62–3

When Marcus Licinius and Lucius Calpurnius were consuls [AD 27], an unforeseen calamity matched the disasters of the greatest of wars. Its origin and outcome became apparent at the same time. For a fellow of freedman origin, named Atilius, had begun the construction of an amphitheatre at Fidenae to put on gladiatorial games and had not laid the foundations on solid ground or built the wooden superstructure with solid bracing, just as one would expect of someone who had undertaken that task not because he had plenty of money or from a desire for small-town popularity, but for squalid profit. Men and women of all age groups flocked in eagerly, because they were held back from such pleasures while Tiberius was emperor, and in all the greater numbers because of the proximity of the site. So the catastrophe was even more immense, as the structure was packed and then torn apart, collapsing inwards or falling outwards, and it dragged with it a huge number of people, watching the games or standing around, and buried them ... Fifty thousand were maimed or crushed to death in that disaster. For the future, a senatorial decree forbade anyone to put on a gladiatorial show whose wealth was less than 400,000 sesterces and that any theatre be erected unless it was built on ground surveyed for its solidity.

1.42 An unsuccessful life

While most monuments celebrate the achievements of the dead, this tomb inscription celebrates the deceased's concern for others in death to compensate for a lack of success while alive. At the conclusion, the extent of the monument and ground is stated to ensure that no one encroaches on the site.

Inscriptiones Latinae Selectae 7519
(Rome, by the via Salaria)

Lucius Licinius Nepos, the son of Marcus, of the Pollian tribe, about whose life no one can rightly complain, [speaks]:

'He hoped that he would become wealthy through his business activities; but he was cheated by his hopes and by many friends, although he served them well. He built this little dwelling in a short period at the end of his life as his abode, with greater care than the cost he could afford. He has erected this stone monument to his dead parents in a secluded spot, underneath which he has ensured that the bones and ashes of his brother Gaius would remain and rest in his city, and through which he can testify with what effort and lack of ease he lived. When he was alive he gave this final hospitality for many friends in time to come; in this shelter they will rest with many grateful friends. He asks them that they make a gift of what they have left over to their folks, for free, and not sell it. Avoid greedy, heedless men, who show no respect for monuments, who do not allow the dead to ever rest.'

Sacred to his spirit. Sir, do not violate this, when you consider that you too will die.
Twelve feet square.

1.43 The honest goatskin seller

While the upper classes might disdain traders, those engaged in trade could take considerable pride in their achievements. In this case, Mithres has acquired sufficient resources to construct a tomb for his entire household and descendants and celebrates this by the literary game of spelling out his name in an acrostic.

Inscriptiones Latinae Selectae 7542
(Maglianum, Sabine territory, Italy)

To the spirits of the dead. The man whose name is spelled out by the first letter of each line built this while he was alive for himself and all his family, his freedmen and freedwomen, and all their descendants.

Liberated for anxieties I will be – note this reader – I, who was
Notable in the holy city for the sale of goatskins. I
Exhibited goods that were suitable for the people's use, I, whose
Rare honesty was praised everywhere and always. My life was
Very fortunate: I built myself a marble home, I was
Steadfast in my actions, as a dealer I always paid my taxes, and
    was honest
In all my business arrangements. I was as
Upright in my dealings as I could be, and often helped those who
    asked, I always
Showed respect to others and was always courteous to my friends.
    Still greater is the
Measure of glory here, and more useful to all as well, that
I arranged such protection for my limbs
That I acted not thinking only about myself alone, but also thought
    about my
Heirs. Whoever lies in his own property,

Retains everything with him.This tale will be told about me:
    I lived as an
Example of honour while life remained, and from my
Solicitude for many, I also created a refuge for many.

L. Nerusius Mithres.

1.44 A humble guild

Some social protection was given to the lower classes by the institution of collegia, guilds that met for social purposes and also ensured proper burial for their members.

Inscriptiones Latinae Selectae 7293 (Potentia, Lucania)

To Mettius Potitus, who lived 18 years. The guild of muleteers and ass-drivers dedicates this.

1.45 A cobbler's tombstone

In addition to the inscription, this tombstone depicts the cobbler sitting by a stool, which has cobbler's tools on it. This is typical of the pride expressed in their trades by many workers in the Roman world (see Joshel 1992).

Inscriptiones Latinae Selectae 7545 (Milan)

Gaius Atilius Iustus, son of Gaius, sandal cobbler, gave instructions in his will that this was to be set up for him and Cornelia Exorata his wife.

1.46 A quarryman's wage receipt from Egypt

This receipt comes from the mines at Mons Claudianus, near the Red Sea. For a detailed explanation, see Cuvigny (1996). The worker will obtain his own food, but in return the cost will be deducted from his wages. The pay rate of 47 drachmae is explained by Cuvigny as one-twelfth of 564 drachmae (= 141 sesterces), a pay rate calculated on an annual contract basis. Almost identical pay rates are known for miners in Dacia, which suggest an empire-wide system of pay scales.

Ostraca Claudiana 4751

Instructions from Pachoumis [to the paymaster] in the month of Thoth.

For pay: 47 drachmae; deduct from this: 20 drachmae in advance payment (you will get a receipt), 3 cotylae of oil, 1 mation of lentils, 1 mation of onions, 1 jar of wine, 3 drachmae for subscription; the wheat to go to the mountain; 4 obols for expenses; the rest to go to the mountain.

1.47 The importance of a trade and retaining one's tools

In the ancient populace there is a clear distinction between those who suffered periods of poverty and those who were permanently indigent. A trade not only gave personal self-esteem, but the possibility of escape from the poverty trap. Those who were forced to sell their tools did so only in the face of absolute necessity.

John Chrysostom, *On Lazarus* 3.2 = *Patrologia Graeca* 48.993

Don't you see how the bronzesmiths, the goldsmiths, the silversmiths, and those who follow any trade at all, when they have all the instruments that are needed for their trade, choose to endure anything – even if hunger forces them, even if poverty grinds them down – rather than part with any of the tools of their trade and so gain nourishment? Certainly many people often prefer to take out loans and so feed their households and children, rather than part with even the least of the tools of their trade. And rightly so, since we know that, if they sold them, their entire craft would be useless to them and their chance of prosperity would have been entirely lost. But, while they still remain, it is possible by continually practising their trade to pay off over time the debt incurred. But if they first hand over these tools to others, they will no longer be able to devise any relief from their poverty and hunger.

1.48 A trustworthy ex-slave and client

This inscription offers an exemplary picture of the relationship between patron and reliable client. Pliny the Elder (*Natural History* 33.139) indicates that 'Clodian' was a type of silver engraving – others included Furnian and Gratian engraving.

Inscriptiones Latinae Selectae 7695 (Rome)

To the spirits of the dead. Marcus Canuleius Zosimus, who lived 28 years. His patron set this up for his freedman who served him well. This man spoke ill of no one in his life, did nothing without his patron's approval, and, although there was a considerable amount of gold and silver in his possession at all times, he never desired any of it. This man surpassed all in the engraving of Clodian bowls.

1.49 The significance of the dream of losing one's head
for various status classes

The manuals of the second-century AD dream interpreter, Artemidorus, by adapting their predictive outcome to the status of the dreamer, offer considerable information on social expectations. In the interpretations below the 'head' is often taken metaphorically. So 'capital' (*kephalaia*) is derived from 'head' (*kephalê*; cf. Latin *caput*, the source of English 'capital') and loss of status is depicted as the same as losing one's head (cf. Latin *capitis deminutio*).

Artemidorus, *On the Interpretation of Dreams* 1.35

To dream that you have lost your head whether from a legal decision or because of bandits or in a gladiatorial fight or in any fashion at all (it makes no difference) is bad for those who have parents alive or children. For the head is like parents as being the source of life, but like children because of the face and appearance. In the past some have been deprived of a wife or a friend or a good steward and no longer possessed a countenance overseeing their property. Some having a house have lost their house, since the head is, so to speak, the home of the senses. But, if someone were to have all these things, it is clear that the dream does not refer to them all, but, as I have observed, to whoever is most cherished, loved, and closely related to the dreamer. This dream is good for someone who is a defendant on a capital charge. For anything that, having occurred once to anyone cannot occur twice, after it has occurred once in a dream, will no longer occur in the future. For it has taken place already. For bankers, moneylenders, fund-managers, shippers, merchants, and all those who are building up their wealth, it indicates loss of their capital because of the similarity of the words. It is good for the indebted for the same reason. The man in a foreign land will return to his own and the man who has a court case about land will win it, because a head cut off falls to the ground and remains there and ensures that the rest of the body will not suffer any more. To a slave in a position of responsibility it indicates being relieved of that responsibility, as no one is decapitated without a court decision or else because someone without a head is not trusted. For the person without status is said to be headless. For all others the dream indicates freedom. For the head is in charge of the body, but when it is removed it indicates that the slave, separated from his master, will be free. Many have bought this very state. But in cases of deciding social standing or money, the dream indicates the loss of the case. The reason is obvious. If someone who is sailing sees this dream, it indicates that the sail yard of the boat will be lost – that is, if one of the sailors should be the dreamer. For I have also seen this indicating death for those in command. For the boatswain is in command of the passengers, the bow officer is in command of the boatswain, the helmsman in command of the bow officer, and the captain in command of the helmsman. One could say that the sail yard was on top of the merchants and passengers. I know of a person who dreamt that his head was cut off and from being a Greek gained Roman citizenship and so had his previous name and standing removed.

To have two or three heads is good for an athlete, for he will win crowns in the same number of competitions. It is also good for a poor man, for, in addition to getting much capital and acquiring much wealth, his children will also be respectful to him and his wife will be compliant. For a rich man it indicates opposition from his relatives. If his previous head is prominent, those opposing him will not overcome him. But, if it is secondary, it indicates danger and death for him.

1.50 A successful harvester

Roman society is sometimes depicted as one in which there was considerable social fluidity, where even the poor might rise to power and wealth. While the opportunities for social climbing may be exaggerated, it is clear that some achieved remarkable success. The harvester of Mactar is a particularly spectacular example, although hard work alone is unlikely to explain his rise to censor in his home town.

Inscriptiones Latinae Selectae 7457 (Mactar, Tunisia)

I was born into a poor dwelling and of a poor father, who had no property or household. From the time of my birth, I lived in the country looking after my business; there was no time off in the countryside and none for me at any time. And when the time of year had brought forth the grain ready for harvest, then I was the first reaper of the stalks. When the sickle-bearing gangs of men had made their way to the fields, whether heading for The Nomads of Cirta or The Fields of Jupiter, as harvester I preceded them all, first into the fields, leaving the packed bands behind my back. I reaped twelve harvests under the raging sun, and afterwards became a work gang leader instead of a labourer. We led the gangs of harvesters for eleven years and our band cut down the Numidian fields. This effort and my frugal lifestyle brought success and made me master of a household and gained me a house, and my home itself lacks nothing. And my life gained the rewards of office: I was myself enrolled among the conscript councillors. Elected by the order [of the decurions], I had a seat in the order's temple and, starting out as a humble country boy, I too became censor. I produced children and saw them grow into young men and saw their children too. In accord with our services in life, we have enjoyed years of fame, which no bitter tongue has hurt with any reproach. People, learn to pass your lives without giving reason for reproach. The man who has lived without deceit has earned meeting his death in such a manner.

1.51 A petition from the tenants of the Burunitan estate, Tunisia (second century AD)

In the countryside, large estate holders had virtually regal power. In the case of the Burunitan estate in North Africa, the lessee of the imperial land had arranged with the procurator in the province for the use of armed forces to compel the tenants to provide labour beyond that specified in their contract. A petition from the tenants made its way to the emperor, Commodus; his response that only customary duties might be enforced was inscribed along with a coda, indicating the accuracy of the correspondence.

Inscriptiones Latinae Selectae 6870 (Soukh el Khmis)

[From this you can understand the collusion of your procurator], which involves not only Allius Maximus our opponent but practically all the lessees, contrary to natural justice and with unceasing harm to your revenues: he has not only avoided considering our case, although we petitioned him more than many years ago and begged him and read out your divine response, but he has even supported to the bitter end Allius Maximus the lessee, who has absolute sway with him by his craftiness, and has sent troops into this same Burunitan estate and ordered that some of us be arrested and harassed, others be placed in chains, and that many, including Roman citizens as well, be beaten with whips and clubs. The only reason why we deserved this was because, in the face of so terrible a wrong, given our modest means, and such a blatant wrong too, when we came to implore your majesty we employed a somewhat hostile tone in our letter. The obviousness of the wrong done to us, Caesar, can be readily judged from the fact that [we are forced] to offer our labour ... This has forced us pitiful folk once again to beg for your divine foresight: we beg you, most sacred emperor, to help us. Since that right has been removed by the section of Hadrian's law cited above, let the right be removed from the procurators, not to mention the lessee, of increasing their share of produce or of increasing their demands for labour or use of animals. The instructions of the procurators, which are in your archive for the Carthaginian district, have specified in them that we should not owe more than two days' ploughing each year, two days of sowing, and two days of reaping. Let that be accepted by all, certainly when the stipulations are engraved on bronze and are furnished by all our neighbours around in all directions in a continuous pattern down to the present and are duly confirmed by the letters of the procurators, which we cited above. Please help: we are impoverished country folk supporting our lives by the work of our hands but unable to match the influence of the lessee with his extravagant gifts before your procurators, a man who is well known to them as they succeed each other through the terms of the lease. Take pity on us and in your sacred response deign to indicate that we do not need to offer more than what is in accord with Hadrian's law and the letters of your procurators, that is, three occurrences of two days' work. So, through your majesty's generosity, we, your rustic house slaves and the foster-children of your estates, may not be troubled further by the lessees of the lands belonging to the treasury . . .

The emperor Caesar Marcus Aurelius Commodus Antoninus Augustus Sarmaticus Germanicus Maximus to Lurius Lucullus and the others in whose name he made his petition: My procurators, in consideration of customary practice and my decision, will ensure that nothing is wrongfully demanded from you contrary to the established measures.

[And written in another hand:] I have recorded this. I have ascertained the accuracy of the record. This is a copy of the letter of the noble gentleman, the procurator. . . .

REFERENCES AND FURTHER READING

Bartsch, S. (1994) *Actors in the Audience: Theatricality and Doublespeak from Nero to Hadrian*, Cambridge, MA.

Bauman, R. (1992) *Women and Politics in Ancient Rome*, London.

Cuvigny, H. (1996) 'The Amount of Wages Paid to the Quarry-Workers at Mons Claudianus', *Journal of Roman Studies* 86: 139–45.

D'Arms, J.H. (1981) *Commerce and Social Standing in Ancient Rome*, Cambridge, MA.

de Ligt, L. (2002) 'Restraining the Rich, Protecting the Poor: Symbolic Aspects of Roman Legislation', in Jongman, W. and Kleijwegt, M. (eds) *After the Past*, Leiden, pp. 1–46.

Erdkamp, P. (2001) 'Beyond the Limits of the 'Consumer City': A Model of the Urban and Rural Economy in the Roman World', *Historia* 50: 332–56.

Finley, M. (1985) *The Ancient Economy*, 2nd edn, London.

Gardner, J. (1993) *Being a Roman Citizen*, London.

Garnsey, P. (1970) *Social Status and Legal Privilege in the Roman Empire*, Oxford.

Giardina, A. (1993) *The Romans*, Chicago, IL.

Gradel, I. (2002) *Emperor Worship and Roman Religion*, Oxford.

Hopkins, K. (1978) *Conquerors and Slaves*, Cambridge.

Hopkins, K. (1983) *Death and Renewal*, Cambridge.

Joshel, S. (1992) *Work, Identity, and Legal Status at Rome*, Norman, OK.

Kaster, R.A. (2005) *Emotion, Restraint, and Community in Ancient Rome*, Oxford.

Levick, B. (1985) *Government of the Roman Empire: A Sourcebook*, London.

Lintott, A. (1993) *Imperium Romanum: Politics and Administration*, London.

MacMullen, R. (1990) *Changes in the Roman Empire*, Princeton, NJ.

Millar, F. (1992) *The Emperor in the Roman World*, 2nd edn, London.

Patterson, J. (1992) 'Patronage, *Collegia* and Burial in Imperial Rome', in Bassett, S. (ed.) *Death in Towns*, Leicester.

Pomeroy, A. (1991) 'Status Anxiety in the Greco-Roman Dream Books', *Ancient Society* (Louvain) 22: 51–74.

Price, S. (1984) *Rituals and Power: The Roman Imperial Cult in Asia Minor*, Cambridge.

Purcell, N. (1983) 'The *Apparitores*: A Study in Social Mobility', *Papers of the British School at Rome* 51: 125–73.

Saller, R. (1981) *Personal Patronage under the Early Empire*, Cambridge.

Talbert, R. (1984) *The Senate of Imperial Rome*, Princeton, NJ.

Veyne, P. (1998) *Bread and Circuses*, Harmondsworth.

2

DEMOGRAPHY

Demography is the study of the structure and dynamics of human populations. If we possessed all the information we needed on the Roman world, we would be able to trace, among other matters, economic trends, the effects of disease and efforts to counter this, and social changes. Unfortunately, given the lack of reliable information available, things are not so simple.

At its most basic level, ancient demography concerns itself with the size of populations, a hotly debated topic since we have little information from antiquity and most of what we do have is contradictory or confused, dealing most often with army sizes. Other avenues of enquiry, based on such factors as the carrying capacity of the land or the quantity of food imports, are unpromising. In general, scholars accept some conclusions (about none of which, however, there is total consensus): that the population of the city of Rome in the early first century AD was most likely around 1 million, that of Italy 5–6 million, and that of the Roman empire as a whole of the order of 50–60 million. The subject has been discussed by Scheidel (2004, 2005), who indicates the lack of reliable evidence for these figures. His conclusions on numbers in the free and slave populations do not differ markedly from standard estimates.

These figures are based on deductions from multiple pieces of evidence. For instance, statements about the size of Alexandria (2.1) and Apamea (2.2) help to set the parameters for city populations in the empire. But, given the lack of publicly circulating statistics, remarks on the size of populations may also be simply conjectures, influenced by factors such as the desire to increase the importance of the town in question (2.3, 2.4). The best evidence available is for Roman Egypt, but even this is not without problems (2.5). Attempts have been made to extrapolate the population of Rome from the number of recipients of food aid (2.6) or the amounts of grain imported (2.7). Information on the city's buildings is given in late antique handbooks (2.8), but the reliability of these accounts is also very uncertain. Perhaps best is simply to accept the general view that it was larger than any other city in the empire (2.9).

43

At a more sophisticated level, demography concerns itself with the structure of populations. Three factors are crucial: mortality, fertility, and migration. Again ancient evidence is sparse and problematic; the ancient demographer has very little in the way of census material, or records of births, deaths, and marriages, with which to work. Most ancient evidence, such as tombstone inscriptions and skeletons, is, unfortunately, of very little value. Over 300 census returns from Roman Egypt have survived and with sophisticated interpretation can yield important clues. But we are most reliant on comparative evidence and tools, for example model life tables, to clarify what is plausible or probable in terms of ancient populations.

The most striking feature regarding Roman mortality is how high its rate was from an early age. In general terms average life expectancy at birth was between 20 and 30 years. This highlights, more than anything else perhaps, the vast difference between ancient times and our own. In this regard the ancient world is more comparable to so-called Third World countries today than to 'developed' countries. The low figure is mainly reflective of very harsh levels of infant mortality, owing particularly to gastrointestinal illnesses. One in three children died in their first year of life – a great proportion within the first few weeks, often depending upon whether or not infants were breastfed immediately. One in two children did not survive beyond the age of 10 years. After that life looks a little brighter. A 10-year-old might expect on average to live another 35–40 years, a 40-year-old at least another 20 years. So some people in the Roman world did survive into old age, but not as great a proportion as do today. Longevity was not necessarily desirable, given physical decline and lack of palliative treatment (2.10). Most older adults would not have parents alive, and would quite likely themselves have lost children. As to mortality differences due to gender, we cannot be certain. It is highly probable that women did not generally live as long as men (maternal mortality is one relevant factor (cf. 2.11), though its level should not be exaggerated), and that males very slightly outnumbered females in the population.

Such high mortality may be attributed to a combination of low levels of hygiene and sanitation (particularly in urbanised areas) and of low standards of medical care, as well as poor nutrition for poorer people. We hear much in the ancient sources of food shortages, epidemics (infectious diseases must have taken a severe toll), and war – Malthus' positive checks (2.12, 2.13). Some areas of the ancient world were felt to be healthier (e.g. Africa (2.14)), while others inherently unhealthy (e.g. Sardinia). While the wealthy might avoid the larger urban areas during epidemics or at times of the year when disease was likely to occur (2.15), the vast majority of the population could do little to improve their living conditions (see Chapter 6).

Modern demographic methods also allow us to glimpse the nature of the living population in terms of age structure, and here another notable difference from our own experience occurs. Ancient populations would have been very young; something like half the population would have been under the age of 25 years at any one time, and only about 7 per cent over the age of 60. Some individuals attained considerable age (2.16, 2.17), but much of our evidence for longevity is fabulous (2.18) or highly suspect (2.19).

To counteract high mortality, fertility levels also needed to be high. A woman in the Roman world on average gave birth five or six times (since many of those born would not survive). Some women produced many more than that; the (alleged) record was thirty births, while one woman in Roman Egypt was said to have given birth to quintuplets on four separate occasions. The level of infant mortality was extremely high (2.20) and complications from delivery might also affect the child throughout its life (2.21). High levels of fertility would also have increased the chance of maternal mortality (2.22) as well as generally reducing female life expectancy (2.23). It is noteworthy that our sources suggest that human sexual activity is unusually high compared to other animals, which would increase the rates of conception (2.24).

However, other women, especially due to quite high levels of infertility, never gave birth at all – such was a constant complaint of Roman upper-class men (women tending to get the blame). On the other hand, we hear quite a lot about contraception (a mixture of magic and medicine: 2.25), abortion, and exposure and/or infanticide (2.26). Poorer families, and even richer families who did not want to spread their wealth too widely, limited their family size by such means. But, even with such relatively high fertility levels, mortality rates ensured that average family size was small. Although some sources suggest population decline (2.27, 2.29) or increase (2.28) in areas of the Mediterranean world at various times, it is difficult to assess the reliability of such evidence.

The emperor Augustus felt that low fertility levels, at least among the Roman upper classes, were such a problem that he introduced legislation to benefit those married with children and penalise those who were married without children or who never even married in the first place (18 BC and AD 9). But never-married adults would have been rare: Romans married routinely, females in their mid- to late teens, males some ten years later. Again, however, mortality would have taken its toll. One or other of the spouses would on average have died within some eighteen years of married life. And it would seem that divorce rates were high as well.

Regarding migration it is more difficult to generalise, since our information is very patchy. Colonisation, widely practised, is the most obvious indication of migration in the ancient world, but most people probably moved little, or at most as young males from countryside to city to find a job or a bride. The slave trade was one of the less subtle forms of migration in the ancient world.

In order to calculate levels of population growth or decline, one needs to be able to measure rates of mortality, fertility, and migration. We do not have the variables to do this for antiquity. We have some information from census data recorded for purposes of taxation (2.30) that give indications of rates of mortality at a particular time and in a particular area. What looks like an actuarial table used for calculating the life expectancy of recipients of bequests (2.31) has attracted considerable attention. However, the steps on this table seem too schematic to be based on reliable data. Attempts to use skeletal remains are also problematic, due to the difficulty in dating the remains and variations in the survival of bone material (2.32). From census returns and literary evidence, it is clear that many in the ancient world would not have had an exact knowledge of their own age (2.33, 2.34).

Overall, it is reasonable to assume that at most periods in ancient history levels of growth were close to zero in the long term. High mortality rates were balanced by high levels of fertility. For ancient people this was the harsh reality of life, as reinforced by the number of funereal commemorations of young children (2.35, 2.36, 2.37, 2.38). 'Carpe diem' was one natural reaction (2.39).

2.1 The size of Alexandria

Diodorus in his universal history describes the founding of the city of Alexandria in Egypt in the fourth century BC; he goes on to consider the city's size in his own day, at the end of the republic.

In the fourth century AD Ausonius (*Ordo urbium nobilium* 1–5) ranks the cities of the empire: Rome, of course, is first, and Constantinople second, with Carthage very close behind, and Antioch (in Syria) and Alexandria next together. Antioch, in the time of Augustus, was nearly equal to Alexandria (Strabo 16.2.5); Herodian 4.3.7, writing early in the third century AD, records that Geta, Caracalla's younger brother, regarded Antioch as a rival to Alexandria, both being second only to Rome. Herodian later relates (7.6.1) that Gordian I regarded Carthage as 'second only to Rome in terms of wealth, population and size', though he notes that Alexandria also rivals for that position. Strabo (above) also notes that the city of Seleuceia on the Tigris is equivalent in size to Alexandria; according to Pliny the Elder (*Natural History* 6.122) the population of the latter's urban plebs was 600,000.

Diodorus' figure of 300,000 has the air of authenticity about it: despite its roundness, it appears to have been based on official figures (however accurate that might make it). See Delia (1988); Bagnall and Frier (1994: 53–6); and Haas (1997: 45–7, 375–6 n. 3).

Diodorus Siculus, 17.52.5–6

On the whole the city has grown to such an extent since its founding that many count it the first city of the civilised world. It is certainly far ahead of all the rest in terms of beauty, size, revenues, and luxury. The number of its inhabitants exceeds that of those other cities. At the time when we travelled to Egypt, those who keep the census records [*anagraphai*] of the inhabitants said that the number of free individuals living there exceeded 300,000.

2.2 The size of Apamea

The equestrian Q. Aemilius Secundus' tombstone (found in Venice) records his career, including the taking of the census of Apamea in Syria, south of Antioch. Quirinius was governor of Syria in AD 6.

Corpus Inscriptionum Latinarum 3.6687 = *Inscriptiones Latinae Selectae* 2683

Q. Aemilius Secundus, son of Quintus, of the Palatine tribe – I was decorated in the service of the divine Augustus under P. Sulpicius Quirinius, Caesar's governor in Syria, with the offices of prefect of the first Augustan cohort and prefect of the second naval cohort. Likewise, by the order of Quirinius I held the census of the *civitas* of Apamea of 117,000 citizens.

2.3 The population of Centuripae

The people of Centuripae, inland from Catania in eastern Sicily, had taken down the statues of their former governor (73–71 BC), the proconsul C. Verres. Verres' successor had ordered them to replace them. Cicero in 70 BC, in his (successful) prosecution of Verres, stresses how admirable the people of Centuripae were.

Cicero, *Verrines* 2.2.163

[If Metellus had not forced the people of Centuripae to replace the statues], I would have remarked on the fact that there are 10,000 citizens of Centuripae and they are our most brave and faithful allies, for all of them had decided that no statue of that man should be set up in their *civitas*.

2.4 Galen on his home town

Galen is writing about his native Pergamum, and about the fact that an individual is not satisfied with being richer than all his fellow citizens. From his account it has been deduced that Pergamum in the second century AD 'had a free adult population of about 80,000, and about 40,000 slaves, implying a total population of about 180,000 including children'. See Duncan-Jones (1982: 260 n. 4); cf. also Harris (1999: 65).

Galen, *De Propriorum Animi Dignotione et Curatione* (On diagnosing and caring for conditions specific to the mind) 9 (5.49 Kühn = *Corpus Medicorum Graecorum* 5.4.1.1.33)

So if our citizens total some four myriads [40,000], and you add women and slaves, you will find yourself not content to be richer than twelve myriads of humans.

2.5 The size of the population of Egypt

Knowing the population of a single province, especially one as large as Egypt, would be very useful for comparative purposes. Unfortunately, Philo and Josephus may be adjusting the numbers, either to suggest that they form a high proportion of the population or to indicate the size of the Roman empire against which the Jewish people had risen in revolt.

A century earlier than Josephus, Diodorus had stated that in the past the population of Egypt had been seven million; he also passes comment on the size of the population in his own day (he visited Egypt in the middle of the first century BC), but the text at that point is hotly disputed by scholars.

(a) Philo, *Against Flaccus* 43

So what did the governor of the country do? He knew that both the city [of Alexandria] and the whole of Egypt had two kinds of inhabitants, us and them, and that there were no fewer than one million Jews resident in Alexandria and the country from the slope into Libya to the boundaries of Ethiopia.

(b) Flavius Josephus, *Jewish War* 2.385

But what need is there to go so far afield to find proof of Rome's power, when I can find it at your very door, in Egypt? This country extends as far as Ethiopia and Arabia Felix, she is the port for India, and has a population of 7,500,000 people (excluding the inhabitants of Alexandria), as is shown by the poll-tax returns. This country does not disdain to submit to Roman domination; and yet what an incentive to revolt she has in Alexandria, with its population, its wealth, and its size.

(c) Diodorus Siculus, 1.31.6–8

In terms of population numbers, Egypt in the past far exceeded all known regions of the inhabited world, and even in our own day it is regarded as being second to none other. For in ancient times it had over 18,000 considerable towns and cities, as may be seen recorded in the sacred archives, while in the reign of Ptolemy [i.e. Ptolemy I Soter, who died in 283/2 BC], son of Lagus, these were reckoned at over 30,000, a number that pertains down to our own day. The total population in ancient times, they say, was around seven million, and in our day it is not less than three [seven?[1]] million.

1 Most manuscripts read *triakosiôn*, that is 'than thirty (myriads)' = three million. But editors now usually change *triakosiôn* to *toutôn*, 'than these', referring back to the seven million of more ancient times.

2.6 The number of recipients of grain distributions at Rome

As to the size of the population of the city of Rome, one method is to try to calculate it on the basis of the so-called corn dole. See Rickman (1980: esp. 8–9). For introductory material on Rome's population, see Hopkins (1978: 96–8).

The maximum number to whom Augustus gave handouts was 320,000. There were males over a certain age, perhaps 14 years. To derive a total urban population number from this datum, one must make calculations for women and children, as well as slaves and resident aliens. And we have no idea what proportion of males did not receive the handouts.

Augustus, *Res Gestae* 15

To each of the Roman *plebs* I paid out 300 sesterces in accordance with the will of my father, and in my own name in my fifth consulship [29 BC] I gave 400 sesterces to each from the spoils of wars; and a second time, moreover, in my tenth consulship [24 BC] I paid out of my own patrimony 400 sesterces as a largesse to each man, and in my eleventh consulship [23 BC] I made twelve distributions of grain, grain bought at my own expense, and in the twelfth year of my tribunician power [12 BC] I gave for the third time 400 sesterces to each man. These largesses of mine reached a number of persons never less than 250,000. In the eighteenth year of my tribunician power, as consul for the twelfth time [5 BC], I gave to 320,000 of the urban *plebs* 60 denarii apiece. In the colonies of my soldiers, as consul for the fifth time [29 BC], I gave 1,000 sesterces to each man from booty; about 120,000 men in the colonies received this triumphal largesse. When consul for the thirteenth time [2 BC] I gave 60 denarii apiece to the *plebs* who were then receiving public grain; these were a little more than 200,000 persons.

2.7 Quantities of grain imported to Rome

Perhaps we can estimate the size of Rome's population from the amount of grain the city imported? (cf. Rickman 1980: 231ff.). Note that in the so-called corn dole at Rome each recipient, from the first century BC on, received 5 modii of grain per month. The calorie count for such a ration is around 3,500 calories per day: a reasonable amount (cf. Duncan-Jones 1982: 147).

(a) [Aurelius Victor], *Epitome de Caesaribus* 1.6

In his [Augustus'] time, 20 million [modii] of grain were imported annually from Egypt to the city [of Rome].

Josephus (*The Jewish War* 2.383–6) has Agrippa say in the first century AD that North Africa provided food for the city of Rome for eight months of every year, with Egypt providing the other four months' supply. Of course there were also other sources of imports available to Rome. And allowance must be made for spoilage, loss to vermin, and shipping losses.

An ancient commentator on Lucan (the scholiast on Lucan *Pharsalia* 1.319, quoted in Weber (1831, vol. 3: 53)) mentions that in the late republic 80,000 modii per day were consumed at Rome.

If (and it is a very big 'if') any reliance can be placed on the *Scriptores Historiae Augustae*, the following passage should probably be related to the fourth century AD, the time of composition, rather than to the reign of Severus.

(b) *Historia Augusta: Septimius Severus* 8, 23

At the beginning of his reign Severus found the grain supply at a minimal capacity. But as emperor he managed it so well that on departing from life he left to the Roman people a surplus equivalent to seven years' tribute ..., enough to distribute 75,000 modii per day.

2.8 The regions of Rome and their buildings

Figures have been derived from the so-called regionary catalogues, the *Curiosum* and *Notitia*. These are lists of buildings and landmarks, arranged according to the fourteen Augustan *regiones* of the city and perhaps used as tourist guides to Rome: there is much about the lists that is debated, including their date (probably fourth century AD), as well as their purpose and the accuracy of the figures. Here we summarise some of the key figures. Where two figures are given side-by-side, the first is that recorded in the *Curiosum*, the second in the *Notitia*.

One of the many vexing questions remains the definition of *insula* here. For example, it has been estimated that the Via Giulio Romano *insula* on the Capitoline had room for 380 occupants: something that size could not be accommodated in such numbers in the *regiones* as here suggested (even if the measurements in Roman feet were accurate for each region). And one must also allow for space used for other purposes, in particular the monumental (especially, one would think, in *regiones* 8 and 10). Most scholars assume that *domus* refers to 'palatial' residences, and *insulae* to the dwellings of the poorer classes. Note that the ratio of total *domus* (1,681 or 1,682) to *insulae* (45,300 or 44,301) is well over 1:26; in *regio* 3, which includes the Flavian amphitheatre, it appears to be as high as

Region		Circuit (Roman *pedes*)	Districts (*vici*)	*Insulae*	*Domus*	Private baths (*balinea*)
1*	Porta Capena	12,211.5/ 12,219.5	10	3,250	120	86
2	Caelimontium	12,200	7	4,600/ 3,600	127	85
3	Isis et Serapis	12,350	12	2,757	60	80
4	Templum Pacis	13,000	8	2,757	88	65/ 75
5*	Esquiliae	15,600	15	3,850	180	75
6	Alta Semita	15,700	17	3,403	146	75
7*	Via Lata	13,300	15	3,805	120	75
8	Forum Romanum	14,067/ 13,067	34	3,480	130	86
9*	Circus Flaminius	32,500	35	2,777	140	63
10	Palatium	11,510	20	2,742/ 2,643	89	44
11	Circus Maximus	11,500	21/ 19	2,500/ 2,600	88/ 89	15
12*	Piscina Publica	12,000	17	2,487	113	63
13*	Aventinus	18,000	18/ 17	2,487	130	44/ 64
14*	Transtiberim	33,000/ 33,488	78	4,405	150	86
Totals (according to the *Breviarium*)			423/ 424	46,602	1,790	856
Actual totals			307/ 304	45,300/ 44,301	1,681/ 1,682	942/ 972

Note: *Regions outside the Servian walls.

1:46. Of course, as the totals help illustrate (first the number as recorded as the total, then the total from the figures recorded for the fourteen regions), numbers are notoriously subject to corruption in manuscript traditions (note too the repetition of the numbers 2,757 and 2,487 under *insulae*).

The figures we give in the above table are derived from the text published by A. Nordh, *Libellus de Regionibus Urbis Romae* (Lund, 1949). Among much scholarly discussion, see especially Hermansen (1978: 129–68), and also most recently Guilhembet (1996: 7–26), as well as Lo Cascio (1997: 58–63).

2.9 Impressions of the size of Rome

Cassiodorus (sixth century AD) reflects on the size of Rome in the distant past, while the *Scriptores Historiae Augustae* (fourth century) offers a typical comic take on the problem.

(a) Cassiodorus, *Variae* 11.39.1–2

It is clear how great the population of the city of Rome was, seeing that it was fed by supplies provided even from far-distant regions, and that the provinces around Rome provided only enough food for foreign residents, while the imported abundance was reserved for the Roman people themselves. A people who ruled the world could never be small in number! The huge extent of the city walls also bears witness to the multitudes of citizens, and so does the swollen capacity of the entertainment venues [*spectacula*], the amazing size of the public baths, and the great number of mills that were provided, of course, especially for the food supply.

(b) *Historia Augusta: Elagabalus* 26.6

The emperor Elagabalus used to play jokes on his slaves, and he even sent them off around the city of Rome to collect a thousand pounds of cobwebs, offering a prize; they returned, it is said, with ten thousand pounds of the stuff. Elagabalus deduced from this that Rome was indeed a big place.

2.10 The horrors of old age

Pliny the Elder, *Natural History* 7.168

It is certainly true that Nature has granted to humankind no more precious gift than shortness of life. The senses grow sluggish, limbs grow numb, sight, hearing, walking, even teeth and the digestive tract, all die before their time – and yet people count this as a part of life.

2.11 The tombstone of a centurion's wife

While tombstones are often inscribed with conventional praise of the dead (for instance, a wife's loyalty to her husband), they may also offer indications of infant and adult mortality.

Corpus Inscriptionum Latinarum 3.3572
(Aquincum, Pannonia Inferior)

Here do I lie at rest, a married woman, Veturia by name and descent, the wife of Fortunatus, the daughter of Veturius. I lived for thrice nine years, poor me, and I was married for twice eight. I slept with one man [*unicuba*], I was married to one man [*uniiuga*]. After having borne six children, one of whom survives me, I died. Titus Iulius Fortunatus, centurion of the Second Legion Adiutrix Pia Fidelis, set this up for his wife: she was incomparable and notably respectful to him [*incomparabili et insigni in se pietate*].

2.12 Disease and natural disasters at Rome

Living in a large city such as Rome exposed its inhabitants to calamities such as fire and building collapse, the effects of Nature through storm and floods, and susceptibility to infectious diseases. In some years, all these misfortunes might occur, each exacerbating the effects of the others.

(a) Cassius Dio, 53.33

Livia [wife of Augustus] was accused of the death of Marcellus, for the reason that he had been preferred before her sons. This suspicion was much disputed, however, because of the climatic conditions both of that year [23 BC] and of the subsequent one, which proved so unhealthy that great numbers died in both. And just as always tends to happen before such events, a wolf was caught in the city, fire and storm damaged many buildings, and the rising of the Tiber carried away the wooden bridge [the *Pons Sublicius*], and for three days made the city navigable for boats.

(b) Suetonius, *Nero* 39.1

To these terrible and shameful calamities caused by the emperor were added certain ones caused by chance, including a plague in which in a single autumn 30,000 deaths were recorded in the temple of Libitina.

(c) Tacitus, *Annals* 16.13

The gods too marked this crime-stained year with storms and pestilences. Campania was laid waste by a tornado, which smashed asunder villas, plantations, and crops and the violence of which reached as far as the neighbourhood of the city of Rome, in which a terrible plague was devastating the entire mortal population – and yet there was no visible blight in the air. But the houses were packed with lifeless bodies, the streets with funerals. Neither sex nor age was exempt from danger. Slave and free were snatched off suddenly, amidst the laments of wives and children who themselves, while sitting alongside, while mourning, were often cremated on the same pyre.

2.13 Plagues at Rome and elsewhere in the empire

The outbreak of infectious diseases during certain periods of the year (e.g. Autumn) was so common that only particularly severe epidemics are noted in our sources. Famine too is only occasionally recorded, although food shortages are likely to have been common. In his *Chronographia*, Theophanes the Confessor (eighth–ninth centuries AD) mentions a severe famine in the East under AD 331/2. This may have strongly contributed to the plague mentioned by Jerome in **2.13b** below.

In AD 189, during the reign of Commodus, the so-called Antonine plague (perhaps smallpox), which had first come to Rome from the East in 165 and which raged till 180, was back with a vengeance; its effect on the population was clearly catastrophic. See most recently Frier (2000), Scheidel (2002), and Bagnall (2002).

(a) Jerome, *Chronicle* 188h Helm (AD 77 ?)

A great plague [*lues*] occurred at Rome, so great that for many days nearly 10,000 names of dead people were recorded in the register.

(b) Jerome, *Chronicle* 233e Helm (AD 333)

A countless multitude died from pestilence and famine in Syria and Cilicia.

(c) Cassius Dio, 72.14.3–4 (AD 189)

And a plague occurred, the greatest plague I know of. At any rate two thousand individuals regularly died at Rome in a single day. And what is more many people, not only at Rome but allegedly through the whole empire, were killed at the hands of criminals who smeared deadly poisons on tiny needles and were paid to infect people in this way. The same thing had apparently happened before in the reign of Domitian [see Dio 67.11.6].

2.14 The effect of locality on life expectancy

While life in the large cities of the Roman world was notoriously unhealthy, some geographical areas had a reputation for prosperity. Writers regularly remark on the fertility of the soil and the people of Africa, and Africans were proverbially long-lived. In the north, the Thracians are regarded as healthy because of the freshness of the air and the lack of contact with more civilised peoples.

(a) Sallust, *Jugurthine War* 17.6

The inhabitants of Africa are healthy, swiftfooted, and of great physical endurance. Most of them die gradually of old age, unless they are killed by the steel or wild beasts, for disease rarely overcomes anyone. Moreover, there are many species there of dangerous wild animals.

(b) Ammianus Marcellinus, 27.4.14

It is well established (as constant reports have spread about) that almost all the rural people who dwell in the mountain areas throughout the regions just described enjoy far better physical health and chances for a longer life than we do. This they believe is a result of the fact that they tend to avoid too many hot foods and that cold sprinklings of dew constantly keep their bodies fresh. They also enjoy the sweetness of a purer air and they are the first of all people to feel the sun's natural life-giving rays before they are infected with the taint of human affairs.

2.15 Rural retreats and infectious diseases

One response to urban living conditions was for the wealthy to retire to their country estates in the stifling heat of summer. Although Seneca insists that from a psychological viewpoint all sites are equivalent, most ancients attributed ill-health to geographical factors.

Still some diseases were known to be spread by contact (and thus avoidable), as Pliny the Younger's comments on dermatitis indicate. Suetonius, *Tiberius* 34.2, mentions that Tiberius issued an edict against 'everyday kissing' (*cotidiana oscula*).

(a) Pliny, *Letters* 5.6.5–6

Summers there are wonderfully temperate. The air is always being stirred up by some spirit, though more often a breeze than a wind. Hence the many old people [*senes*] – you can see there the grandfathers and greatgrandfathers of people who are themselves adults, and you can hear stories from days gone by and words of our ancestors; being there is like living in an earlier age.

(b) Seneca, *Letters* 104.1

I have fled to my villa in Nomentum [modern Mentana, close to Rome]. Fled what, you ask? Rome? No, a fever, and one that was really working its way in. It had already taken hold of me. My doctor said the early signs were there: irregular pulse, its natural rhythms upset. At that I ordered my carriage got ready forthwith; although my Paulina held me back I insisted on driving off. I kept saying the same thing my *dominus* Gallio [i.e. his older brother] said when he began to feel feverish in Achaia; straightaway he went on board ship, insisting that the sickness lay in the place, not in his body.

(c) Pliny the Elder, *Natural History* 26.3

This plague [*lues*] was unknown to our fathers and forefathers, and it first stole into Italy in the middle of the principate of Tiberius Caesar, when a certain Roman equestrian from Perusia, the secretary of a quaestor, introduced the contagion from Asia where he had served. Women, slaves, and the lower and middle classes [*plebes humilis aut media*] did not suffer from the ailment, but the upper classes [*proceres*] were very much affected through the swift contact of the kiss.

2.16 Longevity

Of the c.10,000 tombstone inscriptions from Rome contained in *Corpus Inscriptionum Latinarum*, volume 6, the oldest person recorded, a freedman, died, it is said, at the age of 113 years. The inscription comes from a *columbarium*. The former owner of this freedman, L. Sempronius Atratinus, may be identified as the suffect consul of 34 BC who himself died at the age, it would seem, of 79 years. See Syme (1986: 329).

Corpus Inscriptionorum Latinarum, 6.6835

Lucius Sempronius Lethaeus, the freedman of Atratinus, lived 113 years.

2.17 Long-lived women

On occasion women also feature in lists of *makrobioi* (long-lived individuals).

Pliny the Elder, *Natural History* 7.158

Livia, the wife of Rutilius, exceeded 97 years; Statilia, a member of a noble family in the reign of Claudius, 99 years; Terentia, Cicero's wife, 103; Clodia, wife of Ofilius, 115 – she also actually gave birth fifteen times. The mime actress [*mima*] Lucceia gave a reading on stage at the age of 100. Galeria Copiola, the actress of interludes, was 104 years of age when she was brought back onto the stage in the consulship of Gaius Poppaeus and Quintus Sulpicius [AD 9] as part of the votive games celebrating the safety of the divine Augustus.

2.18 Fabulous long-lived men

Pliny the Elder, on the topic of human longevity, reflected that various fabulous ages attributed to legendary figures are 'uncertain' because of problems of chronology (*inscitia temporum*). He dismisses (7.154) such legends as Arganthonius, king of the Tartesians of southern Spain in the sixth century BC, living to the age of 150 years (as recorded by Anacreon); a few paragraphs later, however, he turns to 'facts'. It seems fairly certain to Pliny, apparently, that Arganthonius lived to at least the age of 120 years.

For these and other such examples, see Parkin (2003: esp. ch. 2). Specifically on Arganthonius, see Parkin (2003: 323 n. 16).

Pliny the Elder, *Natural History* 7.156

But let us cross to admitted facts [*confessa*]. It is almost certain that Arganthonius of Gades [Cadiz] reigned for 80 years; they believe he took up his rule in his fortieth year. It is beyond doubt that Masinissa ruled for 60 years, and that Gorgias of Sicily lived for 108 years.

2.19 Long-lived individuals recorded in the census

The figures recorded by Pliny the Elder, and, somewhat differently, by Phlegon (*Die Fragmente der griechischen Historiker* 257 F 37), were apparently derived from the Roman census of AD ·73/4. An incredible number of centenarians is reported for the eighth *regio* of Italy, up to the age of 150 years. See Parkin (2003: 185–7).

Pliny the Elder, *Natural History* 7.162–4

We also have examples from the most recent census, held within the last three years by the imperial Caesars Vespasiani, father and son [Vespasian and Titus] as censors. And there is no need to search through all the records: we shall only produce cases from the middle region between the Apennines and the Po. Three people at Parma declared themselves as 120 years, at Brixellum one; two people at Parma as 125; one man at Placentia and one woman at Faventia as 130; Lucius Terentius, son of Marcus, of Bononia as 135; and Marcus Aponius 140 and Tertulla 137 at Ariminum. In the hills this side of Placentia is the township of Veleia, in which six declared themselves to be 110 years old, four 120, one (Marcus Mucius Felix, son of Marcius, of the Galerian tribe) 150. And, so as not to delay ourselves any further over a matter of admitted fact, in the census of the eighth region of Italy there were registered fifty-four persons of 100 years of age, fourteen of 110, two of 125, four of 130, the same number of those aged 135 or 137, and three of 140 years.

The figures from both Pliny the Elder and Phlegon from the census may be summarised thus:

Age in years	Number of individuals in Pliny	Number of individuals in Phlegon
100–109	54	63
110–119	14	5
120–129	10	1
130+	12	1
Totals	90	70

2.20 Infant mortality

Popular superstitions may often reveal underlying social and cultural realities, in this case the perception of relatively high levels of maternal and neonatal mortality, as well as attitudes towards gender differences.

Pliny the Elder, *Natural History* 7.37–8, 41, 42

At the birth of twins it is [said to be] rare for the woman giving birth or one of the twins to survive, but if twins are born, one of each sex, it is even more unusual for *either* to survive. Girls are born more swiftly than boys, just as they age more quickly. Males more often move in the womb; males tend to be carried on the right side, females on the left ... A child born before the seventh month is usually stillborn ... A woman bearing a male child has a better colour and an easier delivery; there is movement in the womb on the fortieth day. A woman bearing a girl has totally the opposite symptoms: the weight is hard to carry, there is a slight swelling of the legs and groin, and the first movement is not till the ninetith day ... If the woman breathes [presumably at the final moment of delivery] delivery is more difficult. Indeed *oscitiatio* [yawning or gaping] during delivery can be lethal [namely, for the infant], just as a sneeze after copulation causes abortion.

2.21 Difficulties in childbirth

Note that, despite his words below, Pliny the Elder goes on to reflect that Agrippa was not really such a great success story, given that he was lame as a youth, he lived amidst danger and death all his life, his daughters produced two of the worst emperors, Gaius (Caligula) and Nero, and Agrippa himself lived to be only 50 and suffered from his wife Julia's adulteries. Pliny also notes that Nero was said to have been born feet-first.

Pliny the Elder, *Natural History* 7.45

To be born feet-first is against nature. Those born that way have the name 'Agrippa', as being born with difficulty [*aegre partos*]. Marcus Agrippa is said to have been born in this way. He is almost the only case, among all those born in this way, of someone being successful.

2.22 The effects of multiple childbirth on the mother

Ovid, *Art of Love* 3.81–2

Childbearing makes the hours of youth more brief: with continual harvests the field ages.

2.23 Natal mortality

The fear for the life of a woman at delivery must have been a common one, even if demographically maternal mortality was not as significant as some have supposed (cf. Parkin 1992: 103–5). This letter also highlights the difficulty for the elite (including Pliny the Younger himself) in ensuring a robust line of succession: see Hopkins (1983: esp. ch. 3). On the particular example Pliny cites here, that of the Helvidiae, see Rawson (2003: 103).

Pliny, *Letters* 4.21.1–3

Pliny to Velius Cerialis.

How tragic and how cruel is the demise of the sisters Helvidiae. Both sisters gave birth to girls, and both sisters died giving birth. I am very upset, and my grief is not immoderate, for I think it is truly grievous when motherhood snatches away two very noble girls in their first flower. I grieve too for the plight of the infants, deprived of their mothers immediately at birth, I grieve for their excellent husbands, and I grieve too on my own account. For my affection for their deceased father [the younger Helvidius Priscus, executed in AD 93] remains as strong as ever, as my defence of him and my published works bear witness. Now only one of his three children survives, left alone to prop up and sustain a *domus* that not so long ago was secure in its many supports.

2.24 The belief that humans are uniquely ready for repeated sexual intercourse

In **2.24a**, Pliny the Elder, discussing human fertility, has recounted the birth of twelve infants, but that they were all still-born. In **2.24b**, he is discussing the reproductive methods of a variety of animals.

(a) Pliny the Elder, *Natural History* 7.48–9

When, however, a moderate interval of time separates two conceptions, both may be successful, as was seen in the case of Hercules and his brother Iphicles, and in that of the woman who bore twins of whom one resembled her husband and the other an adulterer; and also in that of a serving-girl who, as a result of sexual intercourse on the same day, bore one twin resembling her master and another resembling the steward [*procurator*].

(b) Pliny the Elder, *Natural History* 10.171–2

The human being is the only biped who produces live births. And it is only the human being who feels regret after engaging in sexual intercourse for the first time; this is certainly an augury for life, deriving from a regrettable origin. All other animals have fixed seasons in the year for mating, but the human being, as has already been said [*Natural History* 7.38] mates at every hour of the day and night. All other animals derive satiety from having mated, whereas the human being gets almost none. Messalina, the wife of Claudius Caesar, thinking this would be a royal triumph, held a competition in it, and chose from the corps of professional prostitutes a servant girl who was absolutely notorious for acts of prostitution, and in a night and a day she beat her with twenty-five men. In the human race men have devised every imaginable form of sexually deviant behaviour, crimes against nature; but women have invented abortion. In this area how much more guilty are we than are wild animals! Hesiod [*Works and Days* 586] records that men are keener on sex in winter, women in summer.

2.25 A recipe for a contraceptive

Papyri Osloenses 1.1.321–32 (= *Papyri Graecae Magicae*, ed. K. Preisendanz 36.321–32, fourth century AD)

This is a spell for the prevention of conception – the only one in the world [that works?]. Take some bitter vetch seeds, as many as the number of years you want to remain sterile. Wet them in the menses of a menstruating woman; let her wet them in her own vagina. Then take a live frog and throw the bitter vetch seeds into its mouth, so that it swallows them down. Then release the frog – still alive – from the spot where you caught it. Next take a seed of henbane, and wet it in mare's milk; also take the nasal mucus of a cow, along with some grains of barley[1] and toss them in a piece of deer skin; bind this up on the outside with the skin of a male mule. Wrap this around you when the moon is waning in a female sign of the zodiac on a day of Kronos or Hermes [i.e. the planets Saturn and Mercury]. Mix in also with the grains of barley some earwax from a female mule.

1 Frog excrement? The original editor, S. Eitrem, read *kopron*; amended in *Papyri Graecae Magicae* to *krithôn*.

2.26 Infanticide in the Roman world

(a) Seneca, *On Anger* 1.2

We dispose of mad dogs ... we even drown children when they are born weak or abnormal.

(b) Livy, 27.37 (discussing the events of 207 BC)

They were disturbed afresh by news from Frusino of the birth of a baby as big as a child of four – and its size was not the strangest thing about it, for it was also of indeterminate sex, like the baby born at Sinuesa two years earlier. Soothsayers called in from Etruria pronounced it to be a portent of a repulsive and horrible kind, which must be removed from Roman territory and sunk in the sea, away from all contact with the land. It was accordingly put in a box alive, taken offshore, and thrown overboard.

(c) Philo, *On Special Laws* 3.114–15

Some carry out the crime with their own hands ... and smother and suffocate the newly born child as soon as it draws breath. Others throw them in a river or into the depths of the sea after attaching to their bodies a heavy object ... Others expose them in a deserted place so as (one might think) to give them a chance of safety – whereas in fact they are exposing them to the most cruel of misfortunes. For all wild animals that are fond of human flesh come to prey on them ... Carrion birds get the left-overs.

(d) Tacitus, *Histories* 5.5

[On the peculiar habits of the Jews, including the fact that] they see to it that their numbers increase; for they consider it a crime to kill any child born after a father has made his will [*agnatus*].

(e) Tacitus, *Germania* 19

To limit the number of children or to kill any child born after the father has made his will is regarded as criminal, and good habits there have more force than good laws elsewhere.

2.27 Depopulation of Greece in the second century BC

Writing in the second century BC and referring to the middle of that century, the Greek historian Polybius speculates on the causes of phenomena such as drought and plagues. He criticises those who are too ready to attribute divine causes to events the explanation of which may be evident. On this passage, see first Walbank's commentary (1979: 678–81), and note also Scheidel (2001a: 41).

Polybius, 36.17.5–10

Let me give you an example. In our own time the whole of Greece has been subject to childlessness and a basic shortage of population. As a result cities have become deserted and agricultural production has declined, even though we have no continuous wars or epidemics. Now suppose someone had advised us to send and ask the gods about this, and find out what we ought to say or do so as to increase our number and make our cities better populated: that would be seen as absurd, would it not? The cause of the catastrophe is obvious and the remedy is clearly in our own hands. The evil rapidly grew and took us over without us knowing, as people had fallen into such a state of pretentious extravagance, avarice, and sloth that they did not wish to marry, or if they did marry they refused to rear the children born to them; or at most they generally raised only one or two of them, so as to leave these well off, to be brought up to squander their inheritance. In cases where there were only one or two children, and one was carried off by war and the other by sickness, it is clear that their homes must have been left empty, and, just as with swarms of bees, so little by little cities lost their resources and became feeble. In these circumstances there was no point at all in asking the gods for suggestions as to how we might be rescued from such a catastrophe. For any ordinary person would tell you that the most effective cure had to be people's own action, in either striving after other objects, or if not, in passing laws making it compulsory to rear children.

2.28 Malthusian views of the Roman empire

These passages from Christian African authors (Tertullian writing c. AD 210–13; Cyprian around 250) appear to confirm crises in the third century AD. However, it is difficult to separate this from Christian views on the approaching end of the world. See Parkin (1992: 59–63).

(a) Tertullian, *On the Soul* 30.3

Certainly it is obvious enough, if one looks at the whole world, that it is becoming daily better cultivated and more fully populated than in ancient times. All places are now accessible, all are well known, all are open to commerce; very pleasant farms have obliterated all traces of what were once notorious wastelands; cultivated fields have tamed forests; flocks and herds have put to flight wild beasts; sandy deserts are sown; rocks are planted to mark boundaries; marshes are drained; and where once were hardly solitary cottages, there are now great cities. No longer are islands dreaded or rocky shores feared; everywhere are houses, everywhere are inhabitants, everywhere are settled communities, everywhere is life [*ubique domus, ubique populus, ubique respublica, ubique vita*]. The ultimate evidence of our teeming population is that we are a burden to the world, which can hardly supply us from its natural elements; our wants grow more and more keen, and our complaints more bitter in every mouth, while Nature fails in affording us her usual sustenance. It is very clear that pestilence, famine, wars, and earthquakes have to be regarded as a remedy for nations, as the means of pruning the overbearing human race.

(b) Cyprian, *To Demetrianus* 3

The world has now grown old, and does not stand as strong as it stood in former times. It does not have the vigour and robustness that it formerly possessed. Even were we silent, even if we adduced no testimony from the holy Scriptures and from the divine prophecies, the world itself is now announcing, and bearing witness to its decline by the evidence of its own failing state. In winter there is not such a plentiful supply of rain for nourishing the seeds; in summer the sun has not so much heat for ripening the crops; in spring the cornfields are not so joyous; and autumn is not so fruitful in its leafy offspring. The layers of marble are dug out in less quantity from the disembowelled and wearied mountains; the diminished quantities of silver and gold suggest already the exhaustion of the mines, and the impoverished veins are straitened and decreased with each passing day; the farmer fails in the fields, the sailor at sea, the soldier in the camp, innocence in the forum, justice in the court, concord in friendships, skilfulness in the arts, discipline in morals.

2.29 A possible decline in population in Alexandria

This passage is from a letter written by Dionysius, bishop of Alexandria, to the bishop Hierax elsewhere in Egypt, around AD 261/2, at the time of plague and sedition in the Egyptian capital.

If we suppose the population of Alexandria (see passages above) was of the order of half a million, then a reasonable estimate of the proportion of this number aged between 40 and 70 years, male and female, assuming for the moment a stationary population with average life expectancy at birth of around 25 years ($e_0 = 25$), would be 25 per cent, that is, 125,000 individuals aged between 40 and 70 years. Now if 125,000 was the total number of people aged between 14 and 80 years in c. AD 262, then this would suggest a total population (if the 14 to 80 age group represented about two-thirds of the population) of only 190,000, a fall from the earlier figure of 310,000, or 62 per cent. See Parkin (2003: 39–42).

Eusebius, *History of the Church* 7.21.9–10

People wonder and are at a loss as to the reason for these continuous pestilences, these chronic illnesses, all these kinds of deadly diseases, this varied and vast destruction of humankind; they cannot understand why this very great city of ours no longer bears in it as great a number of inhabitants as before, from infant children right up to the most advanced in age, as it once supported of those whom it called 'hearty old men' [*ômogerontas*]. But at that time those aged between 40 and 70 years were so much more numerous that now their number cannot be filled out when all those from 14 to 80 years of age are enrolled and counted together for the public grain distribution, and those who appear youngest have become, as it were, the contemporaries of those who in the past were the oldest. And thus, on seeing the human race on the earth constantly diminishing and wasting away, they do not tremble, though their complete obliteration is increasing and advancing.

2.30 Provincial censuses

On the Roman provincial census (as distinct from the census of Roman citizens, last held in the empire under Vespasian and Titus), see references in Parkin (2003: 382). Some 320 copies of census declarations from Roman Egypt survive (examples are given in Chapter 3). From these declarations data about gender and age of individuals may be derived, as follows, calculated from (corrected) figures in Scheidel (2001b: 256–8).

(a) *The Gospel of Luke* 2.1

During that time an order went out from Augustus Caesar to subject the entire world to a census. This first census occurred when Cyrenius was the governor of Syria. Everyone went off to be listed on the census, each going to his own city. Joseph too went up from Galilee, from the city of Nazareth, to Judaea and the city of David, called Bethlehem (since he was from David's household and clan), in order to be taxed, along with Mary, his fiancée, who was pregnant.

(b) The Egyptian census data

Age	Males	(%)	Females	(%)	Sex ratio	Uncertain sex	Total	(%)
0–9	99	(26.8)	71	(20.1)	139.4	7	177	(23.7)
10–19	60	(16.2)	74	(21.0)	81.1	4	138	(18.5)
20–29	58	(15.7)	69	(19.5)	84.1	6	133	(17.8)
30–39	52	(14.1)	59	(16.7)	88.1	4	115	(15.4)
40–49	47	(12.7)	32	(9.1)	146.9	–	79	(10.6)
50–59	28	(7.6)	26	(7.4)	107.7	–	54	(7.2)
60–69	14	(3.8)	13	(3.7)	107.7	2	29	(3.9)
70–79	11	(3.0)	9	(2.5)	122.2	1	21	(2.8)
80+	1	(0.3)	–		–	–	1	(0.1)
Totals	370	(49.5)	353	(47.3)	104.8	24 (3.2)	747	

2.31 A possible life table from Roman legal sources

For the context of this text, and its potential demographic significance, see Frier (1982: 213–51) and Parkin (1992: 27–41).

Aemilius Macer, *On the 5 Per Cent Inheritance Law* (*Digest 35.2.68, praef.*)

For computation to be made in the matter of maintenance [*alimenta*], Ulpian describes the following formula [*forma*]: from birth to the 20th year, the amount of 30 years' maintenance will be calculated and the Falcidian portion of this [*quantitatis Falcidia*] will be due; from 20 years to the 25th year, [the amount of] 28 years [will be due]; from 25 years up to 30 years, 25 years; from 30 years up to 35 years, 22 years; from 35 years up to 40 years, 20 years. From 40 years up to 50 years, the computation will be made by the number of years as are lacking at this age from the 60th year, with one year's remission; then, from the 50th year up to the 55th year, [the amount] of 9 years; from 55 years up to the 60th year, 7 years; and from 60 years, whatever the age, [the amount] of 5 years. Ulpian says that we use this same rule for the computation of a usufruct. However it has been [is?] the practice [*solitum est*] for the computation from birth to the 30th year to be of 30 years, but from 30 years the computation is of as many years as are lacking from the 60th year. Therefore the computation never goes beyond 30 years. Thus, in the same way, if a legacy of a usufruct is made to the state, whether without restriction or for the provision of games, the computation will be of 30 years.

2.32 Evidence from skeletal remains

Regarding skeletal evidence for demographic information, this quotation from St Augustine seems quite apposite. For discussion of skeletal evidence, see Parkin (1992: 41–58). Presently, efforts are being made to use datable bone remains to derive evidence about the health of populations in the Roman world.

Augustine, *City of God* 15.9

The great size of ancient bodies is disclosed even to much later ages by the frequent discovery of bones, for bones are long-lasting. On the other hand, the longevity of people in those days cannot now be determined by any such evidence.

2.33 Approximation in the recording of ages

	Papyri Michigan 176 April 91	Papyri Michigan 177 December 104	Papyri Michigan 178 April 119
Horos	20 years	34 years	48 years
Horion	7 years	20 years	35 years
Thenatumis	–	25 years	31 years

2.34 A dispute over the age of a wealthy matron

C. AD 155 Apuleius (at the time around 30 years old), on his way from his native Madauros in Africa to Egypt, fell ill in the town of Oea (Tripoli). He was visited by his much younger friend, Sicinius Pontianus. The latter's mother, Aemilia Pudentilla, had been a widow for thirteen years, and was now betrothed to her brother-in-law, Sicinius Clarus, whom Pontianus disliked intensely (as well as fearing that the new husband would get the family fortune, some 4 million sesterces). Pudentilla, who has a mind of her own, doesn't want to marry her ex-husband's brother either, and looks for a husband of her own choosing (not only, we are told, because she is lonely, but also on the advice of her doctors).

Pontianus is alarmed at this independence shown by his mother, and he invites Apuleius in his sick-bed to come and stay with his family. In time Apuleius gets better, and is well enough to give public lectures in Oea. His audience loves him, and he is offered citizenship in the town. Pontianus seizes this opportunity and urges Apuleius to marry his mother. Though hesitant, Apuleius finds Pudentilla both attractive and wealthy, and, about a year after he first arrived in Oea, he marries her.

Another brother of Pudentilla's first husband (i.e. Pontianus' uncle), Sicinius Aemilianus, takes Apuleius to court, saying he won Pudentilla by magic. The case was tried at Sabrata by the proconsul of Africa, Claudius Maximus, c. AD 158. We have Apuleius' purported defence speech, his *Apologia*, a tongue-in-cheek defence of the scholar-philosopher, and incidentally a rather clever parody of Plato's *Apology*. As far as we know Apuleius was acquitted.

Apuleius, *Apologia* 89

Now as to Pudentilla's age, about which after those things you lied with such assurance that you even asserted that she was 60 years old when she married, about this I will reply to you in a few words: for on such an obvious matter it is [not] necessary to argue at any length.

Her father made the usual declaration that a daughter had been born to him. Her registers [*tabulae*] are preserved partly in the public registry [*tabularium*] and partly at home, and these [the latter?] are now being presented before your faces. Pass those *tabulae* over to Aemilianus: let him inspect the seal, let him examine the *signa* which have been stamped there, let him read the names of the consuls, let him count the years, the sixty that he assigned to this woman. Let him prove she's 55: he has still lied by a lustrum. But this is not enough, I will treat him more generously: for he himself has granted Pudentilla many years, so in return I will give him back ten years; along with Ulysses, Mezentius [Aemilianus] has gone astray: let him show at least that the woman is 50 years old. But why speak at length? To deal with him as I would with a fourth-partner [public informer], I will double the five years twice over, and in one swoop strike off twenty years. Order the consuls to be reckoned, Maximus: unless I'm mistaken, you will now find that Pudentilla does not go much beyond her fortieth year in age. Oh audacious and outrageous lie, oh falsehood that warrants as punishment a twenty-year exile! You lie by a half, Aemilianus, then you dare to increase them by one and a half again.

2.35 A child's epitaph

This marble tablet from a columbarium, found in a vineyard near the Appian Way in AD 126/7, is in the Vatican. The tablet includes the picture of a boy in a tunic and toga, with a *bulla* around his neck. The epitaph itself is in dactylic hexameters – rather imperfect, it must be said, but then he was only 6 years old when he died! See also Gordon (1951: 48–9).

Corpus Inscriptionum Latinarum 6.7578 = *Carmina Latina Epigraphica* 422

I, Marcianus, am here in this tomb, deceased for eternity.
Not yet had I been expecting to visit Persephone's realm.
I was born when the consuls were Severus (for the second time)
and Fulvus [destined to be the emperor Antoninus Pius] together, and
    from the start was held sweet.
When the sixth year had passed, I began to grow weak as the year
    advanced.
O cruel ninth dawn for my parents, that which stole me
from the lamentations, alas, of both my poor mother and father.
How great had been the hope placed in me, if only my fates had
    allowed me.
The Muses had granted that as a boy I was eloquent.
Lachesis envied me, cruel Clotho slew me,
nor did the third Fate allow me to repay my mother for her *pietas*.
How dutifully [*pie*], how densely-packed came the entire Sacred
    Way,
and the huge crowd wept as it attended my funeral.

They called it a day of death, with solemn gatherings,
because treacherous hope had snatched the years from one so tender
   of age.
And the entire neighbourhood came from all around
to see in me the flower dying by fate.
O eternal one, do give comfort always to the dutiful [*piis*]
and preserve the life of the dutiful [*piorum*], and that of all their
   descendants[?].

2.36 A girl's epitaph

For the sentiment of line 3 see similarly *Corpus Inscriptionum Latinarum* 6.29609 = *Carmina Latina Epigraphica* 974; it also occurs in earlier Greek lyric poetry.

Corpus Inscriptionum Latinarum 6.35887 = *Carmina Latina Epigraphica* 1532 = *Inscriptiones Latinae Selectae* 8168 (Rome)

I lived dear to my own people, as a virgin I gave up life,
I am here dead and I am ash, this ash is earth,
but if earth is a goddess, I am a goddess, I am not dead.
I ask you, guest, not to harm my bones.
Mouse [*Mus*] lived 13 years.

2.37 Children's epitaphs

(a) *Corpus Inscriptionum Latinarum* 2.5477 = *Inscriptiones Latinae Selectae* 8483 (Cadiz)

L. Cornelius Drosus [*sic*], one year old.

(b) *Corpus Inscriptionum Latinarum* 6.14094 = *Inscriptiones Latinae Selectae* 8496 (Rome, just outside the Appian Gate)

To the spirits of the deceased.
To the divine Calistinus, my sweetest and most devoted master, he
   lived 4 years, 4 months, 4 days, and 10 hours.

2.38 Monuments to dead wives

(a) *Corpus Inscriptionum Latinarum* 6.19128 = *Inscriptiones Latinae Selectae* 8451 (Rome)

Of Graxia Alexandria,
outstanding as an example
of modesty,

who even reared her sons
at her own breasts.
Pudens her husband, freedman of Augustus,
set this up for her, well deserving; she lived 24 years, 3 months,
16 days.

(b) *Corpus Inscriptionum Latinarum* 6.20427 = *Inscriptiones Latinae Selectae* 8480 (Rome)

The bones
of Iulia Donata, freedwoman of Gaius;
she died after the birth of a boy
and his naming.

(c) *Corpus Inscriptionum Latinarum* 3.6759 = *Inscriptiones Latinae Selectae* 1914 (Ancyra)

Sacred to the spirits of the deceased.
For his well-deserving wife
Aeturnia Zotica,
Annius Flavianus, decurial lictor of Fufidius
Pollio [*ordinary consul* AD 166], governor of Galatia,
set this up;
she lived 15 years, 5 months,
and 18 days; she
died on the 16th day
after giving birth for the first time,
leaving behind a son.

(d) *L'Année Epigraphique* 1985, no. 355

To the spirits of the deceased.
I, Herennia Cervilla, daughter of Lucius,
a wife, lived 18 years and
30 days.
I left behind three children,
I finished my life in pain.
My dear husband placed this
as a memorial for me when he was alive,
so that it might be of use for such an
inscription to follow her
in the realms above, Gaius Carrenas
Verecundus to his incomparable
and well-deserving wife.

2.39 A nihilistic approach to life

Corpus Inscriptionum Latinarum 6.23942 =
Inscriptiones Latinae Selectae 8160
(Rome, trans Tiberim)

To the spirits of the deceased
of Sextus Perpenna Firmus.
I lived as long as I wished.
Why I am dead, I know not.

REFERENCES AND FURTHER READING

Bagnall, R.S. (2002) 'The Effects of Plague: Model and Evidence', *Journal of Roman Archaeology* 15: 114–20.

Bagnall, R.S. and Frier, B.W. (1994) *The Demography of Roman Egypt*, Cambridge.

Brunt, P.A. (1971) *Italian Manpower, 225 BC–AD 14*, Oxford (reissued with postscript, 1987).

Delia, D. (1988) 'The Population of Roman Alexandria', (*Transactions of the American Philological Association*) 118: 275–92.

Duncan-Jones, R.P. (1977) 'Age-rounding, Illiteracy and Social Differentiation in the Roman Empire', *Chiron* 7: 333–53.

Duncan-Jones, R.P. (1980) 'Demographic Change and Economic Progress under the Roman Empire', in Gabba, E. (ed.) *Tecnologia, economia e società nel mondo romano, Atti del Convegno di Como*, Como, pp. 67–80.

Duncan-Jones, R.P. (1982) *Economy of the Roman Empire*, 2nd edn, Cambridge.

Frier, B.W. (1982) 'Roman Life Expectancy: Ulpian's Evidence', *Harvard Studies in Classical Philology* 86: 213–51.

Frier, B.W. (1983) 'Roman Life Expectancy: The Pannonian Evidence', *Phoenix* 37: 328–44.

Frier, B.W. (2000) 'Demography', in *The Cambridge Ancient History*, vol. 11, 2nd edn, Cambridge.

Gordon, A.E. (1951) 'The Epitaph of Marcianus,' *Archaeology* 4: 48–9.

Guilhembet, J.-P. (1996) 'La densité des *domus* et des *insulae* dans les XIV régions de Rome selon les *Régionnaires*: Représentations cartographiques,' *Mélanges de l'École française de Rome: Antiquité* 108: 7–26.

Haas, C. (1997) *Alexandria in Late Antiquity*, Baltimore, MD and London.

Harris, W.V. (1999) 'Demography, Geography, and the Sources of Roman Slaves', *Journal of Roman Studies* 89: 62–75.

Hermansen, G. (1978) 'The Population of Imperial Rome: The Regionaries', *Historia* 27: 129–68.

Hopkins, M.K. (1964–5) 'The Age of Roman Girls at Marriage', *Population Studies* 18: 309–27.

Hopkins, M.K. (1965–6) 'Contraception in the Roman Empire', *Comparative Studies in Society and History* 8: 124–51.

Hopkins, M.K. (1966–7) 'On the Probable Age Structure of the Roman Population', *Population Studies* 20: 245–64.

Hopkins, M.K. (1978) *Conquerors and Slaves*, Cambridge.

Hopkins, M.K. (1983) 'Brother–Sister Marriage in Roman Egypt', *Comparative Studies in Society and History* 22: 303–55.

Lo Cascio, E. (1994) 'The Size of the Roman Population: Beloch and the Meaning of the Augustan Census Figures', *Journal of Roman Studies* 84: 23–40.

Lo Cascio, E. (1997) *Le Rome impériale: Démographie et logistique*, Rome.

Nordh, A. (1949) *Libellus de Regionibus Urbis Romae*, Lund.

Parkin, T.G. (1992) *Demography and Roman Society*, Baltimore, MD and London.

Parkin, T.G. (2003) *Old Age in the Roman World*, Baltimore, MD and London.

Rawson, B. (2003) *Children and Childhood in Roman Italy*, Oxford.

Rickman, G. (1980) *The Corn Supply of Ancient Rome*, Oxford.

Sallares, R. (1991) *Ecology of the Ancient Greek World*, London.

Sallares, R. (2002) *Malaria and Rome*, Oxford.

Saller, R.P. and Shaw, B.D. (1984) 'Tombstones and Roman Family Relations in the Principate: Civilians, Soldiers and Slaves', *Journal of Roman Studies* 74: 124–56.

Saller, R.P. (1994) *Patriarchy, Property and Death in the Roman Family*, Cambridge.

Scheidel, W. (ed.) (2001a) *Debating Roman Demography*, Leiden.

Scheidel, W. (2001b) *Death on the Nile: Disease and the Demography of Roman Egypt*, Leiden.

Scheidel, W. (2002) 'A Model of Demographic and Economic Change in Roman Egypt After the Antonine Plague', *Journal of Roman Archaeology* 15: 97–114.

Scheidel, W. (2004) 'Human Mobility in Roman Italy, 1: The Free Population', *Journal of Roman Studies* 94: 1–26.

Scheidel, W. (2005) 'Human Mobility in Roman Italy, 2: The Slave Population', *Journal of Roman Studies* 94: 64–79.

Syme, R. (1986) *The Augustan Aristocracy*, Oxford.

Walbank, F.W. (1979) *A Historical Commentary on Polybius*, vol. 3, Oxford.

Weber, C. (1831) *Lucani Pharsalia*, Leipzig.

3

FAMILY AND HOUSEHOLD

The family in Roman society was, both in repute and in reality, the most basic social unit. Within it, its members shared shelter and protection (a theme still existing in the maxim 'A man's home is his castle'; cf. 3.1). It was also the basis of social obligations, the means by and through which both status and wealth were essentially transmitted. As a microcosm of society (3.2), it was also held to be fundamental to the survival of the wider society, and not just in demographic terms.

It is vital that we remember that legal definitions and restrictions (3.3) need not reflect social reality. For example, though women and grown children may be seen to have a quite inferior legal status, nonetheless the reality, even as it may be discerned in aristocratic literature, suggests that they often enjoyed considerable freedom of action. Similarly, marriage ideals, as expressed in legal texts or in tombstone inscriptions, may not always reflect day-to-day reality.

Glossary of key terms relating to the Roman household and to family structures

familia: A group of persons subject by nature or law to the power (*potestas*) of the male head of the group (the *paterfamilias*); i.e. children and descendants derived by nature, and those derived from law, such as wives and slaves. For the marked differences between the terms 'family' and '*familia*', see the classic passage from Ulpian (3.4) and Gardner (1998: 1).

domus: The household, home; used more often than *familia* to refer to the basic household unit, but like *familia* could refer to kin outside the household. *Domus* included all relatives linked through women, whereas *familia* typically referred only to relatives linked to the family through male descent (*agnates*). A daughter's children or a mother's blood kin were excluded from the *familia*, but included in the *domus*. Literary texts suggest that in the late republic and early empire *familia* was increasingly superseded by *domus*. See especially Saller (1984a).

paterfamilias: The male head of the *familia*; traditionally said to have had the power of life and death (*ius vitae ac necis*) over all those under his jurisdiction.

dominica potestas: The power held by the *paterfamilias* over his slaves (as *dominus*, 'master').

patria potestas: The power held by the *paterfamilias* over his descendants (as *pater*, 'father').

manus: The power held by the *paterfamilias* over his wife, if the marriage was a *manus* (lit. 'hand', i.e. in one's hand, 'under one's thumb') marriage, which increasingly in this period it was not.

sui iuris: Legally independent.

conubium: The capacity to contract a legitimate marriage (*iustum matrimonium*) – not held, for example, by slaves, whose marriages were not legally recognised and whose children were therefore illegitimate. Legitimate children belonged to the family of the father, illegitimate children to that of the mother.

sponsalia: The betrothal ceremony in which a ring was given to a prospective bride (*sponsa*) to put on the finger nearest to the little finger of the left hand (the Romans thought that a nerve ran from this finger to the heart). This ceremony gave the girl a precise social status and imposed fidelity.

confarreatio: The oldest marriage rite (involving the consumption of *far* – 'spelt', or grain) in Roman law, which by the classical period had become rare.

coemptio: Transfer of a woman to a new family; the 'sale' of a woman to the buyer in the presence of a person holding scales in which the husband as purchaser put down the price of the object (i.e. the wife).

usus: Acquisition of property by the use (*usus*, 'squatter's rights') of the object (wife) over a period of time. Thus a man acquired *manus* (see above) over a woman after she had been 'used' for one year (the same as for movable goods). But, if at the end of each year the woman spent three nights away from her husband's home, he lost his *manus* over her. Thus a father might retain financial control over his daughter.

It would appear that *manus* marriages became less common in the late republic and early empire (3.5). In such a case the wife remained under the *potestas* of her father, and effectively remained within the original *familia*, while living in the home of another.

In the classical period marriage was recognised as legal if:

1   Both partners were citizens and had *conubium* (see above).
2   They lived together with the intent of being husband and wife (*affectio maritalis*).

3 They performed marriage ceremonies that proved publicly the *affectio maritalis* (**3.6**); the husband might marry in absentia (**3.7**).
4 The woman showed willing adoption of the role of *matrona* (i.e. respectable married woman).
5 The woman was supplied with a dowry, *dos* (though this was not mandatory) (**3.8**).

Hence there was no requirement for a legal document proving married status. Furthermore, divorce meant only that the couple had ceased to live together (the husband saying to the wife the formula 'Take your belongings and go'). See Treggiari (1991).

Pietas

This is a sense, quasi-legal, quasi-religious, of reciprocal devotion or dutiful respect towards those to whom it is owed – gods, country, kin.

This concept is fundamental to Roman ideas about family obligations. Saller (1988).

The nuclear family

It has become increasingly clear over recent decades that the nuclear family structure was the norm among Roman citizens in the classical period, at least in the western half of the empire. The classic article illustrating this, by means of the statistical scrutiny of epitaphs (tombstones being afforded by not just the very wealthy but also those of more moderate means), is Saller and Shaw (1984), which remains essential reading.

Key to Saller and Shaw's method is the analysis of the commemorator's relation to the deceased. Epitaphs, unless they were set up by the person him- or herself while still alive (*se vivo*), typically refer to commemorations between husband and wife, parents and children, or brothers and sisters; much less often are there mentioned relationships between extended kin (grandparents, uncles, etc.). Indeed, in civilian populations (as compared with populations of soldiers), friends, patrons, freedmen, masters and slaves – that is, individuals unrelated by blood – feature more frequently than extended kin.

For example, from a total of 666 relationships as evidenced from civilian tombstones from Regio XI of Italy, 146 represent husband to wife or vice versa, 68 parent(s) to son or daughter, 87 son or daughter to a parent, and 30 of siblings. In other words, 331 of 666 'commemorate' a nuclear family relationship. In 99 cases no commemorator relationship is indicated, and in 147 cases the commemoration is made by the person him- or herself while still alive (cf. **3.36**). Of the remaining 89, a mere 20 are commemorating relationships within an extended family setting; 1 is of an heir,

17 of *amici* (friends), 23 of patron to freedman, 1 of master to slave, and 27 of freedman to patron.

This suggests very strongly that the focus of obligations, where possible, was usually between close familiar members: what we would now call the nuclear family group, rather than the extended kin grouping. In a society where the *paterfamilias*, as oldest living male relative, in theory maintained complete control over the family grouping, this pattern displayed by the tombstones is very surprising, and telling.

When examining the practical realities of marriage in the Roman world, we often find that they are quite different from modern romantic notions about emotional partnerships. Marriage might be necessary simply to maintain the family line (3.9). Although marital harmony was highly desirable (3.10), the Stoic Musonius' list of attributes that he considered unnecessary (including wealth, beauty, and birth) (3.11) indicates what was normally sought in a partner. Pliny the Younger's letter of recommendation for Salinator (3.12) stresses his birth and education; the description of Calpurnia (3.13) emphasises that interest in her husband's career on the part of a wife is an important factor in marital harmony (cf. 3.14). Of course, fertility was also very much desired (3.15), even though it might lead to health concerns (3.16). A bad wife might damage a husband's reputation by her actions (3.17); a good one, by sharing the hazards of life, enhanced the standing of both partners (3.18).

Epitaphs offer the opportunity to examine family patterns in society outside the aristocratic unions that dominate our literary sources. In particular, they offer considerable information on the lives of freedmen and freedwomen. This includes the murky world of the Junian Latins (3.19, 3.21; cf. 5.21), mixed family units of slave and free (3.20), as well as more 'traditional' families where both husband and wife are freeborn or have become free by the time of marriage (3.22, 3.23, 3.24, 3.25). As well as husband commemorating wife (3.27, 3.28, 3.30, and, in particular, 3.37), there are funeral monuments set up from outside the nuclear family, such as sister to sister (3.21), patron to freedman (3.26), or father-in-law to daughter, along with husband (3.29). The model wife who acted as loyal companion is a common motif (3.31, 3.32, 3.33, 3.34). Less commonly, wives commemorate husbands (3.35) or both partners erect a monument during their lifetime (3.36). Patrons, who may themselves be ex-slaves, set up tombs for their freedmen and their *familiae* in turn (3.38, 3.39). Combinations of these themes still exist, as when a tomb is set up for husband and (still living) wife by a female heir who will also, along with her freedmen and those of the deceased, take care of memorial rites at the site (3.40).

That Roman marriages were not always as harmonious as epitaphs may suggest is shown by Tacitus' contrasting description of marital practices among barbarian tribes (3.41). Cicero's letters describing the marriage of his brother Quintus to Pomponia, the sister of his closest friend, Atticus, offer a case study of a failed partnership (3.42, 3.43). An epitaph from Lyons offers a particularly striking warning of the possibilities of domestic violence (3.44). Seneca suggests that divorce and adultery were commonplace among the upper classes (3.45), but provision must be made for satirical and moralising intent in such passages.

While the emperor Augustus sought to restore traditional Roman morality (3.46, 3.54–7), it is apparent that infidelity (defined as female infidelity only) was a matter of concern. The Augustan adultery laws limited the family's (that is the father's and husband's) responsibility for handling such matters, but also greatly extended the state's involvement in domestic affairs by making infidelity a criminal offence (3.47). Divorce was commonplace (3.48) – it might be no-fault (3.49) or even instigated by a *paterfamilias* who still had control over his daughter (3.48). While some might have the joy of leaving their property to a natural heir (3.50), even the emperor Augustus was finally forced to adopt his stepson, Tiberius, who was not of his bloodline, in order to ensure a successor (3.51). Childlessness could also have its benefits, increasing the attention of relatives and others who might hope to gain from the distribution of property after one's death (3.52). Because of the importance of transferring family name and property, the legitimacy of an heir needed to be beyond dispute (3.53), a process that was enhanced by the Augustan marriage legislation (3.54, 3.55). This is a remarkable piece of state intrusion, setting restraints on the power of the *paterfamilias* (3.55). Parents of children were rewarded with particular inheritance rights over the childless (cf. 3.55m). It was only after Augustus' death that exemptions were made for the elderly who could not be expected to produce children (3.56). Other privileges included advancement in political office, both at Rome and in the municipalities throughout the empire (3.57). For the childless male, adoption was a possible resort, although it removed the adoptee from his natural family (3.58). Women, however, would not normally have even this opportunity, except through imperial dispensation (3.59).

While the *paterfamilias* is sometimes portrayed as having absolute power over his family (3.59, 3.60), Roman law limited his powers by statute in many cases (e.g. 3.48f); it was also possible to seek legal redress if his behaviour would not conform to social norms (3.61). His wife, while not enjoying equal legal powers, nevertheless held a special status within the household (3.62) and in traditional aristocratic families played a considerable role in the upbringing of her children (3.63, 3.64). By at least from the time of the late republic, however, it was much more common for slave nurses to take care of infant children from birth (contrast the practices of the Germans: 3.65) and their education was generally entrusted to outsiders, such as tutors or schoolteachers. Roman families could limit their offspring by abortion or exposure (3.66), but, once the child was acknowledged, there was established a reciprocal bond of *pietas* that required parents and children to provide for each other's well-being (3.67).

Exceptions to the nuclear family, such as brothers living together or multiple generations of a family sharing the same dwelling, are recorded, but do not appear common among the Roman upper classes (**3.68**). In Egypt, however, census returns offer considerable evidence for extended family groups (**3.69**).

Finally, it must be remembered that all children required a legal guardian (**3.70**). With males, tutelage ended with puberty. Females never escaped the need to possess a tutor (**3.71**), although they might earn the right to choose this guardian themselves (**3.57h**), thus creating effective emancipation.

3.1 The theoretical sanctity of the *domus*

After his return from exile in 57 BC, Cicero attacked his bitter enemy P. Clodius Pulcher, who, among other things, had caused Cicero's house on the Palatine to be destroyed.

Cicero, *On His Own Home* 109

What is more holy, what better defended by a sense of religious awe than the *domus* of each individual citizen? Here the altars, here the hearths, here the household gods, here the sacred objects, the religious observances and rituals are contained; this is the sanctuary, so holy to everyone that it is considered sacrilege to tear anyone away from there.

3.2 The centrality of the *domus*

This well-known passage highlights contemporary aspects and conservative concerns. The importance of *amicitia* and patronage has been explored in Chapter 1. Note the clear reference to M. Antonius in section 57.

Cicero, *On Duties* 1.53–8

53. Now there are a number of degrees of association [*societas*] among human beings. Moving from the one that is unlimited, there is a closer one of the same race and tribe and language, by which people are particularly linked to one another. Closer still is that of the same community [*civitas*], for citizens enjoy many things in common, the forum, temples, porticoes, streets, laws, rights, courts, voting powers, as well as customs and friendships, and the matters and businesses many conduct with many others. A still closer tie is that involved in the association of relatives [*propinqui*]; hence, from that immense association of the human race, one ends up with a tiny and narrow one.

54.   For since it is natural to all living creatures to have the urge to procreate, the first association is in marriage itself, the next in children, then the single house [*domus*], with all things held in common. That indeed is the basic principle of the city and, as it were, the nursery of the state. There follow the bonds between brothers, and after them those between cousins, who can no longer be contained within a single *domus* and go off into other *domus* as if into colonies. Then follow marriages and ties by marriage from which still more relatives arise. Such propagation and progeny are the origin of public life. What is more, shared blood links people by good will and affection.

55.   For it is a great thing to have the same ancestral monuments, to practise the same sacred rites, and to have tombs in common . . .

56.   . . . Important is the fellowship that comes from kindnesses given and received, back and forth; so long as they are reciprocal and welcome, they bind together those involved in a firm association.

57.   But when you have surveyed all aspects reasonably and thoughtfully, of all associations there is none more serious nor more cherished than that which each one of us has with the state. Parents are cherished, children, relatives, and acquaintances are cherished, but our country has embraced all such affections of everyone within herself. What good man would hesitate to face death on her behalf if it would be to her advantage? It makes all the more detestable the savagery of those men who have tortured this country with every evil deed and who are, and always have been, bent on her utter destruction.

58.   But if there should be a debate about and comparison of those to whom we ought to offer the greatest duty [*officium*], then in the first rank are one's country and one's parents, to whose good services we have the deepest obligations; next come our children and the entire *domus*, which looks to us alone and can have no other refuge; then come relatives, with whom we get on well and with whom even our fortunes are generally held in common. So the necessities of life are owed in particular to those I have just mentioned; but life itself, and shared living, along with plans, conversations, encouragement, comfort, and sometimes even rebukes, flourish particularly in friendships; and the most pleasing friendship is that which is bound together by similarity of character.

3.3 Degrees of dependence

Gaius, in his introduction to Roman law, written probably late in the second century AD, is discussing the divisions in the law of persons; he has already dealt with the fundamental difference between free and unfree.

Gaius, *Institutes* 1.48–55

Next comes another division in the law of persons. For some persons are independent [*sui iuris*], and others are dependent on another [*alieni iuris*]. Of those dependent on another, some are in *potestas*, others in *manus*, and others in *mancipium* . . . Slaves are in the *potestas* of their masters . . . Also in our *potestas* are the children whom we beget in legitimate marriage. This right is peculiar to Roman citizens; for scarcely any other people have over their sons a power such as we have.

3.4 The legal definition of *familia*

For the uses of *familia* and *domus* (both having senses of 'household'), see the Glossary at the beginning of this chapter. As Ulpian indicates, the main uses of the term *familia* are for the male line of a family and for groups of slaves (whether owned by individuals or corporations), which vary considerably from our notions of a household.

Digest 50.16.195–6

195. Ulpian, *On the Edict*, Book 46. Utterances using the male form generally apply to both sexes.

1. Let us consider what the term *familia* means. In fact, it has different meanings. Thus, it applies to both property and individuals. For property, for example, in the Twelve Tables, 'the nearest agnate [male relative] should have the *familia*'. The signification *familia* may also refer to individuals, as when the law talks about patron and freedman, 'from one *familia* into another *familia*'. Here it is agreed that the law is talking about particular individuals.

2. The label *familia* also refers to the indication of a particular group, which is either defined by particular rights of the persons or by a shared bond of wider kinship.

   (a) In the sense of particular rights, we call several individuals, subject to the power of one by nature or law, a *familia*. For example: a *paterfamilias*, a *materfamilias*, a *filiusfamilias* [son under his father's power], a *filiafamilias*, and whoever takes their place in succession, e.g. grandsons and grand-daughters and so on. Besides, whoever has power [*dominium*] in a household [*domus*] is called the *paterfamilias* [father of the *familia*], even though he may not have a son. For we are not indicating his personality alone, but also his legal powers. Consequently we can even call a minor a *paterfamilias*. When a *paterfamilias* dies, whoever were under his control start to have their own *familiae*, as each individual takes on the title of *paterfamilias*.

The same thing will occur in the case of a person who is emancipated, since as an outcome of being *sui iuris* he has his own *familia*.

(b)   By shared bond of kinship we are referring to the *familia* of all agnates. For, although when the *paterfamilias* dies they have their own individual *familiae*, still all those who were under the power of one person are rightly described as being members of the same *familia*, since they originate from the same household [*domus*] and family [*gens*].

3.   We also customarily speak of slave *familiae*, for example in the Praetor's Edict, 'On Theft', where the praetor refers to the tax collectors' *familia*. Here it is not all their slaves that are indicated, but a particular group of slaves readied for this particular purpose, that is for tax collection. In other sections of the Edict, all slaves are grouped together, e.g. 'on unlawful assembly and goods taken by force', or 'return of goods' – if property is reduced in value due to the action of the buyer or his *familia*. In the Interdict, 'Concerning use of force', the term *familia* covers all one's slaves – as well as including sons.

4.   A group of several individuals who are descended from the bloodline of a distant founder are also called a *familia* (for instance, we speak of the Julian *familia*), as if springing from a particular recalled origin.

5.   A woman is both the start and finish of her *familia*.

196.   Gaius, *On The Provincial Edict*, Book 16. The head of the *familia* is himself included in the term *familia*. Women's children are clearly not in their *familia*, since once they are born they pass into their father's *familia*.

3.5 Getting married

Gaius provides clear evidence that *manus* marriages were no longer the norm in the imperial period.

Gaius, *Institutes* 1.111

A woman used to pass into *manus* by *usus* if she remained with him for an uninterrupted year, for thus she was, as it were, acquired by a usucapion of one year, and in this way she passed into her husband's *familia* and held the place or rank [*locum*] of a daughter. So it was provided by the Twelve Tables that if any woman did not wish to come under her husband's *manus* in this manner, she should be absent for three nights annually and thus interrupt the *usus* of each year. But this entire legal institution has been in part removed by laws and has in part been obliterated through simple disuse.

3.6 Professed attitudes towards marriage:
a satirical approach

In his famous sixth satire (early second century AD), Juvenal rails against women, wives in particular. Quite apart from expressing a stereotype and introducing the standard theme of adultery being rife, he also provides incidental details of the marriage process.

Juvenal, *Satires* 6.21–8

It is an ancient and long-established tradition, Postumus, to rattle the bedposts of another and to pour scorn on the genetic sanctity of the marriage-bed. Every other offence appeared later, courtesy of the Iron Age: the Silver Age saw the first adulterers. But here you are in our own day and age, making arrangements for engagement, dowry, and marriage contracts. Soon you'll be being preened by some master-barber. I suppose you've already put the ring on her finger? Postumus, you used to be quite sane. Why are you now getting married?

3.7 Marriage in absentia

It appears that a bridegroom did not have to be present at his wedding; a bride did, in order to be led to the husband's house (cf. Paul, *Sententiae* 2.19.8; Treggiari 1991: 164–7).

Digest 23.2.6, Ulpian

According to Cinna, when a man married a wife *in absentia* then died returning from dinner next to the Tiber, he had to be mourned by his wife.

3.8 The dowry in Roman law

By the terms of classical Roman law the dowry passed into the control and effective ownership of the husband; increasingly it became defined as only belonging to the husband, however, for as long as the marriage lasted. See Cicero's letter to Atticus (**3.43**).

Digest 23.3 and 24.3, various authors

(a) *Digest* 23.3.1–2, Paul

The right to a dowry is perpetual, and, in accordance with him who gives it, it is to be so agreed that it should always be in the husband's possession. It is in the interest of the state that women have their dowries safe, for it is these that make it possible for them to marry.

(b) *Digest* 23.3.7.3, Ulpian

If property is given as a dowry, I believe it becomes part of the husband's estate.

(c) *Digest* 23.3.69.8, Papinian

If property has been valued and handed over as a dowry, although it remains in the wife's use, ownership should be seen to have passed to the husband.

(d) *Digest* 23.3.75, Tryphoninus

Although a dowry is in the estate of the husband, nevertheless it belongs to the wife.

(e) *Digest* 24.3.1, Papinian

An action for the dowry is always and in every case the primary one, for it is in the public interest for women to keep their dowries, it being absolutely essential for women to have dowries in order to ensure the production of offspring and to replenish the state with children.

(f) *Digest* 24.3.2, *praef.*, Ulpian

Where a marriage is dissolved the dowry must be returned to the woman.

3.9 Why marry?

This is an extract from a speech by (according to Gellius) Metellus Numidicus, censor 102–101 BC, on marrying and why one should.

Livy, *Periocha* 59 records that a speech 'urging all men to marry in order to produce children' was delivered by the censor Q. Metellus (i.e. Q. Caecilius Metellus Macedonicus, censor in 131–130 BC and uncle of the Metellus to whom Gellius refers). Suetonius, *Augustus* 89 also relates that the speech was delivered by Q. Metellus and states that it was entitled 'on the increase of offspring', and that this speech was later read to the senate (and people?) by Augustus. Hence, it is likely that Gellius has confused the two famous Metelli.

Aulus Gellius, *Attic Nights* 1.6

If, men of Rome, we could live without a wife, we would all avoid that annoyance. But, since Nature has so arranged it that it is impossible to live very comfortably with them, and not at all without them, we must look to our long-term well-being rather than to short-term pleasure.

3.10 What is the chief end of marriage? Procreation is not the whole answer!

C. Musonius Rufus, an equestrian from Volsinii, lived from before AD 30 to before AD 101. A Stoic philosopher writing in Greek, he took Greek philosophical ideas and adapted them for a Roman audience.

Notice the point he raises that reproduction could take place outside marriage. This is of course true, and Romans were well aware of it; the difference marriage made, quite apart from what Musonius says, had to do with legitimacy.

Musonius Rufus, 13a

Husband and wife ought to unite one with the other on these terms: both to live with one another and to produce children; to regard everything as shared and nothing as belonging to the individual, not even their bodies themselves. For, while the birth of a human is a great thing and that is the result of this union, it is still not sufficient reason in itself for marrying, since this can also occur without marriage when people simply have intercourse, just as animals too have intercourse with one another. But in a marriage there must be a total union and concern of man and woman for one another, both in health and sickness and at all times: through aiming at this, just as at the production of children as well, they will enter into a marriage. So where this concern is achieved and those uniting together bring about its achievement, each striving to outdo the other, this marriage is suitably arranged and worthy of emulation. For such a union is a fine thing. But where one partner looks out for themselves without regard for the other – or, good heavens, both are like this – and they inhabit the same house but in their thoughts look outward, without a willingness to strain and breathe in unison with their yoke mate, then it is impossible for the union not to be destroyed and the affairs of those united not to be in bad shape, and they will either finally be divorced or maintain a union more lonely than solitude.

3.11 How should one choose a partner?

The criteria Musonius rejects were clearly those commonly applied in Roman society, at least by some.

Musonius Rufus, 13b

So those marrying should not consider their partner's background to see if they are of noble birth, nor consider wealth and how much they have acquired, nor their bodies and whether they are beautiful. For neither wealth nor beauty nor nobility can add anything more to a union than can concord nor can they in any way increase the production of children. Rather in marriage one should look for bodies that are sufficiently healthy, of average appearance, and capable of taking care of themselves – these will be less likely to be open to the wiles of the dissolute and will be more able to undertake the physical demands and achieve success in producing children. We should consider that the most suitable souls are those that have a natural bent towards sensible behaviour, justice, and virtue in general. What kind of marriage is fine unless it is harmonious? What kind of partnership is worthwhile without this? How could bad people share their thoughts with one another? This is no more likely than a bent piece of wood could fit with a straight one or two bent pieces with one another. For a bent piece cannot be fitted to a similarly bent piece and even less so to its opposite, a straight piece. The bad man is also no friend of the bad nor is he in agreement with him – and even less so with the good.

3.12 The benefits of getting married

Around AD 107 Pliny the Younger congratulates a distinguished friend on the forthcoming marriage of his daughter (nameless) to an up-and-coming pupil of Pliny's. The friend is L. Iulius Ursus Servianus, destined to be thrice consul: consul I 90, II *ordinarius* 102, and III *ordinarius* 134 at the age of 87 or 88 years; he was Hadrian's brother-in-law and it was he who secured the *ius liberorum* for Pliny in AD 98.

Gnaeus Pedanius Fuscus Salinator, the young man in question, was probably in his mid-twenties at the time, a man ripe for marriage in Roman terms, by age and status. He subsequently enjoyed a distinguished career, including as *consul ordinarius* in 118 with the new emperor Hadrian.

The letter demonstrates several aspects of the reality (or the desired reality) of aristocratic marriage and family life: in particular that the marriage is arranged, that such a marriage was clearly designed to enhance the family status and links, and that the desire for children, and grandchildren, was paramount. *Letters* 1.14, where Pliny has been asked to search for a husband for a friend's niece (his brother's daughter), includes an illuminating list of features considered worthy of mention (including the prospective husband's good looks, not to mention his family's wealth).

Pliny, *Letters* 6.26

To Iulius Servianus.

I am delighted and I offer my congratulations that you have settled on Fuscus Salinator for your daughter. His is a patrician *domus*, his father is a most highly respected gentleman, and his mother is equally highly thought of. He himself is scholarly, well read, and indeed eloquent; he combines a childish simplicity with the charm of a young man and the seriousness of an elder. And I am not letting my affection for him cloud my judgement. Yes, I love him dearly (he has earned such strong feelings through his services), but I also can pass judgement on him – indeed, the more I love him, the keener is my judgement. Knowing him as well as I do, I can assure you that in him you will have a son-in-law who is better than you could ever have prayed for. It only remains for him to make you a grandfather as early as possible, with children who take after their father. What a happy time that will be, when, as if they were my own children or grandchildren, I can take from your embrace his children, your grandchildren, and hold them as if they were my own.

3.13 A new wife

There are innumerable literary and, in particular, epigraphical sources that illustrate marital bliss, precisely because they were written in part to parade marital bliss. We shall see the evidence of epitaphs shortly; first, some further examples from literature, and in particular from the well-known but still highly revealing and suggestive letters of Pliny the Younger, mostly written very early in the second century AD. On the theme of coniugalis amor, see especially Treggiari (1991: ch. 8).

Pliny is writing to Calpurnia Hispulla, aunt of his new, third, and much junior wife, Calpurnia: partly this is Pliny boasting of his devoted new wife (and this is clearly not a political marriage), perhaps even reassuring himself; partly it is to assure her relatives, and his wider audience perhaps, what a good husband he is to her. Along the way we learn of the expectations a husband and society might have of an upper-class wife, particularly that she not be seen too much in public, and, presumably, does not discuss public life with her husband (contrast, e.g., Cicero's Terentia and Augustus' Livia). It is also worth noting that Pliny is proud of the fact that she has learnt to love him. But what is perhaps most striking to a modern reader is how little appreciation Pliny expresses for Calpurnia's own qualities, as opposed to those she has learnt from her aunt and husband.

Pliny, *Letters* 4.19

You are a model of *pietas* and loved your excellent and most affectionate brother as dearly as he loved you, and you also love his daughter as your own and are not only an aunt to her but also you take the place of the father she has lost. So I have no doubt that you will be absolutely overjoyed to learn that she has turned out worthy of her father, worthy of you, and worthy of her grandfather. She is extremely clever and a model of modest living. She loves me, which is a sign of her uprightness. On top of all this she is interested in literature, something that has developed though her devotion to me. She has copies of my books, which she reads repeatedly and even memorises. How concerned she is when I look like I'm about to plead a case, and what joy she shows when I have finished. She arranges for people to tell her what reception and applause I enjoy and how the case turns out for me. On the occasions when I am giving a recitation, she sits close by, hidden behind a curtain, and welcomes with most eager ears the praises we receive. In fact she even sings my verses and accompanies herself on the lyre; no professional has taught her, only love, the best of all masters. All this leads me to the very safe and secure hope that our harmony [*concordia*] will last forever and will increase with each passing day. She loves not my age or my body, which is slowly dying and ageing, but my reputation [*gloria*]. Nor would anything else be fitting for a girl brought up under your direction and trained in your precepts, who has seen nothing in your company except that which is holy and upright, and who in short learned to love me on your recommendation. For you always respected my mother like a daughter, you always influenced and encouraged me from early childhood, and you always forecast that I would become the sort of man I now seem to be to my wife. So we rival one another in our gratitude to you: I because you gave her to me, she because you gave me to her, as if you had chosen us for one another.

3.14 Companionship in marriage

Pliny the Younger is writing to his wife Calpurnia, with whom he was apparently keeping up a steady stream of correspondence when she was in the country recovering from an illness; business affairs meant he could not accompany her. See *Letters* 6.4, 6.7.

Pliny, *Letters* 7.5

It is incredible how much I long for you. There are two causes: my love for you, and because we are not used to being separated. So it is that I spent a great part of each night sleepless, picturing you; and so it is that, during the day, at the times when I was accustomed to visit you, my feet lead me to your room – I swear it's true. Then, sick and depressed, like one shut out on an empty doorstep, I wander away. The only time I am free of these torments is when I am wearing myself out in the forum, pleading cases for my friends. So you can guess what my life is like, when I find rest in work and solace in misery and cares.

3.15 The hope for children

This letter is addressed to Calpurnius Fabatus, his wife's grandfather. It is a fairly clinical and somewhat chillingly brutal letter, in which it is clear that the main concern is that this marriage has not yet fulfilled its most immediate purpose: to produce descendants.

Pliny, *Letters* 8.10

You are keen to see great-grandsons from us, so you will be that much sadder to hear that your granddaughter has had a miscarriage. In her girlish way she did not know she was pregnant, and so she didn't do what pregnant women are supposed to do to protect the unborn child, and did things that she shouldn't have done. She has learnt some tough lessons, and indeed almost paid for her mistake with her own life. Therefore, although you must find it hard at your advanced age to lose descendants who were already on their way, as it were, you should at least give thanks to the gods that, while they have denied you great-grandchildren for the present, they have saved your granddaughter. They will grant us children in the future; our hope for them is now more firm thanks to this evidence of her fertility, even though it is evidence that did not come to happy fulfilment. I am encouraging, advising, and reassuring you now with the same words with which I do myself. For you cannot desire great-grandchildren any more ardently than I do children. For them it is clear, thanks to their lineage on my side and on yours, that the road to public office is straightforward; I shall leave them a quite famous name and an ancestry that is well established. Only let them be born and let them turn this grief of ours into joy.

3.16 The health of a wife

By way of contrast to the previous letter (**3.15**), this quite touching one is addressed to Calpurnia Hispulla, Pliny's wife's aunt, and in it Pliny displays a good deal more concern for his wife. The contrast between *Letters* 8.10 and 8.11 is extremely telling, especially in terms of the expectations and concerns of two different parties.

Pliny, *Letters* 8.11

I realise that your affection towards your brother's daughter is even more gentle than a mother's indulgent feelings, so I think I should give you first the news that really should come second, so that happiness may step in first and leave no room for concern. But I fear that after a sense of relief will come fear again and that at the same time as you rejoice that she has been freed from danger you will shudder at the dangers she faced. Already she is becoming cheerful again, as she begins to be restored to her old self, as well as being restored to me, and to measure the danger she has been through by her progress towards recovery. And there is no question but that the danger was extreme – it is now safe to admit that – through no fault of her own, except perhaps of her age. Hence her miscarriage, a sorry proof of unsuspected pregnancy. So, although it is not yet fated that a grandson or granddaughter of your brother's may comfort you for his loss, nonetheless remember that this solace is postponed rather than cancelled. For she on whom hope rests is safe. Meanwhile excuse the mishap to your father; pardon for this sort of thing is more readily conceded among women.

3.17 Wives and extrafamilial reputations

Tacitus records speeches delivered in the senate in AD 21 as to whether wives should accompany their husbands as governors to their provinces (*Annals* 3.33–4, and see Livy 34.2–7, the debate several centuries earlier over the *lex Oppia*, for evident parallels). It is proposed by A. Caecina Severus (*consul suffectus* 1 BC) that wives should stay in Italy: he himself has had six children by his wife, and never took her with him on his forty overseas campaigns. Taking women on campaign leads to softness – and intrigues ('If senators thought about it, they would realise that whenever individuals were on trial for extortion, most of the charges related to their wives . . . Women have now cast aside their chains and reign in the homes, the courts, and the armies.'). By contrast M. Valerius Messalla Messalinus (consul 3 BC) argues for the benefits of keeping one's wife with one: 'Much of the old-fashioned toughness has been changed for something better and happier.' It is a good thing that wives may accompany their husbands, he argues. A few husbands may not be able to control their wives, but everyone else should not be penalised for them: if women are left behind, it is asking for trouble – they are weak and extravagant.

Martial sums up the attitude very concisely, in an epigram on the wife of the governor of an African province, a woman apparently notorious for her 'giving' nature.

Martial, 2.56

Among the peoples of Libya your wife, Gallus, has a bad reputation, basely charged with immoderate avarice. But these stories are nothing but pure lies. It's not her habit at all to take. What then is her habit? To give [*dare*].

3.18 Wives as companions, even unto death: Arria as exemplar

Roman myths and ancient history, such as that preserved in the time of Augustus by Livy, provided abundant evidence – for both genders, and doubtless from an early age – of how wives (and husbands, less often) were meant to act. One famous example from more contemporary history was that of Arria, whose final words were *Paete, non dolet* ('Paetus, it doesn't hurt') as she handed her husband, A. Caecina Paetus (*consul suffectus* AD 37) the dagger she had just withdrawn from her own breast.

On a tombstone inscription of Oppia, Arria is clearly as proverbial a wife as Laodamia, the widow of the first Greek to die at Troy, Protesilaus. In view of the Augustan marriage legislation (see **3.47**), one might suppose this senator was not married to Oppia.

Pliny the Younger, writing to Calpurnius Macer, wishes to publicise a little-known example of truly wifely devotion.

(a) *Corpus Inscriptionum Latinarum* 10.5920 = *Inscriptiones Latinae Selectae* 6261 = *Carmina Latina Epigraphica* 423 (Anagnia, Italy, c. AD 100)

To Lucius Cominius Firmus, son of Lucius, grandson of Lucius, of the Palatine tribe, praetor, quaestor of the treasury and of the child allowances, and to Oppia Eunoea, freedwoman of Sextus and Gaia. Mourn, the model of a chaste girl, has perished. Oppia is no longer, Oppia has been snatched from Firmus. Receive this soul and increase the Roman consecrated group, Arria, and you, Laodamia, the Greek. Surviving renown preserves this epitaph for you through your merits. To themselves, their *familia*, and their descendants.

(b) Pliny, *Letters* 6.24.2–5 (c. AD 106)

I was sailing over our Larian lake [Lago di Como, N. Italy], when an older friend pointed out to me a villa, and indeed a bedroom looking out over the lake. 'It's from there,' he said, 'that a woman from our town once threw herself with her husband.' I asked why. The husband had been suffering from a long-standing illness, with festering sores covering his private parts. His wife demanded an inspection, on the grounds that no one could give a franker indication of whether he could be cured. She looked and gave up hope, and urged him to die; she herself was his companion in death, in fact she led the way, providing example and compulsion. For she tied herself to her husband and jumped into the lake. Even I, who came from the same town, had never heard of this deed until very recently, not because it was less important than that very famous deed of Arria's, but because the woman was less important.

3.19 Members of a family within a household

Ironically, epitaphs provide important information about the living, albeit through generalised and stereotypical phraseology. The prevalence of death in this section on marriage also highlights a very real aspect of Roman married life: that it was often short (as well as death, one must consider the effects of divorce, and, for slaves, the whims of a master). For inscriptional evidence for family life, see Saller (2001).

This epitaph, from the via Appia at Rome, is from a large family tomb – that of the Volusii. It illustrates a number of features: a fairly ordinary family, about which we have very limited information, and a family based around slavery, and very dependent on the generosity of their master. Note also that Volusia Prima and Volusia Olympias have been freed, though under the age of 30 years (which would mean they were Junian Latins, unless perhaps they were related by blood to Quintus; compare Gaius *Institutes* 1.19, with Weaver (1990)). Epaphroditus appears still to be a slave.

Corpus Inscriptionum Latinarum 6.9326 = Inscriptiones Latinae Selectae 7864

Epaphroditus, steward of our Quintus [perhaps Q. Volusius Saturninus, consul AD 92], to Volusia Prima, his most cherished wife, and to Volusia Olympias [Who is she? Perhaps most likely the sister of Prima, or perhaps of Epaphroditus. Note that no date of death is given for her, unlike the other two]; and Epaphroditus the son, to Epaphroditus, steward of our Quintus. This spot was given by our Quintus. Prima lived 20 years, 9 months, and 24 days, and was buried on October 21 in the year when Fulvus and Atratinus were consuls [AD 89]. Olympias lived 25 years, 10 months, and 5 days. [Epaphroditus?] lived 41 years and died in the year of the emperor Nerva's third consulship [AD 97].

3.20 Families and slaves: the difficulty of determining status in epitaphs

An epitaph at Rome for Sex. Caecilius Thallus and his family. If not for the gap in the fourth line, in the hope of the father's manumission, we would never know that he was still a slave when his sons were born and that they were therefore illegitimate. The father's name is added at the end (in the dative) after he gained his freedom. If he had instead filled in the gap in the nominative we would not have known that Felix was born while Thallus was a slave. Thallus was still a slave when Felix died; the other son was also born illegitimate. (For marriage among the 'lower classes', including this example, see the classic paper by Beryl Rawson (1966).)

Corpus Inscriptionum Latinarum 6.13738

To the spirits of the deceased, of Sextus Caecilius Felix, most dutiful and sweet son, Caecilia Epigone and [. . .] Thallus, his parents, and Sextus Caecilius Frugi for his sweetest and most dutiful brother, who lived 23 years, 7 months, 11 days, purchased this shrine themselves both for themselves and for their family and for their descendants, a spot 3 feet in front and 3 feet in depth, and for Sextus Caecilius Thallus.

3.21 Two sisters

Corpus Inscriptionum Latinarum 6.27856
(Rome, first or second century AD)

To the spirits of the deceased. For Tutilia Supera, who lived 35 years, 9 months, 17 days, Ampliata, her sister, made this for her, well deserving.

3.22 A freed couple

Corpus Inscriptionum Latinarum 6.23324
(Rome: Porta Latina, first century AD)

For C. Octavius Trypho, freedman of Marcella, Aelia Musa made this for her deserving husband.

3.23 A man of substance and his wife

This is a marble tablet, now in the Vatican, from a columbarium at Rome. It would appear that Vinicius has an urn set aside for his wife; or possibly that his remains occupy[?] two urns. Cf., for example, *L'Année Epigraphique* (1910) 69: 'Euhemerus the driver – three urns'.

Corpus Inscriptionum Latinarum 6.28965 =
Inscriptiones Latinae Selectae 7906 (Rome)

To the spirits of the deceased of Marcus Vinicius Secundus, who lived 40 years, and has taken possession of [?] two urns. Procula his wife made this for her well-deserving husband.

3.24 Two freed people and their son

Corpus Inscriptionum Latinarum 6.27109 = *Inscriptiones Latinae Selectae* 7965 (Rome: trans Tiberim)

To the spirits of the deceased. For L. Tarquitius Marcianus, most sweet son, who lived 9 years, 6 months, 19 days, and 11 hours, L. Tarquitius Trophimus and Tarquitia Eutychia, his parents, set this up for their most sweet son.

3.25 A wife longs to be with her murdered (?) husband

Corpus Inscriptionum Latinarum 6.18817 =
Inscriptiones Latinae Selectae 8006 (Rome)

To honour his sacred spirit, to the spirits of the deceased, I, Furia Spes, [set this up] for my most dear husband, L. Sempronius Firmus. As I realised, both boy and girl are equally bound by love. I lived with him for the shortest time, and at that time when we should have been living, we were separated by an evil hand. So I beg you, most holy spirits, to keep my beloved in your care and to be willing to be most indulgent to him, so that in the hours of night I may see him and he might even be able to persuade fate on my behalf [?] so that I too may be able more sweetly and more swiftly to come and be with him.

3.26 A patron honours a freedman

This is from a marble altar from Rome, from the Forum Boarium behind the round temple of Vesta, in a garden. This epitaph is included to remind us that individuals may be buried by members outside the family, and that *pietas* applies here just as within the nuclear family grouping. One might assume that this freedman had no family of his own.

Corpus Inscriptionum Latinarum 6.28790 = *Inscriptiones Latinae Selectae* 8041

For the memory and devotion [*pietas*] of Q. Vibius Crescens, Q. Vibius Cerinthus made this for his most dear, most faithful, and well-deserving freedman.

3.27 A husband honours a dutiful wife

The adjectives to describe the woman are standard, and abbreviated. Either the husband is unnamed or, less likely, Sempronia is the wife of a Moschis.

Corpus Inscriptionum Latinarum 6.26192 = *Inscriptiones Latinae Selectae* 8398 = *Carmina Latina Epigraphica* 368 (Rome)

Here she is buried, the devoted, frugal, chaste, modest Sempronia [wife or daughter?] of Moschis, to whom for her deserving qualities thanks are given by her husband.

3.28 Another model wife

Corpus Inscriptionum Latinarum 6.11602 = *Inscriptiones Latinae Selectae* 8402 = *Carmina Latina Epigraphica* 237 (Rome, Hadrianic period)

Here is buried Amymone, [wife] of Marcus, best and most beautiful, a worker-in-wool, devoted, modest, frugal, chaste, a stay-at-home [*domiseda*][1].

---

1 The adjective *domiseda* (meant as a compliment, of course) occurs only in one other place in the entire body of Latin texts, and that is in another inscription – an epitaph to, presumably, the same woman (*Corpus Inscriptionum Latinarum* 6.34045), and quite possibly a modern forgery: 'Here lies Amymone, wife of a barbarian, most beautiful, devoted, frugal, chaste, a worker-in-wool, a stay-at-home.'

3.29 A woman commemorated by her father-in-law and husband

This woman is possibly from a Christian family. Note the different names (if that is indeed what they are) for father and son.

Corpus Inscriptionum Latinarum 12.832 = *Inscriptiones Latinae Selectae* 8439 (Arelate, Narbonese Gaul, second or third century AD)

To Iulia Tyrrania, daughter of Lucius, who lived 20 years and 7 months and who served as an example equally in habits and in discipline to all other women, Autarcius set this up for his daughter-in-law, Laurentius for his wife.

3.30 A husband commemorates a loving wife

It is common to see reference to the blissful harmony a couple long enjoyed.

Corpus Inscriptionum Latinarum 9.3215 = *Inscriptiones Latinae Selectae* 8443 (Corfinum, central Italy)

Sacred to the spirits of the deceased. For Caecilia Festiva most beloved wife and sweetheart [*monna*[1]], who lived with me for 21 years without an argument. Pomponius Antiochus her husband set this up for her, well deserving through her labours.

1 *Monna* appears to be a term of endearment for a woman; the *Oxford Latin Dictionary* gives this meaning, but inappropriately cites *Corpus Inscriptionum Latinarum* 8.14911 (= *Inscriptiones Latinae Selectae* 4481), where *Monna* would appear to be a woman's name.

3.31 A woman's *cursus honorum*

Corpus Inscriptionum Latinarum 8.11294 = *Inscriptiones Latinae Selectae* 8444 (Byzacena, N. Africa)

Sacred to the spirits of the deceased. Postumia Matronilla, an incomparable wife, a good mother, a most devoted grandmother, modest and reverential, hard-working, frugal, efficient, watchful, concerned, married to one man, slept with only one man, a matron of complete industry and trustworthiness, she lived 53 years, 5 months, and 3 days.

3.32 Dedication to a like-minded wife

Corpus Inscriptionum Latinarum 8.5798 = *Inscriptiones Latinae Selectae* 8447 (Sigus, Numidia, N. Africa)

Sacred to the spirits of the deceased. To the memory of Iulia Rogata, wife; she always enjoyed one mind, one opinion with me for 40 years; she lived

65 years, may her bones rest in peace. Of the Gargilii, L. Gargilius Venator, son of Lucius, of the tribe of Quirina, set up this grave while he was still alive and remained among those living above, so that he might enjoy good things for the remaining time.

3.33 Another model wife

Corpus Inscriptionum Latinarum 6.29580 = Inscriptiones Latinae Selectae 8450 (Rome)

Sacred to the spirits of the deceased. To Urbana, most sweet, most chaste and most rare wife, than whom I am certain nothing has been more splendid, she certainly deserved to be honoured by this inscription, she who lived with me with the utmost pleasantness and simplicity every day of her life, with both wifely affection and hard work in the manner of her own people. I have added these words in this way, so that those who read may know how much we loved one another. Paternus made this for her, well deserving.

3.34 A companion – and business partner?

These are dactylic hexameters (of a sort); despite Lucius' undoubted abilities as a businessman and husband, he was not a gifted poet. Note the acrostic. One is reminded somewhat of Trimalchio's Fortunata in Petronius' *Satyricon*.

Corpus Inscriptionum Latinarum 8.152 = Carmina Latina Epigraphica 516 (N. Africa, second–third century AD)

Urbanilla, my wife, a woman of complete modesty, is buried here,
Rudder for my enterprises, supported by parsimony, my companion
    at Rome.
But when, having success in all my enterprises, I returned to my
    homeland with her,
Ah, Carthage snatched away my pitiful companion from me.
No hope of livelihood remains to me without such a wife:
In my home she supported me, in my plans she assisted me.
Light-deprived, she pitifully finds her rest shut up in marble.
Lucius, your husband, here has covered you with marble.
Afore we were born, fate allotted this lot to us.

3.35 Faithful unto death

This is a heartfelt and evocative, albeit again not very eloquent, epitaph.

Corpus Inscriptionum Latinarum 5.2108 = Inscriptiones Latinae Selectae 8453 (N. Italy)

... who lived more or less 40 years. His dear wife Martina set this up, she came from Gaul and travelled 50 days' journey, in order to commemorate the memory of her most sweet husband. May you rest well, my most sweet husband.

3.36 An enduring bond

Such tombs in anticipation of death are not uncommon.

Corpus Inscriptionum Latinarum 10.4273 = Inscriptiones Latinae Selectae 8459 (Capua)

Sacred to the spirits of the deceased. L. Papinius Verus and Campania Felicissima made this for themselves while alive. They have lived between them [?] 68 years and 10 days.

3.37 A one-woman man

For a woman to be *univira* – married to only one man in her lifetime – was regarded as exemplary (e.g. **3.31** above). For one husband, at least, it worked the other way, or perhaps the wife's primary concern was that a stepmother would enter the family (although no children are mentioned).

Corpus Inscriptionum Latinarum 11.1491 = Inscriptiones Latinae Selectae 8461 (Pisa)

To the spirits of the deceased. To Scribonia Hedon, Q. Tampius Hermeros made this for his most dear wife, with whom he lived for 18 years without a quarrel, and at whose wish he swore that he would not have a[nother] wife after her.

3.38 A freedman and his wife together after death

The inscription is of interest, not only for the wish that the couple be buried together (cf., similarly, *Inscriptiones Latinae Selectae* 7354 = *Corpus Inscriptionum Latinarum* 6.9290), but also that the wish is carried out by the patron, their former master (if that is M. Volcius Cerdo, son of Marcus; he could in theory be the son of the buried couple).

Corpus Inscriptionum Latinarum 6.29460 = Inscriptiones Latinae Selectae 8466 (Rome)

M. Volcius Euhemerus, freedman of Marcus, asks that after his death the remains of his body be put in a single urn along with [those of] his wife Volcia Chreste. M. Volcius Cerdo, son of Marcus, gave satisfaction to the spirits of the deceased.

3.39 A freedman patron in another freedman's *familia*, including the latter's freedmen

From Rome, mid–late second century AD [?], this marble tablet is from the pagan cemetery excavated in 1940–9 under St Peter's. A patron, probably a freedman, is buried by his own freedmen, who also set up the tomb for their own families, for several generations, and for their own freedmen. Jane Gardner suggests that the two Matuccii could even be the freed sons of the deceased.

A.E. Gordon, *Illustrated Introduction to Latin Epigraphy*, 1983, no. 70 (Rome, second century AD)

For T. Matuccius Pallas, best patron, the two Matuccii, Entimus and Zmaragdus, sellers/weavers of linen, made this tomb for both themselves and their children and their [the children's] descendants, and their own freedmen and freedwomen.

3.40 A husband and wife, and another woman

A man sets up his funeral monument, with instructions to his heirs. The man's wife is still alive. The co-heiress Novia Trophime appears to be a close friend. It was not unusual for an heir to be requested to set up and maintain a tomb.

L'Année Epigraphique 1945, no. 136 (Rome, second century AD)

From the codicil [to the will], in triptych, of Popilius
Heracla,
Gaius Popilius Heracla, to his heirs, greetings.
You, my heirs, I ask and order
and trust to your good faith
to make for me a tomb on the Vatican [Hill]
near the Circus [of Gaius and Nero] next to the tomb of Ulpius
Narcissus, at a cost of 6,000 sesterces, for which purpose
Novia Trophime will pay 3,000 sesterces
and her co-heir 3,000 sesterces; and there I wish to be placed
my remains and those of my wife Fadia Maxima,
if anything should happen to her in the manner of human beings;[1]
I bequeath the legal control of this tomb to my freedmen and freedwomen and to those whom I shall manumit by will,
or to anyone else whom I have left in the status of freedom, and
    furthermore
to Novia Trophime and her freedmen and freedwomen,
and to the descendants of the above-named; and may she [*sic*] be permitted
to go to and enter and walk around in order to make sacrifices at this
    tomb.

1 *humanitus*: a euphemistic reference to death.

3.41 Ideal marriage – among barbarians

Tacitus describes the good, and enviable, albeit strange (and quite different from those of contemporary Romans, according to Tacitus), habits of the Germans: whatever the degree of reality regarding the German tribes, the passage certainly reflects Roman ideals and moralising standards.

Tacitus, *Germania* 18–19

18. Among them the tie of marriage is a strict one, and indeed nothing else in their characters is more worthy of praise. They are practically the only barbarians who are content with one wife each; there are very few exceptions, and these are the result not of lust but relate to those for whom polygamous marriage is sought because of their high birth.

As for the dowry, it is not given by the wife to the husband, but by the husband to the wife. Parents and relatives are present to approve these gifts, gifts that are not designed as womanly luxuries nor to adorn new brides, but things like cattle, horse and bridle, or a shield with special spear and sword. In return for such gifts is the wife acquired, and in turn she herself brings some type of weapon for the man. This is considered the strongest bond, these the sacred rites, these their gods of marriage. In case a woman might think herself exempt from thoughts of manly deeds or from the perils of battle, she is warned by the very rites that initiate marriage that she comes as an ally for him in toil and danger, that she will suffer and risk the same as he in peace and in war. This is the meaning of the yoked oxen, the bridled horse, the gift of arms. Thus must she live, thus must she give birth. What she receives she must hand on, intact and unblemished, to her children, to be handed over in turn to her daughters-in-law and passed on again to her grandchildren.

19. They lead lives of sheltered chastity, not corrupted by any of the enticements of public performances [*spectacula*] or any of the temptations of dinner parties. Men and women alike know nothing of the secrets of letters. Amidst so numerous a people adulteries are very few; the punishment for adultery is immediate and at the discretion of the husband: her hair is shorn, she is stripped, and in the presence of relatives she is thrown out of the *domus* by the husband, who drives her through the entire village with a whip. For prostituted chastity there is no pardon; with neither beauty nor youth nor wealth will she find a husband. No one there finds vices amusing, no one calls corruption inflicted or suffered 'the way things are nowadays'. Better still are those tribes in which only virgins marry and the hopes and prayers of a wife are done with once and for all. So they take only one husband just as only one body and only one life, so that they have no other thoughts beyond him, no further desire, so that, as it were, they love not the one they have married so much as the state of being married.

3.42 Another side to being married

Cicero is writing to his friend Atticus in early May 51 BC. Cicero is on his way, unhappily, to his province of Cilicia; hence, perhaps, his rather testy nature. In any event, the private correspondence gives us an insight into Roman family relations that the more public literature refrains from doing. On the conflict within the family of Cicero's younger brother Quintus and his wife Pomponia (sister of Cicero's correspondent, Atticus), see Dixon (1997).

Cicero, *Letters to Atticus* 5.1.3–4 (S-B 94)

I come now to that aside at the end of your letter, the little note in which you remind me about your sister. Here's how things stand in that regard. When I got to Arpinum and my brother came to see me, we first talked a great deal about you; following on from that I brought up what you and I had said at my Tusculan estate about your sister. I have seen nothing as gentle, nothing as peaceable, as my brother was then towards your sister. Even if he had taken offence at all for some reason, it didn't show. That's what happened on that day. On the next day we set out from Arpinum. The holiday meant Quintus had to stay in Arcanum. I stayed at Aquinum, but we had lunch at Arcanum (you know his farm). When we got there, Quintus, in the most kindly of tones, said 'Pomponia, you ask the women in, and I'll see to the boys [i.e. the servants and farm-workers].' Nothing, at least as far as I could see, could have been sweeter, both in what he said and in regard to his intent and demeanour as he said it. But she replied, in our hearing, 'I am a guest here myself.' This was in reference, I think, to the fact that Statius [Quintus' trusted freedman] had gone on ahead to see to our lunch. Quintus then said to me, 'There you go, this is what I put up with every day.'

Now you will say, 'What on earth was wrong with that?' A great deal; it certainly upset me myself. Her response, both in what she said and how she said it, was so ridiculous and rude. I concealed my emotions, painful though they were. We all took our places at table – except for her. Quintus had some food sent to her all the same. She refused it. In short, nothing could have been gentler than my brother, nothing ruder than your sister, it seemed to me – and I'm passing over many details that irritated me more than they did Quintus himself. I went from there to Aquinum. Quintus stayed in Arcanum and came to see me at Aquinum the next morning; he told me she had refused to sleep with him and that at the time of her departure she acted in exactly the same way as I'd witnessed before. Well then. As far as I'm concerned, you can tell her to her face that I regard her manners on that day to have been quite lacking. I have written this to you – perhaps at greater length than was called for – so that you may see that there is also room for you to do some instructing and advising.

3.43 The expense, for a husband, of being married

This was written on 26 April 44 BC, i.e. less than 7 years after the previous passage. Cf. also Cicero's own divorce from Terentia and the financial cost involved for him. See Dixon (1984: esp. 88–97).

Cicero, *Letters to Atticus* 14.13.5 (S-B 367)

Now you write that there are rumours that I'm on the point of selling the place I have at the lake [the Lucrine lake], or at any rate to hand over my really rather small villa to Quintus, even at a considerable price, so that he might bring in (as young Quintus [brother Quintus' son] will have told you) Aquilia with her dowry. But I really am not giving a thought to selling, unless I find something I like better. As for Quintus, he's far from thinking about buying at the moment; he's got enough problems repaying the dowry, in regard to which he's enormously grateful to Egnatius. And, as for getting married, he's so averse to that that he says he prefers nothing to a single bed.

3.44 The cost, for a wife, of being married

For a more usual risk involved in marriage, cf. the epitaph of Veturia (**2.11**).

Corpus Inscriptionum Latinarum 13.2182 = *Inscriptiones Latinae Selectae* 8512 (Lugdunum)

To the spirits of the deceased and for the eternal rest of Iulia Maiana, a most holy woman, who was killed at the hand of a most cruel husband. She died before fate had decreed it. She lived with him for 28 years, and by him gave birth to two children, a boy aged 19 years and a girl aged 18 years. O faithfulness, o devotion! Iulius Maior, brother, for his sweetest sister, and Ingenuinius Januarius, her son, saw to the setting up of this and dedicated it while still under construction.

3.45 *O tempora, o mores!*

By publicising vices such as ingratitude we make them more common, preaches Seneca. Look at how common divorce and adultery are nowadays!

Seneca, *On Benefits* 3.16.2–3

Is there any woman who blushes at divorce, ever since certain famous noble women calculated their age not by the number of consuls but of husbands, and leave home in order to marry, and marry in order to be divorced? They were afraid of such behaviour in the past, for as long as it was a rare occurrence; but since there is not an issue of the public gazette without mention of a divorce, they have learned to do what they used to hear about so often. Is there any shame at all now attached to adultery, ever since it has come about that no woman has a husband except to annoy her adulterer? Chastity is simply a proof of ugliness. You will never find a woman who is so poor, so filthy, as to be satisfied with a single pair of adulterers, unless she has one booked in for every hour. And the day is not long enough for them all, unless she is carried by litter to one and stays overnight with another. She is stupid and behind the times who thinks that marriage is simply having only one lover. Since the shame attached to such immoralities has now vanished, ever since the practice has spread more widely, so you will make ingrates more numerous and more important if they have begun to count their number.

3.46 The most exemplary husband of them all?

Augustus was proud to boast of his social legislation as one of his achievements. Contrast the accounts of his love-life in Suetonius' life of the emperor (*Augustus* 62 ff.).

Augustus, *Res Gestae* 8.5

By new laws passed on my authority I brought back into use many exemplary practices of our ancestors that were becoming forgotten in our time, and in many ways I myself handed down to later generations exemplary practices for them to imitate.

3.47 Curbing adultery

The following texts illustrate aspects of Augustus' legislation of 18 BC, *lex Iulia de adulteriis*, attempting to control adultery. The meaning of *stuprum* varies in different contexts, but basically in legal terminology refers to illicit sexual intercourse apart from adultery. See, for example, *Digest* 48.5.6.1, Papinian, *On Adultery*:

> The law refers to *stuprum* and *adulterium* indiscriminately and in rather inapplicable contexts. But strictly speaking *adulterium* is committed against a married woman, the name being derived on account of the offspring conceived by another [*alter*], whereas *stuprum* is committed against a virgin or a widow.

(a) *Digest* 48.5.13, Ulpian

These are the words of the law: 'Henceforth no one shall commit adultery [*adulterium*] or *stuprum* knowingly or with malice aforethought.' The terms of this law apply both to him who abets and to him who commits the *stuprum* or adultery.

(b) Justinian, *Institutes* 4.18.4

Under the Julian law to control adultery, the crime of *stuprum* is punished, when anyone seduces and violates [*stupro*], even without force, either a virgin or a respectable widow.

(c) *Mosaicarum et Romanarum Legum Collatio* 4.2.3, Paul (*Fontes Iuris Romani Anteiustiniani*[2], 2.553)

But in the second section of the law it allows a father who has his daughter in his *potestas* or whose daughter has gone, with his authority when she was in his *potestas*, into the *manus* of her husband, if he catches his daughter's seducer, in his own home or in his son-in-law's home, or the latter calls in his father-in-law, to kill the adulterer without risk of prosecution, provided that he kill his daughter at the same time.

(d) *Digest* 48.5.25, preface, Macer

A husband is permitted to kill his wife's seducer ... He is permitted to kill a pimp, actor, gladiator, criminal, freedman, or slave who is caught in the act of adultery with his wife in his own home, but not in the home of his father-in-law ... And he must divorce his wife without delay.

(e) *Digest* 48.5.30, preface, Ulpian

A husband who does not divorce his wife when she has been caught in adultery, and who allows the adulterer to go unpunished, is himself punished as a pimp; for he ought to have avenged himself on the man and also vented his rage on his wife, who has violated his marriage.

(f) *Digest* 48.5.30.3, Ulpian

A husband who makes any profit from the adultery of his wife is to be flogged.

(g) Paul, *Sententiae* 2.26.14

Women convicted of adultery are punished by confiscation of half of their dowry, and a third of their property, and by exile to an island. The male adulterers are punished by a similar exile to an island[1] and by confiscation of half their property.

1 Presumably to a different island from that of the woman.

(h) *Digest* 23.2.26, Modestinus

Women accused of adultery cannot marry while their husbands are alive, even before conviction.

3.48 Divorce in Roman law

On the subject of Roman divorce see especially Treggiari (1991). The legal texts give us no indication of the frequency of divorce, but the literary texts, many of a moralising character, give the impression that it was very rife indeed. Again, reality may have been different, but clearly the perception that it was common had an effect on the mechanisms of, and controls over, Roman society (see Dio on Augustus, **3.54a** below).

(a) *Digest* 24.2.1, Paul

Marriage is dissolved by divorce, death, captivity, or any other kind of slavery of either of the parties.

(b) *Digest* 24.2.3, Paul

It is only a true divorce if there is the intention to remain apart permanently. So anything that is done or said in the heat of the moment is not effective until it has been shown by persistence that this was an indication of true intention.

(c) *Digest* 24.1.60.1–61

Cf. *Digest* 24.1.64 (Iavolenus, quoting Labeo) on a gift given by a husband (Maecenas) to a wife (Terentia) after divorce to persuade her to return; she returns, then divorces him; is the gift valid? In other words, was the first divorce valid?

(i) *Digest* 24.1.60.1, Hermogenian

In the event of divorce gifts are permitted between a husband and a wife. It often happens that on account of a priesthood or even sterility.

(ii) *Digest* 24.1.61, Gaius

. . . or old age or illness or military service, it is not possible for a marriage to be conveniently maintained.

(d) *Digest* 43.30.1.1, 5

This is Ulpian, citing decrees and rescripts of Pius, M. Aurelius, and Severus.

If anyone wishes to take away his daughter who is married to me or wishes her to be produced for him, may a defence be granted against the interdict, if the father should happen to wish to dissolve a harmonious marriage [*concordans matrimonium*], perhaps supported by children too? We follow the fixed rule that marriages that enjoy true harmony should not be disturbed by the exercise of the right of *patria potestas*. But this is to be applied by persuading the father not to exercise his *patria potestas* harshly.

(e) *Codex Iustinianus* 5.24.1

This is a rescript of the emperors Diocletian and Maximian to a woman named Caelestina, in AD 294. On divorce children would typically stay with the father, their *paterfamilias*.

Although it is provided by no constitution of ours or of our divine parents that the division of children between parents according to sex should be practised, nevertheless the presiding magistrate will judge whether children [*filii*] should stay and be reared with the father or with the mother.

3.49 Divorce – one Greek's view of Rome

Lucius Aemilius Paulus was consul in 182 and 168 BC, and was the father of Q. Fabius Maximus Aemilianus and P. Cornelius Scipio Aemilianus (note also his ill-starred gamble with his four sons). The passage provides a necessary contrast to ideals of life-long marriage without any disharmony [*sine ulla querella*].

Plutarch, *Aemilius Paulus* 5.1–2

Paulus married Papiria, the daughter of Maso the ex-consul [C. Papirius Maso, consul 231 BC]. After he had lived with her a long time he divorced her, even though he had by her become the father of very fine children: for she was the one who bore for him the very illustrious Scipio and Fabius Maximus. No reason for the divorce has come down in the written sources to us, but there seems to be some truth in the following story told about divorce. A Roman man divorced his wife, and his friends rebuked him, saying: 'Isn't she a sensible woman? Isn't she pretty? Isn't she fertile?'

He then held out his shoe (what the Romans call a *calceus*) and said, 'Isn't this a good-looking shoe? Isn't it new? But not one of you knows where it pinches my foot.' For to be sure it is great and obvious faults that lead to some wives being separated from their husbands, but the small and frequent causes of friction, arising from some unpleasantness or disharmony and unnoticed by everyone else, also produce irreparable alienations in those who live together.

3.50 The joys of descendants, for all sorts of reasons

These lines come from Catullus' *Epithalamium* or wedding hymn, written in the first century BC; for identification of the Torquati here, and the extinction of the patrician line, see still Mitchell (1966).

(a) Catullus, 61.209–13

I want a tiny Torquatus to stretch out his tender hands, reaching from his mother's lap towards his father, smiling sweetly at him with half-open little lips.

(b) Catullus, 68.119–24

Nor so dear to her age-stricken father is the head of the late-born grandchild that his only daughter nurses, who, scarce at length appearing as an heir to ancestral wealth, and having his name brought into the witnessed tablets, puts an end to the unnatural joy of the kinsman, now in his turn derided, and drives away the vulture that waits for the hoary head.

(c) Pliny the Elder, *Natural History* 7.58–60

Cf. also Pliny the Elder, *Natural History* 7.43.139–41 (L. Caecilius Metellus, consul 251, 247): among the greatest blessings known to man is to have many children (others include success in war, politics, and oratory).

One of the many exceptional circumstances connected with the deified Augustus was that he lived to see his granddaughter's grandson, Marcus Silanus [*neptis suae nepotem*, M. Iunius Silanus, *consul ordinarius* AD 46; *Prosopographia Imperii Romani*[2], I 833], who was born in the year of his [Augustus'] death ... Quintus Metellus Macedonicus [consul 143 BC][1] died leaving six children and eleven grandchildren; counting daughters-in-law and sons-in-law, the total number who greeted him with the title of father was twenty-seven. In the *acta* in the time of the reign of the deified Augustus is found the statement that in his twelfth consulship, when Lucius Sulla was his colleague [5 BC], on April 11 a freeborn plebeian from Faesulae

[Fiesole] named Gaius Crispinius Hilarus went in procession preceded by eight children, including two daughters, twenty-seven grandchildren, eighteen greatgrandchildren, and eight granddaughters by marriage, all of whom offered sacrifices on the Capitol.

1 Note his speech *de prole augenda*, mentioned in **3.9** above.

3.51 Another side to Augustus: not so lucky?

A quite different account may be found in Tacitus, *Annals* 1.3.

Plutarch, *Moralia* 508a ('On Garrulity')

Fulvius, the friend of Caesar Augustus, heard the emperor, who was by now an old man, lamenting the emptiness of his *oikos*: two of his grandsons [Gaius and Lucius Caesar] by his daughter were dead, and Postumius [Postumus Agrippa], the only grandson left alive, was in exile because of some slander against him; and so he was being forced to bring his wife's son [Tiberius] into the succession to the throne, although he pitied his grandson and was planning to recall him from exile. Fulvius divulged what he had heard to his wife, and she reported it to Livia. Livia then bitterly rebuked Augustus . . . So when Fulvius came to Augustus in the morning, as was his custom, and said, 'Greetings, Caesar,' Augustus replied, 'Farewell, Fulvius.' Fulvius understood and went straight off home; he sent for his wife and said, 'Caesar has found out that I have not kept his secret and so I intend to kill myself.' His wife replied, 'So you should; you have been living with me for such a long time and yet you have not learnt to guard against my big mouth. But let me go first.' And she took the sword and killed herself before her husband.

3.52 The joys of childlessness

Despite the views expressed about the joys of having children, the opposite view is also frequently and strongly expressed. Various reasons for childlessness may be adduced: the upper-class Roman, in a system of partible inheritance, may not have wanted to see his estate split up among too many children after his death and so may have attempted to limit the size of his family (cf. **3.66** – though Musonius' views can hardly be held to be typical); and Seneca, *ad Helviam* 16.3. Polybius 36.17.5–8 is explicit for Hellenistic Greece (see Chapter 2). The father then ran the risk, of course, that what children his wife did bear may die at an early age, thus effectively terminating the family line. (Cf. Brunt (1971: 141–2) and Hopkins (1983: ch. 3) for the disappearance of families, due not only to poverty or political retirement.)

In any event, it became proverbial that wealthy and childless old Roman men and women could expect a large host of 'friends' to surround them, in the expectation that they would look kindly on these flatterers in drawing up a will and would not live too long after performing this duty. This individual, the *captator* or inheritance-hunter, was a favourite target of the satirist. Many literary (but not legal) references to *captatio*, particularly from Martial, Juvenal, and Lucian, may be adduced. Keith Hopkins (1983: 96–7), warns against regarding literary references in this context as representative of general reality. Indeed A.R. Mansbach, in her unpublished doctoral thesis '*Captatio:* Myth and Reality' (1982), argues that *captatio* was more a literary topos than an historical reality. This may be true, but what is important here is that some of the elite class at Rome at least thought that *captatio* was a real threat (or promise) in old age. Apparently inheritance-hunting was a very profitable profession. See also Champlin (1991: 22 and 87–102).

(a) Horace, *Satires* 2.5.45–50

[Teiresias gives advice to Odysseus on how to get wealthy.] 'Now if someone's loaded but acknowledges a son who's sickly, he's the man to go for – rather than grovelling to one who has no children. You can worm your way gently into his confidence and aim to be named as his second heir. Then, if the lad happens to meet his maker, you can fill his place. This trick seldom fails.'

(b) Martial, 2.26

Because Naevia gasps for breath, because she has a dry cough, and often sprays saliva into your lap, do you suppose you've got the matter sewn up, Bithynicus? You're wrong. Naevia is leading you on, not dying.

(c) Seneca, *Consolatio ad Marciam* 19.2

Seneca seeks to give consolation to the noble Marcia, one of whose sons has died. Seneca mentions the advantages childlessness holds in society – not a creditable consolation, he admits, but a true one.

In our state childlessness now confers more influence than it snatches away, and loneliness, which used to make old age such a curse, now makes older people so powerful that they actually feign hatred for their sons and disown their children – and thus make themselves childless by their own act.

(d) Pliny, *Letters* 8.18

Gnaeus Domitius Tullus (consul II 98; *Prosopographia Imperii Romani*[2], D 167); Konrad (1994: 141), was an otherwise apparently despicable character who cultivated the flattery of many a *captator*, we are told. He disappointed them all in his will, and left his wealth to his (second) wife and descendants – a praiseworthy, if somewhat surprising, display of *pietas*, remarks Pliny. Despite his wealth, he is a hopeless invalid, fortunate only in that he has a wife and slaves to tend him. Even allowing for the fact that in antiquity a groom would typically have been a number of years older than his bride, the literary depiction of an elderly man with a young wife was not infrequently harsh. Tullus' wife, we are told, was criticised severely for having married him in the first place, and particularly now that he is so decrepit. The physical and mental decrepitude of Tullus is described in brief but vivid and disgusting detail.

It is definitely untrue, what is commonly believed, that people's wills are a mirror to their character. For Domitius Tullus has shown himself to be much better in death than in life. For, although he had encouraged inheritance-hunters, he left his daughter as his heir, the daughter he shared with his brother (for he had adopted his brother's daughter).[1] He also left his grandchildren, as well as a great-granddaughter a great many very welcome legacies. In fact the whole will was overflowing with *pietas* – and so that much more unexpected … His will is all the more praiseworthy because it was *pietas* and *fides* and *pudor* that wrote it. In it he basically expresses his gratitude to all his relatives for their services to him, and to his wife. She receives his very lovely villas, and a good sum of money – she, the best and most enduring of wives – she deserved this and more from her husband inasmuch as she was so severely criticised for marrying him in the first place. For it did not seem at all suitable for a woman of her distinguished birth and faultless character, getting on in years, long a widow, a mother in the past, to be married to a wealthy old man so wasted by illness that even a wife whom he had married when he was young and healthy could have found him repulsive. Deformed and crippled in every limb, he could only enjoy his enormous wealth by contemplating it and could not even turn in bed unless he was manhandled. He also had to have his teeth cleaned and brushed for him – a squalid and pitiful detail. When complaining about the humiliations of his infirmity, he was often heard to say that every day he licked the fingers of his slaves. Yet he continued to live, and wanted to continue to live, thanks in particular to the support of his wife, who by her *perseverantia* turned criticism for having entered the marriage into renown.

---

1 Her father had emancipated her, and her uncle had adopted her, to get around her difficult maternal grandfather: see Gardner (1998: 105 n. 197).

3.53 The importance of legitimacy

These passages are on the examination of the womb and the guarding of childbirth. These legal texts illustrate the absolute necessity for legitimacy and confidence in paternity.

(a) *Digest* 25.4.1, praetor 1, Ulpian

In the time of the deified brothers, it happened that a husband said his wife was pregnant, and the wife denied it. Having been consulted, the emperors addressed a rescript to the urban praetor, Valerius Priscianus, which stated: 'Rutilius Severus seems to be asking for something new, to set a guard over his wife, a wife whom he had divorced and who asserts that she is not pregnant, so no one will be surprised if we also suggest a new plan and remedy. So if he persists in the same request, it will be most fitting that the house of a most respectable woman be chosen, in which Domitia may come, and there three midwives, proven in both skill and trustworthiness and engaged by you, examine her. Then if all three of them, or two of them, declare that she appears to be pregnant, then the woman is to be persuaded to allow in a guard just as if she had wanted this herself. If she does not give birth, the husband should realise that his reputation and honour are at stake, so that, not unjustly, he could be seen to have made this up in order to inflict some damage on this woman. If, however, all three women or the majority of them announce that she is not pregnant, there will be no need for the guarding.' 1. It is made extremely clear from this rescript that the decisions of the senate regarding the acknowledgement of children do not apply if a woman pretends that she is not pregnant or even denies it, and with good reason, for the offspring, even before it is born, is part of the woman or her insides. After the child is fully born, the husband has the right to request the child from the woman by means of an interdict [formal request via the praetor], or to have the child shown to him, or to be permitted to lead the child away.

(b) *Digest* 25.4.1.10, Ulpian

As regards the inspection of the womb and the guarding of the birth, the praetor says the following: 'If a woman whose husband has died says that she is pregnant, she must see to it that it is announced to those to whom this matter will be of relevance, or their procurators, twice within a month, so that, if they so choose, they may send people to inspect her womb. Free women may be sent, up to a maximum of five, and they should all examine her at the same time, provided that none of them in the process of examination touches the woman's womb against her wishes. The woman is to give birth in the house of a very respectable woman as determined by me. Thirty days before she thinks she is going to give birth, the woman is to announce to those to whom this matter is of relevance, or to their procurators, so that, if they so choose, they may send people to guard the womb. The room in which the woman is going to give birth must have no more than a single mode of entry; if there are more than one, they are to be boarded over on both sides. In front of the door to this room, three free men and three free women, with two companions, are to keep guard. Whenever this woman goes into the room or into another room in order to have a bath, the guards, if they so chose, may inspect it before she enters, and may search those who go in. The guards, who have been positioned in front of the room, may, if they so choose, search all those who enter the room or the house. When the woman begins to go into labour, she must announce it to those to whom it is relevant, or their procurators, so that they may send people to be present when she gives birth. Free women may be sent, up to a maximum of five, so that in that room, as well as the two midwives, there are not more than ten freeborn women and no more than six slave women. Those woman who are about to enter that room are all to be searched in case any of them is pregnant. There are to be no fewer than three lights there,' for of course darkness is better suited to substitution. 'When something [sic] is born, it is to be shown to those to whom this matter is relevant, or to their procurators, if they wish to inspect it.'

3.54 The Augustan legislation on marriage and childbirth: aims and resistance

Augustus' marriage legislation (*lex Iulia de maritandis ordinibus*, 18 BC, and *lex Papia Poppaea*, AD 9) may not have succeeded in its apparent aims, to increase the legitimate birth rate of the free, but it did exert considerable influence, at least among the affluent.

(a) Cassius Dio 54.16 (18 BC)

Augustus introduced a number of laws, among them one that debarred from magistracies for five years any individuals who had given bribes in order to gain office. He imposed more severe penalties on unmarried men and women, whereas he offered rewards for marriage and childbearing. Now since among the wellborn [freeborn?] there were far more males than females, he allowed those men who wished (apart from senators) even to marry freedwomen and he ordered that their offspring were to be legitimate. Meanwhile there arose an outcry in the senate about the unseemly behaviour of women and young men, this being alleged as a motivation for their reluctance to enter into lawful marriage. The senators urged him to put this right too, with snide references to his many extramarital affairs with women. At first he replied simply that regulations had been laid down to deal with the most essential points and that for every other detail legislation could not possibly be enacted in the same way. But then he was forced to add the comment that 'you yourselves ought to give advice and orders to your wives as you see fit, just as I do myself'. Well, when they heard that, they pressed him much more, wanting to learn what advice it was that he gave to Livia. With reluctance he said a few things about women's attire and other forms of adornment, and also about their going out in public and their modest behaviour; he was not at all concerned that his own actions did not lend credence to his words ... Since some men were betrothing themselves to baby girls and were thus enjoying the rights of married men without actually carrying out their duties, he ordered that no betrothal would be valid unless the man married the girl within two years; in other words, a girl had to be at least ten years old when a man was betrothed to her if he was to gain any benefit from the alliance, for, as I have already said [in a passage now lost], girls are thought to be of a marriageable age on the completion of their twelfth year.

(b) Horace, *Carmen Saeculare* 17–20
(17 BC)

O goddess may you produce offspring and make prosperous the decrees of the senators concerning the joining of women in marriage and the marriage law productive of new offspring.

(c) Suetonius, *Augustus* 34

The laws that he revised and others that he created anew included those on extravagance, adultery, chastity, bribery, and the regulation of marriage. The marriage laws he amended to make them more severe than the others, but in the face of the tumult of those refusing he could not make it work, except by withdrawing or lightening part of the penalties and the three-year moratorium given, and by increasing the rewards. But the equestrians obstinately demanded at a public spectacle the abolition even of this, so he sent for the children of Germanicus and when they arrived he displayed them, one sitting on his knee, the other on his son's, signifying by his gestures and expression that they should not find it a hardship to imitate the young man's example. When he realised the force of the law was being eluded by the immaturity of betrothed girls and by frequent changing of marriages, he shortened the time of betrothal and imposed a limit on divorces.

(d) Cassius Dio 56.1–10 (AD 9)

During the triumphal games the equestrians were very insistent that the law affecting the unmarried and the childless should be repealed, Augustus assembled in one part of the forum all the unmarried ones and in another part those who were married, including those who also had children. When he saw that the latter were much fewer in number he was very upset, and addressed them as follows ...

Dio provides, 56.2–3, a fairly brief speech praising those who have 'done their duty' by the state, in emulation of the gods and of the Romans' own ancestors, thus ensuring the ongoing strength of the Roman people, as well as domestic bliss:

'For there is nothing better than a wife who is faithful, domesticated, a good housekeeper and childrearer; she makes you happy in health and takes care of you in sickness; she is your partner when times are good, and consoles you when hard times come, there to restrain your youthful passions and in time to temper the untimely harshness of old age. Think too of the pleasure of acknowledging a child endowed with the qualities of both parents, to raise and educate it, one's own physical and spiritual image, so that as it grows another self develops. Think of the tremendous blessing that, on leaving this life, you leave behind as successor and heir to your blood and your property one who is arisen from your own line, from your own being. In effect it is only the mortal part of you that passes away, for you still live on in that child as your successor . . .

Dio then presents a rather longer speech, 56.4–9, to the other, larger group, the unmarried equestrians, upbraiding them for not performing their duties as men and citizens, and seeming bent on the annihilation of the Roman race. For example, 56.5.2–3:

'For you are committing murder in not fathering in the first place those who ought to be your descendants. You are committing sacrilege in cancelling out the names and honours of your ancestors, and you are guilty of impiety in that you are destroying your families that were set up by the gods and you are obliterating the greatest offerings that can be made to them, namely human life, and you are thus overturning their holy rites and temples. And what is more you are destroying the state by disobeying her laws, and you are betraying your country by rendering her barren and without offspring; in fact, what is even worse, you are razing her completely to the ground, making her empty of future inhabitants. For it is of course human beings who make up a city, not houses or porticoes or marketplaces empty of men.

Dio then has Augustus, after a great deal of impassioned rebuke of this kind, justify his harshness and his actions, 56.6.4–7.4:

'For it was not permitted to anyone in the past to neglect childbearing and marriage. Even from the very beginning when the first government was established, strict laws were laid down in these regards, and following that many decrees were passed by the senate and the people, decrees that there is no need to detail here now. I have increased the penalties for those who

111

do not obey, so that through fear of being liable to them you will come to your senses, and to those who do obey I have instituted prizes that are more numerous and more substantial than those offered for any other act of manly virtue, so that for this reason, if for no other, you might be persuaded to marry and have children. But you have not made an effort for any of these rewards nor expressed any fear of any of these penalties; instead you have shown scorn for them all and have trampled on them all as if you were not living in a civilised community. Yes, you talk about the unencumbered and carefree way of life you have adopted, without wives and children, but in fact you are no different from robbers and the most wild of animals. 7. For surely it is not your delight in celibacy that leads you to live without wives, nor does any single one of you eat alone or sleep alone; rather what you want is complete licence to lead a life of unrestrained violence and debauchery. And yet I allowed you to court girls who were still of tender age and not yet ripe for marriage so that, having the title of fiancés, you might live as family men should, and I allowed that those who were not in the senatorial order could marry freedwomen, so that anyone, whether through love or through any sort of attachment, who wanted to take such a course could do so lawfully . . . But all my threats and encouragements and extensions of time and pleading have come to nothing. For you yourselves can see how much more numerous you are than those who have married. By now you should have produced for us as many descendants as yourselves, or rather many times more. For how else can families continue. How else is the commonwealth to be preserved, if we do not marry and have children?'

Augustus, as Dio has him speak, admits that there are inconveniences to marriage and child-rearing, but states that the advantages are greater than the disadvantages:

Thus he addressed both groups of equestrians. He subsequently increased the rewards for those who had children, and for the others he introduced a distinction between those who were married and those who were not by inflicting different penalties on them . . . The *lex Papia Poppaea* was drawn up by M, Papius Mutilus and Q, Poppaeaus Secundus, who were consuls during part of that year. It so happened that both these men were not only childless but not even married.

(e) Isidorus, *Origines* 5.15.1

Under Octavian Caesar the suffect consuls Papius and Poppaeus introduced a law which is called, after their names, the *lex Papia Poppaea*, containing rewards for fathers for raising children.

(f) Tacitus, *Annals* 3.25.1

The laws to increase the birthrate, Tacitus asserts, merely increased the rate of litigation.

The *[lex] Papia Poppaea* had been passed by Augustus in his later years, after the Julian measures, to increase the penalties for those without children and to enrich the treasury.[1] It did not make marriage and the rearing of children more popular; childlessness held too strong a sway. On the other hand the multitude of those at risk of being prosecuted continued to increase, since every *domus* was being overturned by informers' spin on things; as a result, whereas before society suffered from its vices, now it suffered from its laws.

1 *augendo aerario*: see the perceptive comments in Woodman and Martin (1996).

(g) Tertullian, *Apologeticum* 4.8 (c. AD 197)

As for those absolutely absurd Papian laws, which require people to have children at an earlier age than the Julian laws require them to be married, did not that most valiant of emperors, Severus, clear them out only yesterday, for all their old age and authority?

3.55 The Augustan legislation on marriage and childbirth: basic terms of the laws

Legal sources focus not on the unpopularity of the legislation, nor on their morality, but on precise aspects of the laws themselves, as they survived into later generations.

(a) *Digest* 23.2.19, Marcian

According to chapter 35 of the *lex Iulia*, persons who wrongfully prevent children whom they have in their *potestas* to marry, or who refuse to give them a dowry in accordance with a constitution of the deified Severus and Antoninus, are forced by the proconsuls or governors of provinces to arrange the marriage of and to endow them. Those who do not seek to arrange a marriage are also held to prevent it.

(b) *Digest* 23.2.20, Paul

It is to be noted that it is not the duty of a curator to see that his female ward is married or not, because his duties only relate to the transaction of business on her behalf. This Severus and Antoninus stated in a rescript in the following words: 'It is the duty of a curator to administer the affairs of his ward, but the ward can marry, or not, as she sees fit.'

(c) *Digest* 23.2.21, Terentius Clemens, *On the 'lex Iulia et Papia'*, book 3

A son who is in *patria potestas* is not forced to marry.

(d) *Digest* 23.2.22, Celsus

If, under force from his father, a son marries a woman whom he would not have married if the choice had been left to him, the marriage will nonetheless be legally contracted; because it is not contracted against the consent of either party, and the son is held to have preferred to take this course.

(e) *Digest* 23.2.23, Celsus

It is provided by the *lex Papia* that all freeborn men, except senators and their children, can marry freedwomen.

(f) *Digest* 23.2.24, Modestinus

Living with a free woman is not considered concubinage but as marriage, if she does not make money by means of her body.

(g) *Digest* 23.2.25, Modestinus

A son who has been emancipated can marry even without the consent of his father, and any son that he may have will be his heir.

(h) *Digest* 23.2.27, Ulpian

If any man who has senatorial rank has a freedwoman as wife, though she is not his wife in the meantime, nevertheless she is in that position and, if he loses his rank, she will become his wife.

(i) *Digest* 23.2.28–29, Marcian, Ulpian

A patron cannot marry his freedwoman against her will.

And Ateius Capito is said to have decreed this in his consulship. This ruling must be observed unless the patron freed her so that he could marry her.

(j) *Digest* 23.2.35, Papinian

A *filius familias* who is a soldier cannot marry without his father's approval.

(k) *Digest* 23.2.41, Marcellus

It is held to be disgraceful for women to live in a shameful way [*turpiter*] and to earn money by prostitution, even if they do not do so openly. 1. If a woman should live in concubinage with someone other than her patron, I say that she does not possess the integrity of a *mater familias*.

(l) *Digest* 23.2.42, Modestinus

In unions of the sexes, it should always be considered not only what is legal, but also what is decent. 1. If the daughter, granddaughter, or great-granddaughter of a senator should marry a freedman, or a man who practises the profession of an actor, or whose father or mother did so, the marriage will be void.

(m) *Epitome of Ulpian* 16 (*Fontes Iuris Romani Anteiustiniani*[2], 2.278–9)

On complete capacity for inheritance between husband and wife: the benefits of having children.

1. Sometimes husband and wife can receive from each other the entire inheritance, if, for example, both or either of them are not yet of the age by which the law requires children, that is, if the husband is less than 25 years or the wife is less than 20 years of age; also if both have in the course of their marriage exceeded the ages set as limits by the *lex Papia*, that is, the husband 60 years, the wife 50; likewise, if relations [*cognati*] up to and including the sixth degree have married one another, or if the husband is absent, both while he is absent and up to a year after he has ceased to be absent. 1ᵃ. There is also complete freedom of making a will between themselves if the privileges attached to having children [*ius liberorum*] have been obtained from the emperor, or if they have a son or daughter in common, or have lost a son of the age of 14 or a daughter of age 12 years, or if they have lost two children of the age of 3 years, or three after the naming-day, provided nevertheless that even one child of any age lost before puberty gives them the right of complete capacity within one year and six months [of the death]. Likewise if the wife, within ten months following the death of her husband, bears a child by him, she takes the whole of his goods.

2. Sometimes they can take nothing from one another, that is, if they have contracted a marriage contrary to the *lex Iulia et Papia Poppaea*, for example if someone has married a woman who is of ill repute [*famosa*, basically a woman who practises a 'dishonest' profession, such as a prostitute, a brothel keeper, a female gladiator, or an actress], or a senator has married a freedwoman.

3. A man who has conformed to neither law within his sixtieth year, or a woman who has not done so within her fiftieth, although after this age exempt according to the laws themselves, will still be liable to the standing penalties by reason of the *senatus consultum Persicianum*. But by the *senatus consultum Claudianum* a man over 60 who marries a woman under 50 will be treated just as if he had married while under 60 years of age. But if a woman over 50 is married to a man under 60, the marriage is styled 'unequal', and by the *senatus consultum Calvisianum* it is ordered that such a case is of no avail in the taking of inheritances and legacies. Therefore on the woman's death her dowry will lapse [i.e. go to the *fiscus*, the imperial treasury].

3.56 The Augustan legislation on marriage and childbirth: upper age limits

As the previous passage has illustrated, Augustus' laws went through a variety of amendments and refinements, both during his lifetime and long after his death.

The *Gnomon of the Idios Logos* provides important evidence of how Roman law was applied in the province of Egypt. The copy we have dates from the second century AD, but fragments of it have also been found from as early as the reign of Tiberius.

(a) Suetonius, *Claudius* 23

Claudius nullified a clause added to the *lex Papia Poppaea* by Tiberius, which had implied that men in their sixties could not father children.

(b) *Gnomon of the Idios Logos* 24–7

The dowry brought by a Roman woman over 50 years of age to a Roman husband under 60 years of age is after death confiscated by the *fiscus*. That likewise is confiscated which is brought by a woman under 50 years of age to a husband over 60 years of age.

And if a Latin woman over 50 brings any property to a husband over 60 years, it is confiscated.

Whatever property a Roman man, who is 60 years of age and who is childless and without a wife, inherits, is confiscated. If he has a wife but no children and declares his position, he is allowed to take the half.

(c) *Codex Iustinianus* 5.4.27 (a rescript of Justinian, AD 531/2)

In the case of males and females older or younger than 60 or 50 years of age, we authorise those who so desire to contract marriages, marriages that had been prohibited by the Julian or Papian law. By no manner and by nobody are such marriages to be prevented.

3.57 The Augustan legislation on marriage and childbirth: privileges granted to those who have three children (*ius iii liberorum*)

(a) Aulus Gellius, *Attic Nights* 2.15.4–7

In chapter 7 of the *lex Iulia* priority in assuming the consular fasces is given not to the older of the two consuls but to the one who has more children in his power than his colleague or has lost them in war. But, if both consuls have an equal number of children, the one who has a wife or who is held to have one is preferred. But, if both have wives and have the same number of children, then the ancient system of precedence stands and the older of the consuls is the first to assume the fasces. If, on the other hand, both consuls do not have wives and have the same number of sons, or have wives but do not have children, there is no provision in that law regarding age. I am told, however, that it was usual for those who had legal priority to hand over the fasces for the first month of office to colleagues who were considerably older or of much higher pedigree or who were entering a second consulship.

(b) *Flavian Municipal Law (lex municipalis Malacitana)* 56

This is on preference in elections being given on the basis of marriage and childbirth.

If in any curia two or more candidates shall have secured the same number of votes, the person holding the election shall show preference to, and announce first, a married man or one who counts as married over an unmarried man without children and who does not count as married, a man with children over a man without children, and a man with more children over a man with fewer children, provided that two children lost after the giving of the name or one male child over puberty lost or one female child over puberty lost are to count as one surviving child.

(c) Martial, 11.53

May the gods look favourably on her, a young but fertile wife, for having given children to her faithful husband and because she hopes for sons, and daughters-in-law. So I pray the gods above will grant that she enjoy one husband alone – and three sons.

(d) Martial, 2.91

Caesar, sure saviour of the world, glory of the lands, through whose survival we know the great gods exist, if my poems, so often collected in hasty little volumes, have detained your eyes, permit to be seen what fortune forbids to occur, that I may be believed to be the father of three children. If I have caused displeasure, let this be my consolation; if I have given pleasure, let this be my reward.

(e) Martial, 2.92

The *ius trium natorum*, at my request, he alone who had the power granted, a reward for my poetry. Farewell, wife. The gift of the *dominus* must not be wasted.

(f) Pliny, *Letters* 10.2.1 (AD 98, to Trajan)

I am not able to express in words, *dominus*, how much joy you have given me in judging me worthy of the *ius trium liberorum*. For, although you have granted it at the prayers of Iulius Servianus, an excellent man and most devoted to you, nevertheless from the wording of your rescript I understand that you were the more willing to do this for him because his request was on my behalf. So I feel like I have achieved the answer to all my prayers, since you, at the beginning of your most auspicious reign, have shown that you consider me worthy of your personal indulgence. Still more now do I desire children, whom I wanted even during that most depressed time,[1] as you can see from my two marriages. But the gods knew better, reserving all these good things wholly for your generosity. I would much rather become a father now when I know I shall be safe and happy.

---

1   Reign of Domitian: cf. *Letters* 4.15.3, on Asinius Rufus doing his duty by having children when, according to Pliny, most people find childlessness such an advantage they do not want even one child.

(g) Pliny, *Letters* 10.94–5

Gaius Pliny to the emperor Trajan.

Suetonius Tranquillus is a most upright, noble, and learned man. I have long admired his character and his scholarship. I have formed a close association with him, and the more of late I have got to know him better, the more fond of him I feel. There are two reasons why he needs the *ius trium liberorum*: it would be just reward for the high repute he enjoys with his friends, and his marriage has not been as blessed as it might be, and he can only obtain from your generosity, via us, his friends, that which the cruelty of fortune has denied to him. I know, *dominus*, what a great favour I am seeking, but I seek from you who have always shown indulgence in granting all my requests. You may gather how much this means to me by the fact that I should not ask such a thing while abroad if my desire for it was only half-hearted.

Trajan to Pliny.

You are at least well aware, my dearest Pliny, how sparingly I grant these sorts of benefits, since even in the senate I make a habit of asserting that I have not exceeded the number that I announced before that most august body would suffice for me. Nevertheless I endorse your request and I have ordered that it be recorded in my *commentarii* that I have granted the *ius trium liberorum* to Suetonius Tranquillus on my usual conditions.

(h) Paul, *Sententiae* 4.9

(1) It is sufficient for mothers – and this includes not only those who are freeborn, but also freedwomen who are Roman citizens – in order to be entitled to the *ius liberorum*, to have given birth three or four times provided that they were born alive and after full term.

(2) A woman who has three children at a birth is not entitled to the *ius liberorum*, for she did not give birth three times; rather she is considered to have had only one birth, unless she should happen to have had them at intervals.

(3) If a woman brings forth a monster or a prodigy [*monstruosum aliquid aut prodigiosum*], this is of no avail, for creatures having forms contrary to that of the human race are not children.

(9) A mother is entitled to the *ius liberorum* who either has, or has had, three sons, even though she may not have them, nor has had them. She has them when they survive, she has had them after she has lost them; and she neither has, or has had them, when, through the kindness of the emperor, she obtains the *ius liberorum*.

(i) *Codex Iustinianus* 8.58.1 = *Codex Theodosianus* 8.17.3

In AD 410, the need to apply to the emperor for the *ius liberorum* was removed.

From now on no one is to seek from us the *ius liberorum*; by this law we grant this right to everyone.

3.58 Adoption, Roman style

In Roman law adoption could only take place between two Roman citizens. There were two quite different procedures. *Adrogatio* was by the authority of the people, for a person already *sui iuris*, who thus entered another *familia* along with everyone in his power; and *adoptatio* by a magistrate, when the adoptee was still in *potestas* and was given by his *paterfamilias* to another. See Gardner (1998: ch. 2).

(a) Justinian, *Institutes* 1.11.4

It is not permitted that a younger person adopt [*adoptare*] an older person; for *adoptio* imitates nature and it would be monstrous that a son be older than his father. Therefore, he who makes another his son by adoption or adrogation should be of full puberty [i.e. at least 18 years of age].

(b) Aulus Gellius, *Attic Nights* 5.19

When outsiders [*extranei*] are taken into another *familia* and into the place of children, it either happens through the praetor or through the people. If it is done through the praetor it is called *adoptatio*, through the people, *adrogatio*. Now individuals are adopted by *adoptatio* when by a thrice-repeated sale they are surrendered in court by the parent in whose *potestas* they are, and they are claimed by the one who adopts them in the presence of the magistrate before whom this legal action takes place. On the other hand, individuals are adopted by *adrogatio* when they are *sui iuris* and they hand themselves over to the *potestas* of another and are themselves the instigators of this act. But adrogations are not undertaken offhandedly or without investigation. For the so-called *comitia curiata* are summoned by the authority of the pontifices and consideration is given as to whether the age of the one who wishes to adrogate is not suited rather to begetting his own children,[1] and that the property of the one who is to be adrogated is not being sought under false pretences. And an oath is sworn during the process of adrogation, an oath that is said to have been composed by Quintus Mucius [Q. Mucius Scaevola, consul 95 BC, pontifex maximus 89–82, one of the republic's greatest lawyers] as pontifex maximus. No one can be adrogated who has not yet reached the age of puberty [*vesticeps*]. It is called 'adrogation' because this type of transfer to another *familia* is done through a rogation or request to the people. The words of this request are as follows: 'May you wish and may you order that Lucius Valerius be the son of Lucius Titius as justly and lawfully as if he had been born from that father and the mother of his *familia*, and that Titius have the power of life and death over Valerius just as a father has it over his son. This, just as I have said, I so request of you, fellow Romans.' Neither a ward [*pupillus*] nor a woman who is not in the *potestas* of a parent can be adrogated, since women have no role in the *comitia* and it is not right for tutors to have so much authority and power over wards as to subject to another's control a free individual who has been entrusted to their own protection. Freedmen, however, can be legally adopted by free people, as Masurius Sabinus [a jurist of the time of Tiberius whom Gellius is fond of quoting; cf. Gaius 1.102, however, on adrogation of *pupilli*] has written. But he also says that it is not permitted and thinks that it never should be permitted that people of freed rank should by adoptions usurp the rights of free people. 'Furthermore,' he says, 'if the very antiquity of that law is to be preserved, even a slave can be given into adoption through the praetor.' And he states that several ancient legal authorities have written that this can be done. I have noticed in a speech of Publius Scipio, 'On Morals', which he delivered as censor to the people, that among the things he criticised on the grounds that they occurred contrary to the practices of our ancestors, he also found fault with the following, that an adopted son benefitted the adoptive father in terms of the rewards for fathers. The words from this speech are as follows: 'A father votes in one tribe, a son in another, an adopted son is as of much benefit as if one had one born to oneself; those absent are ordered to be counted in the census, so it is not necessary for anyone to come to the census.'

1 *Digest* 1.7.15.2 (Ulpian) states that the adrogator should normally be at least 60 years of age, since before that age 'he should rather be attending to begetting his own children,' unless illness prevents this. Cf. also Cicero, *On His Home*, 13.34–14.38, with reference to Clodius.

(c) Pliny, *Letters* 8.18

See **3.52d**.

(d) Valerius Maximus, *Memorable Doings and Sayings* 5.10.2

This is from the chapter entitled 'On Parents who have Borne the Death of Children with a Brave Heart'. L. Aemilius Paulus Macedonicus made an unlucky gamble with his four sons: he gave the older two in adoption, making it easier for the other two to advance from his own resources: but the younger two died early. Paulus is celebrating his victory against Perses, the last king of Macedonia, defeated by Paulus at Pydna in 168 BC.

Aemilius Paulus, a very famous model of a father who was one minute most happy, the next minute most wretched. He had four sons of singular beauty and outstanding ability. Two of these, by the law of adoption, passed into the Cornelian and Fabian family groupings, and thus Aemilius by his own act denied himself of them. Fortune snatched the other two from him. One of them preceded his father's triumph by his own funeral three days before. The other breathed his last two days after being seen in the triumphal chariot. Thus he who had so many children that he could afford to give them away found himself suddenly abandoned and childless. With what strength of mind he endured this fate he made very clear to all in the speech that he delivered before the people on his achievements, by adding the following final sentences: 'In this so great growth of our good fortune, Roman citizens, I was concerned that Fortune may have something bad in store for us, so I prayed to Jupiter Best and Greatest, to Queen Juno, and to Minerva, that, if any adversity threatened the Roman people, it might all be diverted onto my *domus*. And so all is well. By assenting to my prayers they make sure that you should grieve for my fate rather than I should groan over yours.'

(e) *Codex Iustinianus* 8.47(48).5

Women could not adopt, since they could not have *potestas* over any other free person, not even over their own children (Gaius 1.104). But even here there could be an exception, as this rescript of Diocletian to Syra, dated to December AD 291, shows. Presumably the son is born from Syra's husband's previous marriage; she is now a widow (cf. Justinian, *Institutes* 1.11.10: 'Women are not able to adopt because they do not have even natural children in their *potestas*, but by the indulgence of the *princeps* they are able to adopt as a solace for lost children.').

Now it is definite that a person cannot be adrogated by a woman who does not have even her own children in her *potestas*. But, since as a consolation for your lost children you desire to have your stepson [*privignus*] in place of legitimate offspring, we agree to your request according to the terms that we have set out in our *adnotatio*, and we permit you to have him just as if he were born from you, as an honorary [*ad fidem*] natural and legitimate son.

3.59 The ultimate power of the *paterfamilias*

Writing in the time of Augustus, Dionysius, a Greek teacher at Rome, is describing the early origin of the Roman father's power, supposedly deriving from the time of Romulus (laws that, according to Dionysius, are superior to the laws of the Greeks, particularly in the severity of the punishments).

Dionysius of Halicarnassus, 2.26.4

The Roman lawgiver gave practically total power over the son to the father, and throughout the former's whole life, if he chose to imprison him, flog him, put him in chains for forced labour, even kill him; and this applied even if the son was already engaged in public life, even if he was counted among the highest offices and was celebrated for his zeal for the state . . . I forbear to state how many good men, driven on by their valour and zeal to perform some noble deed that their fathers had not ordered have been killed by their fathers – such a story is told of Manlius Torquatus, among many others.[1]

---

1 Torquatus was executed for killing a Latin in single combat, against the express orders of his father, the consul of 340 BC (but, for the degree of reality or otherwise underlying these traditional powers, see now the important article by Brent D. Shaw, 'Raising and Killing Children: Two Roman Myths' (2001). On the question of whether one must obey one's parents under all circumstances, see Musonius Rufus 16.

3.60 *Patria potestas*

Digest 50.16.195.2, Ulpian

Someone is called the *paterfamilias* if he holds power [*dominium*] in the *domus*, and it is quite right to refer to him by this title even if he does not have a son, for we do not mean only his person but also his legal status ... And when the *paterfamilias* dies, all those individuals who were under his power begin to have separate households [*familiae*] of their own; for as individuals they each enter into the category of *paterfamilias* [in Roman terms, such individuals usually became legally independent, *sui iuris*]. The same thing also happens in the case of someone who is emancipated,[1] for when this individual becomes *sui iuris* he [or she] has his own *familia*.

1 I.e. formally released from *potestas* while the *paterfamilias* is still alive, through a fictitious sale, and thereby made *sui iuris*.

3.61 The reality of being *paterfamilias*

The traditional and theoretical powers of the *paterfamilias*, it is now clear, were not as extreme or as austere as dry legal texts might suggest. All the same, it may sometimes have been the case that offspring resented the influence and authority a father in particular might exert over them even in the younger generation's adult years.

Pliny the Younger is telling an old friend, Voconius Romanus, about a wonderful speech that Pliny has enclosed and that he recently delivered in a dramatic case of *querela inofficiosi testamenti*, i.e. the contestation of an unduteous will, which typically related to situations where children had been disinherited by a father, contrary to usual, generalised notions of *pietas*. Clearly the case was of wide interest, if we can believe Pliny. See most recently, with references, Dixon (1997).

Pliny, *Letters* 6.33

This speech was delivered on behalf of Attia Viriola, and it was remarkable through the high standing of the individual, the rarity of the type of case, and the great size of the court. For this woman, of equestrian standing and married to a man of praetorian rank, had been disinherited by her octogenarian father within eleven days of his falling head over heels in love and bringing home a stepmother for her. She was now suing for her patrimony in a 'fourfold court'. One hundred and eighty judges were sitting (this is how many they total when all four panels are joined together); on both sides there were huge teams of legal assistants and packed seats of supporters as well as a close-packed ring of spectators, several rows deep, lining the very spacious courtroom. The bench was also crowded, and from the upper gallery of the Basilica men and women were hanging over the edge, keen to hear (not an easy thing) and to see (which was easy). Great was the suspense among fathers, daughters, even stepmothers . . .

3.62 Definition of a *materfamilias*

Digest 50.16.46.1, Ulpian

We ought to regard as the *materfamilias* she who has not lived dishonourably [*non inhoneste*]. For *mores* distinguish and separate a *materfamilias* from other women. It makes no difference whether she is married or a widow, freeborn or freed; for neither marriage nor birth makes a *materfamilias*, but good morals.

3.63 The ideal mother

Gnaeus Iulius Agricola, AD 40–93, was Tacitus' father-in-law, and, at one stage, governor of Britain; cf. *Agricola* 6 on Tacitus' wife.

Tacitus, *Agricola* 4.2–4

The mother of Agricola was Iulia Procilla, a woman of exceptional moral integrity. He spent his boyhood and adolescence close by her side being gently trained in every aspect of honourable achievement. He was sheltered from the enticements of immorality not only by his virtuous and upright nature, but also because, as a young boy, he had as his residence and as a model for behaviour Massilia [Marseilles], a town that provided a mixture and blend of Greek refinement and provincial frugality. I remember that he himself said that he had, in his early youth, been more absorbed with philosophy than was proper for a Roman and a senator until his mother's good sense brought under control his ardent and passionate nature.

3.64 Raising children the old-fashioned way

Here is the conservative Vipstanus Messalla on why eloquence has declined.

Tacitus, *Dialogue on Oratory* 28.2–29.2

Everyone knows that eloquence and the other arts have fallen from their former high renown not through a lack of people but through the laziness of the young[1] and the neglect of parents and the ignorance of instructors and the decay of ancient morals. Such evils first were born in the city of Rome, subsequently spread throughout Italy, and now are seeping into the provinces . . . I shall speak about Rome and those native, home-grown vices that take hold of us the minute we are born and build up through every single stage of life. But first I shall say a few words about the strictness and discipline that our ancestors employed in the raising and training of children. In former times every man's son, born to a properly married couple, was raised not in the tiny chamber of some hired nurse but in the lap and embrace of his mother, whose special praise it was to watch over the *domus* and devote herself to the children. Moreover, an older female relative used to be chosen, a woman of tried and tested character, to look over all the offspring in the same *familia*. In her presence it was unheard of for any base word to be said or for any wrong deed to be seen to be done. With a certain religiosity and modesty she regulated not only the boys' studies and occupations but also their recreations and games. Thus, we are told, Cornelia, mother of the Gracchi, thus Aurelia, mother of Caesar, thus Atia, mother of Augustus, directed their sons' upbringing and reared their children as leaders. The object of such strict discipline was so that their nature, pure and natural, not warped by any depraved tendencies, might immediately and with its whole heart seize on virtuous pursuits, and, whether its bias was towards the military art or legal science or the pursuit of eloquence, it might aim for this alone and imbibe it to its fullest.

29.   But nowadays the newborn infant is handed over to some little Greek slave girl, to whom is attached one or other of all the other slaves – and as a rule the very worst of them all, quite useless for any serious service. Their stories and fantasies from the very first fill the children's green and unformed minds. And not a single person in the whole *domus* cares less what he says or does in the presence of his baby master. Indeed, even the parents themselves make no effort to train their little ones in honesty and modesty, but rather in wantonness and raillery. Thus gradually they lose all sense of shame and grow to feel contempt for themselves and for others.

1   Cf. Columella 12.preface10 on elite women's lazy vices and the contrast between then and now.

3.65 Raising children the natural way

Tacitus, *Germania* 20

In every *domus* they grow up, naked and filthy, into these limbs, into these bodies that we hold in awe. The mother breastfeeds her own children: they are not handed over to servant women and nurses.

3.66 Should every child that is born be raised?

Musonius Rufus, 15

Haven't all the lawmakers, who have this very task of examining and scrutinising what is good for the city and what is bad, what benefits and what damages the community, judged that filling up the houses with citizens is most advantageous to cities and emptying them out is the most harmful? And didn't they consider that not having children or having small families [*oligopaidia*] among the citizens was disadvantageous, but having children and indeed many was advantageous? They prohibited women from having abortions and imposed a penalty on those who disobeyed; then they dissuaded them from preferring childlessness and preventing conception; and they set rewards for large families [*polypaidia*] for husband and wife and imposed penalties for not having children. So wouldn't we be doing wrong and acting against the law if we did what was contrary to the wishes of the lawmakers, godlike men beloved by the gods, men whom we believe it is fine and advantageous to follow? We would be doing the opposite if we kept ourselves from having large families . . . That raising many children is a fine and advantageous thing can be ascertained if you consider that the man who has many children is held in esteem in the city for offering a lesson to his neighbours, since he has more influence than all his peers who do not have an equivalent abundance of children . . . This seems to me most shocking: it is not those who have the excuse of poverty, but those who have plenty of resources, some of them quite wealthy, who nevertheless dare not to raise their later children, so that the earlier born may have more wealth, thus ensuring their children's prosperity in an unholy manner. But they do away with their children's brothers so that the children may have a greater share of their parents' property, failing to notice that having many brothers is a far better thing than having plenty of wealth. For wealth stirs up scheming among one's neighbours, while brothers can protect you from schemers.

3.67 *Pietas*

(a) Valerius Maximus, *Memorable Doings and Sayings* 5.4.7

The prize of dear *pietas* is cheapened by no bitterness of fortune nor meanness of station [*sordibus*] . . .

A praetor had handed over a woman of free birth found guilty at his tribunal of a capital crime to the triumvir to be executed in prison. When she was received there, the head warder had pity on her and did not strangle her immediately. He even allowed her daughter to visit her, but only after she had been thoroughly searched to make sure she wasn't bringing in any food; for the warder expected that the prisoner would die of starvation.

But, after a number of days had passed, he asked himself what could be sustaining her so long. Observing the daughter more closely, he noticed her putting out her breast and relieving her mother's hunger with the succour of her own milk.

This novel and remarkable spectacle was reported by him to the triumvir, by the triumvir to the praetor, and by the praetor to the board of judges. As a result, the woman's sentence was remitted.

Whither does *Pietas* not penetrate, what does she not devise? In prison she found a new way to save a mother. For what is so extraordinary, so unheard of, as for a mother to be nourished by her daughter's breasts? This might be thought to be against Nature, if to love parents were not Nature's first law.

(b) Pliny the Elder, *Natural History* 7.121

Of *pietas* there have, it is true, been unlimited instances all over the world, but one at Rome with which all of the rest could not compare. A plebeian woman of low position, and therefore unknown, had just given birth and had permission to visit her mother who had been shut up in prison as a punishment, and was always searched in advance by the doorkeeper to prevent her carrying in any food; she was caught feeding her mother at her own breasts. In consequence of this marvel the daughter's *pietas* was rewarded by the mother's release and both were awarded maintenance for life; and the place where it occurred was consecrated to the goddess concerned, a temple dedicated to *Pietas* being built on the site of the prison, where the Theatre of Marcellus now stands, in the consulship of Gaius [Titus] Quinctius and Manius Acilius.[1]

1 150 BC; the temple was in fact dedicated in 181 BC, by a different Acilius: Livy 40.34; Valerius
   Maximus, *Memorable Doings and Sayings* 2.5.1.

(c) *Codex Iustinianus* 5.25.2 (AD 161)

This is from the chapter 'On Support for Children and Parents'.

Marcus Aurelius and Lucius Verus to Celer.
The competent magistrate will order that you be maintained by your son, if he has the means to be able to provide support for you.

3.68 Beyond the nuclear model?

See further Bradley (1991).

(a) Plutarch, *Crassus* 1.1

Marcus Licinius Crassus, consul in 70 and 55 BC, was best known as a member of the so-called first triumvirate, and for his enormous wealth.

Marcus Crassus was the son of an ex-censor who had enjoyed a triumph, and yet he was raised in a small home along with two brothers. His brothers married while the parents were still alive, and they all shared the same table, which is clearly one of the main reasons why Crassus was sensible and moderate in his lifestyle. When one of his brothers died, Crassus married the widow and had children by her.

(b) Plutarch, *Aemilius Paulus* 5.4–5

One of Aemilius' daughters became the wife of Aelius Tubero, a very fine man who, more than any other Roman, combined the greatest dignity with poverty. For there were sixteen people living together, all Aelii. All they had was a very small house, and a small farm sufficed for them all, where they maintained a single hearth for so many wives and children . . . But nowadays brothers and other kin relatives never stop quarrelling, unless their joint inheritances are separated out by slopes and rivers and walls and they have wide open spaces to keep them apart from one another.

(c) *Digest* 7.8.5–6, Paul, Ulpian

Paul: Indeed a father-in-law may be living with his daughter-in-law, at least, if her husband is there too.

Ulpian: A woman may be able to live not only with her husband but also with her children and freedmen, as well as her parents.

3.69 The family in Egyptian census returns of the Roman period

See Bagnall and Frier (1994) and Rowlandson (1998).

(a) *Michigan Papyri* 176 (AD 91)

To Horos, son of Haruotes, registration officer of Bacchias, and Apunchis, son of Onnophris, and the other elders [*presbuteroi*]. From Peteuris, son of Horos, a resident of the village of Bacchias. There belongs to me in the village a fourth part of a house in which I dwell, and I register both myself and those of my household for the census of the past ninth year of imperator Caesar Domitian Augustus Germanicus. I am Peteuris, son of Horos, the son of Horos, my mother being Herieus, the daughter of Menches, a cultivator of state land, 30 years old without distinguishing marks, and [I register]: my wife Tapeine, the daughter of Apkois, 25 years old, and my full brothers: Horos, 20 years old, and Horion, another, 7 years old. And there belongs to my brother the . . . of a fourth part of the aforesaid house and courtyard in which we live. I, Peteuris, the aforesaid, have submitted the declaration, and I swear by imperator Caesar Domitian Augustus

Germanicus that the foregoing statements are true and that I have falsified nothing. Aphrodisios, secretary of the village, wrote for him as he is illiterate. The tenth year of imperator Caesar Domitian Augustus Germanicus. Pachon 15 [10 May 91].

(b) *Michigan Papyri* 178 (AD 119)

To Lucretius Cerialis, strategos [administrative governor], and Pasion, royal secretary of the division of Herakleides of the Arsinoite nome, and Areios, village secretary, and Apollonios and Patron, registration officers [*laographoi*] of the village of Bacchias. From Peteuris, the son of Horos, the son of Horos, his mother being Herieus, daughter of Menches, a resident of the aforesaid village. There belongs to me and to my brothers in the village a fourth part of a house and courtyard in which we dwell, and I register both myself and those of my household for the house-by-house census of the past seventh year of imperator Caesar Nerva Trajan Augustus Germanicus Dacicus. I am Peteuris, the aforesaid, a cultivator of state land, 44 years old, without distinguishing marks, and [I register]: my brother Horos, 34 years old, with no distinguishing marks, and Horion, another brother, 21 years old, with no distinguishing marks, and his [Horion's] wife Thenatumis, daughter of Chariton, her mother being Tapetosiris, 25 years old, and in the same village a share of building sites.

[2nd hand] We, Apollonios, registration officer of the village of Bacchias, and Patron, registration officer, have entered [the declaration] through Petesouchos, secretary. The eighth year of imperator Caesar Nerva Trajan Augustus Germanicus Dacicus. Choiak 5 [1 December 104].

[3rd hand] I, Areios, village secretary for the eighth year, have signed it.

(c) *Michigan Papyri* 178 (AD 119)

To Eudemos, strategos, and Hermaios, also called Druton, royal secretary of the division of Herakleides of the Arsinoite nome, and Ptolemaios, village secretary, and Aunes, son of Aunes, and Orsenouphis, son of Orsenouphis, registration officers of the village of Bacchias of the same division. From Horos, the son of Horos, the son of Horos, his mother being Herieus, daughter of menches, of the aforesaid village of Bacchias. There belongs to me and my brother Horion in the village a fourth part of a house and courtyard in which we dwell, and I register both myself and those of my household for the house-by-house census of the past second year of Hadrian Caesar our lord. I am Horos, the aforesaid, a cultivator of state land, 48 years old, with a scar on my left eyebrow, and [I register]: my wife Tapekusis, daughter of Horos, 45 years old, and our own child, Horos, a son, ... years old, with no distinguishing marks, and Horion, another son, 1 [?]

year old, with no distinguishing marks, and my aforesaid brother Horion, 35 years old, with a scar in the middle of his forehead, and his wife Thenatumis, daughter of Chariton, 39 [?] years old, with no distinguishing marks, to whom belongs a half share of a house and courtyard in which we dwell, and their own son Horos, 1 year old, with no distinguishing marks. I, Heras, nomographos of Bacchias, wrote it.

[2nd hand] I, Orsenouphis, registration officer, have recorded it through Melanas, secretary.

[3rd hand] I, Aunes, son of Aunes, registration officer, have recorded it through Epimachos, secretary. The third year of Hadrian our lord. Pachon 10 [May 5 119].

[4th hand] I, the village secretary, have recorded it. Pachon 10.

From the Roman Egyptian census returns, we also have nine examples of upwardly extended families where a husband's or, less frequently, wife's mother or father resides with the younger family. They range in age from 50 to 75 years (in two of these cases the age is lost); on three occasions it is the older person who files the return. (See Bagnall and Frier (1994: 62) and cf. 146–7 on three-, and in one case, four-generation households.)

Here are some further examples:

1. *Berliner Leihgabe griechscher Papyri*. III.52B, AD 147: there are at least five co-resident siblings, all declared as *apatores* (i.e. illegitimate), ranging in age from 30 to 14, two married to each other, and the oldest married to an outsider.

2. *Berliner Leihgabe griechscher Papyri* I.17, AD 161: three brothers and two sisters live in a house that they rent off two wards of one of the brothers; all five siblings are (or have been) married, two of them to each other (but now divorced), and two of the brothers to two sisters. All have children; a divorced or widowed sister lives in the house with her child. The ex-wife of one of the brothers also lives there, with a child. Finally there are two slaves (mother and son) of that child.

3. Compare *Papyri Rylands* II.111, AD 161, for a similarly complex situation, where a man's former wife (his sister) and their children co-reside with the man's new wife and their children; in total twenty-seven individuals are in the household.

4. *Papyri Osloenses* III.99, AD 161: a married couple, the husband 72, the wife 57, have two children, aged 40 and 8 years; if (and it is a big 'if') the ages as

stated are accurate, the woman was married by the age of 16, the marriage has lasted at least forty years, and the second child was born to the woman when she was 49 years old. It is also striking that apparently the 40-year-old daughter is living in her parents' home and is not currently married.

5. *Papyri Bruxellenses* 1.10, AD 174: four brothers live together in a *frérèche* with their wives (one of whom is also a sister) and children. Two of the brothers also have children in the house from previous marriages. There are seventeen family members in all.

6. *Berliner griechischer Urkunde* I.115 i, AD 189: a 50-year-old male lives with his wife (who is also his sister and who is 54); they have eight children, five boys and three girls, the youngest 7, the oldest 29. The 29-year-old son has married his sister, and their two 1-year-old sons live in the house; another brother, aged 26 years, has married, this time outside the family, and also has two sons, the older 13 years old (which means this brother became a father at the age of 13). In this household twenty-seven people reside (at least five of them named Heron!), including some lodgers who are also related by blood.

7. *Tebtunis Papyri* II.322, AD 189: a 61-year-old man lives with what appears to be his third wife, who is 41. They have a 5-year-old daughter. Also in the house are children from the man's two earlier marriages, and two of these half-siblings have actually married each other. Added to that are two children from the wife's previous marriage.

8. *Berliner griechischer Urkunde* II.577, AD 203: a 74-year-old woman lives with her three children, two sons aged 56 and 46, and a 56-year-old daughter; the older son has a 26-year-old son, who in turn has a 6-year-old daughter.

3.70 Growing up

Tutela was the legal guardianship of a minor (i.e. males under the age of 14 years, and females of any age, who were not under the 'protection' of a father – or, in the case of a woman married *cum manu*, husband).

Cura was a lesser form of guardianship, available for males from the age of 14 to the age of 25 years, and also for spendthrifts (*prodigi*) and lunatics (*furiosi*).

(a) Gaius, *Institutes* 1.142–5

Now let us pass to another division [of persons]. Of these persons who are neither in *potestas* nor in *manus* nor in *mancipium*, some are in *tutela* or in *curatio*, others are held under neither institution ... Now it is permitted to parents to give to children whom they have in their power tutors by will, to males below the age of puberty, to females of whatever age, even if they are married. For men of old decided that women, even if they were of full age, should be in *tutela* on account of their lightness of mind [*animi levitas*]. Therefore, if a man has given a tutor to his son and daughter by will, and both reach the age of puberty, the son ceases to have a tutor, but the daughter nonetheless remains in *tutela*. For it is only by the *lex Iulia et Papia Poppaea*, by the rights attached to having children, that women are freed from *tutela*.

(b) *Epitome of Ulpian* 11.1 (*Fontes Iuris Romani Anteiustiniani*[2], 2.273)

Tutors are appointed both for males and females, but for males only when they are below the age of puberty on account of their infirmity of age, but for females both before and after the age of puberty, both on account of their infirmity of gender and on account of their ignorance in business and legal matters.

3.71 The tutorship of women

(a) *Epitome of Ulpian* 11.27 (*Fontes Iuris Romani Anteiustiniani*[2], 2.276)

Women require the authority of a guardian in the following matters: if they are engaging in a legal case or a lawsuit, if they are undertaking a legal or financial obligation, if they are transacting civil business, or if they are permitting their freedwoman to cohabit with another's slave, or if they are alienating something that is owned under *mancipium* [i.e. under solemn or ritual ownership].

(b) Gaius, *Institutes* 1.171

The *tutela* of agnates [i.e. relatives in the male line who, from the time of the Twelve Tables, automatically become tutors if no other tutors are named in a will] over women has been removed by a *lex Claudia* [a law passed in the reign of the emperor Claudius].

(c) Gaius, *Institutes* 1.189–91

That persons below the age of puberty should be *in tutela* is common to the law of all states, for it is consonant with natural reason that a person who is not of full age should be governed by the *tutela* of another. And there can hardly be another state in which it is not permitted to parents to

132

give a tutor to their under-age children by will, although, as we have said above, only Roman citizens seem to have their children in *potestas*. But hardly any valid reason seems to exist in favour of women who are of full age being in *tutela*. That which is commonly believed, that they are typically deceived through lightness of mind and that it was only fair that they be governed by the authority of tutors, is more specious than true. For women who are of full age conduct their own business affairs for themselves, and in certain cases the tutor interposes his authority *gratia*, as a matter of form, for often he is forced by a praetor to give his authority even against his will. That is why no action on the *tutela* lies at the suit of a woman against her tutor. But when a tutor manages the business affairs of a male or female ward, after the ward reaches the age of puberty the tutor is held to account by the action relating to *tutela*.

REFERENCES AND FURTHER READING

Arjava, A. (1996) *Women and Law in Late Antiquity*, Oxford.

Bagnall, R.S. and Frier, B.W. (1994) *The Demography of Roman Egypt*, Cambridge.

Bannon, C.J. (1997) *The Brothers of Romulus: Fraternal* Pietas *in Roman Law, Literature, and Society*, Princeton, NJ.

Bauman, R.A. (1992) *Women and Politics in Ancient Rome*, London.

Blok, J. and Mason, P. (eds) (1987) *Sexual Asymmetry: Studies in Ancient Society*, Amsterdam.

Bradley, K.R. (1991) *Discovering the Roman Family: Studies in Roman Social History*, Oxford.

Brunt, P.A. (1971) *Italian Manpower, 225 BC–AD 14*, Oxford (reissued with postscript, 1987).

Burguière, A., Klapisch-Zuber, C., Martine Segalen, M., and Zonabends, F. (eds) (1996) *A History of the Family*, vol. 1, Cambridge.

Champlin, E. (1991) *Final Judgments*, Berkeley and Los Angeles, CA.

Clark, G. (1989) *Women in the Ancient World*, Oxford.

Clark, G. (1993) *Women in Late Antiquity: Pagan and Christian Life-styles*, Oxford.

Cooper, K. (1996) *The Virgin and the Bride: Idealized Womanhood in Late Antiquity*, Cambridge, MA.

Cornell, T. and Lomas, K. (eds) (1997) *Gender and Ethnicity in Ancient Italy*, London.

Crook, J.A. (1967) *Law and Life of Rome*, London.

D'Ambrosio, A. (2001) *Women and Beauty in Pompeii*, Los Angeles, CA.

Dixon, S. (1984) 'Family Finances: Terentia and Tullia', *Antichthon* 18: 78–101.

Dixon, S. (1988) *The Roman Mother*, London.

Dixon, S. (1992) *The Roman Family*, London.

Dixon, S. (1997) 'Conflict in the Roman Family', in Rawson, B. and Weaver, P. (eds) *The Roman Family in Italy: Status, Sentiment, Space*, Oxford, pp. 149–68.

Dixon, S. (ed.) (2001) *Childhood, Class and Kin in the Roman World*, London.

Evans, J.K. (1991) *War, Women and Children in Ancient Rome*, London.

Evans Grubbs, J. (1995) *Law and Family in Late Antiquity: The Emperor Constantine's Marriage Legislation*, Oxford.

Evans Grubbs, J. (2002) *Women and the Law in the Roman Empire: A Sourcebook on Marriage, Divorce and Widowhood*, London.

Eyben, E. (1972) 'Antiquity's View of Puberty', *Latomus* 31: 677–97.

Eyben, E. (1993) *Restless Youth in Ancient Rome*, London.

Flemming, R. (2000) *Medicine and the Making of Roman Women*, Oxford.

Foxhall, L. and Salmon, J.B. (eds) (1998a) *Thinking Men: Masculinity and its Self-representation in the Classical Tradition*, London.

Foxhall, L. and Salmon, J.B. (eds) (1998b) *When Men Were Men: Masculinity, Power, and Identity in Classical Antiquity*, London.

Gardner, J.F. (1986) *Women in Roman Law and Society*, London.

Gardner, J.F. (1993) *Being a Roman Citizen*, London.

Gardner, J.F. (1998) *Family and Familia in Roman Law and Life*, Oxford.

Gardner, J.F. and Wiedemann, T.E.J. (eds) (1991) *The Roman Household: A Sourcebook*, London.

Hallett, J.P. (1984) *Fathers and Daughters in Roman Society*, Princeton, NJ.

Harlow, M. and Laurence, R. (2002) *Growing Up and Growing Old in Ancient Rome: A Life Course Approach*, London.

Hawley, R. and Levick, B. (eds) (1995) *Women in Antiquity: New Assessments*, London.

Hopkins, K. (1983) *Death and Renewal*, Cambridge.

Huskinson, J. (1996) *Roman Children's Sarcophagi: Their Decoration and its Social Significance*, Oxford.

Joshel, S.R. and Murnaghan, S. (eds) (1998) *Women and Slaves in Greco-Roman Culture: Differential Equations*, London.

Kampen, N. (1981) *Image and Status: Roman Working Women in Ostia*, Berlin.

Kertzer, D. and Saller, R. (eds) (1991) *The Family in Italy from Antiquity to the Present*, New Haven, CT.

Konrad, C.F. (1994) '"Domitius Calvisius" in Plutarch', *Zeitschrift für Papyrologie und Epigraphik* 103: 139–46.

Krause, J.-U. (1992) *Die Familie und weitere anthropologische Grundlagen*, Stuttgart.

Lefkowitz, M.R. and Fant, M.B. (eds) (2005) *Women's Life in Greece and Rome*, 3rd edn, Baltimore, MD.

McGinn, T.A.J. (1998) *Prostitution, Sexuality, and the Law in Ancient Rome*, Oxford.

McGinn, T.A.J. (2004) *The Economy of Prostitution in the Roman World*, Ann Arbor, MI.

Mansbach, A.R. (1982) '*Captatio*: Myth and Reality', unpublished doctoral thesis, Princeton University, NJ.

Mitchell, J.F. (1966) 'The Torquati', *Historia* 15: 2–31.

Moxnes, H. (1997) *Constructing Early Christian Families: Family as Social Reality and Metaphor*, London.

Pomeroy, S.B. (ed.) (1991) *Women's History and Ancient History*, Chapel Hill, NC.

Porter, J.I. (ed.) (1999) *Constructions of the Classical Body*, Ann Arbor, MI.

Rawson, B. (1966) 'Family Life among the Lower Classes at Rome in the First Two Centuries of the Empire', *Classical Philology* 61: 71–83.

Rawson, B. (1974) 'Roman Concubinage and Other De facto Marriages', *Transactions and Proceedings of the American Philological Association* 104: 279–305.

Rawson, B. (ed.) (1986) *The Family in Ancient Rome*, London.

Rawson, B. (ed.) (1991) *Marriage, Divorce and Children in Ancient Rome*, Oxford.

Rawson, B. (2003) *Children and Childhood in Roman Italy*, Oxford.

Rawson, B. and Weaver, P. (eds) (1997) *The Roman Family in Italy: Status, Sentiment, Space*, Oxford.

Rousselle, A. (1988) *Porneia: On Desire and the Body in Antiquity*, Oxford.

Rowlandson, J. (ed.) (1998) *Women and Society in Greek and Roman Egypt: A Sourcebook*, Cambridge.

Saller, R.P. (1984a) '*Familia, Domus*, and the Roman Conception of the Family', *Phoenix* 38: 336–55.

Saller, R.P. (1984b) 'Roman Dowry and the Devolution of Property in the Principate', *Classical Quarterly* 34: 195–205.

Saller, R.P. (1987a) 'Men's Age at Marriage and its Consequences in the Roman Family', *Classical Philology* 82: 20–35.

Saller, R.P. (1987b) 'Slavery and the Roman Family', in Finley, M.I. (ed.) *Classical Slavery*, London, pp. 65–87.

Saller, R.P. (1988) '*Pietas*, Obligation and Authority in the Roman Family', in Kneissl, P. and Losemann, V. (eds) *Alte Geschichte und Wissenschaftsgeschichte: Festschrift für Karl Christ zum 65. Geburtstag*, Darmstadt, pp. 393–410.

Saller, R.P. (1994) *Patriarchy, Property and Death in the Roman Family*, Cambridge.

Saller, R.P. (2001) 'The Family and Society', in Bodel, J.P. (ed.) *Epigraphic Evidence*, London and New York.

Saller, R.P. and Shaw, B.D. (1984) 'Tombstones and Roman Family Relations in the Principate: Civilians, Soldiers and Slaves', *Journal of Roman Studies* 74: 124–56.

Shaw, B.D. (1984) 'Latin Funerary Epigraphy and Family Life in the Later Roman Empire', *Historia* 33: 457–97.

Shaw, B.D. (1987) 'The Family in Late Antiquity: The Experience of Augustine', *Past and Present* 115: 3–51.

Shaw, B.D. (2001) 'Raising and Killing Children: Two Roman Myths', *Mnemosyne* 54: 31–77.

Skinner, M.B. (ed.) (1987) *Rescuing Creusa: New Methodological Approaches to Women in Antiquity*, Lubbock, TX.

Treggiari, S. (1991) *Roman Marriage*, Oxford.

Watson, P.A. (1995) *Ancient Stepmothers: Myth, Misogyny and Reality*, Leiden.

Weaver, P. (1990) 'Where Have All the Junian Latins Gone? Nomenclature and Status in the Early Empire', *Chiron* 20: 275–305.

Wiedemann, T. (1989) *Adults and Children in the Roman Empire*, London.

Woodman, A.J. and Martin, R. (1996) *The Annals of Tacitus, Book 3*, Cambridge.

Wyke, M. (ed.) (1998) *Gender and the Body in the Ancient Mediterranean*, Oxford.

4

EDUCATION

Some rudimentary education is likely to have often been instilled in the household by parents, nurses, and pedagogues (slave childminders who also had the duty of ensuring that children behaved, and who might look after their charges until they had come of age: **4.1**). But it is likely that most children would have learned the elements of reading, writing, and basic arithmetic under a schoolmaster (*magister*), probably meeting in a public place. The message was regularly reinforced by thrashings (**4.2**), sometimes with fennel canes or even with eel skins (**4.3**). Although educationalists might frown on such practices as uncivil (**4.4**), they appear to be the noisy accompaniment of most learning in the Roman world.

For more advanced education, students would need to seek out a teacher of grammar or a teacher of rhetoric (although these too would often need to reinforce elementary education). Smaller centres might not attract such teachers, so the students would often need to travel to larger cities and seek an appropriate instructor. Such youths away from parental control would be difficult to control (**4.5**). An alternative was to set up a public trust to employ educators in smaller towns – this might also appeal to the wealthy as a means of displaying civic euergetism (public service) or philanthropy (**4.6**). But the possible continuing expense to the community and dangers of towns vying to capture the students in their areas led to intervention by the Roman authorities to limit the number of publicly employed teachers (**4.7**).

Most educators seem to have led a hand-to-mouth existence, dependent on the regular payment of fees by their pupils' parents, which explains the high percentage of ex-slaves among the teachers who are recorded. But a few were spectacularly successful, such as Remmius Paleamon, who also showed his entrepreneurial skills in the rag trade and in viticulture (**4.8**). Greek educationalists could also prosper in the bilingual environment of Rome, as is illustrated by the career of the Alexandrian freedman, Epaphroditus, who flourished in the second half of the first century AD (**4.9**).

Those with advanced education in literature and public speaking gained considerable social cachet (cf. the sorry efforts of Calvisius Sabinus to imitate his betters: **5.2**) and were likely to find it much easier to gain entry to positions in the public service (cf. **8.7**). Others might express their resentment in *scholastikos* jokes (**4.10**) or attempt to gain an equivalent education on their own. Such a course risked ridicule from the litterati who would seek to defend the exclusivity of their club (**4.11**).

Hermeros, in Petronius' *Satyricon*, instead offers a defence of 'practical' education against the pretensions of his social superiors (**4.12**), regarding elementary training as sufficient for most purposes. Indeed, from Artemidorus (**4.13**), it is clear that many of his customers would not even possess a minimum level of literacy. Soldiers who could read and write well were welcome recruits (**4.14**), but it is unlikely that all, or even most, would have this skill. For important documents, it would be as well to use the services of a scribe, who would not only be able to write correctly, but would also know the format of documents such as wills (**4.15**). While it might appear useful to have literate slaves in positions of responsibility, there were also advantages in not giving too much power to the overseers by enabling them to control the finances and management of the estate by themselves (**4.16**).

The level of literacy in the Roman world continues to be a topic of considerable debate. Yet it is clear that many of the public monuments, dedications, and civic records were little more than 'urban wallpaper', rarely accessible to most of the Roman public and poorly archived by the Romans themselves (**4.17**). In these circumstances, the lack of regular use of such sources by Roman writers is hardly surprising and the occasional citation of inscriptions by historians and biographers all the more meritorious.

4.1 The pedagogue

Romans of upper-class families would often employ slaves as guardians of their children, not only protecting them from outside influences, but controlling their conduct. Martial here humorously depicts an imaginary freedman, whose desire to control his ward has long overstayed its welcome.

Although many children must have retained a soft spot for their nurses and pedagogues when they grew up, there could also be conflict between the free child and the social inferiors who disciplined them. This is clear in Martial and the similarly comic case of Claudius' pedagogue.

(a) Martial, *Epigrams* 11.39

You were the hand that rocked my cradle, Charidemus,
And the guardian and constant comrade of my boyhood.
But now my towel is black with the shaving from my beard
And my girlfriend complains that my kisses prickle.
But to you I haven't grown up: my supervisor is afraid of you,
And my accountant and the entire household are scared of you.

You don't allow us to play and be lovers.
You don't want to allow anything to me, but everything to you.
You criticise, oversee, complain, sigh away,
And your anger barely draws a line at caning.
If I put on Tyrian attire and perfume my locks,
You declare, 'Your father never did anything like that.'
And you keep a count on our glasses of wine with furrowed
    brow –
As if the wine jar had come from your own cellar.
Stop it! I can't abide a freedman playing at Cato.
My girlfriend will tell you that I am now a man.

(b) Suetonius, *Claudius* 2.2

For a long time – and even after he attained his majority – he was under guardianship and in the charge of a pedagogue. Claudius himself complained in a petition that the man was a barbarian, a part-time muleteer deliberately entrusted with him, to discipline him as savagely as possibly for any reason under the sun.

4.2 The noise of the schools at Rome

Martial's depiction of the noise of the schools at Rome may be typically exaggerated, but should serve to remind us that education was usually carried on outdoors in the ancient world. His offer to pay off the primary schoolmaster (the *ludi magister*) also recalls that fees were paid on a short-term basis only and were notoriously low.

Martial, *Epigrams* 9.68

What is your beef with us, ratbag schoolmaster,
A hateful sight to boys and girls alike?
The crested cocks have not yet broken the silence
But you are already thundering with savage roar and whips.
It's as loud as the echo of bronze struck on the anvil,
When a workman is preparing to place a lawyer on the middle of
    his horse.
There is less mad shouting in the great amphitheatre
When the winning Thracian is cheered on by his crowd of
    supporters.
We neighbours of yours plead for some, not a whole night's, sleep:
It's nothing to be woken, but to be always awake is a pain.
Send your pupils home. Would you be willing to take as much,
Loudmouth, as you get for shouting simply to shut up?

4.3 The use of eel skins for punishment

Corporal punishment was normally restricted to slaves and non-citizens as demeaning for Romans. However, as children were regular thrashed as part of their upbringing, citizen children (*praetextati*) too could be flogged rather than suffer the normal monetary penalty for misdemeanours.

Pliny the Elder, *Natural History* 9.77

Vedius Pollio, a Roman knight who was one of the friends of the divine Augustus, found in this animal [the moray] a way to display his cruelty, tossing condemned slaves into fish pools full of them. It wasn't because land animals were insufficient for this purpose, but because there was no other way that he could view the whole man being torn apart at once. They say that they are particularly driven into a fury by the taste of vinegar. Their skins are particularly fine, while those of common eels are thick, and so Verrius says that they were regularly used for flogging the children of citizens [*praetextati*] and, hence, it was unusual for them to be fined.

4.4 Advice to avoid the use of force in education

Although thrashing seems to have been a regular part of primary education (**4.2** and **4.3** above; there is a tablet in the Berlin Staatsmuseen with the line to be copied: 'Pay attention, boy, or else you will get it'), writers on educational principles were less happy at treatment that equated children with slaves and tended at best to decrease their sense of responsibility and might even lead to worse consequences.

(a) Pseudo-Plutarch, *On the Education of Children* 8f

In addition, I assert that one should lead children to decent behaviour by encouragement and advice, and certainly not by blows and humiliations. For this seems to be more appropriate to slaves than to the freeborn. As a result they act stupefied and shudder at their tasks, partly from the pain of the blows and partly because of the indignity of it all. But praise and criticism are more useful than any ill-treatment in the case of the free, the former encouraging them towards the honourable, the latter holding them back from what is disgraceful.

(b) Quintilian, *The Education of the Orator* 1.3.14–17

In fact I am in no way in favour of the thrashing of pupils, although that is the established practice and Chrysippus is in favour of it, first because it is ugly and only fitting for a slave and definitely an outrage (this would be

139

accepted if you changed the age of the sufferer). Then there is the fact that, if anyone is so base in spirit that he cannot be corrected by reproof, he will also be hardened to blows like the worst sort of slaves. Next, there will not even be any need for chastisement if a supervisor continuously keeps watch on his studies. Now by the inattention of their pedagogues things are usually turned around so that children are not forced to do what is right, but are punished because they haven't done it. Finally, when you have controlled the small child by thrashing, what will you do with the youth, to whom you cannot apply this terror and who must be taught more important things? In addition, many things that are unpleasant to mention and that will be a matter of shame in the future often happen to those who are beaten from pain and fear – the humiliation breaks and crushes their spirit and encourages a disgust with and willingness to flee life itself. If then there has been insufficient care in evaluating the character of their guardians and teachers, I will hesitate to mention the vile acts those unspeakable creatures use that power of beating to achieve and what opportunities this fear among the pitiful children also on numerous occasions offers to others. I will not dwell on this topic – that's more than enough for it to be understood. So it is sufficient to say this: no one ought to be allowed too much power over those of a tender age who are open to damage.

4.5 A schoolboy's letter to his father

The following letter shows the problems faced by a student who has gone off to a larger urban centre for higher education: uncertainty about obtaining an adequate teacher of whom his father will approve and a concern not to waste his money on fees. He appears to be in contact with a friend of his father's or relative (Philoxenus) who can offer some advice, and has the services of a slave, who could bring in some revenue to offset the cost of rent. He also has the occasional food parcel from home. Still, there are signs that all is not as it appears: suggestions of bad behaviour in the theatre, the slave running back to the father to report on his charge, and money being saved on fees and grooming that is presumably being used for other activities. See Rea (1993).

Oxyrhynchus Papyrus 18.2190 (c. AD 100)

To Theon, my lord and father, greetings.

You have rescued us from the greatest despondency by showing us that what happened in the theatre is of no concern to you, but I hoped by hurrying in sailing down that I would find fine opportunities – but what have I achieved for my enthusiasm? Even now I am looking for a teacher [*philologus*] and I have discovered that Chairon the teacher [*kathêgêtes*] and Didymus, son of Aristocles, with whom I have hoped that I might make progress, are no longer in the city, but only junk [*katharmata*] through whom most have taken the direct road to ruin. Previously I wrote to you, just as I wrote to Philoxenus and company, to deal with the matter, and I was introduced by them to someone who looked suitable. But you immediately rejected him, although he had begged for Theon's pardon, on the ground that you know him personally and he is totally lacking in ability. When I passed on your judgement to Philoxenus, he thought the same, saying that he pitied the city only for this lack of rhetors, but Didymus had sailed down [to Alexandria], apparently a friend of his who ran a school and would look after the others – and in particular he persuaded the pupils of Apollonius, son of Herodas, to transfer to him. They have up to now been seeking such a teacher of a higher education after the teacher they had enrolled with had died. But I, having prayed not to even look at Didymus from a distance if I found teachers worth mentioning, am depressed by this very fact: that he who used to teach in the country is setting himself up in competition with the others here.

So knowing this – that, apart from paying more fees in vain, I have gained nothing from my teacher but have achieved something by myself – please write back as soon as possible saying what you think. I have Didymus, as Philoxenos will also say, always available to me and offering whatever help he can. Furthermore, by auditing the public performances, including those of Poseidonius, if the gods are willing I will quickly make good progress.

But it is my despondency about those things that forces me to disregard my physical appearance, as it is not necessary for those who are not engaged in work to care about these things, especially when they don't have anyone to bring in some money. For once upon a time after a few days the helpful Heracles – woe of woes – would bring in some obols, but now along with his being put into restraints by Isidorus, he has run away and gone off, so it appears, to you. Be well aware that he isn't averse to plotting against you if he has the opportunity. For he is not ashamed especially to spread tales of events in the theatre and the city with alacrity and to babble out lies that no prosecutor would declare – and he has done this although he hasn't suffered anything such as he deserved, but had been let roam and was acting like a free person in all matters.

But all the same you can hire him out to a builder if you don't send him back, as I hear that a young man can make 2 drachmas a day. Or assign him some other task, where he can earn more money, so that the wages collected by him can be sent to us from time to time. For you know that Diogas is studying literature as well. In the time it takes you to send the young fellow, we will look for a bigger place in a private house: in order to be Dionysius' neighbours, we have been living in a very small place.

We received the basket that had all that you wrote about safe in it: all the jars with the half-cadus, in which we found not 18, but 22 choes. And

I sent a half cadus with a letter to all you wrote about. I got the six measures of whole lentils and a Coan jar full of vinegar, and 126 pieces of salted meat, plus those in the jar, and 30 pieces of cooked meat.

Farewell. [30 November]

4.6 Setting up a public trust fund to hire an educator

The difficulties in finding suitable teachers who would stay in an area and the problems associated with sending youths off to be educated (as seen in the previous passage), often led to the establishment of permanent positions in education in the major cities of the Roman world. While, at Rome, these were imperial benefactions, in other cities (and even minor towns such as Comum) these were supported as acts of philanthropy. As with his fund for support of the children in his hometown, Pliny the Younger is here seeking to ensure the appropriate expenditure of his funds in the future by involving the locals in his trust.

Pliny, *Letters* 4.13

Gaius Pliny to his friend Cornelius Tacitus, greetings.

I am glad that you have come to the city safely; besides, you have now come, if ever, at a time when I especially need you. I will still linger on for a few days at my Tusculan villa to complete the little piece that I have in my hands. For I'm afraid that, if I put off this effort when it is now approaching completion, I will have difficulty in turning back to it. In the meantime, in case my bustle should cool down, I am going to ask in this letter that is acting as a forewarning the advice that I will seek from you when I am present. But first let me tell you the reason for asking, then what it is I am after.

Recently, when I was in my hometown, the young son of a townsman of mine came to greet me. 'Are you studying?' I asked. He replied, 'Certainly.' 'Where?' 'Milan.' 'Why not here?' His father, who happened to be with him as he had brought the boy personally, replied, 'But we have no teachers here.' 'Why don't you have any? It's of the utmost importance to those of you who are fathers' – there happened to be a number of fathers listening – 'that your children are educated here for preference. Where can they stay more happily than in their hometown or be kept under better moral control than under the eyes of their parents and with less expense than at home? It is a tiny outlay to pool your resources and hire teachers and to add on by way of payment the money that you now spend on board, travel costs, and everything that is costly to buy (anyway, everything *is* costly to buy). So then, I myself who have no children am however ready to give to you, for the upkeep of my town, as if for a daughter or a parent, a third of what you decide to contribute. I would promise the lot, except that I'm afraid that my gift might in the future be ruined by self-interest, as I have seen occurring in many places where teachers are hired by the community. There is only one cure for this problem: for the right of hiring to be left to the parents alone and if they have added to their duty of making the right choice the need to contribute to the cost. Those who might be unconcerned about others' money will certainly take good care of their own and will make every effort that only a worthy applicant will receive my money, if he is also going to receive theirs. So talk it over and come to a joint decision, and take heart from my aim – I want the sum I need to contribute to be as large as possible. You cannot make a more noble contribution for your children or one more appreciated by your town. Those who are born here will be educated here and right from infancy will learn to love and enjoy their native soil. If only you were to bring here teachers so famous that the people in the neighbouring towns would seek their education here and, just as now your children head off for foreign places, so foreigners will soon head to this place!'

I thought that these things should be traced far back, almost to their source, so you would be more aware of how grateful I would be if you were to undertake what I'm imposing on you. I am making this imposition and requesting in accordance with the importance of the matter that from among the crowd of the educated, who flock to you from their admiration for your intellect, you should look for teachers whom we can approach – but with this proviso, that I will not offer my guarantee to anyone. I am keeping everything open to the parents: they will decide and they will choose; I am only claiming the supervision and expenses for myself. Hence, if you should find anyone who trusts in his talent, he should go there on this condition, that he is bringing nothing settled except for his faith in himself.

Goodbye.

4.7 Public appointments in the empire and their limitations

Competition for the services of teachers and doctors, which might increase the status of small towns such as Pliny the Younger's Comum, could also be financially ruinous. Hence the limitations set down in the second century by Antoninus Pius.

Digest 27.1.6.1–2, Modestinus, *Excuses* book 2

Teachers of grammar, teachers of rhetoric, doctors of the type called general practitioners have immunity from tutelage and curatorship, just as they are exempt from other impositions. The number of rhetors and doctors in each city who have exemption from liturgies amid their selection is limited by law, as is shown by the letter of Antoninus Pius written to the province of Asia, but applicable to the whole empire. This is the main injunction:

The smaller cities are able to have five doctors exempt, and three teachers of rhetoric and an equal number of teachers of grammar. The larger cities may have five physicians and four teachers of either type. The greatest cities may have ten doctors and five teachers of rhetoric and an equal number of teachers of grammar. Not even the largest of cities may offer immunity in excess of this number.

It is probable that the largest number applies to capitals of provinces, the middle number to cities that have legal assizes, and the third to the rest.

4.8 A non-conformist teacher

The career of the slave Palaemon ('Wrestler'), who was probably born at the end of the first century BC and lived under all the Julio-Claudian emperors, is portrayed as not only revealing an intelligent slave's inventiveness (combining a career in clothing manufacture with one in education), but also a 'freedman's temperament'. His arrogance is matched only by his extravagance; his entrepreneurial skills (including success in the risky business of viticulture) go hand in hand with a vulgar lewdness. As with other successful freedmen (cf. **1.41**, **3.27**), his very success is likely to have inspired stereotyping anecdotes. Jokes about teachers were also a favourite theme in the ancient world (see **4.10**).

Palaemon is viewed by Suetonius as a teacher of literature and grammar, a *grammaticus*, rather than a teacher of oratorical skills (*rhetor*), especially as such education would be seen as the preserve of the freeborn. In reality, the two professions tended to overlap and it is clear that Palaemon's ability encouraged the enrolment of children of sufficiently high status in his school to earn the disapproval of two emperors.

As is the regular Roman fashion, the name of his mistress is not given, but it is likely that she was the daughter of a Quintus Remmius – hence Palaemon's freed name.

Suetonius, *On Teachers of Grammar and Rhetoric* 23

Quintus Remmius Palaemon, from Vicetia, was a houseborn slave of a woman. He first (so it is said) learnt to be a weaver, then, while accompanying his mistress's son to school, learnt to read and write. Later, when he had been freed, he taught at Rome and achieved the top rank among teachers [*grammatici*], although he was held in ill repute for every type of vice and Tiberius and later Claudius had publicly stated that there was no one less to be entrusted with the education of boys or young men. But he would win men over by both his memory of details and his fluent speaking style and even used to produce poetry on the spot. In fact he wrote in all sorts of difficult metres. Such was his arrogance that he called Marcus Varro

144

'the pig', boasted that literary appreciation was born and would die with him, and declared that his name didn't occur in the Eclogues by accident, but that Vergil was predicting that one day a Palaemon would be the judge of all poets and poetry. He even used to boast that brigands had once spared him because of the glory of his reputation. He so indulged his extravagance that he would bath several times a day, and, although he earned 400,000 sesterces annually from his school and almost as much from his private investments, it did not cover his expenses. He took especial care of these private investments: he ran workshops that produced garments for sale and paid such attention to his land holdings that it is accepted that a vine planted by his own hand produced grapes 365 days a year. But he paid greatest attention to his desires – in the case of women, even earning a reputation for oral sex. It is said that he was put down by a very funny remark coming from someone who was unable to avoid him in a group, although he had turned away when Palaemon was approaching to kiss him: 'Professor,' he said, 'do you like to swallow every time you see someone in a rush?'

4.9 The life of a Greek teacher

Most of our knowledge of *grammatici*, who taught principles of grammar and literary criticism, is derived from Suetonius' work on Roman teachers. But there were also their Greek equivalents, such as Epaphroditus, an Alexandrian ex-slave who moved to Rome under the patronage of Mettius Modestus and who wrote commentaries on Homer and Callimachus' Aetia, as well as a general work (*Lexeis*) on linguistic questions. His statue with inscription is preserved in the Villa Altieri at Rome: from his extant memorial, his ability to own two houses, and his extensive library, it is clear that Epaphroditus was much more successful than most teachers, who were often regarded as leading a hand-to-mouth existence in the capital.

(a) Suda, *sv Epaphroditus*, e 2004

Epaphroditus: from Chaeroneia, a teacher of grammar. The foster-child of Archias, a teacher of grammar from Alexandria; educated by him, he was purchased by Modestus, the prefect of Egypt. After educating Modestus' son, Petilius, he was held in high regard at Rome from the time of Nero up to that of Nerva [c. AD 54–98]. This was the period of Ptolemy, the son of Hephaistion, and many other famous names in education. He continually bought books and owned more than 30,000, including significant and recondite works. He was tall and dark, like an elephant. He lived in the area called Faenianocoria [Hay-hides] where he owned two houses. He died aged 75 after falling ill with dropsy. He left a fair number of works on grammar.

(b) *Corpus Inscriptionum Latinarum* 6.9454

M[arcus] METTIVS
EPAPHRODITVS
GREEK TEACHER OF GRAMMAR
M[arcus] METTIVS GERMANVS HIS FREEDMAN SET THIS UP

4.10 Some student (*scholastikos*) jokes

A series of jokes from an anthology compiled in late antiquity (but as old as the hills) not only mocks students but also casts light on other social material (for instance, the treatment of animals, the purchase of slaves, manumission, and eagerness to claim inheritances). The *scholastikos* mocked has been translated as 'student', although the term covers anyone claiming higher knowledge (the absent-minded professor as well as the know-it-all of modern humour).

Philogelos, (fifth century AD)

9.   A student who wanted to teach his ass not to chew on things stopped giving him food. When the ass died from hunger, he said, 'What a disaster! Just when I had taught him not to chew, he goes and dies on me.'

12.   A friend asked a student who was travelling overseas, 'Could you please buy me two slaves, each 15 years old.' He replied, 'If I can't find what you want, I'll buy you one who is 30.'

13.   A couple of good-for-nothing students were complaining to one another that their fathers were still alive. One said, 'How about we each kill our father?' 'No way,' said the other. 'That would make us parricides. But if you like, I'll kill yours and you can kill mine.'

16.   A student had been looking for his book for many days and unable to find it. He just happened to eat a salad and turned around and and saw the book lying in a corner. Later he met a friend who was crying because he had lost all his clothes. 'Don't be down-hearted,' he said, 'but buy a salad and eat it; then turn around and look in the corner: you'll find them there.'

18.   A fellow ran into a student and said to him, 'The slave you sold me has died.' 'By the gods,' he replied, 'he never did anything like that when he was with me.'

25.   A student was on a voyage and a storm sprang up. When his servants started wailing, he said, 'Don't wail. I've left you all your liberty in my will.'

32. A student invited to a meal didn't eat. When one of the guests asked him why he wasn't eating, he replied, 'In case I appear to have come for the food.'

54. A student writing to his father from Athens, thoroughly proud of what he had learnt, added, 'I hope I will find you charged in a capital case, so I can show you my skill as a lawyer.'

57. When a student produced a child by a slave girl, his father advised him to kill the infant. But he replied, 'When you've first buried your own children you can then tell me to get rid of mine.'

61. A student who was working as an elementary teacher [*khamaidida-skalos*] suddenly glanced at the corner and roared, 'Dionysius in the corner is acting up.' When someone said that he was absent, he replied, 'Well, he will be when he's here.'

4.11 The self-educated as obscurantists

Writing in the second century AD, Aulus Gellius frequently mocks the culturally ignorant and partially educated – a similar butt of humour to the *scholastikos* of Philogelos. In particular, the self-educated are satirised as the *nouveaux riches* of the literary world, interlopers who have not undergone the full programme of indoctrination of schooling under the grammarian and rhetor. Like Sabinus (**5.2**), the subject of this passage has not adequately internalised the rules of the game and so uses outrageously archaic words in an attempt to impress. A *bovinator* is probably a 'blusterer', but the actual meaning of the word was clearly long lost by the second century AD when Gellius was writing.

Aulus Gellius, *Attic Nights* 11.7

The use of words that are either too archaic and recherché or unusual and harsh and unattractive in their novelty appears to be the equivalent of a mistake. But in fact I think it is nastier and more blameworthy to utter words that are invented, unknown, and obscure, than ones that are common and coarse. By 'appearing to be novel' I also mean words that are unusual and obsolete, even if they are of old ancestry. Indeed that is a regular fault of self-education, which the Greeks call late learning [*opsimathia*] – to make the utmost effort, whenever you have first learnt them, to utter, at every opportunity and when talking about any subject, words that you have never learnt and of whose existence you have long been in ignorance. So at Rome in our presence a man who had long been eminent in legal affairs, but possessed a rather haphazard education, was speaking before the urban prefect. He wanted to say that someone was living a poverty-stricken, pitiful life and eating bread made from bran and drinking wine that had been belched up and stank. 'Here is a Roman knight eating *apluda* and drinking the *flocces* of the wine.' All those in attendance looked at one another, initially with a confused look as if wanting to know what each of those words meant; then they all burst out laughing, as if he had spoken something in Etruscan or Gallic. He had read that the country folk in the old days had called grain bran *apluda* and that word was used by Plautus in one of his comedies (that is, if the play called 'Astraba' belongs to Plautus). Likewise he had heard that *flocces* was an archaic word to indicate the dregs of the wine made from the skins and pips, just like the pips [*fracces*] from olives. He had read that in Caecilius' *Polumeni* and had kept those two words to use to embellish his speeches.

Another vulgarian also from a similar lack of education, when his adversary asked for a postponement of the case, said this, 'Please, praetor, help me out and come to my rescue! How long is this *bovinator* going to delay us?' And he bawled out loudly that phrase, 'he's a *bovinator*', three or four times. A murmuring began among all those who were present as if they were amazed at this prodigy of a word. But he, proud of himself and eager to show off, declared, 'Haven't you read Lucilius, who calls someone who avoids the issue a *bovinator*?' Indeed in Book 11 of Lucilius there is this verse:

'If a shifty type or unabashed *bovinator* with shameless mouth . . .'.

4.12 A defence of self-education

At the banquet put on by the freedman, Trimalchio, well-off ex-slaves and well-educated, but financially imperilled, free men are depicted as mixing uneasily. Hermeros, one of the freedmen, has taken offence at Ascyltos, who has been mocking Trimalchio's witticisms. In turn, the slave boy Giton cannot restrain his laughter, which provokes Hermeros to an enraged defence of his old-fashioned, yet practical education (a basic literacy and arithmetic sufficient to engage in trade).

Petronius, *Satyricon* 58

When this was said, Giton, who was standing at my feet and had restrained himself for ages, burst out in the rudest of laugher. When Ascyltos' adversary noticed this, he directed his anger at the boy. 'What are you laughing at, you curly-haired onion? Io Saturnalia – tell me, is it December? When did you pay your 5 per cent manumission tax? What's the matter, you titbit from the cross, you crow's meat. I'll make sure that Jupiter hates you – and the fellow who's not controlling you . . . Obviously, like master, like slave . . . I'll make sure that Athena hates you and the fellow who first made you such a curse. I haven't learnt geometry, literary studies, and senseless rubbish. But I know how to read inscriptions; I can give you fractions up to a hundred in bronze, weights, and money. To be brief: if you'd like, let's make a bet. I've come forward and anteed up. Now you'll find that your father wasted his money, even if you know the art of rhetoric. Here it is:

Which of us am I? I come long, I come broad. Solve me.

'I'll tell you which of us runs and doesn't leave the spot; which of us grows and shrinks at the same time. You're running around, your mouth wide open, you're as busy as a mouse in a chamberpot. So either shut up or don't annoy someone better than you, who doesn't even care whether you were born. Unless you're thinking I'm worried about the boxwood rings that you stole off your girlfriend. May Lucky Break be on my side! Let's go to the forum and borrow money – then you'll know that this iron ring has credibility. Bah! A dripping fox is a fine thing. As sure as I'll make a profit and die in such fine circumstances that the people will swear by my end, I'll hunt you down everywhere with your toga on backwards. He's a fine thing too, the fellow who taught you, an imbecile, not a teacher. We were taught differently. Our teacher used to say, "Have you got everything? Then straight off home. Don't look round; don't speak ill of your betters." But now they are pure junk heaps. But I, just as you see me right now, thank the gods for my learning.

4.13 Dreaming of learning to read

Artemidorus recognises that he will have both literate and illiterate customers and interprets dreams of reading and writing as either a reversion to childhood (with all the unpleasantness of school discipline) or as indicative of learning new ways, most commonly in the interchange of Greek and Roman culture in the Roman empire, but also including other 'barbarian' customs.

Artemidorus, *Interpretation of Dreams* 1.53

Learning to read signifies for the illiterate something good to come to the dreamer along with toil and fear. For learners experience fear and suffering at the same time, even though they are learning something valuable. If someone who is literate, however, learns to read, one should consider this as something bad and unusual, as learning is a childish thing. Hence it signifies unemployment, along with fear and suffering. Such a dream is only good for someone who desires a son: it will not be he himself, but his son, who will learn to read. If a Roman learns to read Greek or a Greek to read

Roman writing, the former will come into Greek society, the latter into Roman. Also many Romans have married Greek women and Greeks Roman women after seeing a dream of this sort. I know of someone who dreamt that he was learning to read Roman writing and was sentenced to [public] slavery. For a slave is taught nothing in Greek. To dream of being able to read barbarian writing well and fluently indicates coming into barbarian territory and society and doing something significant there. To read barbarian writing badly indicates doing badly among the barbarians or to be delirious when ill, because of the strangeness of the sounds. If someone is unable to write or read writing, he will be unemployed according to the writing: if it is only a little, it will be for a few days; if more, for months.

4.14 The value of literate soldiers

Although the handbook of Vegetius dates from the late fourth century AD, its comments on the need for literacy among at least some of the legionaries must apply to earlier periods also. Because of the need to communicate with other centres and to maintain appropriate accounts, it is likely that the army would have a higher level of basic literacy than the general civilian population, a view that is reinforced by the generally greater epigraphic remains from military provinces (Harris 1989).

Vegetius, *Handbook of Military Matters* 1.2.6, 19, 20

6.   It should be understood that there must be ten cohorts in a legion. But the first cohort surpasses the others in number and quality of soldiers: it requires the best soldiers in terms of physique and literacy ...

19.   Since there are numerous training schools in the legions, which require literate soldiers, it is reasonable for those who check the recruits to consider their height, physical strength, and mental agility in all cases, but to single out some of them on the basis of knowledge of the alphabet and their ability to calculate and reckon ...

20.   ... In addition [to the individual accounts for each of the ten cohorts] there was an eleventh one to which the whole legion contributed for burial costs: so if any of their comrades died, the costs of his burial were provided from the eleventh account. This account was kept in a strongbox by those who are now called standard-bearers. And so not only reliable, but also literate men were chosen as standard-bearers so they would know how to guard the deposits and offer an account to each soldier.

4.15 An Italian writer of wills

While wills might be made orally in front of witnesses, it was simpler for the illiterate or those not used to writing regularly to hire the services of a scribe, such as the freedman Philadespotus, whose pride in having mastered the legal form is shown on his tombstone. Cf. **8.12**, where Castor has written his will himself.

Inscriptiones Latinae Selectae 7750 (Venafrum)

TO PUBLIUS POMPONIUS PHILADESPOTUS
FREEDMAN OF PUBLIUS
SCRIBE, WHO WROTE WILLS
FOR 25 YEARS
WITHOUT USING A LAWYER

4.16 The importance of having some literate overseers on the farm estate

The level of literacy among the Roman workforce, particularly the overseers, is the subject of controversy. While Cicero expects the heads of an urban or rural workforce to be literate, it is clear from Columella that many would prefer their overseers to be skilled managers, but ones who would be limited in their ability to control the business by their lack of writing and mathematical skills. Tenants on Pliny the Younger's estates could regularly send him requests (although they may have used scribes to draft their petitions).

(a) Cicero, On the Republic 5.3.5

Scipio: 'So just as the overseer [*vilicus*] knows agriculture and the accountant [*dispensator*] knows how to read and write, but both of them turn back from the pleasure of their knowledge to the practicalities of making use of this. So too our ruler will be interested in the law and in studying individual laws, and will certainly have looked at the reasons why they originated, but he will not tie himself up in giving opinions and reading and writing to prevent himself from acting as a virtual steward of the state and its bailiff, so to speak . . .'

(b) Columella, On Agriculture 1.8.1–4, 12–13

So it's my advice not to choose an overseer from slaves of the handsome sort, and certainly not from the type who have the refined skills of the city – they are a lazy, drowsy type of slave, used to leisure, the Campus, the circus, the theatres, gambling, fast-food joints, and the brothels, who dream about nothing other than the same sort of nonsense. If they are transferred to farming, the master will take a loss not as much with respect to the slave himself as in his whole estate. You should choose a man who is hardened to country labours from childhood and tested by practice. If there is no such man, put one of those in charge who have withstood hard labour, who has now left his youthful period behind, but has not yet entered old age. This is so that youth does not lessen respect for his authority, as older workers disdain obedience to a young man, and in case his age is unable to cope with the most physical of tasks. He should be of an age between these two and of strong physique, skilled in agriculture and of the utmost diligence, so he picks things up very quickly: it's not our method of working to have one man giving orders and another telling the workers how to do the task. A man who learns from a subordinate what needs to be done and how is incapable of properly controlling the work. He may even be illiterate: as long as he has a very reliable memory, he can reasonably control affairs. Cornelius Celsus says that an overseer of this type more often than not brings in money, rather than just the ledger to his master: because he is illiterate, he is too frightened to cook the books himself and do it through another because this involves an accomplice in his fraud ... He should not allow anyone to leave the estate unless he has sent him and he should not send him unless there is a very good reason indeed. He should not do business on his own behalf or invest the master's funds in animals or other transferable goods. This type of business diverts the supervisor's attention and prevents him from balancing the master's books – when an audit is made, he will produce goods, not cash.

(c) Pliny, *Letters* 9.15

Pliny to his friend Falco, greetings.

I had taken refuge on my Tuscan estate to be able to do every thing as I wanted. But I couldn't achieve that even in Tuscany. I am being bothered by numerous petitions from the country folk, full of such complaints, which I read considerably more against my will than my own compositions. I am handling appeals over little squabbles, which after the passage of time is a nasty, thankless task. The accounts are being ignored, as though I was an absentee landlord. Sometimes I mount my horse and play the head of the household to the extent that I travel through part of the farm holdings for exercise. Make sure you follow your habit and send a detailed account of urban affairs to us the country bumpkins.

4.17 Inscriptions and dedications in public areas

Although there were numerous honorary decrees and inscriptions throughout the civic centre of Rome, it is clear from the passage below that copies were not regularly preserved in the state archives and in the event of a catastrophe (such as the fire that destroyed the temple of Jupiter to whose walls the bronze tablets would have been attached) would need to be restored from copies in the possession of the honorands. Their practical application could only be haphazard, as when the cities of Asia vied for the glory of being the site of a temple to Tiberius and his mother, each using republican decrees to support their case (Tacitus, *Annals* 4.55–6).

Suetonius, *Vespasian* 8.5

The city was looking dreadful from fires and collapses from long ago. Vespasian allowed anyone to take squatter's rights over empty lots and build on them, if the owners were no longer to be found. He himself undertook the restoration of the Capitol and made the first effort in clearing the debris, taking away some material on his own shoulders. He undertook the restoration of 3,000 bronze tablets that had burnt along with the Capitol, searching out copies from everywhere. These were the finest and oldest documents of the Roman empire, in which were contained, dating back from nearly the origin of the city, decrees of the senate and decisions of the people about alliances, treaties, and privileges granted to various individuals.

REFERENCES AND FURTHER READING

Bonner, S. (1977) *Education in Ancient Rome*, London.
Bowman, A.K. and Woolf, G. (eds) (1994) *Literacy and Power in the Ancient World*, Cambridge.
Cribiore, R. (2001) *Gymnastics of the Mind*, Princeton, NJ.
Harris, W.V. (1989) *Ancient Literacy*, Cambridge, MA.
Humphrey, J.H. (ed.) (1991) *Literacy in the Roman World*, Ann Arbor, MI.
Kaster, R. (1995) *Suetonius, De Grammaticis et Rhetoribus*, Oxford.
Morgan, T. (1998) *Literate Education in the Hellenistic and Roman Worlds*, Cambridge.
Rea, J.R. (1993) 'A Student's Letter to his Father: *P.Oxy.* XVIII 2190 Revised', *Zeitschrift für Papyrologie und Epigraphik* 99: 75–88.
Saller, R. (1994) *Patriarchy, Property, and Death in the Roman Family*, Cambridge.
Schulten, P. (2002) 'Ancient Humour', in Jongman, W. and Kleijwegt, M. (eds) *After the Past*, Leiden, pp. 209–34.
Too, Y.L. (ed.) (2001) *Education in Greek and Roman Antiquity*, Leiden.
Too, Y.L. and Livingstone, N. (eds) (1998) *Pedagogy and Power*, Cambridge.

5

SLAVERY

The institution of chattel slavery is one of the most striking features of Roman society. Slaves were an almost totally malleable product: they could be used to display the wealth of their owner (5.1) or for the most specialised purposes, such as being virtual talking books (5.2). The Roman upper classes were aware of this reliance and not uncommonly expressed concern at this dependence on those beneath them (5.3). The demand for slave labour was supplied by domestically bred slaves and also by the purchase of considerable numbers of imported slaves, some from outside the empire, but most from within the area of Roman rule. Baby farming is particularly noticeable in Egypt (5.4). From Egypt, too, we have a considerable number of records of the sale of slaves (5.5, 5.6, 5.7). A section from the *Digest* of Roman law that discusses the right of return of unsatisfactory goods according to the edict of the aediles (who supervised the Roman market) offers a fascinating depiction of Roman expectations of slaves (5.8).

Routine comments on runaway slaves and reward notices (5.9, 5.10, 5.11), not to mention collars for captive fugitives (5.12), indicate that attempts at escape were not uncommon. The collars, which were perhaps preferable to branding slaves who had a history of escaping, also show that the Christian church accepted slave ownership as a normal part of life. Punishment of slaves appears to have been commonplace – it was even possible to hire professionals to do the job, such as the funeral service (the employees of Libitina) at Puteoli (5.13). On occasion, there are reports of slaves reacting violently, but the severity of punishment inflicted on these occasions would have been a major deterrent. The famous case of the execution of the entire household of Pedanius, in the reign of Nero (5.14), and the detailed provisions of the *senatus consultum Silianum*, discussed at length by the legal experts (5.15), show how concerned Roman masters were to ensure their daily safety.

Other aspects of slave treatment are hardly reassuring. Living conditions for slaves might not be much better than those enjoyed by the farm animals, as Columella's recipe for a slave-prison (*ergastulum*) indicates. His suggested measures for economising (such as using the kitchen as the main source of heating for the slaves in winter) also indicate a very marginal concern with slaves' welfare (**5.16**).

Slaves in domestic service who were close to their owners, and imperial slaves especially (**5.17**), had a better chance of advancement or even gaining their freedom. It was not uncommon to free slaves when they were on the brink of death (**5.18**, **5.19**), or else posthumously in one's will (**5.20**), as these actions cost the owner himself nothing. Manumission by terms of a will was restricted by Roman law in the time of the emperor Augustus (**5.21**), but these provisions could be evaded by informal arrangements or by specific legal procedures. Still, care had to be taken to ensure that the freed slave was publicly seen to have been freed (**5.22**, **5.23**) or, at best, they might only obtain the status of Junian Latins (**5.21**). At worst, they might find it difficult to prove their freed status against future claims. Some freeborn individuals might be raised as slaves and later claim their rights of free birth (**5.24**), but measures were taken against those who tried to use this as a legal loophole to avoid the stigma of being freed (**5.25**). And freedom for an ex-slave was not absolute: in the Greek-speaking part of the Roman world, it was common to 'free' slaves on condition that they remained with their owners for a period of time, sometimes up until their deaths (**5.26**). At Rome, it was established that slaves owed an agreed number of days of service to their ex-owners, their patrons. The nature of these services could be the butt of ribald humour (**5.27**) or be the subject of learned legal discussion (**5.28**). Because of the Roman custom of allowing slaves, like other members of the household under the power of the *paterfamilias*, to maintain their own resources (*peculium*, literally 'pocket-money'), slaves could take this with them as seed-capital when they were freed or even use this to arrange for others to buy them and free them. This latter process relied on the good faith of the buyer, which could lead to complications (**5.29**; cf. **5.14**).

5.1 The importance of slaves for display among the Romans

About 200 AD, Athenaeus composed an eclectic work that is structured around the learned dinner conversation of a group of philosophers. In particular, they consider the means of maintaining a luxurious lifestyle, quoting from various authors. In this context, the use of slaves is considered: after Masurius has described the use of slaves in Greece, Larensius discusses the use of slaves in republican Rome. The tone is clearly moralising, emphasising the show value of slaves, rather than their value in the workforce. But, as can be seen from **5.14** below, large slave households were common, indeed expected, among the upper classes at Rome.

Athenaeus, *Deipnosophistae* 6.272c–273a

Every Roman is in possession of as many slaves as possible. Every single one of them owns ten thousand, twenty thousand, or even more. It is not for the income, as in the case of Nicias, the richest of Greeks [fifth century BC] – most of the Romans have the majority of their slaves as advance attendants. By contrast, most of the tens of thousands of slaves in Attica worked the mines in chains. Posidonius says that as a result, when they revolted, they killed the guards at the mine, but seized the fortifications at Sounion and plundered Attica for a long period. This was the time when the second slave uprising occurred in Sicily [104–101 BC]. Spartacus the gladiator, after escaping from the Italian city of Capua, attracted to him a great number of slaves [73–71 BC]: he was himself a slave, of Thracian race. He overran all of Italy for some time as many slaves poured in to join him each day. If he had not died in battle with Licinius Crassus, he would have caused our people considerable effort, as did Eunous in Sicily [135–132 BC].

5.2 Slaves custom-made for literary reference

Seneca the Younger, writing at the time of Nero, mocks the pretensions of a *parvenu*, Calvisius Sabinus. As the upper classes liked to pepper their dinner conversation with literary references and quotations (cf. Athenaeus, **5.1** above), Calvisius tried to emulate this behaviour, but his methods of doing so were regarded as extreme. Satellius Quadratus plays the role of the *parasitos* in this anecdote, the habitual dinner guest whose task it was to offer witty comment – here, at the expense of his host. (See Gowers 1993.)

The reference to the three names refers to the traditional naming practice at Rome: a first name (praenomen, e.g. Marcus), a clan name (nomen, e.g. Tullius), and a family name (cognomen, e.g. Cicero, distinguishing this group from other Tullii).

Seneca, *Letters* 27.5–8

We remember Calvisius Sabinus, the millionaire. He had the wealth and the intellect of an ex-slave: I've never seen a more disgustingly lucky individual. He had a memory that was so poor that he would forget the name of Odysseus, or Achilles, or Priam – characters whom he knew as well as we know our slave attendants. No geriatric name-keeper [*nomenclator*], who doesn't recall the three names but imposes them on somebody, ever ran through his greetings to the tribes of men as badly as Sabinus did with the Trojans and Greeks. All the same, he wanted to seem to be educated. So he thought up this shortcut: he bought slaves at great expense, one to recall Homer, another to recall Hesiod, and he assigned one to each of the nine lyric poets. There's no reason why you should be surprised that he bought these at considerable cost: he couldn't hunt them up, but had to contract out their creation. After he had obtained this group of slaves, he started to bother his fellow diners. He used to keep the slaves at his feet: while he continually sought from them verses for quotation, he often forgot them in mid-line. Satellius Quadratus, who made a habit of dining out on the dumb rich and, as follows, of laughing along with them, and, the corollary of these two, of getting his laughs in against them, offered the suggestion that he should get table-cleaners trained as language-experts. When Sabinus said that each slave had cost him 100,000 sesterces, he declared, 'You could have bought as many cases of books for less.' Yet he was fixed in his belief that he knew what each person in his household knew. Satellius also started encouraging him to engage in wrestling, although he was sickly, pale, and weedy. When Sabinus answered, 'How can I? I can hardly stay alive', he declared, 'Please, don't say that. Don't you see how many slaves of the sturdiest disposition you own?'

5.3 Over-reliance on slaves and freedmen (including doctors)

In a satirical entry in his encyclopaedia, Pliny the Elder mocks the arrival of the medical profession at Rome. Not only was the quality of service so poor that it might be joked that doctors were the Greeks' revenge for the Roman conquest, but the members of the profession were usually outsiders and often from the lower levels of society. Hence the concern at having to rely on their opinion, which is here contrasted with considered Roman judgement at the census or in legal matters. The reliance on slaves for transporting litters, for providing the names of clients (**5.2** above), and for other daily services conflicted with ideas of self-reliance that were both part of the traditional Roman belief system (as seen in the works of the Elder Cato) and adopted from the Hellenistic schools of philosophy.

Pliny the Elder, *Natural History* 29.19

We still don't take any notice of this [i.e. doctors' tendency to kill their patients]: the sweetness of hope each has for his own life is so overpowering. Besides, there is no law that punishes fatal negligence and no precedent for legal redress. The doctors learn at our risk and carry out their tests by killing us – there is total immunity for a doctor to have merely killed a man. No, instead, the blame moves on and our intemperate lifestyle is censured: those who have died are attacked instead. Jury panels are scrutinised at imperial censuses for their lifestyle, inquiries are held within the household, judges are brought in from Cadiz and the pillars of Hercules to make commercial rulings, indeed in cases which might result in exile no vote is taken unless there are forty-five picked jurors. But they go off from the judge, as others go out to consider their verdict, to start slaughtering straightaway. And rightly so, given that none of us wishes to know what will cure him. We walk around on other folks' legs, we recognise each other through others' eyes, we greet each other through others' memory, and we live by others' efforts: natural effort and the proof that we're alive has disappeared. The only thing we keep for ourselves is our pleasures.

5.4 Cancellation of contract for raising a foundling slave (Alexandria, 5 BC)

Given the number of slaves required for work and display in the Roman world (estimates have placed the number of slaves in Italy as high as a third of the population), there was always a concern for replacement. Many might be house-born and trained in the *familia* (the *vernae*, who often record this status with pride); others might be enslaved in war or sold into the empire, probably as the result of inter-tribal conflict. From Egypt, we also have evidence of baby-farming: foundlings (exposed children who had been collected) might be raised by wet-nurses in expectation of later sale. The contract below annuls a contract between Harpocration, the slave speculator, and Apollonias, who is engaged to raise the slave girl, Agalmation, for him.

Corpus Papyrorum Graecarum 1.11

To Protarchus from Harpocration, of imperial employ, and from Apollonias daughter of Panotes with her guardian and fiancé, Chaeremon, son of Petesis. Since Harpocration happens to have given to Apollonia the foundling slave of his who is still breastfeeding, named Agalmation [Statuette], to be nursed by Apollonia herself by her own milk for the agreed time and, since before the weaning of the slave named Agalmation had been completed, Apollonia's milk has dried up, we have come to an agreement among ourselves on these terms: Apollonia has been paid in full by Harpocration, both by direct payment from his estate and partially from the bank for the nursing costs of eight months and will make no claim on Harpocration for this in any fashion.

5.5 Sale of a slave (Egypt, AD 129)

Among the papyrus remains from Egypt are a number of receipts associated with the sale of slaves. As a major item, subject to sales tax, the transfer of slaves was recorded in the public archives, indicating the contract between the buyer and seller and guarantees given. In the following typical sale, a guarantee is given that the slave was acceptable at time of sale; if, however, she later turns out to have epilepsy or to be subject to a claim from a third party, the buyer may return her for a full refund.

Oxyrhynchus Papyrus 1.95

In the thirteenth year of the emperor Caesar Trajan Hadrian Augustus, 29 Pauni, in the city of Oxyrhynchus in the Thebaid. Agathos Daimon, also called Dionysius, son of Dionysius, grandson of Dionysius, whose mother is Hermione from the city of Oxyrhynchus agrees in public [lit. 'on the street'] with Gaius Iulius Germanus, son of Gaius Iulius Domitianus, that through this agreement, which was made by Agathos Daimon, also called Dionysius, with Iulius Germanus on the twenth-fifth day of the month Tubi of the thirteenth year [of Hadrian's reign] in progress, that he has witnessed the sale recorded in the handwriting of the purchaser, previously owned by Heracleides, also known as Theon Machon Sosicosmeios, also known as Althaieus, of the slave, Dioscoroutes, approximately 25 years old, which then Iulius Germanus received from him just as she was, free from defect, unless she has epilepsy or is subject to external claim, for the price of 1,200 minted drachmas, which at that time Agathos Daimon, also called Dionysius, received from Iulius Germanus along with the handwritten bill of sale. From this Iulius Germanus has paid out the cost of the education of that same slave Dioscoroutes on the third of the month Phanemoth of the same year, in accordance with the agreement made with him; the guarantee of the same slave Dioscoroutes in all respects is incumbent on Agathos Daimon, also called Dionysius: the handwritten bill of sale also covers this. If she happens to have epilepsy or have any other defect, Iulius Germanus does not need [to retain the slave?] . . .

5.6 Sale of a child slave

The following receipt, valid when registered in the local archive, shows that even very young slaves might be sold. The description of distinguishing features of the slave, along with guarantees, shows considerable similarity to contracts for the sale of farm animals. It is likely, in fact, that slave contracts, showing the sale of 'speaking tools' (*instrumenta vocalia*), were adapted from traditional practice with animals: see Litinas (1999), who discusses sales receipts that likewise record age, colour (cf. remarks on complexion in slave sale deeds), scars, and guarantees of freedom from disease.

Note too the common practice of having another write the receipt. This may not indicate that Libelarius is unable to read, but that he is uncertain about the proper form of the document and has chosen someone with knowledge in the area.

Bodleian Papyrus 1.44 (Egypt, AD 310)

I acknowledge that I have sold to you from now in perpetuity the female slave that I own [Name], who is at present 3 years old, honey-complexioned, at a price agreed between us of . . .ty [i.e. 30–90] talents of silver coin, which I have received in hand in full here, in return for which [she will remain with you and] you will have control and ownership of the purchased goods and the right to supervise and manage her however you like: I guarantee this in perpetuity.

This written contract with the signature of the person signing on my behalf shall be valid when lodged in the public archive [*demosia*] and, when asked, I have agreed that this is so.

In the consulship of Statius Andronicus and Pompeius Probus [AD 310], the most illustrious prefects of the sacred Praetorium . . .

I, Aurelius Libelarius, the aforementioned have [agreed to the sale of the aforementioned slave] and have received the aforementioned . . . talents of silver coin and will furnish to you every guarantee as aforesaid.

I, [. . .], ex-magistrate, have written this for him as he is illiterate.

5.7 Mandate empowering the sale of a slave

Whereas the slave sold above may have been a foundling, the following shows clearly the sale of a houseborn slave (*verna*) at a young age, via a third party.

Sammelbuch Griechischer Urkunden aus Aegypten 5.7573 (Egypt, AD 116)

In the twentieth year of the emperor Caesar Trajan Optimus Augustus Germanicus Dacicus Parthicus, 7 December, at [. . .] in the Thebaid, notarised by [. . .], son of Ammonius, and [. . .], son of Gaius.

Taverseious, daughter of Onnophris, whose mother is Tanese from Elephantine, for 41 drachmas agrees . . ., with Pachompaonnophres the priest of the great god Ammon acting as guardian, to appoint Pachompetenephotes, son of Onnophris, whose mother comes from Tisa, the priest of the great goddess Isis, so he can be sent to sell the houseborn slave that she owns, named Narcissus, approximately 8 years old, with a scar on his right hand, the child of her slave that she owned and is now dead, Aphrodite. This is on condition that Pachompetenephotes sells the slave Narcissus and hands over most of his sale price according to his agreement to Taverseious. He will be permitted to proceed with regard to the indicated slave as he wishes and whatever contract he concludes with regard to him will be valid as if she were also present.

5.8 Defects to be declared (or not) before the sale of slaves

The following extracts from the imperial jurists on the right of return of slaves and possible damages against the vendor throw considerable light on Roman society. What can and cannot be considered unhealthy, what activities indicate

160

unsatisfactory mental states, and what actions suggest a likely runaway or a potential truant are considered at some length. Slaves who flee to asylums or to a statue of the emperor are regarded as taking due advantage of the possibility of escape from mistreatment, not as runaways. The significance of nationality, the risks of purchasing a suicidal or felonious slave, the possibility of scams whereby the slave would run back to his original owner, and due respect for familial bonds even among slaves are other topics raised by these valuable passages.

Note, too, the Roman view of biology in 21.1.14.1, which follows the standard ancient view that women merely provided a fertile site for the development of the embryo that they receive from their male partners. In 21.1.23.3, the references to slave suicide suggest that this was not infrequent. This is supported by the provision in the contract for the Guild of Funeral Directors at Puteoli (see **5.13**) that the body of a free man found hanging be removed within the hour, but a slave (male or female), 'if notification is received before the tenth hour, before the second hour on the following day'.

Digest 21.1

21.1.1. Ulpian, *On the Edict of the Curule Aediles*, Book 1. Labeo writes that the edict of the curule aediles applies to the sale of those things that are fixed as much as those that are movable or self-moving. 1. The aediles declare: 'Those who sell slaves should make the buyers aware of each's diseases and defects, which are runaways, which are truants, and which are subject to a claim for damages. They should announce all this openly and plainly when they sell the slaves. If a slave turns out otherwise or things turn out differently from what was said and promised when the sale was being made, we will pronounce as to what is owed in respect of the slave and we allow court action for the return of the slave to the buyer and all those affected by the affair. If the slave has in any respect been damaged after the sale and transfer through the actions of the buyer's household or his agent, or if anything has arisen or been acquired through him after the sale, or if anything else has been acquired in that sale or any profit from it is attained by the buyer, he should make restitution for all this. Likewise, if the seller has provided anything additional, he should get it back. Likewise, if a slave has committed a capital offence or done anything in a suicide attempt or has been presented in the arena to fight it out with the wild beasts, they should announce all this at the sale. So we will allow court action to the buyer in these cases. In addition, if anyone be said to have made a sale contrary to these provisions knowingly and with malice afore-thought, we will allow a court action.'

2. The reason for posting this edict is to block the cheating of sellers and assist buyers who might be cheated by the sellers, to the extent that the seller should be obligated by the edict even if he did not know what the aediles order to be made public. This is perfectly fair: the seller could

161

have discovered these requirements and it makes no difference to the buyer whether he is deceived by ignorance or fraud on the part of the seller. 3. However, it should be understood that these provisions do not apply to sales by the imperial treasury. 4. But if any other state makes a sale, this edict applies ...

6. If any fault or disease in the slave can be recognised (for they generally indicate their faults by various signs), it can be said that the edict is inoperative, since it only considers this point: that the buyer should not be cheated. 7. It should be known that a disease was thus defined by Sabinus: a state of any physique that is unnatural, which makes it inferior for any purpose for which Nature has given us physical health. This can sometimes occur throughout the body, sometimes in part of it (tuberculosis is a disease of the whole body, blindness of a part – even if a man was born blind). A fault is quite different from a disease. Consider the case of a stammerer: he is faulty, rather than diseased. I'm of the opinion that the aediles made the same pronouncement in two ways on the same matter to avoid any confusion. 8. Accordingly if there is any such fault or disease that reduces the use and service of a fellow, this will allow an action for return of property, so long as we remember that not every slight flaw results in him being considered diseased or faulty. So a mild fever or long-standing malarial condition that can be ignored in practice or a mild injury provide no grounds for offence in themselves, even if it was not announced. For these things could be ignored. Let us consider, for example, who is actually diseased or faulty. 9. Vivianus wonders whether or not a slave, if he does not toss his head around like a religious fanatic and make prophetic utterances all the time, is healthy despite these actions. Vivianus declares that he is healthy in spite of this. We ought not, he says, consider people insane because of mental faults; otherwise we would declare many to be insane by this reasoning ad infinitum, such as for being fickle, or superstitious, or bad-tempered, or obstinate, or any similar mental faults. More is guaranteed about the health of the body than about the health of the mind. Sometimes, however, a physical fault spreads to the mind and harms it, as happens to someone delirious, since that occurs as the result of fever. Well then, if a fault was such that it ought to be picked up by the seller and he does not announce it when he is aware of it, he will be liable for a lawsuit over the sale. 10. Vivianus also says that if someone used to rave around shrines and offer prophecies, but does not do so now, there is no longer a fault. There are no grounds for action on the basis that he once did that, no more than that he once had a fever. If, however, he persists in that fault and regularly raves around shrines and gives predictions as if off his head, although that is the result of lack of self-control, it is a fault, but one of the mind, not of the body, and so one cannot return the goods, since the aediles speak of physical faults. All the same, he would allow court action over the sale. He also says that in the case of those who are excessively frightened, greedy or mean, or bad-tempered ...

21.1.2. Paul, *On the Edict of the Curule Aediles*, Book 1. or depressives.

21.1.3. Gaius, *On the Edict of the Curule Aediles*, Book 1. or self-willed or hunchbacked or bent or deformed or suffering from itchy rash or scabby or the deaf and dumb.

21.1.4. ... there is no right of return because of these faults, but he allows a court action over the sale. 1. But if the physical fault penetrates all the way to the mind – if, for example, they are speaking in tongues because of fever or speaking ridiculous things around the city districts like madmen – in the case of those whose mental faults occur from a bodily fault, return of goods is possible. 2. Similarly, Pomponius says that some were of the opinion that compulsive gamblers and alcoholics are not covered by the edict, just as gluttons, fakes, liars, and the disputatious are not either. 3. Pomponius also says that, although a seller does not need to guarantee that a slave is of notable intellect, still, if he sells one who is so stupid or moronic that he is of no use, it will be obviously a fault. We seem to use this legal definition that the words 'fault' and 'disease' only appear to apply to the body. 4. In short, a seller will only guarantee against a fault of the mind if he has promised this; otherwise, he doesn't. So there are specific exceptions for a truant or runaway, since this is a fault of the mind, not the body. So some have said that animals that are shy or prone to kick are not to be listed as diseased, for this is a fault of the mind, not the body. An action in respect of sale can be raised, if the seller has knowingly kept silent about that mental fault. If, however, it is a fault of the body alone or a fault partially of body, partially of mind, then return of goods will apply. 5. It will need to be noted that these statements are about illness in general, not about a disease that would prevent participation in normal duties. Pomponius says that this does not appear surprising: for there is no discussion here about whatever it is that the illness prevents. He also says that not every illness gives an opportunity for return of goods, if you consider the case of a slight eye defect or a slight tooth- or earache or a minor ulceration; furthermore, not every little fever falls under the application of this edict ...

21.1.6. Pomponius rightly says that this edict applies not only to lasting illnesses, but also to transient ones. Trebatius says that someone with impetigo is not ill if he can use the limb where the impetigo is just as well as a healthy man. It seems to me that Trebatius' view is correct: it seems to me that a eunuch is not ill nor really faulty, but healthy, just like a person who has one testicle and can still father children.

21.1.7. Paul, *To Sabinus*, Book 11. But if anyone is a eunuch because the needed part of the body is completely absent, he is ill.

21.1.8. If anyone's tongue has been cut out, there is a question over whether he seems healthy. This inquiry occurs in Offilius, raised in his case over a horse: he says it doesn't seem healthy to him . . .

21.1.11. Paul, *To Sabinus*, Book 11. A man who lacks a tooth is not diseased, for a majority of men lack one tooth or other and are not diseased because of it: particularly when we are born without teeth and not thus less healthy until we have teeth. Otherwise, no old person would be healthy.

21.1.12. 3. It should also be known that a left-handed person is not diseased or faulty, except if he uses the left hand by preference because of weakness in the right one. This person is not left-handed, but maimed. 4. There has been a query over whether the man whose breath smells is healthy. Trebatius says it is not unhealthy for anyone's breath to smell, just as with a person who smells like a goat or a squint-eyed person, for that is the result of the lack of oral hygiene. If that occurred from a physical fault, such as from an illness of the liver, lung, or something else, he is diseased.

21.1.14. There is a question about a woman who always produces still-births as to whether she is diseased. Sabinus says that, if this occurs by a fault of her vulva, then she is diseased. 1. If a woman is sold who is pregnant, everyone agrees that she is healthy, since it is the greatest and particular duty of women to receive and foster the embryo. 2. Childbirth is also healthy so long as nothing external to this occurs that disposes her body to any sickness. 3. Caelius says that Trebatius distinguished the cases of the infertile woman: if she is naturally infertile, she is healthy, if by a physical fault, the opposite is true. 4. There is also a query about a bed-wetter. Perdius says he is not unhealthy because of that if he urinates in the bed when overcome in a drunken stupor or even because he cannot be bothered to get up; but if from a bladder disease he cannot hold on to the collected water, he can be returned – not because he is a bed-wetter, but because he has a diseased bladder . . . 9. If a seller makes an express exception about a disease and says or promises that the slave is healthy in other respects, the agreement must be kept to (a chance to change their minds must not be given to those who have waived their legal rights) unless the seller knowingly and deliberately kept silent about a disease. 10. If a disease is not specifically excepted, but is such a disease that it could be apparent to anyone (think of a blind man on sale or one who had an obvious scar from a life-threatening experience on his head or some other part of the body), Caecilius says that the seller cannot be held accountable for this reason – it is just the same as if the disease was expressly excepted. It must be agreed that the aediles' edict applies to those diseases and faults of which anyone has been unaware or could have been unaware . . .

21.1.15. Paul, *To Sabinus*, Book 11. A woman who menstruates twice a month is not healthy, just as one who does not menstruate at all, unless that is the result of age . . .

21.1.17. Ofilius defines what a runaway is. A runaway is one who, in order to hide himself from his master, remains outside his master's house for the purpose of flight. 1. Caelius in addition says that a runaway is one who departs with the intention of not returning to his master, even if he changes his mind and returns to him: no one stops being guilty of such a crime by a change of heart, he says. 2. Cassius also writes that a runaway is one who leaves his master with deliberate intent. 3. Likewise in Vivianus the opinion is offered that a runaway is generally to be understood from his state of mind, not just from flight: for the man who flees from the enemy or a brigand or fire or building collapse, even though it is a fact that he fled, is not, however, a runaway. Likewise, not even the slave, who has fled from the instructor to whom he has been entrusted for learning a skill, is a runaway, if he happens to be fleeing because he is treating him harshly. The same holds if a slave flees from someone to whom he has been loaned, if he flees for the same reason. Vivianus gives the same judgement if he is viciously treated. This applies if the slave flees these types and returns to his master; if he does not return to his master, he says he is clearly a runaway without any doubt. 4. When the problem was raised, Proculus said the same about a slave who hides at the house for the apparent purpose of escaping when he gains a chance of fleeing. He says that, although he could not be seen to be fleeing if he remained at the house, still he had been a runaway – except that if he had only hidden until his master's anger had subsided, he was not a runaway, no more than he who, when he saw that his master wished to have him whipped, rushed off to a friend to have him intercede on his behalf. Not even that slave is a runaway who has gone as far as to throw himself from a height – he had instead intended to commit suicide (though you might call a slave a runaway who had climbed to a high place in the house in order to leap from there). Proculus also says that what the ignorant say, that the slave who leaves the house at night without any permission from his master is a runaway, is wrong: this should be assessed according to the intent of each. 5. Vivianus also says that, if a slave leaves his master and returns to his mother and there is a question as to whether he is a runaway, if he acted to hide so he could avoid returning to his master, he is a runaway; but, if the reason was to be more readily excused for some mistake through his mother's intercession, he is not a runaway. 6. Caelius also writes that, if you buy a slave who has thrown himself into the Tiber, so long as he left his master with the intention of killing himself, he is not a runaway; but if he first had the intention of fleeing, then changed his mind and threw himself into the Tiber, he remains a runaway. He makes the same decision as well about a slave who has thrown himself from a bridge. All these decisions as provided by Caelius are correct. 7. He also says that, if your slave runs away and takes his underslave [*vicarius*] with him, and if the underslave follows unwillingly or in ignorance and does not make use of a chance given of returning to you, he does not appear to be a runaway. But if, early on when he was running away, he understood what was happening or afterwards recognised what had happened and did not want to return to you when he could, the opposite is the case. He thinks the same decision should be made about a slave whom a kidnapper has abducted. 8. Caelius also says that, if a slave on a farm leaves the farmhouse with the intention of fleeing and someone catches him before he has left the farm, he is clearly a runaway, as his intent was to act as a runaway. 9. He also says that a slave who goes one or two steps or just starts to run away, if he cannot escape his master in pursuit, must be a runaway. 10. He also rightly says that fleeing is a form of freedom of a sort, that is, being free from one's master's control for the moment. 11. A slave given as a surety has the debtor as his owner; but, if he escapes after the creditor exercises his rights over him, he can be regarded as a runaway. 12. Labeo and Caelius raise the question whether, if a slave takes refuge in an asylum or makes for a place where those who demand to be sold off to another master are sold off, he is a runaway. I think he isn't a runaway: he is doing what is generally considered permissible to do. I do not even think the slave who takes refuge at a statue of the emperor is a runaway, since he did not do this with the intention of fleeing. I have the same opinion about the slave who has taken refuge in an asylum or anywhere else, because he has not done this with the intention of fleeing. If, however, he first ran away and afterwards took refuge, he does not any less continue to be a runaway. 13. Likewise Caelius writes that he is of the opinion that the slave is also a runaway who goes to a place where his master cannot recover him and is all the more a runaway if he goes to a place from where he cannot be seized. 14. Labeo defines a truant as a minor runaway, and, conversely, a runaway as a major truant. But we duly define truant as follows: a slave who indeed is not in flight, but regularly wanders around without a reason and having spent the time on unimportant matters comes back to the household late.

21.1.18. Gaius, *On the Edict of the Curule Aediles*, Book 1. If a seller declares something about a slave for sale and the buyer complains that this is not so, he can bring an action for return of goods or for reckoning of the value of the goods (that is, how much less they are actually worth). For example, if the seller declares that the slave is diligent and hard-working or speedy and industrious or that he gained his *peculium* from his own thriftiness and, on the contrary, he turns out to be fickle, mischievous, lazy, inattentive, slow, idle, and wasteful. All this seems to indicate that one should not demand precisely what the seller declares, but allow for some latitude: if he happens to declare that he is diligent, the extreme self-control and restraint of a philosopher should not be looked for; if he declares he is hard-working and industrious, we don't require constant effort day and night from him, but all this should be looked for to a decent extent, reasonably and fairly. We will consider the same to hold about the other things the seller declares. 1. A seller, who says the slave is the finest of cooks, ought to provide one who is top quality in that skill; but one who instead simply says he is a cook, is seen to satisfy that condition even if he provides an average cook. The same goes for other types of skills. 2. Likewise, if anyone simply says the slave has acquired a *peculium*, it is sufficient if he had even the smallest *peculium*.

21.1.19. Ulpian, *On the Edict of the Curule Aediles*, Book 1. It should be realised that there are things that one does not need to provide, if one has said that they are so: certainly this is the case for those things that involve the pure praise of a slave, such as saying he is thrifty, trustworthy, and obedient. For, as Pedius writes, there is a great difference between whether a seller says something to praise a slave or really promises to provide what he has said . . .

21.1.23. 2. [While the return of the slave will normally restore the position of the parties before the sale,] an exception is made for the case of a slave committing a capital offence. To commit a capital offence is wrongfully to commit any such offence as would be punished with the death penalty. In old times they used to put down 'offence', when they meant 'penalty'. We will allow that a capital offence has been committed if it is done with malice aforethought and from wickedness; if anyone does anything mistakenly or accidentally, the edict does not apply. 3. An exception is also made in the case of a slave who has acted in order to bring about his own death. He is considered to be a bad slave when he has done something to remove himself from this world, such as readying a noose or drinking medicine to poison himself or hurling himself from a height or doing anything else after which he hopes that death will result – since he will venture to do anything against another who has dared to do this to himself . . .

21.1.31. 21. Those who sell slaves ought to announce their race at the sale, as the race of a slave generally either encourages or warns off the buyer. So it is important that we know the race, since it is a presumption that some slaves are good, because they are of a respectable race, while others appear bad, because they belong to a less respectable race. But, if there is no such mention of race, an action will be allowed to the buyer and all interested parties for the seller to return the slave . . .

21.1.35. Generally in the case of diseased slaves, healthy slaves are returned as well if they cannot be separated without considerable trouble or without offending feelings of respectability. How about the case where the buyers would prefer to return the parents but retain the son, or vice versa? The same decision ought to be followed in the case of brothers and those linked together in a de facto relationship . . .

21.1.43. Paul, *On the Edict of the Curule Aediles*, Book 1. 1. A slave who takes refuge with a friend of his master to beg forgiveness is not a runaway. In fact, even if he intended not to return home if he did not gain assistance, he is not yet a runaway, because running away is a term not merely for a plan, but also involving a deed. 2. Someone who leaves his master on another's persuasion is a runaway, even if he would not have done that without the advice of the person who persuaded him. 3. If my slave who was in service to you in good faith ran away, whether knowing he was my property or not, he is a runaway, unless he did that with the intention of returning to me. 4. A slave is suicidal if he wants to kill himself because of his wickedness and evil character or because he has committed some crime, but not if he does that because he cannot endure some bodily pain . . .

21.1.51. Africanus, *On Inquiries*, Book 8. When a slave buys a diseased or faulty slave and his master is seeking return of goods or an action with regard to sale, he says that it is totally the knowledge of the slave, not the master, that must be considered. It makes no difference whether he has bought with his own funds or in his master's name, or with specific or general instructions from him, because it is in accord with the principle of good faith that, if the slave, through whom the transaction has taken place, has not been deceived, then his mistake in making the agreement should be suffered by his master. But, if the slave on his master's instructions buys a person whom his master knows to have faults, the seller will not be bound by the edict.

21.1.58. Paul, *Responses*, Book 5. 2. I bought a slave for twice his value who ran away, taking goods belonging to me with him. Later, when he was found and asked in front of respectable witnesses whether he had fled to the seller's house, he replied that he had done so. I raise the query as to whether the slave's reply should be accepted. Paul replied: if other evidence for previous running away exists, then the slave's reply should be credited.

21.1.65. Venuleius, *Actions*, Book 5. It is a fault of the mind rather than the body, if a slave continually wants to sit and watch the games or carefully look at paintings or if he is a liar or suffers from similar faults. 1. Whenever a disease is called serious, Cassius says that indicates one that is damaging; furthermore, damaging is understood as whatever is continuing, not something that is temporary. Any disease that occurs to someone after birth can appear as serious – serious meaning harmful. 2. A slave can be called either experienced or a newcomer. But Caelius says that 'experienced' should not be judged by length of service, but by type and case. So, someone bought from a market for new slaves and put in charge of a duty is immediately one of the experienced. 'Newcomer' is understood not by a lack of education, but in respect to the condition of slavery. So it would be irrelevant whether a slave knew Latin or not – for if he had been educated, he would, following that logic, be one of the experienced.

5.9 A public notice of a missing slave

Notices from Egypt together with Roman legal sources suggest that it was not uncommon for slaves to run away. Likewise, Paul, *To Philemon*, shows the apostle intervening on behalf of a slave who has taken refuge with him. Public notices offer detailed descriptions of missing slaves (in this case, including verging on the insulting) along with offers of rewards. It may be assumed that such slaves felt that they would readily fit in with the society around them and that they could easily pass as free or as working independent of their owner.

Oxyrhynchus Papyrus 51.3617
(Egypt, third century AD)

[A reward is available if anyone finds X] an Egyptian from the nome of Athreibites, who does not know Greek, [and is] tall, thin, bald-headed, with a scar on the left side of his head, of olive complexion, jaundiced, thinly bearded and having no hair at all on his chin, smooth-skinned, narrow-jawed, with a long nose, a weaver by trade, who walks around like he's somebody, rambling on in a high-pitched voice. He is about 32 years old. He is wearing a brightly coloured cloak.

5.10 Runaway slaves: the action for making slaves worse and recovery of slaves

Given the importance of slavery in Roman society, it was important that slaves be kept under control. This meant discouraging them from running away, preventing others from sheltering them, and penalising those who might exert a bad influence over others' slaves (hence the action for ruining a slave). The number of ways a slave might 'go bad' indicates how much independence slaves might have, especially in an urban environment, and their ability to use their *peculium* (see **5.29**). The search for an escapee involves questions of trespass onto other's property and needed to be carefully controlled. Measures also needed to be put in place to hold runaways and return them to their owners – even if they had been performing at the games (and so might have considerable public support). In particular, slaves who passed for free men were to be particularly severely dealt with as undermining the social boundaries between free and servile.

Digest 11.3–4

11.3.1. Ulpian, *On the Edict*, Book 23. The praetor says: 'If anyone with malice aforethought shall be declared to have sheltered another's slave, male or female, or persuaded them to do anything that would make him or her worse, I will give judgement against him at double the value of the cost of the damage.' 1. If someone buys a slave in good faith, he will not be held liable under this edict, but he cannot himself bring a case for ruining a slave, because it is of no importance to him that the slave not be ruined Surely, if anyone allowed this case, it would turn out that two people would be eligible to bring action for the ruining of a slave, which is nonsense. And we are of the opinion that neither can anyone, whom a free man serves in good faith [i.e. acting as a slave], bring this action. 2. Besides, when the praetor says 'sheltered', we take this to mean 'if he had received another's slave into his home' – specifically, 'sheltering' is to offer a slave refuge for the purpose of escaping either on one's land or in someone's place or building. 3. Besides, 'persuading' covers more than a slave being compelled and forced to obey you. Persuading is one of the intermediates [*ta mesa* – neither good or bad in themselves, but dependent on the result], for someone can persuade both by giving good advice and by giving bad advice. So the praetor adds 'with malice aforethought, to make him worse'. For no one commits an offence unless he so persuades a slave as to make him worse. So then anyone who encourages a slave to any wrongful action or intention appears to be covered by this edict. 4. But then will he be so liable if he encourages a reliable slave to commit wrong or indeed if he encourages a bad slave or shows a bad slave how to act? It is reasonable that if he shows a bad slave how to do wrong that he is liable. Indeed, even if a slave was absolutely likely to run away or commit a theft, if someone happened to be there to encourage this idea, he is liable, since one ought not to increase evil-doing by praising it. So whether you make a good servant bad or make a bad servant worse, you seem to have ruined him. 5. Also a man makes a slave worse who persuades him to commit an insult [*iniuria*] or a theft or to flee, or to incite another's slave to do wrong, or to tie up his money [*peculium*], or to turn himself into a lover [keeping an expensive mistress], to go awol [*erro*], or to become a devotee of the black arts or be too keen on the games or a rabble-rouser [*seditiosus*]. A man also makes a slave worse if he persuades an agent [*actor*] by words or inducement to embezzle from his master's accounts or even to falsify the accounts entrusted to him.

11.3.2. Paul, *On the Edict*, Book 19. Or makes him extravagant or insolent, or who persuades him to be the passive partner in a sexual relationship [*stuprum pateretur*].

11.3.3. With the addition of 'malice aforethought' the praetor rebukes the cunning of the person doing the persuading. But, if someone makes a slave worse without malice aforethought, he is not rebuked, and, if he acted in jest, he is not liable. 1. So the question is raised: is someone liable if he persuades another's slave to climb onto a roof or go down into a well and he obeys, goes up or down and falls and breaks a limb or something else or dies. If in fact he did this without malice, he is not liable; if with malice, he is liable.

11.3.4. Paul, *On the Edict*, Book 19. But it is more appropriate that he should be liable for a remedial action [*actio utilis*] under the *lex Aquilia*.

11.3.5. In addition, the term 'malice' must refer to the person who sheltered a slave, so that no one other than a person who shelters a slave with malice aforethought is liable. But if somone shelters a slave to guard him for his master or from kindness or pity or from any other respectable and legitimate reason, he will not be liable ...

11.3.15. Gaius, *On the Provincial Edict*, Book 6. The temperament of a slave is ruined if he is persuaded to despise his owner.

11.3.16. Alfenus Varus, *Digest*, Book 2. A master freed his slave steward and afterwards received the books from him. As these did not add up, he discovered that he had spent the money at the house of a certain 'lady' [*muliercula*]. The question arose as to whether he could bring a suit for ruining a slave against that lady when the slave was now free. I responded that he could, but he could also bring a suit for theft over the money that the slave had paid over to her.

11.3.17. Marcianus, *Rules*, Book 4. An action is available under the heading of 'ruining a slave' to a husband against his wife, even though the marriage is still in place, but, out of respect for marriage, it only allows for simple compensation.

11.4.1. Ulpian, *On the Edict*, Book 1. Whoever hides a runaway is a thief. 1. The senate decides that runaways should not be allowed into the runholds [*saltus*] or protected by the bailiffs or agents of the owners and set out a fine. However, there is an amnesty for their previous actions for those who within twenty days either hand over runaways to their masters or produce them before the magistrates. 2. Besides, this senatorial decree also gives the opportunity for a soldier or civilian to track down a runaway on the property of senators or civilians (the *lex Fabia* and the senatorial resolution passed when Modestus was consul had foreseen this requirement); if they want to search for runaways, they are to be given an introduction to the magistrates, and a fine of 100 solidi is fixed to be levied on the magistrates, if, after receiving the introduction, they do not assist in the search. But there is also the same penalty set for anyone who does not allow a search to be made at his place. There is also a general letter from the deified Marcus Aurelius and Commodus, in which it is stated that governors, magistrates, and soldiers on police duties [*milites stationarii*] ought to help a master in searching for runaways, both in order to return those they have found and to punish those with whom they are hiding if they are open to being charged. 3. Each individual who captures a runaway ought to produce him in public. 4. The magistrates are rightly admonished to guard them carefully, in case they escape. 5. Understand runaway as including anyone awol. Labeo, *On the Edict*, Book 1, writes that the child of a runaway female slave is not covered by the term 'runaway'. 6. They are understood as being 'produced in public' if they are handed over to the municipal magistrates or to the public officials. 7. 'Careful custody' also allows enchaining. 8. Besides, they are to be kept under guard until they can be brought before the Prefect of the Night-watch [*praefectus vigilum*] or to the governor. 8a. Their names, distinguishing marks, and the names of their owners should be related to the magistrates so they can more easily be recognised and apprehended (scars are included under the term 'marks'). It is the same under law whether this is published in writing in public or on a temple building.

11.4.2. Callistratus, *Investigations*, Book 6. Mere runaways are to be returned to their owners; but if they pretend to be free, they should be punished more severely [i.e. crucifixion or condemned to the beasts].

11.4.3. Ulpian, *On the Duties of the Proconsul*, Book 7. The deified Antoninus Pius said in a rescript that a person who wants to search for a runaway on another's property can approach the governor to give him his introduction. If the matter so requires, that same governor should also give him an assistant [*apparitor*] so that he is allowed to enter and search and fix the penalty owed by anyone who doesn't permit a search. Also the deified Marcus Aurelius in a speech delivered in the senate gave the right of entry onto the property of the emperor as well as that of senators and civilians to those wanting to search for runaways and to look for the tracks and lairs of those hiding them.

11.4.4. Paul, *Opinions*, Book 1. Harbour-masters and soldiers on police duty properly keep in prison those who have been apprehended. The municipal magistrates properly send on runaways who have been caught to the base of the provincial governor or the proconsul.

11.4.5. Tryphoninus, *Disputations*, Book 1. Even if a runaway slave has signed up for the arena, he cannot avoid the power of his master over himself by submitting to such a danger, even imperilling his life. For the deified Antoninus Pius said in a rescript that they should be returned to their masters without exception, whether caught before they had fought against wild animals or after the fight, since sometimes after embezzling money or having committed some major felony they might prefer to sign up for the arena to avoid an investigation or undergoing legitimate punishment. So they should be handed back to their owners.

5.11 A parody of the announcement of a runaway slave and offer of reward

In Apuleius' second-century novel of the hero turned into an ass, there is inserted the novella of the love of Venus' son, Cupid, for the mortal girl, Psyche. When Venus is informed of her son's affair, she looks to track down Psyche by using the messenger of the gods, Mercury, as town crier and treating her prospective daughter-in-law as a mere runaway slave.

Note the information on a well-known geographical location where information about Psyche is to be lodged (at the southern end of the circus, where the chariots would round the barrier that included the shrine of the goddess Murcia), and the specification of the actual reward to be received.

Apuleius, *Metamorphoses* 6.7–8

Then in triumph, accompanied by Mercury, Venus immediately left heaven. She spoke her words to him carefully, 'Arcadian brother, I'm sure you know that your sister Venus has never done anything without Mercury being there. And I'm sure, at any rate, that it hasn't passed you by how long it is now that I haven't been able to find my slave girl who's hiding away from me. So there's nothing for it except to use you as a herald to announce publicly the reward for hunting her down. So make sure you're quick about my orders and clearly proclaim the distinguishing marks that enable her to be recognised, in case anyone risks the charge of illegal concealment, thinking he can offer an excuse, using ignorance as his defence.' As she said this, she passed over to him a handbill containing Psyche's name and other details. After this, she immediately went home.

Mercury did not fail in his duty. Passing everywhere far and wide on the tongues of all the nations, he thus carried out his task of making the announcement as charged, 'If anyone can haul back from flight or show where the king's daughter, Venus' slave girl, who goes by the name of Psyche, is hiding, he should meet Mercury the town crier behind the Murcian markers. He will receive by way of reward from Venus herself seven delightful kisses and one deep and honeyed from the insertion of her enticing tongue.' When Mercury made his announcement like this, the desire for such a reward incited the interest of all mortals to compete for it.

5.12 Some slave collars

While runaway slaves might be deterred from repeating the offence by branding, it was also possible to attach metal collars (which appear to have also been used to indicate slaves subject to import taxes and who were marked out for other purposes too). These collars seem to have become particularly common in late antiquity, when the church frowned on disfiguration of slaves, but not their ownership. Simple collars (**5.12a**) indicate only that the slave is a runaway; more usefully, others indicate the owner and where to return the slave (cf. **5.11** above).

Inscriptiones Latinae Selectae 9454, 9455, *L'Année Epigraphique* 1946, no. 211, *Corpus Inscriptionum Latinarum* 15.7192 (a, c–d: Rome, b: N. Africa; fourth century AD)

(a) T.M.Q.F. [*tene me quia fugi*] = 'Grab me, I'm a runaway.'
(b) '[I'm an] adulterous whore; grab me, I'm a runaway from Bulla Regia.'
(c) 'Grab me, I'm a runaway, and recall me to my master the eminent senator [*vir clarrisimus*] Cethegus at the Libianan market in the third region [of Rome]'.
(d) 'Grab me, I'm a runaway, and recall me to Victor the acolyte at the church of Saint Clemens.'

5.13 A contracting service for the punishment of slaves

At Puteoli, the main port of Italy, close to Naples, the contract for removing dead bodies from the city, conducting public funerals, and dealing with punishment of slaves was carried out by a workforce attached to a site sacred to the goddess of death, Libitina. These workers were restricted in their movements inside the city, due to their pollution from handling dead bodies, but this made them very suitable for inflicting torture (cf. **5.15**) or capital punishment, either on behalf of the owners or at the command of the magistrates.

Note the specifications for the physical suitability of the workmen.

Inscription from Puteoli, 'On the Public Funeral Service', *L'Année Epigraphique* 1971, no.88

... The workmen assigned to the task should not live in the tower where the grove of Libitina is today. They should bathe after the first hour of night. They should not come to town except to pick up or dispose of the dead or to inflict punishment. If any of them come in, whenever he enters town or is in it, he should have a coloured cap on his head. None of them should be over 50 years old, or under 20. They should not have sores, be one-eyed, crippled in the hand, lame, blind, or tattooed. The employer should not have fewer than thirty-two workmen.

If someone wants to inflict punishment on a male or female slave privately, he will get the punishment inflicted according to his wishes. If he wants to affix the slave to a cross or gibbet, the contractor should provide planks, chains, and ropes for the whipmen and provide the whipmen. Whoever inflicts such punishment will owe the sum of 4 sesterces to each of the workmen who carry the gibbet, and to each of the whipmen, and also to the executioner.

Whenever the magistrates inflict punishment publicly and give the order, whenever the order goes out, the contractor must be ready to inflict the punishment, to set up the crosses, and he must offer for free nails, pitch, wax, tapers, and whatever are needed for dealing with the condemned. If he is ordered to drag off the body with a hook, a workman dressed in red will drag off the body, or several bodies, to the ringing of bells ...

5.14 The murder of the city prefect and punishment of his slaves

The killing of the city prefect, Pedanius, in AD 61 and its aftermath, the execution of his slave household, was spectacular because of both the rank of the victim and the sheer number of those punished (if the figure of 400 slaves was regular among senatorial households, this would suggest 200,000 slaves in the capital belonging to this group alone). Tacitus' account makes clear the widespread sympathy of the Roman population, many of whom would have known members of the *familia*.

The two possible explanations for the killing are instructive: the favourable view is that this is a case of self-purchased manumission gone wrong (see **5.29**); the negative case is that the slave saw the master as a rival in a love affair (cf. the case of the slave embezzler in *Digest* 11.3.16 – **5.10** above). Gaius Cassius' speech, with its upper-class fear of slave rebellion, bears careful comparison with the attitudes of the jurists (**5.15**). It is probably intended to be reactionary in tone, with jibes at slave behaviour. For instance, the reference to inherited wealth and ancestral property (playing on the ambiguity of the word *mancipium*, which could be either goods or a slave) highlights a slave's legal lack of ancestry. The suggestion that there must have been some forewarning plays on two slave stereotypes: that they were loquacious and that they would normally be cowardly (so a bold stance would serve as a warning).

Tacitus, *Annals* 14.42–5

Not long after this, the city prefect Pedanius Secundus was killed by one of his own slaves, either because he refused to free him after having agreed on a price for liberation, or because the slave was in love with a male prostitute and could not bear having his master as a rival. But, since by ancient custom the entire household that lived under the same roof should be led off for execution, the populace flocked to protect the large number of the innocent and things reached a state of revolution. The senate was besieged: inside they had the support of some who rejected this excessive harshness, while the majority thought that there was no need of change. One of the latter was Gaius Cassius who offered his opinion along these lines:

'Oftentimes, conscript fathers, I have been present in this group when new senatorial decrees contrary to the habits and laws of our ancestors have been called for. And I did not oppose them, not because I wasn't sure that on every matter better and finer arrangements had been made and that everything that was altered was being changed for the worse, but in case I seemed to be publicising my opinion from excessive liking for the ancient methods. At the same time I thought that whatever prestige I possessed should not be reduced by repeated expressions of opposition so that it would remain intact in case the state needed my advice. That has come about today: a man of consular rank has been killed in his own home by a slave ambush, which no one stopped or betrayed, even though the senatorial decree that used to threaten punishment on the whole household was not yet under threat. All right: pass a vote letting them off the punishment. But who will be kept safe by his status, when that won't help the city prefect? Who will be protected by his band of slaves, when four hundred didn't guard Pedanius Secundus? Who will be helped by the household that does not concern itself with the danger to us even when it has something to fear? How about this for a story that some are not ashamed to make up: "The murderer took revenge for a personal wrong, because he had reached an agreement about inherited riches or had been separated from some ancestral goods." We will be freely declaring that the master had been killed with just cause.

'Are you happy to find defences in the fact that the matter has been debated by philosophers? But, even if we were having to come to a decision for the first time now, do you think that a slave would have formed the intention of killing his master without threatening words escaping his mouth or giving some forewarning by his boldness? Let's imagine he hid his plan and readied his weapon surrounded by slaves who were in the dark. Surely he couldn't have got past the watchmen, opened the doors of the bedroom, brought in a light, and carried out the killing without anyone knowing. There are many indicators of a crime. If the slaves reveal these, we can live safely, a few among many, safe among the fearful, or at worst if we have to die, then go having taken our vengeance surrounded by the guilty. Our ancestors did not trust the attitude of their slaves, even when they have been born on the same farms or in the same houses and received the affection of their masters from birth. But after we have taken foreign tribes into our households, who have different customs and outlandish rites or none at all, it's impossible to control that rabble that has been routed; when a decimation occurs, even good soldiers will be drawn by lot. Every great warning has something unfair about it, because the value for the state is measured against the suffering of individuals.'

While no one dared to meet Cassius' opinion head-on, some dissenting voices countered with the number, age, sex, and the undoubted innocence of most of the slaves. Still the group that voted for punishment won the day. But the sentence could not be carried out, since the populace had banded together and was threatening to use rocks and burning torches. Finally the emperor castigated the populace in an edict and closed off under military guard the entire route along which the condemned were led off to punishment. Cingonius Varro had proposed that the freedmen also, who had been living under the same roof, should be banished from Italy. This was vetoed by the emperor so that ancient custom, which had not been reduced through pity, would not be made more harsh by vindictiveness.

5.15 The provisions of the senatorial resolution proposed by Silius (*Senatus Consultum Silianum*) and the Claudian resolution as to whose wills may not be opened

Because the consequences of the Silian resolution were so severe, there is considerable attention to which slaves would be liable to its provisions. Given the state of forensic science at Rome, it might be difficult to tell if a death was homicide or self-inflicted and whether the slaves could have intervened or, indeed, should have intervened in the case of suicide as a response to intolerable pain. The threat of torture (and worse) thus constantly hung over the slave household; yet owners felt this was necessary to protect their persons against their slaves, who they felt were constantly hostile to them. By making rights of inheritance subject to punishment of the household, the Romans also ensured that revenge was duly taken on behalf of a master, even if the heir had nothing to gain (and often much property to lose) by this. Note also the various types of family members who appear in the passage and their significance according to the application of the law (including possible conflict with the Julian Law on Adultery: 29.5.3).

Numerous aspects of Roman law appear in this passage. For instance, the *peculium castrense* is equivalent to money and goods held by a member of the armed forces and not subject to the power of the *paterfamilias*. Various forms of inheritance also appear: in 29.5.3.30 the *heres suus* (e.g. a son) could not refuse an inheritance as being under the control of the deceased. Then death will not extinguish these rights if they could not earlier be used because the legacy could not be accepted for fear of legal action under the Claudian resolution. Cf. 29.5.4, where an heir is created by the will if no other heir exists – which requires consideration as to whether the deceased's wife may still produce an heir. The *ius anulorum* referred to in 29.5.11 is application for equestrian status, i.e. for recognition as possessing the status of free birth, expunging all servile taint (*Digest* 40.10).

Digest 29.5

29.5.1. Ulpian, *On the Edict*, Book 50. Since no household can be safe unless the slaves are forced by the risk of execution to offer protection to their masters from both insiders and intruders, senatorial resolutions have been produced for holding a public investigation into the household of those killed. 1. Someone who has ownership, even if someone else enjoys the profit, is covered under the rubric 'master'. 2. Someone who possesses a slave in good faith [*bona fide*] is not covered by the term 'master', nor is someone who only enjoys the profit from the slave. 3. A slave given as security [*pignus*], as far as the debtor's killing is concerned, is in every respect regarded as if he had not been given as security. 4. Even those who have been left in a will on provision [of testamentary manumission] are covered by the rubric 'slaves', for they belong to the heir in the meantime, nor does a provision whose fulfilment means that they will cease to be the property of the heir bring it about that they do not appear as his in the meantime. The same is true of a slave to be manumitted on fulfilment of conditions [*statuliber*]. 5. But in the case of a slave whose freedom is owed pure and simple under a provision of the will [*fideicommissum*] there is a rescript of the deified Antoninus Pius to Iuventius Sabinus, in which it is pointed out that there should be no rush to torture someone who is owed under a provision of the will; it is preferable that he should not be punished for being under the same roof, unless he was an accomplice in the crime. 6. It must be ruled that under the rubric 'master' is included even someone who is joint master. 7. Also included under the rubric 'master' is the son of the head of the household and other children who are in his power – so the Silian resolution does not apply only to heads of household, but to their sons as well. 8. What will we declare then if the children are not under the power [of the head of household]? Marcellus in *Digest*, Book 12, expresses doubts; I think that it should be taken in a more general sense, so that it even applies to those children who are not under the power [of the head of household]. 9. In the case of one who has been given away for adoption, we don't think that the resolution applies, although it applies to an adopted son. 10. But the resolution does not apply in the case of a slain foster-child. 11. If a son or daughter has been killed there will not be an investigation into the mother's slaves. 12. If a head of household is captured by the enemy and his son is killed, Scaevola acutely states that there will be an investigation into the slaves [i.e. with torture to extract the truth] and punishment inflicted: he also recommends this after the death of a head of household, if the son was killed before he became his heir-in-power [*suus heres*]. 13. The same Scaevola says that the view must be resolutely defended that, when a son has been instituted as heir, an investigation must be held and punishment inflicted on those who were simply left as legacies or manumitted if the son was killed before he entered into the inheritance. For although, if he was alive, when he had become the heir they would not belong to him, still he says, when he died, in that their becoming legacies or manumission has been annulled, the resolution would come into force. 14. If a head of a household is murdered would there be an investigation into the son's slaves if he happened to have these as 'military' property [*peculium castrense*]? It is even more reasonable that there should be an investigation into the slaves of a son and that punishment be inflicted, even if the son was not in his father's power. 15. It is stated that, when a husband or wife has been killed, there is an investigation into their slaves, although the husband's slaves are not technically the wife's slaves, nor the wife's slaves the husband's. But, because the slave household is mixed together and there is one house, the senate decreed that the punishment should be inflicted as if on their personally owned slaves. 16. But the senate decreed that neither when a wife nor when a husband is killed should there be an investigation into the father-in-law's slaves – yet Marcellus in *Digest*, Book 12, rightly stated that the same should apply in the case of a father-in-law's slaves as in the case of the slaves of a husband. 17. Labeo writes that those who are murdered by violence or bloodshed, for instance someone who has had his throat cut, been strangled, pushed from a height, or struck by a rock, club, or stone or slain by any other weapon, come under the rubric of 'killed'. 18. But if anyone has been killed by poison, for instance, or anything else that normally kills secretly, the punishment for their death does not involve this resolution – the reason being that slaves must always be punished for not helping their master whenever they could assist him in the face of violence and have not brought assistance. But what could they do against those who secretly attacked them by poison or any other method? 19. Clearly, if the poison is inflicted by force, the resolution will come into effect. 20. So, wherever force is used that usually kills, it must be ruled that the resolution will come into effect. 21. So then, what about the case where the master is killed by poison, but not by act of violence – will the deed go unpunished? Not at all, for granted that the Silian resolution will not be in force and there will not be an investigation and punishment taken against those who were under the same roof, still if any of them were accomplices or partners in crime, they at least will be executed. The inheritance can be accepted and the will opened even before any investigation is held. 22. If someone commits suicide, the Silian resolution will not come into force, but his death is avenged – for instance, if someone does this in the sight of his slaves and they were able to prevent him from inflicting this frenzied behaviour on himself; but if they were unable to do so, they should be let off. 23. If someone commits suicide not from fear of facing criminal prosecution, but being tired of life or unable to endure the pain, the form of his death does not prevent his will being opened and read. 24. Likewise, it should be understood that, unless it is clear that some-one has been killed, there is no investigation into the slave household. So it ought to be plain that someone has been criminally murdered for the resolution to take effect. 25. Furthermore we understand by investigation not only torture, but every type of inquiry into and avenging of the death. 26. Moreover, this resolution absolutely punishes those who were under the same roof, but not those who were not under the same roof, but in the same area, except if they were accomplices. 27. Let us consider how 'under the same roof' is interpreted: when inside the same walls or, more extensively, in the same room or bedroom or the same house or the same park or the whole country estate. Sextus says that this judgement has often been made: whosoever were in a position to hear a shout are punished, as if being under the same roof, even though some have louder voices and others weaker ones and not everyone can be heard everywhere. 28. Besides, the deified Hadrian appears also to have produced a rescript in these words: 'Whenever slaves can bring help to their masters, they ought not to prefer their own safety to that of their masters. Thus a slave girl, who was in the same room as her mistress, could have helped in the affair, if not by her physical effort but certainly by calling out loud, so those who were in the household or nearby would hear her. That is clear from the very fact she said that the murderer threatened to kill her if she called out. So she deserves to suffer the ultimate penalty if only so that other slaves may not think that they should each worry about themselves in the face of danger to their master.' 29. This rescript covers a great deal: he does not spare someone who was in the same room; he does not spare someone who was afraid of being killed; and the fact that he shows that slaves ought to help their masters if only by shouting. 30. If anyone visiting at his country estate is killed, it is beyond unfair, if he happens to have a widespread estate, to have an investigation into all the slaves who were in that area and inflict punishment. It is enough to have an investigation into those who were with the man who is said to have been killed and who seem to fall under suspicion of the crime or of knowledge of it. 31. When a master is killed on a journey, punishment should be inflicted on those who were with him or who fled, after being with him. But if there was no one with the master when he was killed, those senatorial resolutions are not valid. 32. A slave boy or slave girl who has not yet reached puberty [*impubes servus*, generally 14 for a male, *vel ancilla nondum viripotens*, 12 is the minimum age for a female to marry] are not in the same position, since their age deserves to be excused. 33. However, there is the question whether we should spare an underage slave [*impubes*] only from punishment or in fact from the investigation as well. It seems preferable that no investigation should be held – this custom is followed elsewhere as well, that the underage are not tortured: they are usually just frightened or beaten by a leather strap or a cane. 34. Furthermore, slaves are acquitted who have come to help without malice aforethought [*sine dolo malo*]: for if someone pretends he is helping or has offered it to win credit, this device will not help him. 35. It seems that not only the person who saves his master has offered help – that is, the person who was able to offer help with the result that the master is saved – but also he who did whatever he could, although the master was slain. To wit: if anyone shouts out that the slaves should come together to help or strikes fear into the attackers or if someone assembles a group of slaves or places his body in the way or in some other way brings help through his body. 36. But it is not always the case that someone who shouts appears to have offered help – what about the case where he could physically repel the danger from his master, but he chose to make a useless shout? Certainly he will have to be punished. 37. What if the slaves are wounded when they are protecting their master? It must be ruled that they ought to be spared unless they have inflicted those wounds on themselves so that they won't be punished, or they have suffered such wounds that they could have brought assistance all the same, if they wanted to. 38. If a master has lived on, mortally wounded, and not complained about any of his slaves, even though they were under the same roof, they will be spared all the same.

29.5.2.   Callistratus, *On Judicial Investigations*, Book 5. The deified Marcus Commodus [Marcus Aurelius] sent a rescript to Piso in these words: 'Since it has been established by you, my dearest Piso, that Iulius Donatus was wounded after he had been alarmed by the arrival of brigands and fled his villa and then in his will excused the efforts of his slaves, neither a feeling of duty [to a master] with respect to slaves nor the concern of the heir should bring it about that those whom the master himself has acquitted should be summoned to punishment.'

29.5.3.   Ulpian, *On the Edict*, Book 50. If someone suffering from a severe illness could not have brought assistance to his master, he should be protected. 1. If someone while dying has said that a violent death has been inflicted on him by a slave, it must be stated that a master should not be believed, if he said this while dying, unless it can also be proven. 2. If a husband kills his wife sleeping with him at night in the bedroom or a wife her husband, the slaves will be free from the punishment set by the senatorial resolution. But, if they heard something and did not bring assistance, they will need to be punished, not only if they were the property of the wife, but also if they belonged to the master. 3. If, however, a husband were to kill his wife, having caught her in adultery, because he is excused, it must be ruled that not only the slaves of the husband, but also those of the wife must be freed from this resolution, as long as they did not resist the master carrying out his legal right of revenge. 4. If when all his masters underwent an attack, a slave brought assistance to one, should he be acquitted or in fact should he be punished because he didn't bring it to them all? It is more reasonable that, if indeed he could bring assistance to all, although he brought assistance to some of them, he should suffer punishment. If indeed he couldn't assist them all, he should be acquitted because he brought assistance to some. For it is very harsh to rule that, if, when he couldn't bring help to two, he chose to help one of them, he had committed a crime. 5. So too if a woman's slave was more of a help to his mistress's husband than to his mistress or vice versa, it should be ruled that he ought to be acquitted. 6. Judicial relief is given to those who at the time when their master or mistress was killed

181

were so shut up without malice aforethought that they could not break out to help or to apprehend those who did the killing. It makes no difference by whom they were shut up and held back – but on such condition, however, that they had not intentionally wanted to be locked in so they could not render assistance. We ought to accept as shut in also those who are chained up, on such condition, however, that they could not break their chains in any way and be of assistance. 7. Those are also excused who are worn down by old age. 8. A deaf slave must also be included among the feeble or among those who are not under the same roof, but while they hear nothing because of the distance, he hears nothing because of his illness. 9. A blind slave also deserves to earn an acquittal. 10. We make a similar exception for a dumb slave, but only in the case where only help by shouting was available. 11. There is no doubt at all that an exception is made for the insane. 12. If anyone accepts or hides knowingly and with malice aforethought any slave, male or female, who was guilty of the crime from that slave household, they are in the position of being guilty of the crime as under the law that was passed about murderers [*sicarii*]. 13. If a slave is owed under an agreement and he has informed on the murder of his master and is manu-mitted as a reward for this, an action on the basis of an agreement is not granted to the man who accepted the agreement – the reason is that he also would not be granted an action if he had suffered punishment. But if he wasn't under the same roof, an action on the basis of agreement regarding the value of the slave will be available to the creditor. 14. Besides, there is a question as to whether he alone seems to have given evidence or informed who of his own accord steps forward to do this, or whether the person who turns the charge back on another when he himself is accused also does this. It is preferable to regard he who steps forward to make an accusation of his own accord as [alone] worthy of this reward. 15. Those also who could not otherwise gain freedom – for instance, someone who is excepted by law from being manumitted – are able to gain freedom because of the fact that this is a communal advantage. 16. Punishment must be inflicted on these slaves also who have been liberated by will, as if they were still slaves. 17. In the case of those who have fled before the will of the murdered master or mistress is opened and afterwards, when the will is opened, are found to be listed as freed, an investigation must be held just as in the case of slaves and punishment inflicted. The reason is that it is most reasonable that the generosity of masters should not stand in the way of avenging them – the greater the generosity one has experienced, the greater the punishment he will deserve for his crime. 18. It is forbidden by the edict that anyone knowingly and with malice aforethought should have opened, read, and copied whatever in the way of a will has been left behind by someone who is said to have been killed, before an investigation of his slave household is held following the senatorial resolution and the guilty are punished. 19. Moreover, here a person appears to have opened a will, who opens it in the normal sense, whether the will has been sealed or not, but only closed in the normal sense. 20. We ought to take it that we are prohibited from opening the will either openly in public or in secret, as every opening is forbidden. 21. If anyone opens a will not knowing that the deceased had been killed, he will not be subject to this edict. 22. And if he opens it knowingly, but without malicious intention, he will equally not be subject, as, for example, he opens if through ignorance or lack of education unaware of the praetor's edict and the resolution of the senate. 23. If someone has not opened the tablets in the normal sense, but only cut the cord around it, he will be let off, because someone who hasn't opened the tablets lacks malicious intention. 24. However, if the whole will is not opened, but only part of it, it must be ruled that he who has opened it is subject to the edict; for it makes little difference whether the whole or part is opened. 25. If someone opened the codicils but did not open the will, he is subject to the edict, for the codicils as well are part of the general form of will. 26. Likewise, whether what is opened is legally valid or not, still the edict is in operation. 27. The same method is followed as well in matters pertaining to the case of substitution, if a minor, male or female, under care of a guardian [*pupillus pupillave*] is said to have been killed. 28. If one person opens the will, another reads it, and another copies it, all who have done any of these things will be liable under the edict. 29. This edict applies to an inheritance not only from a will, but also from intestate inheritance: no one should accept or seek possession of goods because an investigation is held into the slave household, in case the heir for his own gain covers up the household's crime. 30. Scaevola expresses it elegantly: in order that someone can leave legal rights for action [*actiones utiles*] to his automatic heir [*heres suus*], if the heir happens to have died before taking up the inheritance, it must be investigated whether he did not take up the inheritance because he was deterred by the senatorial decree and edict. 31. If the heirs are told to satisfy a condition within a fixed number of days from the day of death and do not carry this out because they were unaware of the terms, if the ignorance came about from the fact that the will could not be opened from fear of the senatorial resolution, they are assisted in satisfying the condition. 32. If there is also something else preventing the acceptance of an inheritance or opening the will, as well as the senatorial resolution, the fact that the senatorial resolution prevents opening the will has no force if there was some other impediment: for instance, if the wife of the murdered man was pregnant or even thought to be so and so the appointed heir [*heres institutus*] could not accept the inheritance.

29.5.4. Papinian, *Responses*, Book 6. A man who had instituted his children born after the will was made [*postumi*] as heirs; when children were not born, wrote in his wife as heir in the second degree. When he was reported to have been killed by his slave household, his wife had passed away. The woman's heirs asked to be given right to bring suit [*actiones*] according to imperial precedent [*constitutio*]. I gave the response that they should only be heard if the wife, who it was agreed was not carrying a child in her womb, could not have accepted the inheritance because of the senatorial resolution. Otherwise, if she had died pregnant, there would have been no possibility of complaining that there had been a loss of rights [*iniuria*].

29.5.5. Ulpian, *On the Edict*, Book 50. I think that slaves manumitted in the will in order to become heirs [*heredes necessarii*] are covered by the edict, if they get involved in the inheritance. 1. The praetor does not allow application for possession of goods; but I think this edict pertains to all cases of possession of goods. 2. The goods are not confiscated unless it is agreed that the head of the household has been killed and the heir has taken up his inheritance before an investigation of the slave household has been carried out and punishment meted out. 3. Where someone has been killed by negligence or the treachery of doctors, an inheritance can be accepted, but the avenging of his death is incumbent on the heir.

29.5.6. Paul, *On the Edict*, Book 46. Even if the assassin is clear, an investigation must be held all the same to find the instigator of the killing. For sure the assassin himself will be particularly interrogated, even if others are also punished. 1. Although at other times slaves are not tortured when it involves the risk of capital punishment to their owners, still there will rightly be an investigation here, even if they accuse the heir, be he outside the deceased's authority [*heres extraneus*] or one of those subject to his authority [*heres suus*]. 2. If a joint master does not make an appearance, an investigation into his fate should be made through the slaves that are jointly owned. It is better that they be tortured for the rescue or avenging of a master who doesn't appear than to risk the life of one who is present. 3. If a master is attacked but not killed, the resolution of the senate does not apply, since he can punish his own household.

29.5.7. Paul, *On the Silian Resolution*, Book 1. He will also have special assistance against his freedmen.

29.5.8. Paul, *On the Edict*, Book 46. The Pisonian resolution stipulates that, if a slave liable to be punished is sold, when punishment has been inflicted on him, the vendor should pay back the sale price, so that the senate does not appear to have wronged the buyer. 1. If the son of the head of the household, who has made a will bequeathing his 'military' property, is killed, the view must be absolutely defended, that in cases where the goods of the head of the household revert to the treasury, in these cases also his property goes to the treasury, rather than to his heirs who have erred in accepting the property or the like and have not avenged him.

29.5.9. Gaius, *On the Provincial Edict*, Book 17. Since a dead person's goods that cannot be inherited [*bona caduca*] because his death has been unavenged are assigned to the treasury, an action for legacies is permitted against the treasury. In addition, manumission is granted – of course, of those slaves who are exempt from the senatorial resolution.

29.5.10. Paul, *On the Silian Resolution*, Book 1. If a son who has been disinherited is killed before the inheritance from his father is accepted [namely, by someone else], the matter will be considered according to the result – if the inheritance had been accepted, the slaves would seem to have belonged to someone else; but if the will is null and void, everything is dealt with just as if he [the son] had been master because they [the slaves] would have been his if he had been alive. 1. Under the deified Trajan an imperial enactment [*constitutio*] determined that there will be an investigation into the freedmen whom the master had freed while living.

29.5.11. Tryphonius, *Disputations*, Book 2. Likewise, there will be an investigation into those as well, who had applied for equestrian status [*ius anulorum*].

29.5.12. Paul, *On the Silian Resolution*, Book 1. If a slave is left in a will by a testator who is killed and the praetor deciders that he is to be free as a reward, the decision must be given that nothing prevents his freedom.

29.5.13. Venuleius Saturninus, *On Criminal Actions*, Book 2. When investigating a will that has been opened, contrary to the senatorial resolution, of someone who is said to have been killed by his slave household, five years is the time permitted for the investigation by the senatorial resolution passed in the consulship of Taurus and Lepidus [AD 11]. This, however, applies to those outside the household. For one is always allowed by the same senatorial resolution to bring an accusation against those who can suffer the penalty for parricide.

29.5.14. Maecianus, *On Criminal Actions*, Book 11. Underage [*impuberes*] slaves are excluded from the Silian resolution. Still Trebius Germanus as governor ordered an underage slave to be executed and quite reasonably, all the same. For that slave was not far off the age of puberty and was sleeping at the feet of his master and did not reveal his murder afterwards. While it was accepted that he could not have brought him help, still it was certain that he assisted by his silence afterwards; in addition, he believed that only those underage slaves were spared by the senatorial decree who were simply under the same roof. But those who were accomplices or partners in the crime and were of such age, that, although they had not reached puberty, they could form a judgement on the matter, ought not to be spared in the case of a master's murder any more than in any other case.

29.5.15. Marcianus, *On Informers*, Book 1. If the heir in the next degree has avenged the death of a testator, should the inheritance be transferred from the heir in the previous degree to him? Papinian says that this is not the case, for the punishment of the latter ought not to be a reward for the former. 1. When there was a legacy to an heir instituted as having a share [in the estate] and he had failed his duty in avenging the death, the deified Severus and Antoninus stated in a rescript that both his share in the inheritance and his legacy should be taken away from him. 2. Besides, the goods are taken away from heirs who have neglected their duty in avenging the death of the deceased, both in the case of a will and in the case of intestacy. Perhaps this occurs even if he happens to be virtually a patron, although patrons are accepted [as heirs] in their own right.

29.5.16. Marcellus, *Digest*, Book 12. After a master had been killed by his household, a jointly owned slave revealed his murder. Because of the inclination to manumit, he indeed ought to be freed, but the [master's] partner ought to obtain the share of the slave's value that belongs to him.

29.5.17. Modestinus, *Rules*, Book 8. First a slave household should be tortured to give evidence against one another and, if there is a confession, then there should be an investigation as to on whose orders the crime was committed.

29.5.18. Modestinus, *Rules*, Book 9. It is possible both to bring suit that a will was not dutiful [*inofficiosum testamentum*] and to avenge the death of the deceased, and that is Paul's opinion.

29.5.19. Modestinus, *Encyclopaedia*, Book 8. When a master is being killed, the slave household ought to bring him assistance both by action, shouting, and by placing their own bodies in the way. But if someone does not help, when he could, he will rightly be executed.

29.5.20. Papinian, *Replies*, Book 2. An heir, who is bringing a charge of poisoning, is not normally prohibited from dealing with urgent affairs of the inheritance so long as the evidence for proving his case is not harmed.

29.5.21. Papinian, *Replies*, Book 6. The time allowed for asking for a grant of possession [*bonorum possessio*] is not extended because of an inquiry into poisoning, since even when that charge is adjourned one can rightly ask for the grant. The senate decided differently in the case where a master is said to have been murdered by his household, apparently because of the slaves, whose manumission must be put aside for the sake of carrying out the inquiry. 1. A granddaughter, who was asking for a grant of possession of her grandmother's property, had not sought revenge for her death, although she knew she had been murdered. The decision was that a trust [*fideicommissum*], which the grandmother owed the granddaughter in the terms of someone else's will, should not be removed when the property was confiscated to the treasury, on the grounds that the heir's treachery had been punished. If, however, the woman lost the right to gain the property from an oversight, it is reasonable to think that the trust should be withheld because her right to claim what she is owed has been restored. 2. When from the connivance of a judge defendants are acquitted of the charge of committing murder, it appears that it is not appropriate to remove the inheritance from the heirs, who had earnestly fulfilled their necessary duty, even though they had not appealed the case.

29.5.22.   Paul, *Replies*, Book 16. When Joe Bloggs [literally, Gaius Seius] was ill, he complained that he had been poisoned by his slave and then died. His heir, Jane Doe [literally, Lucia Titia], his sister, neglected to follow up this charge of murder and she herself died ten years later. Someone came forward to denounce Joe Bloggs' property [as belonging to the treasury]. My query is: is the charge rendered null and void by the death of Jane Doe? Paul's opinion is that the case in question, since it involves money matters, does not seem to be rendered null and void by the death of an ungrateful heir.

29.5.23.   Maecianus, *Trusts*, Book 13. If the tablets of a will were opened before it became clear that the testator had been killed, then it was clear that this crime had occurred. I think that, after the case has been investigated, the appointed heir must be forced to accept the inheritance, which he said was suspect, and to submit his accounts under the Trebellian resolution.

29.5.24.   Ulpian, *On the Edict*, Book 50. If anyone under compulsion accepts a suspect inheritance, he will not fall under the Edict.

29.5.25.   Gaius, *On the Provincial Edict*, Book 17. Under the Cornelian law provision is made for the rewarding of an accuser, who hunts down and denounces those slaves who have fled from a household before an investigation is held. For each slave whose conviction he obtains, he should receive five gold pieces from the property of the murdered man or, if that amount cannot be provided from there, from the public treasury. This reward is given to the accuser not for every slave who was under the same roof or in the same place, but for those alone who committed the killing. 1. In addition, it is provided that those who have fled before an investigation has been held and are found to be inscribed as free men once the will has been opened should be tried under the homicide law [*lex de sicariis*] – they should plead their case in chains and, if convicted, be punished like slaves, and ten gold pieces should be given from the property of the condemned as a reward to the successful prosecutor. 2. Under this Edict, an action lies against a person who is said to have opened the tablets of a will contrary to the praetor's Edict or is said to have done anything else [illegal]. As is apparent from what has previously been said, there are numerous activities that result in punishment under the Edict. It is clear that this is an action open to everyone, whose penalty could be as much as a hundred gold pieces from the goods of the condemned. From this sum the praetor promises that he will give as a reward half to the person by whose effort the [guilty party] was convicted, and will confiscate the other half to the public treasury.

29.5.26.   Scaevola, *Digest*, Book 34. Joe Bloggs owed John Doe a trust from the will of his cousin; John Doe received this from Bloggs' heirs. The question raised is: when Joe Bloggs' heirs had not avenged his death, can Doe nevertheless lodge an accusation against those heirs as unworthy, because of the fact that they did not avenge his death, and nothing prevent him from receiving the trust from them in accordance with the cousin's will? He replied that nothing had been brought up to prevent him doing this.

29.5.27.   Callistratus, *On the Rights of the Treasury*, Book 1. If a will has been opened by several heirs, some of whom were unwilling or unaware of what was happening, those who are not to blame do not lose their share.

5.16 How to design a farm building for maximum efficiency from the workers

The Spaniard Columella's account of recommended farming practices, written in the time of Nero, provides an insight into upper-class attitudes to agriculture. The passage below recommends the siting of a typical villa to offer best comforts for the owner (this can be compared with Pliny the Younger's descriptions of his villas in his letters), but also that the work quarters be made the most practical. It is noticeable that the prescription for the slave's quarters is immediately followed by those for the (other) domestic animals and a concern that the steward be able to easily supervise the work and workers on the estate.

Note the description of the quarters of the chained slaves, the *ergastulum*, which are clearly unpleasant for the inhabitants, but healthy enough not to reduce their labour output.

Columella, *On Agriculture* 1.6

The nature and number of the parts should fit in with the overall farmstead and be divided into three types: the living quarters [*urbana*], the work quarters [*rustica*], and the storage quarters [*fructuaria*]. The living quarters should as well be divided into winter and summer quarters, with the winter sleeping quarters facing the midwinter solstice rising sun and the dining area facing the midday sun at the equinox. The summer sleeping quarters should face the equinoctial midday sun, but the dining area should face the summer solstice rising sun. The baths should face the setting summer sun so they are lit from after noon to sunset. Porticoes should be aligned with the midday sun of the solstice so they receive the maximum sunlight in winter and the least possible amount in summer. A kitchen should be built in the work quarters of such size and height that the roof will escape the risk of fire and the slaves can hang around in it comfortably at any time of the year. For the slaves who circulate freely, their quarters are best facing the equinoctial midday sun; for the chained slaves there should be work quarters underground that will be quite healthy for the largest number to be expected and that should have narrow windows raised far enough from the ground that they cannot be reached by hands. The stables for the animals should not suffer from heat or cold: for the domestic herd of cattle there should be a summer and a winter shed; for the other animals that need to be inside the estate there should be quarters that are partially roofed and partially out in the open surrounded by high walls so that they can rest there in the first area in winter and in the latter area in summer, untroubled by attacks from wild animals. But these large stables should be so designed that water should not flow into them and that any waste that occurs there should flow away immediately in case the walls are undermined and the hooves of the animals rot. The sheds for the oxen should be 10 or at minimum 9 feet wide – this size will give ready opportunity for the oxen to undergo the yoke and for the ox-keeper to get around them. The steward's quarters should be next to the entrance so that he can see who is entering and leaving; and the agent's quarters should be above the entrance for the same reason – besides, he should keep an eye on the steward from nearby and the storehouse should be near both. All the farm tools should be collected here and inside it there should be an enclosed place for the safeguarding of iron implements. The rooms of the cowherds and shepherds should be near their herds so that they can easily go out to look after them. All should, however, live as close as possible to one another so that the steward's attentiveness is not reduced by making his rounds about widely separated places and so that they should all be witnesses of each other's hard work or laziness.

5.17 A successful freed family

This inscription honouring the ex-imperial slave, Secundus (who has adopted the first two names from his owner, the emperor, on manumission), suggests that he has married another member of the imperial household and that the pair had obtained considerable wealth to afford to erect a tomb for them both and their own slaves and freedmen and descendants.

Note the message of hedonism, an appropriate reminder to 'Seize the day', given that death awaits.

Inscriptiones Latinae Selectae 8157
(Rome, Julio-Claudian period)

To the spirit of Tiberius Claudius Secundus, who lived for 52 years. Here he has everything with him. Baths, wine, and sex wreck our bodies, but baths, wine, and sex make life worth living. Merope, the freedwoman of Caesar, built this tomb for her dear companion, herself, her household, and their descendants.

5.18 Pliny's treatment of his slaves

It is important to remember that most slaves would not have been as successful as Secundus (cf. above **5.17**). Many would not have lived long enough to be freed, as is shown by Pliny the Younger's account of deaths among his household. His solution appears designed to improve the morale of his workers, by manumission just before their deaths (which would have cost him nothing) and by allowing the slaves to transfer their *peculium* within the household (again, not reducing the owner's overall wealth). The comment that slaves saw the household as a virtual homeland owes something to ancient philosophical theory, but is also likely to be true, given the loss of any other country on enslavement and the social bonds within the *familia*.

Pliny, *Letters* 8.16

I'm worn out by the illnesses of my slaves – and deaths as well, including those of some who were quite young. There are two forms of consolation that hardly match such grief, but are consolations nonetheless: one is the ease of freeing slaves (it appears to me that I have not lost them totally prematurely if I have lost them now that they are free); the other that I allow my slaves also to make virtual wills and that I respect them as if they were legal provisions. They can leave legacies and ask that their wishes be carried out as they think right, while I obey as if under injunction. They can share out property, make gifts, and leave inheritances, so long as they stay within the household – for a slave the household is practically his state and a country of sorts. But, although I gain some peace from these consolations, I am weakened and broken in spirit by that same human kindness that led me to allow this very thing. Still I would not like to become more thick-skinned because of that. I am aware that others call events of this sort nothing other than a loss, and so think they are great and wise men. I don't know whether they are great and wise, but they are not men. A man should feel that he is affected by grief, to hold fast all the same and accept consolation, not have no need for it.

5.19 Manumission on the verge of death

This funerary inscription illustrates the practice recommended by Pliny above (**5.18**) and also (as with Pliny too) commemorates the mourning of the slaves' owner.

L'Année Epigraphique 1995 no. 665
(Milan, third–fourth century AD)

To the sacred spirits. I erected this while alive: I, L. Trebius Divus, dedicate this to Septicia Maura, my dearest wife, who lived with me 38 years, 5 months, and 14 days.

Here, where I have packed in my freedmen and they have gone to their destiny before me as my loss, here they lie taken by an undeserved death. Here lie four young slaves manumitted on the one day, with the wife dear to me: Lucius Trebius Chyseros, who lived 18 years, 5 months, 8 days; Benigna, who lived 5 years, 22 days; Felicitas, who lived 4 years, 2 months, 11 days; Postumia who lived 2 years, 8 days. Oh miserable me to have provided for so many cruel funerals. I weep night and day. After this, I cannot provide more for my household for my part apart from an eternal home. Oh what pain that forces a patron's heart to endure this. After this, my wife Flamia has been added. She is on the left; the freedmen are all on the same level on the right, below my first loyal wife. Friends who read this: now I foresee that day coming on which that cruel ruler will appear who will transport me to them.

5.20 A slave is given freedom and specified legacies in a will

Particularly common is the manumission of slaves after the death of the owner, since this involves no cost except to the heir. Note the reference that Psenamounis is literate – this allows a claim that he can write his own will without external assistance.

Papiri greci e latini (*PSI*) 9.1040 (probably AD 216/7)

The will of Psenamounis Harpocrates, son of Harpocrates, mother Thatres from the city of Oxyrhynchus. Literate.

Psenamounis makes his son Aurelius Theodorus, the child of his now-deceased wife Diogenis from the same city, his heir.

Immediately on his death he frees Damais his slave girl, who is approximately 13 years old and releases her from her obligations to her patron and grants her all her *peculium*. He also bequeaths to her control a quarter of the servant's accommodation that he possesses in the same city in the quarter of the theatre of Plataea along with all the household items and at the same time a bed with a mattress on top. This is on condition that she may not rent this out, except to the extent that she may rent it to my brother if she wishes.

5.21 The rules for manumission

The introductory legal handbook attributed to Gaius, apparently written in the late second century AD, offers a basic outline of the rules for freeing slaves. Some slaves (those assimilated to the previous 'surrendered foreigners') might never become Roman citizens; others, freed without undergoing all the legal requirements, will become 'Latins' (i.e. they will be in the position of earlier Roman colonists who lacked full citizen rights). Those in this last group are identifiable by not having the three names that full citizens possess (cf. **5.2** above). They can, however, become full citizens by marrying and having a child or by performing various public services.

Note the limitations placed by the emperor Augustus (via the *lex Fufia Caninia*) on the number of slaves who might be manumitted under a will. Under the *lex Aelia Sentia*, slaves under 30 could not be manumitted without just cause, which would also limit the number of slaves who might be freed. But just cause includes marriage and the need to use an ex-slave as an agent (slaves, having no legal personality, could not normally create legal contracts on their masters' behalf) (1.19).

Also observe the relative ease of manumission before a magistrate, since this might occur simply in passing. This is further discussed in **5.23** below.

If the *Rules for the Undertakers of Puteoli* (**5.13**) paint a lurid picture of the punishment of slaves, the restrictions set out in Gaius 1.53 below suggest that mindless violence by owners against their slaves was not acceptable.

Gaius, *Institutes* 1.9–54

9. And indeed this is the basic division of the law of persons, that all men are either free or slaves. 10. Again, of free persons, some are freeborn, others freedmen. 11. Freeborn are those who were born free; freedmen are those who were manumitted from legitimate slavery. 12. Again, there are three types of freedmen: they are either classified as Roman citizens, Latins, or 'surrendered foreigners'. We will investigate each, but let's begin with the 'surrendered foreigners'.

13. Under the *lex Aelia Sentia*, slaves who have been chained by their masters as a punishment, or who have been branded, or who have been questioned under torture because of some felony and have been found guilty

192

of that felony, or who have been handed over to fight as gladiators or with the beasts and have been placed in a gladiatorial school or prison, and have afterwards been manumitted by that same or a different master, when freed are of the same status as 'surrendered foreigners'. 14. We call 'surrendered foreigners' [*peregrini dediticii*] those who previously had taken up arms and fought against the Roman people, then were defeated and surrendered. 15. So slaves who have undergone this disgrace, in whatever way and at whatever age they are manumitted, even if their masters had absolute rights over them, will never be said to become Roman citizens or Latins, but will be understood to be totally fixed in the ranks of the surrendered. 16. If in fact a slave is in no such state of dishonour, we will say that when he is manumitted he becomes either a Roman citizen or a Latin. 17. For if these three requirements are met in his person – that he is over 30 years old and he is freed under the Roman legal right of his master and by a legitimate and legal form of manumission, he becomes a Roman citizen. But if in fact any of these is lacking, he will be a Latin.

18. That there is a requirement about the age of a slave was brought in by the *lex Aelia Sentia*. For that law wants slaves under 30 years old who are manumitted not to become Roman citizens unless they are freed by a ceremonial assertion of liberty [*vindicta*] after a legitimate claim for manumission has been accepted by an advisory council. 19. A legitimate cause of manumission is, for instance, if someone manumits before the advisory council [*consilium*] a son or daughter or natural brother or sister or foster-child or pedagogue or a slave in order to have an agent [to represent him] or a female slave to marry her. 20. They use as a council at Rome five senators and five Roman knights of adult age; in the provinces, however, they use twenty Roman citizen assessors [*recuperatores*]. That happens [in the provinces] on the last day of the assizes; but at Rome slaves are manumitted before the council on fixed days. 21. But slaves over 30 years old are regularly manumitted at any time and are even manumitted in passing – for instance, when the praetor or governor goes to the baths or the theatre. In addition, a slave freed under 30 years old can be a Roman citizen if he has been left free and made his heir by his master, who is bankrupt ...

22. [Otherwise?] they are called Junian Latins: Latins, because they are assimilated to the Latins in the colonies; Junian, because they have gained freedom under the Junian law, although they appeared to be slaves at one time. 23. Still the Junian law does not permit them to make a will or accept an inheritance from someone else's will or to serve as guardians for an inheritance. 24. Given that we said that they cannot inherit under a will, we mean this: we are saying that they cannot inherit anything under the strict definition of inheritance or bequest, but they can accept a bequest through a trust. 25. But those who are counted as surrendered [*dediticii*]

cannot in any way inherit under a will, no more than any foreigner. Indeed they cannot make a will either, according to the preferable opinion. 26. So the worst form of freedom is that of those who are numbered among the surrendered. For no law or senatorial resolution or imperial legislation can give them a way in to Roman citizenship. 27. Indeed, in addition at Rome they are prohibited from staying within the hundredth milestone of the city of Rome. If they contravene this, it is ordered that they and their goods be sold on the terms that they should not be slaves in the city of Rome or within the hundredth milestone of the city of Rome and they never be freed. If they were freed, it is ordered that they be slaves of the Roman people. These things are covered in this way by the *lex Aelia Sentia*.

28. Latins become Roman citizens in numerous ways. 29. Straightaway under the *lex Aelia Sentia* those under 30 years old who have been freed and become Latins, if they marry Roman citizens or colonial Latins or women of their own status and that has been witnessed by no fewer than seven adult Roman citizens, and if they have had a son, when the son starts to be a year old, are granted the right under that law to approach the praetor or the provincial governor in the provinces and offer proof that in accord with the *lex Aelia Sentia* they have married a wife and have from her a son who is a year old. If the official, before whom the claim is being confirmed, declares this to be so, then the Latin and his wife, if she is of the same status, and his son, if he is of the same status also, are declared to be Roman citizens. 30. We have added [the clause] on the nature of the son, 'if he also is of the same status', because if the wife of a Latin is a Roman citizen, her offspring, according to the recent senatorial resolution, passed with Hadrian's support, is born a Roman citizen. 31. Even though only those freed under the age of 30 and who have become Latins had this right to obtain Roman citizenship, afterwards this right was extended to those over 30 who had become Latins, by a senatorial resolution passed when Pegasus and Pusio were consuls [early 70s AD]. 32. Besides, even if a Latin dies before he can prove his claim of having a 1-year-old child, the mother can offer proof of his claim and so will herself become a Roman citizen, if she was a Latin . . . Even if the son himself was a Roman citizen, because he was the child of a Roman mother, still she ought to prove his claim in order for him to become the heir-in-power [*suus heres*]. 32a. But we will understand what we said about a 1-year-old son is the likewise said about a 1-year-old daughter.

32b. Besides, through the Visellian law, both those under and over 30 who have been freed and become Latins obtain the rights of the Quirites [*ius Quiritum*], that is, they become Roman citizens, if they serve at Rome in the night-watch [*vigiles*] for six years. A senatorial resolution is said to have occurred later in which Roman citizenship is given to those who serve in the military for three years.

32c. Likewise, by the Claudian edict Latins gain the rights of the Quirites if they build a sea-going ship that can take no less than 10,000 modii of grain and that ship or another substituted for it brings grain to Rome for six years. 33. Besides, Nero promulgated a measure that, if a Latin who had a fortune of more than 200,000 sesterces built a residence at Rome, on which he spent no less than half his fortune, he would obtain the rights of the Quirites. 34. Finally Trajan promulgated a measure that if a Latin had operated a mill in the city for three years that ground more than 100 modii of bread a day he should be entitled to the rights of the Quirites . . .

35. Besides, those manumitted when older than 30 who have become Latins can gain the rights of the Quirites by repeating the processing [and following due measures . . . So the slave who has been] freed by assertion of liberty or at the census or in a will becomes both a Roman citizen and the freedman of the person who has freed him on this second occasion. So, if a slave is among your possessions but [technically] mine under Roman law, he can be made a Latin by you but can be freed again by me – but that cannot be done by you and so he is my freedman. And even if he gains the rights of the Quirites by other means, he is still my freedman. However, possession of the goods that [he owns] when he dies will be given to you, no matter what way he has achieved Roman citizenship. But, if he belonged to someone both by possession and under Roman law, when freed by that same act he could of course both become a Latin and achieve citizen rights.

36. Not everyone, however, who wants to manumit is allowed to. 37. For a person who manumits to defraud a creditor or to defraud his patron achieves nothing, because the *lex Aelia Sentia* stops the manumission. 38. Likewise under the same law, a master under 20 years of age is not allowed to manumit, except if before an advisory board [*consilium*] a legitimate reason for manumission is proven. 39. Legitimate reasons for manumission are, for instance, if someone is manumitting his father, mother, pedagogue, or foster-brother [*conlactaneus*]. But those reasons, which we have set out concerning slaves under 30 years old, can also be applied to this case that we are discussing. Likewise, in reverse, these reasons that we have brought up in the case of a master who is under 20 years old, can be extended to a slave under 30 years old as well. 40. So since there is a fixed limit to manumission by masters under 20 years old set by the *lex Aelia Sentia*, the result is that someone over 14, although he can make a will and in it set up an heir for himself and leave legacies, if he is under 20 years of age still

cannot give freedom to a slave. 41. And, although a master under 20 might like to create a Latin, nevertheless he is obliged to prove his case before an advisory council and so afterwards manumit in the presence of friends.

42. In addition, by the *lex Fufia Caninia* a fixed limit is set for freeing slaves in one's will. 43. Permission is given for someone who has more than two, but fewer than ten, slaves to manumit up to half of them; but, for someone who has more than ten, but no more than thirty slaves, to manumit up to a third of that number; yet for someone who has more than thirty, but no more than a hundred to manumit up to a quarter. Finally permission is given for someone who has more than a hundred, but not more than five hundred, to manumit no more than a fifth of them. No account is taken of someone having more than five hundred for the fraction of that number to be fixed; but the law prescribes that no one is allowed to free more than a hundred slaves. But, if someone has one or two slaves in total, that does not fall under this law and so he has unrestricted power of freeing them. 44. And this law does not in any way affect those who manumit slaves apart from by their will. So those who free slaves by assertion of liberty or at the census or among friends are allowed to free their whole family – so long as, of course, no other reason stands in the way of their freedom. 45. But we understand what we have stated about the number of slaves who may be manumitted that no fewer are permitted to be manumitted from that number, from which half, a third, a quarter, or a fifth can be freed, than permitted from the previous number. For it would clearly be ridiculous if a master was allowed to free five out of ten slaves because he was permitted to manumit up to half of that number, but someone having twelve slaves was not allowed to manumit more than four . . .

46. For, if freedom was granted in a will to slaves by a circular list, because no set order of manumission can be found, none will be free, because the *lex Fufia Caninia* annuls any actions committed to evade its provisions. There are even particular senatorial resolutions through which those schemes are annulled that have been thought up to evade that law. 47. Overall, this must be known: the provision of the *lex Aelia Sentia* that those who are manumitted to defraud creditors do not become free also applies to foreigners, but the other rights under that law do not apply to foreigners.

48. Another distinction follows regarding the law of persons. Some persons act under their own free will [*sui iuris*], others are subject to others' will [*alieno iuri*]. 49. Again, of those persons who are subject to others' will, some are in the power of others [*in potestate*], others under their control [*in manu*], others part of their property [*in mancipio*]. 50. Let us now look at those who are subject to others' power. For, once we have recognised

who those persons are, we will at the same time understand who act under their own free will. 51. First let us glance at those who are under others' power.

52. So, slaves are in the power of their masters. Indeed this power is part of universal law [*ius gentium*], for in all peoples equally we can note masters having the power of life and death over their slaves and that whatever is acquired by a slave is acquired by the master. 53. But at this time neither Roman citizens nor any other people who are under Roman rule are allowed to act cruelly without limitation or without reason against their slaves. For, by legislation of the most sacred emperor Hadrian, anyone who kills his slave without reason is subject to the same provisions as if he had killed someone else's slave. Also aggravated cruelty by masters is checked by this same legislation. For, when some provincial governors queried him about slaves who take refuge at the shrines of the gods or at statues of the emperors, he gave instructions that, if the cruelty of their masters appears unbearable, they should be forced to sell their slaves. In both cases, the result is right: for we ought not to misuse our free will (for this reason, the hopelessly extravagant [*prodigi*] are forbidden to administer their property). 54. But, among Roman citizens there is a double form of ownership (for a slave is understood as belonging to someone as (1) being in his possessions or (2) from citizen rights[1] or (3) from both of these). So, finally, we say a slave is in his master's power if he is among his possessions, although at the same time he might not belong to him through citizen rights. The person who simply has citizen rights over a slave, is not regarded as having actual power over the slave.

---

1 *ius Quiritium*, i.e. having rights to property that have not yet been extinguished by an appropriate Roman legal method. So simple sale would not extinguish the former owner's power (*potestas*) over a slave, although in practice it would have this effect.

5.22 Manumission record

In order to safeguard the future liberty of a slave, it would be helpful to follow due procedure for manumission (here by *vindicta*, before a council of three *agoranomoi* (market officials)) and have the full details of the case recorded. In this case, the freed slave has been jointly owned and so there has been more than one manumission ceremony to achieve her freedom.

Oxyrhynchus Papyrus 4.722 (AD 91)

In the tenth year of the emperor Caesar Domitianus Augustus Germanicus, 6th of the intercalendary month Hyperberetaeus, the imperial holiday (the

6th of the intercalendary month Caesareus, the imperial holiday), in the city of Oxyrhynchus in the Thebaid, before three *agoranomi*, each named Psammis.

We – Achilleus, around 20 years old, of medium height, of olive complexion, long features, with a scar in the middle of his forehead, and Sarapas, around . . . years old, of medium height, of olive complexion, long face and scar on his left . . ., both sons of Ammonius, with Sarapous their mother, citizens of the city of Oxyrhynchus – have set free before Zeus, Earth, and Sun, in public, the third of the slave Apollonous owned by them in common (the other two-thirds having already been freed), who is around 25, of medium height, olive-complexioned, long face, with a scar on the right foot. While she has been two-thirds freed for . . . talents, for the last third being freed the fee is . . . drachmae, 4 obols of silver coin, out of which Heraclas, the son of Tryphon, son of . . ., whose mother is Taonnophris, daughter of Panesieios from the same city, aged about 31, of medium height, olive complexion, long face, with a scar above the right knee, has paid to Achilleus and Sarapas for manumission 200 drachmae of imperial silver coins, of copper . . . talents, 1,000 drachmae. It is not permitted for Achilleus or anyone else to demand back from Apollonous any of the aforementioned manumission fee . . . Certifier of the manumission . . ., son of Peteesis, whose mother is . . ., from the same city, approximately 40 years old, of medium height, olive complexion, long face, with a scar on the front of the shin, in public at the same time.

I, Achilleus, with my brother Sarapis, have manumitted in a third part the slave Apolionous and have received the manumission fee of 200 drachmas of silver, of copper . . . .

5.23 Public manumission on legal fiction (*vindicta*) before the magistrates

Other specific examples of manumission are provided by the *Digest*. For instance, the possibility of a magistrate manumitting his own slaves is upheld, as is the practice of manumission as a magistrate passes by (not requiring him actually to be holding court). It is also indicated that this is a purely ceremonial affair, with attendants (lictors) making the due legal claims to the liberty of the slave but the master not actually participating in these procedures.

Digest 40.2.5–9, 23

5. Julianus, *Digest*, Book 42. It has often been queried whether the person who provides the council can use it to manumit in his own presence. Since I remembered that Iavolenus my teacher had manumitted his own slaves both in Africa and in Syria when providing the council, I followed

his precedent and both in my praetorship and consulate freed some of my slaves by public assertion of liberty [*vindicta*]. I also gave the same advice to various praetors who consulted me about this.

6. Julianus, *To Urseius Ferox*, Book 2. It is indisputable that a slave jointly owned by owners who are under 20 years old can be manumitted before a council, even though only one of the partners has proved his case.

7. Gaius, *Daily Matters or Golden Remarks*, Book 1. It is not entirely necessary to manumit before a magistrate's tribunal. So slaves are commonly manumitted in passing, when a praetor or proconsul or imperial legate goes out to wash or take a walk or see the games.

8. Ulpian, *On the Edict*, Book 5. I myself, when I was at my country estate with the praetor, allowed slaves to be manumitted before him, although there were no lictors present.

9. Marcianus, *Institutes*, Book 13. There is a legitimate reason for manumission, if a slave has freed his master from a deadly peril or from disgrace.

23. Hermogianus, *Epitome of Law*, Book 1. Today manumission is customarily carried out by lictors with the master silent, and, although the due utterances are not spoken, they are taken as having been spoken.

5.24 A poor person taken as a slave and later freed by restoration of his free status

Free children might be brought up with slaves as their childhood companions and remember them when they have become adults. In the following case, Tatianus has not simply manumitted his companion in his will, but restored his freeborn status by a posthumous *vindicta*. This suggests that Aurelis was indeed originally free, but from such impoverished circumstances that his parents would have preferred him to be treated as a slave. Note the considerable family attached to Aurelis who celebrate this good fortune, including his foster-mother, Prima, who would appear to have acted as nurse to Tatianus in Aurelis' household after he was separated from his natural parents, Epinicios and Zenodote.

L'Année Epigraphique 1998 no. 1322
(Maionia, province of Asia)

In the year 327 [of the Sullan era = AD 242/3], in the month of Hyperberetaios, on the third day of the waxing moon.

Aurelis Procopton has done well in service to Tatianus, his childhood companion [*syntrophos*]. Tatianus, recalling Aurelis' devotion to him, when he died left him free with the standing of a freeborn citizen by restoration of his status [*ingenuus per vindictam*] and left to him the legacy specified in his will.

His [biological] parents Epinicios and Zenodote have erected this in honour of Procopton; also Prima in honour of the child she reared, and Damianus in honour of the slave who grew up with his father, and Aurelis Romanus, his brother, and his concubine Tatias; also his children have erected this in honour of their father – Zenodote and Tatianus and Procopton and Epinikos and Euphemia; also Zenodote and Socrates in honour of their brother; and Alexandros, his uncle.

In memorial.

5.25 The law prevents granting free birth status to slaves via the legal fiction of being of free birth

As descent from a slave would disqualify members of the family from becoming senators for the next two generations, it might seem worthwhile to allow a claim of original free birth as a means of freeing a slave. This loophole was closed in the reign of Domitian; instead, in exceptional cases, ex-slaves might be granted the *ius anulorum*, the right to wear the rings that marked equestrian status (see **1.25** above).

Digest 40.16.1

Gaius, *On the Edict of the Urban Praetor, Section on the Case for Freedom*, Book 2. In case the excessive indulgence of some masters towards their slaves should disgrace the most illustrious order [of the senate] by allowing their slaves to profess free birth and gain judgement as being free, a senatorial resolution was passed in the time of Domitian, which enacted that, if anyone proved that anything had occurred through the collusion [of master and slave], if the person involved is [actually] a slave, he should become the slave of the person who unmasked the collusion.

5.26 A *paramone* contract (i.e. the slave remains with the ex-owner) from Macedonia

Freedom was not absolute for an ex-slave. In some cases (especially in the Greek East), actual liberation was delayed until the fulfilment of some condition or until the death of the previous owner. In this example, this guarantees the owner support in her old age.

Supplementum Epigraphicum Graecum 46 (1996) 745, from the sanctuary of Enodia in Macedonia

AD 223, February.

As there was a festival and assembly, I, Aurelia Iulia, previously called the daughter of Amyntas, have made a gift to the goddess Enodia of Hermes, my slave. I want him to remain with me for the length of my life and support me in my old age, obedient to the goddess on terms set out publicly, but to be unclaimable [by my heirs] after my death.

5.27 *Operae* – what can be expected of an ex-slave?

More common in the Latin West was the need for the ex-slave as client to provide services for the previous master, now their patron. This close bond could easily be mocked and portrayed as an overly familiar relationship, as occurs here.

Seneca the Elder, *Controversiae* 4 Praef.10

I remember that, when he was defending a freedman on trial who was being accused of being his patron's lover [*concubinus*], Haterius declared, 'Sexual laxness is a charge against a free man, but an absolute necessity for a slave, and a service [*officium*] from a freedman.' The matter turned into a joke: 'You aren't servicing me' and 'he spends a lot of time servicing him'. As a result, the promiscuous and queer [*inpudici et obsceni*] were for some time regularly called 'serviceable' [*officiosi*].

5.28 The law on days of work owed (*operae*)

Traditionally, work was measured as full days of employment (see Matthew 20.16 in **6.8**). This applied to contract work (indeed hired hands were often simply termed as *operae*), to labour to be provided to the landlord from a tenant, and to the services of a client/freedman. But, from the viewpoint of public interest, services that were disreputable or undignified could not be offered or demanded.

Digest 38.1.1, 3, 16, 17, 34–5, 38, 45–6

1. Paul, *On Different Readings*, the one book. Days of work owed [*operae*] are a full day's service [*officium*].

3. Pomponius, *To Sabinus*, Book 6. Once you have agreed on days of work owed you are not allowed to ask for the work for that day until the day is complete. 1. But it is not possible to pay off part of the work owed by hourly work, because it is a full day's service. So a freedman who was present for six hours before midday only will not get let off that day's obligation.

16. Paul, *On the Edict*, Book 40. A freedman owes the provision of work [*operae*] in that trade that he has learnt after his manumission, if it is of a type that can be offered respectably and without imperilling his life, rather than always the work that he owed at the time of manumission. But, if he starts to practice a shameful type of work afterwards, he ought to provide the work that he offered at the time of manumission. 1. Such work owed is given to the ex-master [*patronus*] as ought to be assessed as suitable according to age, status [*dignitas*], health, need, promises, and other considerations of this type for each of the persons involved.

17. Paul, *On the Rights of Patronage*, the one book. An ex-master should not be granted a hearing if he demands work that would be rejected on grounds of age or cannot be undertaken because of physical weakness or that would harm the manner or pattern of the client's life.

34. Pomponius, *To Quintus Mucius*, Book 22. It should be known that sometimes the duties of work owed can be reduced, increased, or changed. So, when a freedman is ill, the work owed to his patron, including that which had already begun, is cancelled. If a freedwoman who promises her work rises to such a status that it would be undignified for her to offer work to her patron, the work is terminated on the basis of equity [*ipso iure*].

35. Paul, *On the lex Iulia et Papia*, Book 2. A freedwoman over 50 is not compelled to offer work to her patron.

38. Callistratius, *The Monitory Edict*, Book 3. In summary: work duties [*operae*] imposed are understood to be those that can be offered without shame and without peril of life. So, if a prostitute [*meretrix*] was manumitted, she ought not to provide the same services [*operae*] to her patron, even if she still earns her living by her body. Nor should a participant in the games [*harenarius*] who is manumitted offer work of this type, because it cannot be provided without risk to one's life.

45. Scaevola, *Replies*, Book 2. Could the freedman of a clothing manufacturer carry on the same business in the same town and same place against his master's will? He replied there was no reason given why he could not, if the patron suffered no harm from this.

46. Valens, *Trusts*, Book 5. If a freedwoman was in a relationship with her patron equivalent to being married to him, it is agreed that he ought not to be allowed to sue her for services owed.

5.29 The rights of a slave to use his *peculium*, even to acquire his freedom

Slavery at Rome is unusual in that slaves were allowed to possess working capital (either money or property), the *peculium*. This recognition of 'pocket-money' appears to have been originally instituted to allow sons whose fathers were alive, and as *patresfamilias* possessed full power over them, to operate independently and was extended to other members of the household. This *peculium* would revert to the owner on the slave's death, but might be used earlier to 'purchase' freedom. This involved a legal fiction, since slaves, lacking legal identity, could not purchase their own freedom; but, in practice, it was sufficiently common to be granted legal protection. A possible worst-case scenario resulting from this practice has already been seen in the case of the urban prefect, Pedanius (**5.14** above).

Digest 33.8.19, 40.1.4–5

33.8.19.   Papinian, *Replies*, Book 7. When a master wishes to free a slave, he orders him to give an account of his *peculium* and after this the slave receives his freedom. It is clear that anything in the *peculium* that has not been listed in the account does not appear to have been tacitly granted to the freed slave.

40.1.4.   Ulpian, *Matters of Argument*, Book 6. A slave who is bought with his own money is changed, under a letter of the deified brothers to Urbius Maximus, to a status whereby he gains his freedom. 1. First, he does not seem properly described as having been bought by his own money, since a slave cannot have money of his own; but, with a nod and a wink, it should be believed that he was bought by his own money, since he is not purchased by the money of the person who bought him. So, whether he was bought out of his own *peculium* (which is a matter for the seller), or from chance profit, or even by the help and generosity of a friend or by the slave himself offering an advance or promising to pay the money back or by standing surety for accepting the debt, he should be believed to have been bought by his own money. It is sufficient that the person who lends his name to the sale does not spend any of his own money. 2. If he is bought by an outsider, but afterwards he presents his own price, the judgement must be that he should not be granted a hearing: this ought to be dealt with from the beginning, so that the purchase turns out to be fictitious and that it is a case of an arrangement between buyer and slave based on good faith. . . .

5.   Marcianus, *Institutes*, Book 2. If someone says he has been bought by his money, he can remain with his master, on whose honesty he has relied, and lodge a complaint on the grounds that he was not manumitted by him

– at Rome, with the Urban Prefect; in the provinces, with the governors – in accordance with the imperial precedents [*constitutiones*] of the deified brothers. However, there is this injunction: a slave who brings this case and does not succeed will be handed over to the mines unless his master happens to prefer to receive him back and the penalty he would fix because of this case is no heavier [than being sent to the mines].

REFERENCES AND FURTHER READING

Bradley, K. (1989) *Slavery and Rebellion in the Roman World*, Bloomington, IN.

Bradley, K. (1994) *Slavery and Society at Rome*, Cambridge.

Fitzgerald, W. (2000) *Slavery and the Roman Literary Imagination*, Cambridge.

Gowers, E. (1993) *The Loaded Table: Representations of Food in Roman Literature*, Oxford.

Harris, W.V. (1980) 'Towards a Study of the Roman Slave Trade', in D'Arms, J.H. and Kopff, E.C. (eds) *The Seaborne Commerce of Ancient Rome*, Rome, pp. 117–40.

Litinas, N. (1999) 'P. Lond. 111 1128: Sale of a Donkey', *Zeitschrift für Papyrologie und Epigraphik* 124: 195–204.

Patterson, O. (1982) *Slavery and Social Death*, Cambridge.

Scheidel, W. (1997) 'Quantifying the Sources of Slaves in the Early Roman Empire', *Journal of Roman Studies* 87:156–69.

Scheidel, W. (2005) 'Human Mobility in Roman Italy II: The Slave Population', *Journal of Roman Studies* 95: 64–79.

Watson, A. (1987) *Roman Slave Law*, Baltimore, MD.

Weaver, P.R.C. (1972) *Familia Caesaris*, Cambridge.

Wiedemann, T. (1985) 'The Regularity of Manumission at Rome', *Classical Quarterly* 35: 162–75.

Wiedemann, T. (1987) *Slavery*, Greece and Rome New Surveys in the Classics, 19, Oxford.

6

POVERTY

One's opportunities in life in the ancient world differed markedly depending on whether one was a member of the group of the wealthy and respectable or in the much larger group described as the 'humble' or the poor (see Chapter 1). This basic division into two classes underlies, for example, the interpretation of the probable outcome of dreams (6.1). But as 'poor' is simply a relative term in comparison with the 'rich', it covers a wide range from people whom we might consider well off (for instance, the satirist Juvenal talking about himself), to craftsmen and vendors (*pauperes*), to the completely indigent (*egeni*). The latter are even mocked as too poor to be called poor (6.2). In philosophical/ethical writing, it is not uncommon for poverty to be praised as representing a freedom from the dependence on material goods that afflicts the wealthy (6.3; cf. 6.9). This reflects the nature of our sources, who would not consider themselves 'poor' (except in relation to their peers), and whose attitude to the poor is very much based on the maintenance of their own status. Schemes that might appear to offer support for the underprivileged, such as Trajan's alimentary scheme or even the grain 'dole' (*annona*) at Rome, are open to all members of society and select from 'worth' rather than need (6.4, 6.5). Group solidarity meant that the wealthy would first support their own (6.6) and that their philanthropy was likely to be based on personal display rather than the result of concern for the needy (an attitude often criticised in Christian sources: cf. 6.15).

A very few among the poor might react violently, but brigandage was a short-lived response against which there would eventually be heavy reprisals (6.7; cf. 8.22, 8.25). Most obtained a living as they could, chronically underemployed and so open to exploitation in the spot labour market (6.8). While a public speaker such as Dio Chrysostom might offer negative comment on many of the occupations available to the poor, they themselves could hardly be so choosy: apart from well-paid occupations as town criers and entertainers, there were numerous opportunities in despised manual work and the sex industry (6.9). The food intake could be supplemented by public grain handouts in the larger cities or by memorial feasts; public sacrifices and animal hunts at the games would also have provided dietary windfalls (6.10). The indigent might need to look for market scraps (6.11) or even funerary offerings (hence the association of beggars with grave-yards, which might also offer temporary shelter). From John Chrysostom, we have considerable information on those reduced to asking for assist-ance from the more fortunate (6.12), and about the areas in which they operated and their means of shelter (6.13). The use of public facilities (especially the baths) for shelter is also illustrated in Alciphron (6.14), although the desperately ill would even be excluded from these areas (6.13). But even begging was a competitive area: an appeal to the vanity of passers-by would be more likely to be successful, but the best results seem to have been achieved by those who could provide entertainment (6.15), or who suffered from some gross physical impairment (6.16). John Chrysostom offers a gruesome picture of the freak-show performances of some of these unfortunates (6.17).

The vast majority of the populace in the ancient world also did not enjoy the luxury accommodation of the traditional Roman *domus* or villa. Most lived in quite primitive structures (6.18) and life in winter and the wet seasons cannot have been pleasant (6.19). Cities would possess market places, civic buildings, guaranteed water supplies, and entertainment (6.20), but they also presented constant danger from flood, fire, and building collapse (6.21). For most of the population, living in closely packed apartment buildings (*insulae*), there was constant noise from local manufacturers and vendors, street hawkers, entertainers, and beggars; only the wealthy few lived in fine houses on the hills with considerable land around (6.22). Many of the wealthy too would have to put up with these difficult living conditions when they rented the better apartments in *insulae* (although Seneca is probably imagining his quarters in 6.23). It is clear that building techniques were mainly developed to enable buildings to be constructed to the greatest height possible, rather than with safety in mind (6.24). Owners would simply factor into the high rents the risk of loss and seem to have expected a constant need to rebuild (6.25). Fire, in particular, was a major risk that certainly encouraged the wealthy to keep at least a proportion of their capital in agricultural land, rather than engage in high-risk urban investment. Methods of reducing the fire risk were unreliable (6.26), particularly because of the tendency to build with wood on upper floors and the construction of wooden balconies over the roads to nearly touch one another (6.27). Still, the demand for housing both for the urban masses and for rich immigrants, meant that speculation in accommodation might be highly profitable. This was especially the case with Crassus, who exploited cheap property and demand for high-status housing in the late republic to amass enormous wealth (6.28). Despite attempts to improve the plan of the city and to give greater protection from fire, Rome remained in the main a confused urban sprawl (6.29).

6.1 Dreams interpreted differently for the rich and the poor

The second-century dream interpreter Artemidorus regularly notes that dreams vary in their predictive nature according to the character of the dreamer. It is common that a dream will have a completely different meaning for someone with wealth than for a poor person or slave. In the latter cases, even having something to lose portends an improvement in one's lot.

Artemidorus, *Interpretation of Dreams* 2.9 (110–11 Pack), 2.26, 2.54

Lightning falling nearby without any thunder that does not strike the body exiles the dreamer from the place where he is. For no one would stay close to lightning. If it falls in front, it prevents one going forward. Being struck on the top of the head by lightning was given a double explanation by the very oldest interpreters, who said it was good for the poor, but bad for the rich following this rationale. The poor are like bare and humble places, where dung or other worthless material is thrown. But the rich are like precincts dedicated to gods or men, the temples of the gods, groves, or any sort of solemn spot. So, just as lightning makes ignoble places renowned because of the altars set up and the sacrifices on them, while it makes fertile places into untrodden deserts (as no one wants to stay in them in the future), so the dream is of advantage to the poor, but hurts the rich. Furthermore, lightning is nothing other than fire and it is a characteristic of fire to destroy all matter. While the poor man possesses poverty, the rich man has riches – hence it destroys the one's poverty and the other's wealth, since the man struck by lightning suddenly becomes especially notorious. In the same way, the poor man suddenly becoming wealthy and the rich man suddenly losing what he has both become notorious. The first interpreters put their trust in this interpretation.

But those who followed have recently said something about slaves as well, declaring that it is good for slaves to be struck by lightning, because those struck by lightning no longer have masters nor do they toil, but are dressed in white clothing like those who have been freed and men approach them as though they have been honoured by Zeus, just as freedmen have been held in honour by their masters.

Cow dung is good for farmers alone (the same is true of horse dung and all other types except human excrement) – for others it indicates despondency and suffering and, if it besmears, sickness. It is good only for those working in the dirty professions, where it has been observed to be profitable.

Human excrement seen in large quantities indicates many different troubles. This is how: when it appears in a square or market or any public place, it prevents the places in which it is from being used, and often prevents one from advancing. So there are times when it causes those who take no notice to wipe away great wrongs with their own heads. It would be unusual to be besmeared with flowing human excrement from any source.

I know someone who in a dream seemed to defecate on the head of a rich companion with whom he was on intimate terms and who was a friend of his. He received the property and became the heir of his companion. On the other hand, a person dreamed that he was defecated on by a poor person whom he knew and suffered great harm from him and endured a great disgrace. The explanation is that it is reasonable for someone who is prosperous to bequeath his property to the dreamer, but someone who is impoverished who has nothing to leave will despise the dreamer and cover him with disgrace.

To fight wild animals is good for a poor man. For he will be able to nourish many. For the animal fighter nourishes the animals with his own flesh. The dream portends injustice to come for a wealthy man from such a type of man as the animals represent. For many it has portended disease. For the flesh is eaten away by disease, as it is by wild animals. The dream liberates slaves, so long as they are killed by the wild animals.

6.2 Some jokes about the poor

As part of a programme of self-sufficiency, some Hellenistic philosophies recommended an ascetic lifestyle, close to that of the poor. This is particularly true of the Cynics, who adopted the dress of the homeless (staff and pouch) and would loudly accost passers-by, spreading their message. From this and self-publicising habits of carrying out all nature's acts in public, they came to be called 'Doggies' (from the Greek *kynikoi*, 'dog-like'). Other sects, such as the Stoics and the Epicureans, similarly praised poverty and proclaimed not to be afraid of death. Martial reflects a response (also visible in Juvenal's *Satires*) of ridiculing such figures as true beggars, only able to reject traditional values because they were excluded from life's pleasures.

Note the distinction between being poor (*pauper*), an elastic term that denotes anyone who is not rich, and being impoverished (*egenus*), which indicates a lack of clothing, shelter, and sustenance that would reduce the sufferer to relying on random acts of charity.

(a) Martial, *Epigrams* 4.53

The fellow you have often seen in the shrine of our Athena
And at the door of the new temple, Cosmus,
The old guy with staff and pouch, whose dirty white hair
Stands on end, whose filthy beard falls down to his chest,

Who is covered by a yellow cloak that serves as his wife on his
    bare bed,
To whom the passing crowd gives the food he barks for –
You think he's a Cynic, taken in by the feigned appearance.
He's not a Cynic, Cosmus. What is he, then? A dog.

(b) Martial, *Epigrams* 11.32

You have no cloak, nor hearth, nor a bed chewed by bed-bugs,
No mat mended with thirsty marsh reeds,
No slave boy nor even one long in the tooth, no slave girl or child,
No lock or key or dog and dish.
Still, Nestor, you make a pretence of being called and appearing to be
A poor man and look to have some standing in the crowd.
But you're lying and flattering yourself with this empty acclaim.
That's not the definition of being poor, Nestor: 'having nothing at all'.

(c) Martial, *Epigrams* 11.56

Because you praise death too much, like a good Stoic, Chaeremon,
Do you want me to marvel at your spirit and look up at you?
This courage comes from a jug with a broken handle,
A lonely hearth warmed by no flame,
A mat, bed-bugs, and the frame of a bare pallet,
And a toga that is too small, never changed night and day.
O what a grand man you are who can do without
The dregs of red vinegar and beanstalks and black bread!
Well, let's have your mattress stuffed with Leuconian wool,
A couch tucked up with brushed purple covers,
And a slave sleeping with you who, when he mixed the Caecuban
Just before, tortured the guests with his rosy lips.
Oh how much then will you want to live three times Nestor's years
And lose nothing from any day!
In dire straits it's an easy matter to despise life:
He's a real hero who is able to live on in misery.

6.3 A plea for the necessary symbiosis of rich and poor

Christian doctrine, basing its thinking on the belief that all things have been created
by God and so have a purpose, offers a forerunner to modern sociological
discussions of the functional interrelationship between rich and poor. John
Chrysostom's depiction is partly derived from Greek philosophical thinking about
the city (cf. Plato's *Republic* and *Laws*) and partly derived from the diatribes of
popular philosophy (particularly associated with the Cynics) with its paradoxical
views of the value of poverty.

John Chrysostom, *Homilies on First Letter to the Corinthians* 34.4–5 (= *Patrologia Graeca* 61.291–2)

God has neither entrusted everything to man, nor everything to woman, but has divided these things between each, handing over the household to her, and civic business to him. He has the task of feeding, since he is the farmer; she has the task of clothing, since the loom and distaff belong to the woman. He has given to woman the knowledge of weaving. If only the love of money would disappear, which does not allow this division to be seen. For the laziness of the crowd has encouraged men as well to take up the loom and placed shuttles and the warp and the woof into their hands. But all the same the foresight of god's placement shines through. For we not only very much need a woman for other absolutely essential things, but also find ourselves needing our inferiors for the sustenance of our lives. And such is the force of this need that, even if someone were richer than all men, he would not because of this avoid this tie and its most absolute necessity. For it is not only the poor who need the rich, but also the rich who need the poor – indeed the rich need the poor more than the latter need them.

In order for you to see this more clearly, let us create, if you wish, two cities, one only of the rich, the other only of the poor. Let there not be any poor person in the city of the rich, nor any rich man in the city of the poor, but they should each be totally isolated from one another, and let's see which city will be more self-sufficient. So, if we find the city of the poor more able to cope by itself, it will be perfectly obvious that the rich are more in need of them. So in the city of the well off, there will be no carpenter, no builder, no architect, no shoe-maker, no baker, no farmer, no bronze worker, no rope-maker – in fact, no one of this sort. For who among the wealthy would choose to pursue these trades, when indeed those who participate in them, when they have become rich, cannot any longer endure the suffering of these occupations. How then will this city survive? 'By paying money,' it is said, 'the rich will buy these things from the poor.' So they will not be self-sufficient if they need their services. How will they build their houses? Or will they buy them ready built as well? But nature would not permit this. So they will have to summon workmen there and repeal the law that we set up at the start when we established the cities. Recall the time when we said that there should be no poor person inside the city. But look here: necessity, even if we don't wish it, has summoned them and introduced them. From this it is clear that is impossible for a city to survive without the poor. For, if a city remained without accepting any of them, it would no longer be a city, but would have collapsed. So it will not be self-sufficient unless it brings into itself the poor like saviours. But let's also look at the city of the poor to see if it also is in a similar state of dependency when it is deprived of the rich. Let us first clarify wealth by reasoning and let's display it clearly. What then is wealth? Gold and silver, precious stones, and cloaks of silk or dyed purple or with golden thread. So, since what wealth is has been made clear, let's drive it out of the city of the poor, if we are going to make a pure city of the poor, and let not even the dream of gold appear there nor cloaks of those types. If you like, there should not be silver nor silver objects. Well then – tell me what the life of this city will be lacking because of this. Nothing. If we need to build a house, we do not need gold, silver, and pearls, but skill and labour, and not simply labour, but hands with calluses and fingers that are gnarled, but full of strength, and wood and stones. If again we need to weave a cloak, again we don't need gold and silver but, again, hands and skill and female labour. Well, what do we need to farm and dig the earth? Do we need the rich or the poor? It is absolutely clear that it is the poor we need. And when we need to manufacture iron objects or anything else similar, we particularly need this crowd. So where will we need the rich in the future, except in order to destroy this city. For, after they enter and infect them with the desire for gold and pearls, these types of philosopher (for I am calling philosophers those who don't look too deeply into anything), dedicating themselves to laziness and self-indulgence, will destroy everything afterwards.

6.4 Trajan's alimentary scheme

Provision for payments for children is not uncommon in bequests to towns in the ancient world. By the time of Nerva (Pseudo Aurelius Victor, *Epitome de Caesaribus* 12.4) and perhaps even under Domitian, the emperor had begun the practice of making loans to the wealthy throughout Italy who would in return be required to provide the interest for the upkeep of children in their area. So, at Veleia, there is recorded 'the repayments owed on properties for 1,044,000 sesterces, so that by the generosity of the greatest and best emperor, Caesar Nerva Trajan Augustus Germanicus Dacicus, boys and girls may receive child benefits (*alimenta*)' (*Corpus Inscriptionum Latinarum* 11.1147).

Pliny, *Panegyric* 28

You have gladly offered gifts of food [*congiarium*] to glad citizens, acting without fear towards those who need not fear you. What the emperors in the past tossed to the people when their hearts were angry to quell their hatred, you gave free from guilt to a populace equally guiltless. There were just under 5,000 freeborn children, senators, whom the emperor's generosity sought out, found, and adopted. These are being raised as a defence in war and a blessing in peacetime, and are learning to love their country not only as their fatherland, but as their nurturer. From these the camps and the tribes will be filled again, from these children will be born who will have no need of child support [*alimenta*]. May the gods give you, Caesar, the lifespan you deserve and preserve the spirit they have given to you – then how much greater the crowd of children you will order time after time to be placed on the rolls. Their numbers are being added to daily and increasing, not because children have become dearer to their parents, but because the citizens are dearer to their emperor. You may present gifts of food whenever you like, you may present child support whenever you like, but they are being born simply because of you.

6.5 Pliny's provision for an alimentary scheme at his hometown of Comum

Pliny the Younger's provision for setting up a trust to provide child support at Comum shows his serious concerns that money provided to the civic body might be diverted at a later date (as happened in Bithynia). By placing land in trust with the community and renting it back, Pliny guarantees a constant stream of money attached to a specified project. The same approach appears to have been taken with Trajan's scheme, which lent money at excellent rates to local landowners to invest in land, the recipient of the interest being the local community that would spend the money on child support. Under Trajan's scheme there is differentiation between males and females, with males receiving twice the payment of females, and between freeborn and illegitimate (mixed marriage?) children. Nowhere is child support dependent on demonstrated need.

Pliny, *Letters* 7.18

You're asking my advice as to how the money that you have offered to our townsfolk for a memorial feast can be kept safe after you pass away. That is a respectable query and the answer isn't ready to hand. Imagine that you paid out a lump sum of money. Then there's the fear that the capital will shrink. What if you make a donation of land? No attention will be paid to it as public property. In fact I have found no better scheme than what I myself have done. For instead of the 500,000 sesterces, which I had promised for the upkeep [*alimenta*] of freeborn boys and girls, I have transferred to the civic treasurer land from my estate that is worth far more than that. I have obtained the same land back under a rental arrangement, paying 30,000 sesterces a year. This way the income to the municipality is guaranteed and the return is fixed, and the land itself will always find a master to work it because it returns considerably more than the rent. I am aware that I appear to have paid back more that I have given in my grant, since the need to pay rent has reduced the value of this very fertile land. But we should put public benefit ahead of the private and immortal rewards ahead of mortal ones, and we should pay much more attention to our philanthropy than to our wealth.

6.6 The material assistance of a wealthy man to one of his group fallen on hard times

Part of the effectiveness of social groupings in the ancient world was the creation of horizontal links for support. For the humble, this might simply be *collegia*, which would give a feeling of solidarity in life and the assurance of burial after death (**1.44**). For the wealthy, group support meant rescuing members from the disgrace of poverty. In some cases, this resulted in what was almost insurance – for instance, the restoration of fire losses (Juvenal 3.212–22 on Asturicus; cf. the total destitution of Cordus: 3.208–11). In Apuleius, Aristomenus is shaken by the appearance of his friend (contrast the expected reaction to beggars in John Chrysostom's descriptions: **6.12**, **6.15**) and provides him with clothing, bathing (a basic necessity for the good life in Roman times), and shelter.

Apuleius, *Metamorphoses* 1.5–7

So then, thoroughly tired out by my unsuccessful hurrying [to try to complete a business deal], as evening came on I had gone out to the baths. Who did I see but my friend Socrates. He was sitting on the bare ground, half-covered by a torn cloaklet, almost unrecognisable with his sallow complexion, like one of Fortune's prunings who beg for coins at the crossroads. Since he was in this state, I approached him uncertainly, even though he was a friend with whom I had been on the closest terms. 'Hey, Socrates, what's this? What are you going to do? What's this scandal? At home they have by now finished mourning and lamenting for you, your children have been given guardians by decree of the provincial governor, and your wife, who has carried out the duties owed to the dead and looks ghastly from continuous grief and sorrow after crying out her eyes almost to the point of blindness, is being pushed by her own parents to brighten up the misfortune of the household by the joys of a new wedding. But you, to our utmost disgrace, appear here like the image of a ghost.'

'Aristomenus,' he said, 'you should know about the slippy uncertainties of people's luck, their shifting advantages and changing ups and downs', and, as he said this, he covered his face, which had much earlier turned scarlet from shame with his stitched patchwork, with the result that he uncovered the rest of his body from his navel to his loins. I could no longer endure such a miserable display of suffering, placed my hand on him, and tried to get him to rise.

But he, just as he was, with his head covered, replied, 'Please, allow Fortune to enjoy for a while longer the victory trophy that she has planted here with her own hand.'

I got him to follow me and at the same time took off one of my two garments and hastily dressed him (or should I say, covered him up) and immediately transferred him to the baths. I myself provided what he needed

213

for oiling and scraping the dirt off, carefully rubbed away a great heap of dirt, and took good care of him. As I was tired out myself, it was with some difficulty that I helped guide him exhausted as he was to the inn, rested him on a couch, filled him with food, soothed his spirit with drink, and calmed him with stories.

6.7 A Roman Robin Hood

Tales of clever robbers are frequent in antiquity (cf. the tale of Rhampsinitus and the thief in Herodotus 2.121) and it is clear that features of this genre have attached themselves to the historical account of Bulla (e.g. the capture of the centurion hunting him; Bulla's ultimate capture due to a love affair). Still it is clear that Bulla's activities were significant enough to be recorded at length by his contemporary, Cassius Dio. For the means of his death, cf. **8.25**. The suggestion that public slaves and freedmen were not receiving regular pay and so were ready to assist robber bands cannot be confirmed by other evidence but has numerous parallels at other times in history.

Cassius Dio, 76.10.1–7

At this time [AD 206–7], Bulla, an Italian, gathered together a robber band of around 600 men and plundered Italy for two years, although the emperors and large numbers of soldiers were present. He was hunted by many, since Severus was eager to track him down, but when he was seen he was not recognised, nor discovered when he was found, nor captured when they had him in their grasp, such was his skill in bribery and cunning. He would learn about all those who were leaving from Rome or arriving at Brundisium – who they were and what they had on them and how much. He would immediately release the others after taking some of what they had from them, but he would keep craftsmen for some time. Then, after he had made use of their services, he would free them, giving them something extra. Once, when two of his robbers had been captured and were going to be given to the beasts, he came to the prison warden, pretending to be the governor of the country, and asked for some people such as them and so took them away and saved them. He met up with a centurion hunting the band and complained about himself as if he were someone else, and promised that if he followed him he would hand the brigand over to him. So, leading him into an overgrown hollow as if to Felix (he had been given this nickname), he easily captured him. Then he ascended a tribunal, taking on a governor's dress, called the tribune before him and had his head shaven. Then he said, 'Tell your masters, "Feed your slaves or they will become brigands."' In fact he had most of the imperial servants in his employ, since some received little pay and others simply no pay at all. So, when Severus learnt each of these events, he was overcome with rage because he could conquer his enemies in Britain through others, but he was being defeated

214

in Italy by a robber. Finally, he sent a tribune from his bodyguard with a large number of cavalry, having threatened him with terrible consequences if he did not bring the robber back alive. The tribune, when he had learnt that Bulla was having an affair with someone else's wife, promised the woman through her husband immunity if she assisted them. As a result, he was captured when sleeping in a cave. Papinian the prefect asked him, 'Why were you a robber?' He replied, 'Why are you a prefect?' Then, after public announcement had been made, he was given to the wild beasts and his robber band was also broken up. Clearly all the strength of the 600 men lay in him.

6.8 Casual labourers in a vineyard, all paid at the same rate

Labour was rarely hired for extended periods of time in antiquity. This is often explained as being based on a desire by the free not to be associated with the slave population, but, while this attitude might have prevailed among the more privileged, the poorer members of the populace simply had no choice but to take the intermittent work offered. Long-term labour could be obtained by devices such as tenancy contracts, while advantage could be taken of a labour glut by daily hiring at regular sites, such as the market place mentioned below. Pay would be for a day's work from dawn to dusk; additional labour might be obtained later in the day from the desperate at virtually any rate offered (note that no rate is here specified). Most unusually, the owner is here portrayed as offering the same rate of pay (1 denarius = 4 sesterces or 1 drachma) to all, which leads to considerable grumbling among his employees. Although the vineyard owner can claim the right to pay according to individual agreement, there is also an indication here of the public pressure that would be exerted on those who acted outside the expected pattern.

Gospel According to Matthew 20.1–16

The kingdom of the heavens is like master of a household who came at dawn to hire workers for his vineyard. Having reached an agreement with the workers on wages of a denarius a day, he sent them off to his vineyard. Coming at the third hour he saw others standing around idle at the market place. He said to them, 'You too make your way to the vineyard and I will give you what is due.' They went off. Again, coming at the sixth and ninth hours he did the same. Coming at the eleventh hour he found others standing around and said to them, 'Why are you standing around the whole day idle?' They said to him, 'Because no one has hired us.' He said to them, 'You too make your way to the vineyard.' When it was evening, the owner of the vineyard said to his steward, 'Call the workers and give them their wages, starting from the last and going on to the first.' Coming forward those hired at the eleventh hour each received a denarius. Coming

215

forward, the first thought that they would receive more. But they also each received a denarius. Taking this, they grumbled to the master of the household, saying, 'These last hired did one hour's work and you have treated them as equal to us who have endured the heat and burden of a full day's work.' But he spoke in reply to one of them, 'Friend, I am not wronging you. Didn't you make an agreement with me for one denarius? Take what is yours and go. I want to give to this latecomer the same as to you. Aren't I allowed to do what I want on my property? Or do you look askance because I am a good man?' So the last will be first and the first last.

6.9 Jobs for the poor

Dio Chrysostom's *Euboian Oration* is best known for its utopian description of a self-sufficient society of hunters that occupies the first two-thirds of the speech. The theme of self-sufficiency (a major tenet of Stoic thought, but also reflecting aristocratic ideas of independence in ancient society) is then continued in the context of the city. It might seem that the rich would find this ideal easier to achieve (but see John Chrysostom's treatment of the theme in **6.3**), but Dio seeks to show that the poor can also live respectable lives.

Dio's recommendations are most notable for their reflection of aristocratic values. So the assemblymen and jurors of democratic Athens (a long-lost memory) are mocked, along with the occupations that serve the extravagance of the wealthy. Acting and other forms of entertainment are rejected as pandering to the crowd, while more common occupations, such as heraldry, are rejected as too obviously vulgar. Dio also excludes earnings from prostitution, not so much from rejection of sexual acts (indeed some philosophers saw prostitution as a way to release sexual energy), as from the effects of sexual licence on the more important parts of the community. From prostitution it will be a short step to the seduction of unmarried women and to adultery and, from there, to the seduction of the sons of noble families, thus undermining the future rulers of the community.

Dio Chrysostom, *Orations* 7.103–51

So much for this description of the farming, hunting, and shepherding life, which has possibly taken up more time than it deserved since we wanted somehow to show that poverty isn't a problem but provides a livelihood and a lifestyle that befits free men who want to live independently and even leads us on to much greater and more useful works and deeds and ones that are more natural than those in which wealth usually encourages most people to engage.

Well now, we must examine the lifestyle and work of the poor in the city and around the town to see what sort of activity in particular and what types of work they can engage in to live decently and no worse off than the moneylenders who charge high rates of interest and who have a fine knowledge of the numbering of days and months, nor than those who own large apartment buildings [*insulae*] and own ships and numerous slaves.

Granted that, for such people, work in the city will be occasional and needing to be supplemented by outside resources, when they need money to rent shelter and to pay to get everything else – not only clothing and furniture and food, but also wood for daily needs, or if one needs firewood, leaves, or any other cheap requirement: in fact, apart from water they will be required to obtain everything else by paying for it, since nothing is set out in public except, I believe, for numerous expensive things for sale – then it might appear difficult to be self-sufficient in such a life, having nothing apart from their own bodies, especially when we are recommending to them not to pick up whatever work comes along nor to gain money from every possible opportunity. So perhaps we will be forced to expel the self-respecting poor from the cities in our argument, in order that we may produce cities that are really 'well inhabited', as Homer says, as they will be inhabited by only the blessed, and we will allow no free worker inside the walls, so it seems. But what are we going to do with all these poor people of this sort? Will we settle them scattered around the land, as they say the Athenians inhabited all of Attica in the old days and once more after Peisistratus' tyranny? So such a lifestyle was suitable for them and it did not make the character of the citizens ignoble, but in every way better and more sensible than those assemblymen and jurymen and copyists raised in the city afterwards, who were both lazy and menial. There will not be then any great or worrisome danger if all these were to become rustics in all respects. Still I think they will not fail to find nurture even in the city.

But let's consider how they should act and what they should do to live respectably in our eyes and not be forced by sitting around idly to turn regularly to any of the worthless activities. For, out of all the occupations in the city and the many skills of different types, some are very useful to their practitioners (if you consider 'useful' in terms of pay). But it is not easy to list them all individually because of their number and even more because of their oddity. So let's keep the praise and blame of these brief. Whatever things are harmful for the health of the body or for its suitable strength because of the hanging about and sitting down, or which produce a vileness and servility in the soul or are simply useless and good for nothing and have been invented for the debasement and self-gratification of cities – these basically cannot be correctly called skills or occupations. Hesiod being a wise man would not have praised all work alike, if he thought any bad or disgraceful activity deserved this title. If any of these harmful qualities is attached to any skill or occupation whatsoever, the free and decent man will not touch it or be skilled in it himself or teach it to his children, as neither according to Hesiod nor according to us would the person who practised any such thing be a worker, but he would acquire the reproach for sloth and disgraceful earnings that is normally reserved for slaves and be simply called menial, useless, and vile. On the other hand, whatever occupations are not unseemly for those who engage in them and do not produce any vileness in the soul nor cause sickness (including in these sicknesses weakness, cravenness, and softness through excessive resting of the body) and which provide a sufficient amount of the requirements for living – if they engage in all these enthusiastically and diligently, they will never be short of employment and the means of living, and they will not provide the rich with a real opportunity of speaking about them as they usually do and calling them indigent, but on the contrary will instead be providers for them and in no way indigent, to use that term, with respect to any of the things that are necessary and useful.

So then let's recall out of the two categories of occupations, without any particular exactness in talking about individual cases but by general impression, what kinds of things we will not pursue and why and what kinds of things we would tell the poor to engage in with full confidence, taking no notice of the types who simply say this sort of thing. For instance, they are in the habit of regularly criticising to their faces not only their work, which has nothing unusual in it, but also their parents – for example, if one's mother was a day labourer [*erithos*, cf. *operae*] or a grape picker or nursed a parentless child for pay or a child of the rich, or if one's father taught how to write or acted as a child minder. They should take on these people without feeling any such shame. If they speak about these things, they will be talking about them simply as the signs of poverty, clearly disparaging poverty itself and treating it as something bad and unfortunate, rather than any of its deeds. So, as we do not admit that poverty is worse or less fortunate than wealth, but agree that to many, perhaps, it is more advantageous, this reproach is not to be taken any more to heart than that other one. For, if they were required to criticise not by simply naming the object that they are objecting to, but by mentioning the daily events that occur as its result, they would be able to mention many more things that were really disgraceful resulting from wealth, not least what was judged in Hesiod as the worst of all reproaches, that for laxness, saying, 'My dear sir, the gods did not make you a digger nor a ploughman and you merely have hands that are unchafed and soft like the suitors.'

So I think this is clear to everyone and perhaps is often said, that dyers and perfumers, along with hairdressing for women and men, which is pretty much the same nowadays, and virtually all cosmetic improvement, not only in dress, but also for the hair and complexion, by rouge, lead, and every other kind of ointment that results in a false and artificial appearance of youth, and the beautification of the roofs, walls, and floors with colouring, stones, gold, ivory, and the carving of the walls themselves, are best not accepted at all into the cities, but, as far as we are concerned in our present discussion, we should legislate that none of our poor should engage in such activities. It is as if we were now contending against the rich in a chorus, and the contest is not one over happiness – for that prize is not set out for poverty or for riches instead, but is able to be claimed by virtue alone – but merely over the type of lifestyle and its reasonableness.

So we will not accept tragic or comic actors or the creators of unrestrained laughter in certain mimes or dancers or chorus singers – aside for the holy choruses – singing and dancing about the sufferings of Niobe or Thyestes, or lyre or flute players competing for prizes in the theatre – even if some of the renowned cities will be annoyed with us over this, for instance Smyrna and Chios and in fact Argos along with them, since to the best of our ability we will not be allowing them to increase the reputation of Homer and Agamemnon. Perhaps the Athenians will also be angry, believing that we are dishonouring their tragic and comic poets, when we banish their servants and say that they are not providing anything good. It's likely that the Thebans will also be annoyed on the grounds that the victory that they were awarded by Greece in flute-playing is being attacked. They were so fond of this victory when their city had been razed to the ground and even now is only inhabited in a small section, the Cadmeia, that they were not concerned about anything else that had been destroyed – the many temples, columns, and inscriptions – but sought out the Herm and erected it again, which had on it this inscription about flute-playing:

Greece judged that Thebes gained the prize in the flute contest.

Even now this one statue stands in the middle of the old market place amid the wreckage. But we will reject these entertainers, without fear of any of these people nor of those who will reproach us for criticising the most important things in the eyes of the Greeks, but instead showing that all such things are unsuitable for respectable and free men, since there are many nuisances attached to them, most of all shamelessness, when the crowd has a higher regard for itself than it ought to, which would more correctly be called rashness.

So we will not accept our poor becoming heralds of goods for sale or announcing the reward for information about thieves or runaway slaves, proclaiming this on the streets and in the market place with absolute impunity, nor drafters of contracts, legal challenges, and in general the documents for court-cases and challenges, pretending to have legal experience, nor again to be clever and bothersome litigators and advocates, who announce that they will help everyone alike for a fee and especially the guilty and that they will not be ashamed at others' unjust deeds and that they will act like scoundrels and shout and beg on behalf of those who are neither friends nor relatives, even though some of these seem to be very much honoured and famous in the city. We'll offer those jobs to others. Some of them may be forced to become workers, but they are not forced to become speech- and law-workers.

If any of the occupations I have spoken about or will mention seem useful to the cities, as they do to those presently inhabited, such as perhaps the task of writing down laws and treaties and perhaps some announcements, this is not the right time now to decide how or through whom they should occur to be least harmful. We are not at the moment arranging the civic constitution so that it would be best or better than many, but we proposed to talk about poverty, how its circumstances would be bearable, since it seems to many that poverty itself ought to be avoided and is an evil, but in fact it offers innumerable opportunities from earning a living to those who want to work independently that are neither dishonourable nor harmful. From this starting point we pressed on first to narrate at length the account of farming and hunting, and now to talk about occupations in the city and which of them are appropriate and do not harm those who will lead respectable lives and which will make those engaged in them worse.

If much of what has been spoken about is generally useful for the state and for choosing what is appropriate, then it would be right to excuse the length of this speech, on the grounds that it was long but not simply point-less nor rambling on about useless things. The examination of occupations and skills and overall of the lifestyle that is appropriate or not for reasonable men even on its own has shown itself to need considerable detailed consid-eration. So the listener is required to endure digressions with indulgence, even if they might seem very long, but this is not the case with a digression about what is worthless or contemptible or inappropriate, since the speaker is not giving up on his general topic while he goes through what is necessary and appropriate for philosophy. We would not miss the mark if we almost imitated hunters in this respect: whenever they have first picked up a track and following it have along the way come across some more visible prey that is closer, they are not ashamed to follow it too and, after capturing what they have chanced upon, to go off in pursuit of the first quarry. So perhaps one ought not to blame someone who has started to talk about the just man and justice, but, after mentioning the city as an example, has spent much of his speech on political constitutions and has not returned to his subject before he has discussed all the variations and all the forms of political constitutions, showing very clearly and ostentatiously what happens in each case, even if, perhaps, he will be blamed by some for the length of his speech and for the sermon about his example. He may be not entirely unjustly criticised on these grounds, if for anything: that what has been said is in no way relevant to the topic and that what is being investigated, which was the reason at the start for bringing this into the speech, is in no way made clearer by this. So, if we too should appear to be pursuing things that are not appropriate or related to the topic, then we would properly be said to spinning out our speech. But it is unfair to offer praise or blame in respect of the length or brevity of a speech by itself.

As for the other occupations in the city, we should go through them with confidence, mentioning some, but leaving some unmentioned and forgotten.

So there is no need in fact to talk about pimps and brothel-keeping as though there are two sides to every story. We must strongly resist this and speak out against it, saying that no one, neither poor nor wealthy, should undertake this occupation, collecting pay from outrage and profligacy, which must be denounced by all, acting as matchmakers for unerotic unions and loveless lovemaking, offering the captured bodies of women and boys, or ones that have simply been bought for misuse in filthy stalls, which are displayed throughout the city, both at the entrances to the rulers' quarters and in the market places, and by the official buildings and temples, among the holiest of places. They should not inflict on barbarian slaves or Greeks, who rarely experienced this in the past but now frequently and in large numbers suffer slavery, such inescapable outrage, doing something much worse and filthier than what horse breeders and ass breeders do, not mounting animal on animal without compulsion and willing on willing, without any feeling of shame, but mating sex-mad, unrestrained humans with other humans who are ashamed and acting against their will for a futile and fruitless union that will result in the destruction of bodies rather than their generation, feeling no shame before any man or god, neither before Zeus the patron of birth, nor Hera patron of marriage, nor the Fates who bring the term to an end, nor Artemis patron of childbirth or mother Rhea, nor the Eileithuiae who protect human birth, nor Aphrodite whose name signifies the natural connection and union of male with female. The ruler and the lawmaker will not permit such earnings nor set down laws controlling them, whether in cities best arranged to result in virtuous conduct or in the second, third, fourth best cities, or in any at all, if it is in the power of any of them to control such conduct. If he accepts old practices and incorrigible afflictions, all the same he should not completely allow them to be untreated and unchecked, but he should consider what he can repress and check in some fashion, since the bad is not accustomed to remain in the same place, but is always in motion and advancing towards what is even more licentious as it has no essential limit.

We need to take some care that we do not endure too easily or readily violence against the bodies of the lowly and slaves, not only because the whole human race is in common honoured and equally respected by the god who has created it, having the same signs and tokens of being rightly honoured, reasoning and the awareness of what is noble and what is disgraceful, but also keeping in mind that it is difficult to set a limit to violence, fed as it is by permissiveness, which it would not then be afraid to dare to transgress. Rather, gaining uncontrollable strength and force from practice and experience in what seem unimportant and trivial matters, it will no longer spare anything in the future.

So now, most of all, we must think that these obvious acts of adultery committed in public with the lowly without any feeling of shame or any restraint are to a considerable extent to blame for unseen and invisible attacks on noble women and boys, because it is quite simple to commit such outrages when shame is publicly despised. And we must not think, as some do, that this behaviour has been invented for protection and the avoidance of such crimes.

Well then, someone might speak bluntly in this fashion: 'You wise lawmakers and rulers who have accepted such behaviour from the start, and who have discovered this amazing recipe for restraint for your cities, watch out in case these public and unbarred houses open our locked homes and the bedrooms inside and turn outsiders who are clearly acting badly for a small outlay against free and respectable women with greater bribes and gifts, as they will no longer enjoy what is easy to buy and within their means, but head for the very thing that is forbidden in fear and with great expense. You will see clearly the same way as it seems to me if you consider this: where adultery is, as it were, sent on its way with great pomp and circumstance, where it meets with considerable sympathetic understanding, mainly from the stupidity of husbands who do not realise what is going on, but in some cases from husbands agreeing not to notice, accepting adulterers being called guests, friends, and relatives, and sometimes even showing their kindness and inviting them to dine with them at festivals and sacrifices, in the same way as they would treat their nearest and dearest, and setting a limit to their anger in the face of what is absolutely clear and apparent – where these affairs with others' wives are carried on in such a reasonable fashion, it will not be easy there to be confident in the virginity of unmarried girls or to ever believe that the wedding hymn has been sung truly and rightly at the marriage of these girls. Won't it have to be that everything will happen there as in the ancient myths, excluding the wrath and meddling of fathers, when many will imitate the love affairs of the gods that we have heard about? Won't a great deal of gold drip through the roof, quite easily in fact since the houses are not made of bronze or stone; and by Zeus no little silver drip through, not into maidens' laps alone, but into those of their mothers, nurses, and slave guardians; and many other fine gifts make their way in secret through the roofs and sometimes even clearly through their very doors? Well, isn't it likely that in the rivers and at the springs many things will occur like those previously narrated by the poets? Except, I suppose, they will not occur in public or out in the open, but in wealthy homes and in luxurious lodges in parks and on suburban estates, in which grottos of the nymphs and amazing groves have been built, as this will not involve poor girls nor the daughters of impoverished kings, the sort who draw water and play by the rivers, washing in cold baths and on far-stretching beaches, but wealthy girls, the daughters of wealthy parents, in royal residences that have all their private facilities far surpassing and more impressive than those that the state possesses.

'But perhaps nevertheless they will expect children to exist in that city such as Homer described Eudorus, the son of Hermas and Polydora, nicknaming him, I'd guess because of his birth:

> "The virgin's son [*parthenos*], whom Polydora beautiful at the dance gave birth to."

'Among the Spartans too some gained almost the same nickname for those who have been so born, as it was common for them to be called the virgin children [*Partheniai*]. So if most of those born in such extravagant cities do not perish because, I think, they will not receive any divine assistance at all, then there is nothing to prevent everywhere being filled with heroes. But nowadays some perish straightaway, while those they do rear remain hidden under the form of slaves until their old age, because those who have fathered them are unable to help them out.

'Well then, among those who so carelessly look after their daughters, what kind of upbringing and education should we expect their sons to have? Is it possible that all those adulterers would refrain from corrupting and destroying the males, setting this as the clear and sufficient boundary, that which has been set by nature. Wouldn't they, after fulfilling in every way their every lust for women, become sated with this pleasure and seek some greater, even more illegal outrage? Dealing with women and those generally free and virgins has shown itself to be easy and there is no effort involved for anyone who hunts such quarry with money; for anyone who goes after the noble wives and daughters of men who are truly noble with Zeus' invention, gold, in his hands, will never fail. But the future developments I expect will be clear in most respects. The person who insatiably longs for such things, when he finds nothing is rare or hard to get with the female gender, will despise what is easy, reject sex with women as something simple and in reality completely effeminate, and will make for the men's quarters, wanting to disgrace those who will very soon rule and be judges and generals. There perhaps he will find some difficult and hard-to-achieve form of pleasure, having suffered the same fate as heavy drinkers and dipsomaniacs, who, after drinking large quantities of wine unmixed over a long period, often do not want to drink, but create a sufficient thirst by working up a sweat and eating salty and acidic foods'.

6.10 The poor use animal carcasses to supplement their diet

In a series of robbers' tales, Apuleius describes the misfortunes of a band of brigands, who, after disastrous attempts at burglary at Thebes, now seek their fortunes at Plataea, attracted by the report of an exceptional *munus* (see Chapter 9). Apart from famous gladiators, animal hunters, and condemned prisoners, the temporary arena and grandstands are of impressive construction.

Part of this display is the number of large animals to appear in the *venationes*. After beast hunts in the arena, meat from the slaughtered animals was made available to the general populace. In Apuleius' description, the animals unfortunately do not make it as far as the games; still the people have the chance to butcher the animals as they die and take their skins as well (which gives the brigand narrator the thought of disguising one of his band as a bear).

Apuleius, *Metamorphoses* 4.13–14

Then having suffered the blow of our double loss, we now gave up on our attempts at Thebes and made for the next town, Plataea. We had heard a repeated report that a fellow called Demochares was going to put on a gladiatorial show. He was a man of the first rank by birth, exceedingly rich, and of extraordinary generosity and he was preparing public games of a brilliance that would match his wealth. Who would have the talent, who the eloquence to be able to describe the individual forms of the numerous interlinked displays in words that would do them justice? The gladiators were men of renowned deeds, the hunters men who had proven their speed, and elsewhere the condemned with a lack of concern born of hopelessness were at their banquets readying a rich meal for the beasts. There were stage devices linked together, towers of wooden construction made up of interconnected storeys, looking like houses surrounding the market place, and tableaux painted with flowers, worthy holding places for the hunt to follow. Furthermore, what a huge number and what a fine sight of animals was there! For he had brought in with particular effort from elsewhere those funeral processions of noble heads condemned to death. Apart from the rest of the furnishings of these brilliant games, he had used all the resources whatsoever of his wealth to obtain a large number of bears. For, apart from those captured by his own hunting expeditions and those obtained by the generous expenditure of his friends, he also had those offered by various donors in competition with one another, which he carefully looked after in the most expensive confinement.

But those resplendent and glorious preparations for the entertainment of the populace had not escaped the harmful eyes of Jealousy. For the animals, exhausted from their long captivity and also parched by the burning summer heat and listless from lying around sluggishly, fell victim to a sudden infection and almost none returned to duty. Everywhere around the numerous squares you could see strewn the half-dead bodies from those feral shipwrecks. Then the common crowd, whom rude poverty does not allow any choice of food and forces to find foul supplements and free feasts for their shrunken stomachs, rushed up to these banquets set out everywhere.

6.11 The diet of the poor in Corinth

The epistolary fiction of Alciphron (fourth century AD) offers one of the few descriptions of the indigent feeding off food scraps and waste at the market (for which there are numerous parallels in modern Third World societies).

Alciphron, *Letters* 3.24

I am no longer continuing on into Corinth. For I quickly learnt the vileness of the rich there and the wretchedness of the poor. When the rich were taking their baths in the middle of the day, I saw some suave and good-looking young men not going around the houses, but around the Craneion, especially where the bread sellers and fruit vendors usually reside. There one would bend down to the ground and pick up lupin pods, another would carefully examine the nutshells in case any edible bit had been inadvertently left in them, another scraped with his nails the pomegranate rinds that we Athenians are accustomed to call *sidia* to see if he could still extract any of the seeds, others stooped down picking up pieces of bread thrown away and that had now been walked over by numerous feet. Such is the gateway to the Peloponnese and the city sited between the two seas, which has the least charming inhabitants and the least blessed by Aphrodite. Yet they say that Aphrodite, rising from Cythera, embraced the Acrocorinth. Unless, of course, Aphrodite Protectress of the City has been set up for the women, but Famine for the men.

6.12 The preservation of wealth is at the expense of other members of society

While beggars are largely ignored in our sources or mentioned only in passing, John Chrysostom emphasises the details of their lives. They will normally stay close to the market place (*agora*) where they can expect to meet a considerable number of passers-by, particularly the wealthy, but actually accost them in the alleyways where they cannot be avoided.

John Chrysostom, *Homilies on First Letter to the Corinthians* 11.5 (= *Patrologia Graeca* 61.4–5)

What if we say, 'Why do you want to be wealthy through greed? Is it to pile up gold and silver for others, but curses and innumerable accusations against yourself?' The person who has been deprived of these things will be tormented by a lack of necessities and will lament and call down innumerable charges against you, and when evening comes on he will go around the market place and accost everyone in the alleyways, totally indigent and not having enough to be confident of shelter for the night. For how would he rest then, his stomach gnawing at him, unable to sleep, beset by hunger, and when there is often frost or rain falling down on him? But you come back clean from the baths, kept warm by soft garments, happy and in good spirits, heading off for an expensive meal that is all prepared. But he is continually driven everywhere around the market by cold and hunger, and goes around begging, his head bent and his hand outstretched. Unable to rely with confidence on the well-fed person he has stopped, he directs a speech to him about the necessity of nourishment and often goes away with a flea in his ear. But, whenever you go home, whenever you recline on your couch, whenever there is bright lighting throughout the house, whenever there is a costly meal ready, then you should remember that miserable and wretched fellow, going around accompanied by the dogs in the dark alleys and mud – although he often leaves there not to go home to his wife, nor to bed, but to a bed of straw, just as we see the dogs who howl the whole night long. You, if you see one little drip coming from the roof, rouse the whole household, calling on your slaves and setting everything in motion. But he lies in rags on straw and mud, suffering the cold without relief.

6.13 John Chrysostom comforts a sick friend by describing the suffering of the impoverished

In the late fourth century, John Chrysostom wrote three tracts to his friend Stagirus, who was suffering from epilepsy. In particular, he seeks to console him by contrasting the continual (rather than spasmodic) nature of the suffering of the indigent, those suffering from wasting illnesses, and those in the prisons and mines. In brief, Stagirus still has the support of his peers (themselves well off in Antiochene society), while the truly wretched have been cut off from the assistance of family members or friends that might alleviate their sufferings.

John Chrysostom, *To Stagirus, Tormented by a Demon* 3.13 (= *Patrologia Graeca* 47.490)

So that I don't seem to be wearing out my listeners by enumerating each individual who has suffered such things, go to the person entrusted with running the hospice and tell him to escort you to those lodging there so you can see all the roots of suffering, strange types of disease, and all the forms of despondency. Then go to the public prison and find out everything happening in the building. Then make your way to the forecourt of the baths, where people live naked, under straw and dung instead of clothing and housing, beset by continual cold, sickness, and hunger, calling out to the passers-by through their appearance alone, their trembling bodies, and the noise of their chattering teeth – they are unable to make a sound or to extend their hands because they have by now been dreadfully debilitated by their terrible sufferings. But don't stop with these: go off to the refuge

226

for beggars outside the city and then take a careful look, so the depression that seems to hold you will now be but a calm port in life's storm. What description could you give to men nearly consumed by elephantiasis, the women eaten away by cancer? Both of these diseases are slow and incurable. Both of them drive the sufferers out of the city: they are not allowed to partake of the baths or the market or anything else inside the city. And this is not the only terrible feature of their suffering, but that they cannot take comfort in the generosity of their relations. What about those who have been condemned to be imprisoned in the mines, often at random and without any good reason?

6.14 The public baths as shelter

Along with John Chrysostom, Alciphron offers evidence of the use of the baths as shelter in adverse weather, especially in winter. This, however, required the baths to be open and heated (usually through a memorial endowment or by imperial or local euergetism), since even the minimal cost of private institutions might be beyond the truly poor.

Alciphron, *Letters* 3.40

I have never endured such a storm in Attica. For not only did the winds strike us blowing in a broad front, or rather carried along in a column, but now thick snow closely packed first covered the ground. Then it was not only on top of the ground, but a huge mound of fallen snowflakes rose up so high that you would have been happy to open the door of your house and see the alley. But I had neither wood nor a cloak. How then or from where to get this? The snow was sinking into my insides and my bones. So I thought up a plan worthy of Odysseus: to run into the halls of the bathhouse. But my fellow guildsmen wandering around there did not make room for me, as a similar divinity was persecuting them – Poverty. So, when I realised I would not be able to enter these halls, I ran to the bathhouse of Thrasylos, found it empty, gained the blessing of the bathman by paying him 2 obols, and warmed myself until ice followed the snowstorm and the stones were stuck to one another by the freezing of the moisture between them. After the icy fog lifted, the gentle sun revealed that the way was free for me to go and that I could stroll around as I wished.

6.15 A slave girl criticises her mistress for her heartlessness

This imaginary reproach by an inferior summarises much of what we know about the habit of beggars in the Greco-Roman world: appeals to the charity of the wealthy by bestowing compliments (cf. Seneca, *Constantia Sapientis* 13 on the self-satisfaction of those praised by beggars) or attempts to draw attention by performing as street entertainers. Not mentioned is the abuse that might follow those who did not donate (Seneca, *On Clemency* 2.5.2). Large households might employ jesters and dwarfs for entertainment, a practice that is also condemned by John Chrysostom (*Homilies on First Letter to Timothy* 17.2 = *Patrologica Graeca* 62.593).

John Chrysostom, *Homilies on First Letter to the Thessalonians* 11.3 (= *Patrologia Graeca* 62.465)

Beggars are sitting here who have lost the use of their feet, watching you rush past. Then, since they cannot follow you on foot, as if using a hook, they expect that they can halt you by the dread of their appeal and stretch out their hands and call out for you to give them just one or two obols. But you rush by, although you have been appealed to in the name of your Master [i.e. Christ]. If a beggar appeals to you before the eyes of your husband who is out in public, or of your son or your daughter, you immediately relent and your heart is immediately uplifted and warmed. But, if he appeals in the name of the Lord, you run on. I know many, who, on hearing the name of Christ, hurry by, but, when their beauty is praised by those they meet, melt in spirit, soften their hearts, and extend their hands. Indeed they force the wretched poor to this – to become clowns. For, when they cannot latch onto your souls by vehement and biting comments, they take that path by which they will give the greatest pleasure. The man in misfortune, tortured by hunger, is forced by our absolute worthlessness to deliver encomia of our beauty as a way of begging. If only this was the limit – there is another form worse than this. It forces the poor to be conjurers, dirty-joke tellers, and clowns. Whenever they tie cups, bowls, and drinking vessels to their fingers and play the cymbals attached to their bodies, holding a flute and playing on it disgraceful songs full of love-themes, and sing out in a loud voice – then many people will stand around them and some will donate soft bread, others an obol, others something else. They stop there for a long time, and men and women enjoy themselves. What is worse than this? Don't they deserve much lamentation? They are small things and are thought of as small things. But they give birth to many things that harm our morals.

6.16 An imagined debate (*declamatio*) over a man who earned a living turning children into crippled beggars

The suggestion that child beggars might be deliberately crippled appears common across numerous cultures and time periods. While the authenticity of the practice cannot be established (and is of little concern for the imaginary debates recorded by Seneca the Elder), there is no doubt that there was a market for the castrated in the Roman world. This practice was limited by Domitian's legislation outlawing castration (Suetonius, *Domitian* 7 – but note that this law may have only applied to the areas of the empire where Roman law prevailed). The illegal holding of the free in slave prisons was a constant abuse (cf. Suetonius, *Augustus* 32) and the attraction of the gladiatorial schools needed to be subject to senatorial legislation (**1.17**).

Seneca the Elder, *Controversiae* 10.4, preface 17–18

The Crippled Beggars

A case may be brought on the grounds of harming the state.

A man would maim children who had been exposed, force them as cripples to beg, and demand money from them. He is accused of harming the state.

... Labienus argued as eloquently for the case of the man who crippled them as anyone did for the other side, although all the most eloquent speakers had spoken on that side to display their ability. He declaimed this topic with particular force: 'It's amazing that folks have time on their hands to contemplate this and worry what a beggar man does among beggars! Our leading men use their riches to defeat Nature: they have herds of eunuchs, they castrate their boyfriends to suitably suffer their lechery for longer, and, because they are ashamed of being men, they see to it that men are as rare as possible. No one helps these darlings and crippled pretty boys. You've got the idea of worrying about who is taking away from lonely places babes who will perish if they're not removed. But you don't worry that your rich types have their lonely places worked by slave prisons full of the freeborn, you don't worry that they play on the innocence of unfortunate youths and throw the most handsome and most suitable for fighting into the gladiatorial schools. You have got it into your minds to pity these people because they do not have limbs – how about pitying those who do?' By attacking the vices of the age in this fashion, through the excellence of his theme, he was able to defend a besmirched and infamous defendant by highlighting the lack of punishment of greater crimes.

6.17 Poverty in Antioch in the fourth century AD

It is a regular part of the practices of the early Christian church to devote alms to the upkeep of the needy (beggars and widows, in particular). The charitable practices of the church conflicted with the traditional system of euergetism or philanthropy, which were based on individual displays of generosity (for instance, the provision of games or feasts) that took little account of the need of the recipients.

John Chrysostom, *Homilies on First Letter to the Corinthians* 21.5–6 (= *Patrologia Graeca* 61.176–7)

'Who says this?' someone replies [to the message that the congregation is ignoring the advice to give away their riches]. Well, this is particularly terrible, because this is spoken not in words, but in deeds. For it would be less terrible if only spoken in words, rather than occurring in deeds. Does not that inhuman and cruel tyranny, the love of money, announce this every day to her prisoners: 'Let sustenance be provided for the informers, the brigands, and those plotting against you to make them fat, but not for the poor and for those in need.' Well, isn't it you who create brigands? Well, isn't it you who provide sustenance for the fire of the slanderers? Don't you yourselves create runaways and those who plot against you, setting forth your wealth like bait for them? What sort of madness is this? For it is clearly madness and insanity to fill up chests with cloaks, but to disregard a man who has been made in the image and likeness of God, naked and trembling from the cold and finding it hard to stand up.

'But,' someone says, 'has he an excuse for his trembling and weakness?' So aren't you afraid that lightning from above kindled by these words might strike you? I'm at bursting point with anger – please forgive me. You, who have your bellies full and are well fattened, who extend your drinking sessions well into the night, who are kept warm by soft coverings, don't you deserve to be punished for so criminally using God's gifts? For wine is not intended to make us drunk nor nourishment to swell our bellies, nor food to extend our stomachs. But will you examine, question, and interrogate the poor man, the wretch who is no better than a corpse and not fear that dread and fearful court of Christ? For, if he were to reply, he would answer that his trembling and weakness came from need and necessity because of your cruelty and inhumanity, which demands such an appearance, since it is not inclined to pity. For who is so wretched and miserable that he would look so miserable, be so smitten, and endure such a trial for a single loaf of bread unless necessity forced him to do so? Your questioning of him goes around with you as the herald of your inhumanity. For, since by pleading, begging, uttering pitiful words, wailing and crying, and following you he cannot obtain the nourishment he needs, he has perhaps invented this scheme, which does not bring shame and condemnation as much to him as to you. He has the right to be pitied as having come to such a state of need. But we deserve innumerable punishments for forcing the poor to endure such things. Even if we were favourably disposed from a feeling of contentedness, he would never choose to suffer these things.

Why do I mention nakedness and trembling? I will tell you about something more blood-chilling: that some have been forced to maim their children while they are still in infancy in order to overcome our lack of concern. And, when looking like this and going around naked they have not been able to attract the pitiless by their age and fate, they have added another worse tragedy to such ills: in order to stop their hunger, they think that it would be easier to be deprived of the light shared by all and the light of day given to everyone than to wrestle with constant hunger and suffer the most pitiful of deaths. Since you have not learnt to pity poverty, but to enjoy misfortune, they fulfil your insatiate desire and kindle for themselves and for you a blaze worse than that of Hell.

So you may know that such things as these occur, I will give you an example that has been witnessed and that no one will deny. There are other poor people, simple and bewildered in mind, who do not know how to endure hunger, who would rather suffer anything but this. After they have regularly met you with pitiful expressions and words and have achieved nothing, they give up on such supplication and thereafter surpass the conjurers, some chewing the leather of worn-out shoes, others piercing their heads with sharp nails, others going into water that is icy from the cold up to their naked stomachs, and others enduring still more bizarre things than these, in order that a wretched audience may gather around.

But you, when this is going on, stand around laughing and admiring this, priding yourselves in the misfortunes of others, while our common nature is disgraced. What thing worse than this could a wild demon create? Then, so that he will do this with more spirit, you give him money in abundance. But you do not deign to reply or to look at one who offers prayers and calls on God and approaches you humbly, but even direct those vulgar expressions at him when he continually annoys you. Should this fellow be alive? Should he be fully breathing or looking upon this sun? You are proud and arrogant before them, like a producer of that ridiculous and satanic disgracefulness. So it would be more reasonable if these words were spoken to those putting on these contests and not donating anything until they see others suffering: are these alive and fully breathing? Should they look upon this sun who are committing a crime against our common nature and creating a disgrace in the eyes of God? And when God says, Give charity and I will give you the kingdom of heaven, you do not listen. But when the devil shows you a head with nails in it, you suddenly become proud. The scheme of the wretched demon that has so much harm is more attractive than the promise of God bringing innumerable blessings. When it is necessary, even if you had to spend money to prevent these things and not see them occurring, to do and endure everything to remove this great insanity, you do everything and make every effort to ensure that they occur and that you watch them happening. Then you will ask me, 'Why is there a Hell?' Don't ask this in future, but why there is only one Hell.

6.18 The development of shelter

The original invention of common objects or practices was a common theme in ancient antiquarian and philosophical writings (cf. Lucretius, *On the Nature of Things* 5, especially 1011–1457). Vitruvius follows the common practice of induction, reasoning back from primitive habitation in the present to imagine early forms of shelter from which man has progressed to more complex (and possibly more extravagant) forms.

Vitruvius, *On Architecture* 2.1.3–6

Since humans have the ability to learn and imitate, each day they would boast of their discoveries and show one another the results of their building methods. By so applying their talents in competition, they improved their decisions daily. First they put forked branches upright and placed twigs in between and covered these walls with mud. Others dried lumps of clay and built walls, binding them together with wood, and covered them with twigs and leaves to avoid rain and heat. After these constructions were unable to withstand the water from winter storms, they created roof ridges and sloping roofs plastered with clay, and ran out the rainwater.

We can deduce that these things were created from the beginnings described above because, up till this day, buildings are created out of these materials in foreign countries, such as using oak shingles and thatch in Gaul, Spain, Lusitania, and Aquitaine. Among the Colchian people in Pontus there is an abundance of wood. So they place tree trunks horizontally along the ground on the left and the right, leaving a space in between that is enough for a tree length, and at the ends of them they place tree trunks at right angles, which enclose the middle of the dwelling. Then they join the corners by lying beams one after another on each of the four sides. By making walls of trees in this way rising directly from the base, they create towers of considerable height, and they block up the spaces left in between by the unevenness of the wood with wedges and mud. They construct the roofs in a similar way, cutting the beams at the far ends and gradually bringing them together, and so from the four sides they construct cones in the middle at the top, which they cover with foliage and mud and in barbarian fashion create the tortoiseshell roofs of their towers.

The Phrygians, however, who live in flat areas and lack wood because of the scarcity of trees, choose natural mounds and open them up in the middle by digging and then by boring paths through they clear out as large an area as the nature of the place permits. They bind branches together above and create cones, which they cover with rushes and brushwood, and raise up particularly large hillocks of earth above their dwellings. Their method of building makes their winters thoroughly warm and their summers perfectly cool. Some build huts of marsh grasses. Among other nations as well the construction of their cottages is achieved in a comparable fashion by use of similar rush material. Likewise, even at Marseilles we can observe rammed earth and straw roofs instead of tiles. At Athens on the Areopagus, there is an example of ancient construction surviving to this day that is roofed with clay. Likewise the house of Romulus on the Capitol and the roofs of shrines made of thatch in the Citadel can remind us and illustrate the manners of the past. In this way we can from this evidence make our judgements on the ancient discoveries and deduce that they were of this sort.

6.19 The life of a gardener and his ass

While the housing of the wealthy and apartment buildings have left considerable archeological traces, the shelter for perhaps the majority of those living in the ancient world has left little or no trace as it was rapidly degradable. There would be little to distinguish a storehouse from living quarters and, indeed, many such huts would have served both purposes.

Apuleius, *Metamorphoses* 9.31–2

Finally I myself was bought by a poor gardener for 50 drachmas, a large amount, so he said, but he paid it to get a partner to bind to himself by their shared labour. The situation seems to me to demand that I expound the pattern of my enslavement.

In the morning the master used to lead me, loaded down with plenty of vegetables, to the nearest town and, when he had handed over the goods to the buyers, he would mount my back and so return home. While he was digging or watering or kept busy bent over with other tasks, I was free for this period and rested in gentle repose. But, after the fixed wanderings of the stars through the due measure of months and days, the turning year changed from the delights of autumn with its unfermented wine to the winter's frosts under Capricorn and to continual rain and heavy dew at night under an open sky. Shut in an unroofed stable, I was tortured by the unceasing cold, since my master because of his extreme poverty could not obtain any bedding or the slightest covering for himself, let alone me. Instead, he endured this period, content with the leafy shade of his little hut. In addition, in the morning I would struggle my way through, walking with bare hooves on mud that had frozen solid and sharp bits of ice and could not even fill my stomach with my normal fodder. For my master and I had equivalent and quite similar meals, which were quite meagre: old and bitter greens, which, because of the long time since they had been sown, had almost turned into branches and had matured to become bitter and rotten with slimy juices.

6.20 The basic amenities of a city negatively defined

It is instructive to contrast Panopeus, utterly lacking in expected amenities, with the civic heart of Rome at the forum, the numerous theatres and Flavian amphitheatre for entertainment, its baths, and abundant water supply from its aqueducts.

Pausanias, *Guide to Greece* 10.4.1

There is a distance of 20 stades [about two and a half miles] from Chaeroneia to Panopeus, the city in Phocis, if in fact one was to refer to as a city even people who have no civic buildings or gymnasium, no theatre and no market place, no water running into a fountain, but live there in a ravine in dwellings that are round quite like huts in the mountains. Still they have boundary stones with those with whom they share borders and they too send representatives to the assembly of the Phocaeans.

6.21 Building and building restrictions at Rome

Part of the Greek reaction to Rome's conquest of the Mediterranean was an attempt to explain the reasons for this success. An initial explanation was the favourable geographical site of the city, underpinned by the labour and courage of the inhabitants. This resulted in Rome's growth to the largest city in the Mediterranean, which, however, produced problems of ensuring the food supply and coping with the need for constant large-scale building.

Strabo, *Geography* 5.3.7

This was no chance discovery of a good site [for Rome] that would be favoured in the future. As the place was supportive of bravery and toil, there was an inrush of gains that exceeded all natural advantages. The city, having grown so much because of this, can cope partly through its food supply and partly by using wood and stone for building, which is continual because of collapses, fires, and sales, which are also continual. In fact the sales are a type of voluntary collapse, as they tear down and rebuild one building after another according to their desires. In addition, there are numerous quarries and forests, and navigable rivers are in amazing supply: first the Anio flowing from Alba, the Latin city facing the Marsi, through the plain beneath it to its confluence with the Tiber, then the Nar and the Teneas, flowing through Umbria into the same Tiber river, and the Clanis running through Etruria and Clusium. Caesar Augustus showed his concern about such losses in the city: to combat fires he established a military force recruited from freedmen to assist; to combat collapses he reduced the height of new buildings, legislating that those beside public streets should not exceed

70 feet in height. Despite this, the rebuilding programme would not be sufficient except that the quarries, forests, and the ease of navigation enable them to cope with this.

6.22 Living conditions at Rome

Martial's complaints about the noise at Rome show a set of stereotypes of lower-class occupations: the schoolmaster (see Chapter 4), millers, copper- and goldsmiths, money changers, the priests of Bellona (the castrated Galli), firewood sellers (or is this person selling eye salves?), Jewish beggars, and shipwreck survivors with their evidence of misfortune. He is presumably living in an apartment building (*insula*), but can escape to his country farm. The really wealthy (such as Sparsus) have their own free-standing houses (*domus*) on the hilltops at Rome and gardens (*horti*) around them, which, it is claimed, allows for all the pleasures of the country within the city. The extent of such estates may be seen in the *horti Sallustiani* (gardens originally owned by the nephew of the historian Sallust), which became a major public park, or Hadrian's Villa at Tivoli (which has paths for wheeled vehicles within the estate).

Martial, *Epigrams* 12.57

Are you asking me why I often head for
My little farm at dry Nomentum and the humble Lar at my
    farmstead?
There is no chance in the city, Sparsus, for a poor man
To think or rest. The schoolmasters in the morning
Prevent one from living, the millers at night,
And the hammers of the coppersmiths all day long.
Here an idle money changer shakes
His rough table with a pile of Neronian coins;
Over there the hammerer of Spanish gold dust
Beats his worn stone with gleaming cudgel.
Nor does the frenzied mob of Bellona desist
And the gabbing shipwreck survivor with his wrapped beam,
And the Jew taught to beg by his mother,
And the blear-eyed merchant of sulphured wood.
Who can count the numerous ways to lose deep sleep?
He will be able to tell you how many hands strike brass in the city
When the moon is flogged into eclipse by the Colchian rhombus.
But you, Sparsus, don't know any of this – nor could you,
Leading the life of Riley on your Petilian estate,
Whose home all on one level looks down on mountain tops,
Who has country life in the city and a vinedresser at Rome
(There is no greater harvest on the Falernian hills)

And a wide path for your chariot inside your threshold,
Deep sleep and rest broken by no tongues,
And no daylight unless it has been allowed in.
We are woken by the laughter of the passing crowd
And Rome lies at our elbow. Whenever we are exhausted with
    tiredness
And wanting to sleep, we head off to our farm.

6.23 The noise above a bathhouse

Seneca suggests the freedom from concern with everyday life (*ataraxia*) open to the Stoic philosopher by depicting himself as living above a bathhouse. It is unlikely, given his enormous wealth, that Seneca actually lived this way, but the depiction of commonplace activities in the baths, including the plucking of armpits, is a particularly vivid snapshot of daily life.

Seneca, *Letters* 56.1–5

I'll be damned if silence is as much a necessity as it appears for those who withdraw to study. Look, all sorts of uproar surround me from all sides – I'm living above the bathhouse itself. Now assemble all the sorts of noises that can rouse the ears to hatred. When the strongmen are exercising and heaving up their arms weighed down with lead, I hear the grunts when they are straining or pretending to be straining, their whistles and harsh wheezing, whenever they release the breath they've been holding in. When I run into a lazybones who is satisfied with the ordinary rubdown, I hear the thud of hands on his shoulder blades, giving out a different sound depending on whether they come down flat or cupped. But if a ball player takes over and starts to call the balls, that's the end! Now toss in the brawler, the thief caught in the act, and the guy who likes the sound of his own voice in the baths, and toss in the folks who jump into the pool with a huge splash as they hit the water. Apart from them (their voices are at least natural), think of the armpit plucker continually letting out his high-pitched and shrill cry to catch everyone's attention, never stopping except when he is plucking armpits and making someone else scream out instead of him. Then there's the array of calls from the drinks seller, the sausage seller, the bun seller, and all the employees of the hot-food shops selling their wares each with their own distinctive inflexion.

'You're an iron man – or deaf,' you reply, 'when you can keep your head amid such an array of different noises, when the constant stream of well-wishers drove our leader Chrysippus to his death.' Good lord, I am no more concerned about that babble than about the flow and ebb of water – although I have heard that one race had this single reason for moving their city: that they could not bear the noise of the Nile going over the falls. A single voice, it seems to me, is more distracting than any uproar, as the former distracts the mind, while the latter merely fills the ears and hands them a beating. I include in the things that roar around me without distracting me the carriages rushing by, the local builder and the man sawing in the neighbourhood, and the fellow here who is trying out pipes and flutes by the Meta Sudans, not playing a tune but blaring away. Again, I find the sound that stops from time to time to be more annoying than one that goes on continuously. But I have by now hardened myself against all those annoyances so I can even listen to a coxswain setting time for the rowers in a thoroughly shrill voice. I am making my mind focus on itself and not be distracted by things outside. Everything can be reverberating outside, so long as there is no uproar inside, so long as desire and fear are not brawling with one another, so long as greed and extravagance are not at loggerheads, and it's not one thing upsetting another. What's the use of silence throughout the whole district, if the emotions are roaring away?

6.24 Building materials in apartment blocks

As Strabo noted (**6.21**), building space was at a minimum at Rome and so construction needed to rise to several levels at least. The construction of stone, brick, and wood permitted this, but also provided a fire risk. Furthermore, unbaked or poorly baked brick would decay easily through weathering or floods, creating a risk of building collapse (*ruina*) such as happened to Cicero's shops (**6.25**).

Vitruvius, *On Architecture* 2.8.17–20

The public regulations do not allow walls of a greater thickness than 18 inches if they are shared with another building. The other walls are built of the same thickness so that the space inside isn't reduced. But brickwork that is not two or three bricks deep but only of 18 inches in thickness cannot support more than one storey. But given the grandeur of Rome and the unending multitudes of citizens there is a need to construct countless dwellings. So, as the flat areas cannot allow this enormous crowd to live in the city, the situation has forced them to turn to height to help with building. So by stone pillars, fired-brick construction, and rubble walls they have built up high structures of apartments assembled with numerous wooden floors, which offer the finest conveniences and produce views down over the city. So, by using walls supported by wooden floors, they multiply the ground space high in the air and the Roman people have wonderful living conditions without any problems.

Since we have explained why, at Rome, because of the requirements of the limited space, brick walls are not allowed, when they need to be used outside the city, this is the method to use so there will not be any faults that will reduce their useful life. At the top of walls, a fired-brick construction should be used for the last 18 inches under the tile roofing and there should be projecting cornices. In this way you can avoid the regular faults in these walls: when the tiles on the roof are broken or torn off by the wind, so water from rainstorms can flow through them, the brick protection will not allow the wall to be harmed – the projecting cornices will throw off the rainwater beyond the straight line of the wall and in that fashion preserve the construction of the brickwork walls intact.

No one can give an immediate judgement on burnt brick as to the best type and what is wrong for building, because only when it is set on a roof and exposed to weathering and the effects of time is it revealed whether it is strong enough. For it is only then that brick that is not made of a good mix or insufficiently fired will show itself to be faulty when it is affected by ice and frost. So the brick that cannot take the strain on roofs cannot be strong enough for load-bearing in building. So, in particular, roofs of old tiles and walls made of old baked brick will be able to offer solidity.

But I wish that wattlework construction had never been discovered. The more it assists in speed of construction and freeing up space, the more it lends itself to greater disaster for everyone, as it is like kindling readied for a fire. So it seems more reasonable to have the expense of using burnt brick in the building costs, rather than to take risks by saving through wattlework. It also causes cracks in the plasterwork by the arrangement of upright and cross pieces. For when it is plastered, it swells from the moisture it absorbs, then shrinks as it drys and having been weakened like this, cracks the solidity of the plastering. But as the need for haste or lack of funds or the partitioning of an overhanging space forces many to use this method, this is the way to work. The foundation should be raised so that it does not touch the rubble or the pavement. If wattlework is fixed in [the ground], it becomes weak with age; then it starts to incline as it sinks and breaks the surface of the plaster.

6.25 The lack of concern of a landlord for his tenants

It is clear that Roman senators regularly speculated in urban property for the high rental returns, as well as investing a considerable proportion of their wealth in safer rural assets. Not only was there risk from fire (**6.26** and **6.27**), but also from flooding of the valleys in the city, and also from the collapse of buildings, either after floods had weakened the foundations or from the strain on the construction from excessive numbers of storeys. Cicero jokes about the matter – whether his tenants were so happy is another matter – but the regular collapse of buildings also offered opportunities for rebuilding on an even greater scale in the prosperous economies of the late republic and early empire.

Cicero, *Letters to Atticus* 14.9
(Puteoli, 17 April, 44 BC)

I have learned a great deal about public affairs from your letters, which in fact I received simultaneously in a bundle from Vestorius' freedman. I will briefly reply about the things you are asking about. First I am very pleased by my Cluvian property. But since you are asking why I summoned Chrysippus: two of my shops have collapsed and the others are showing cracks in them. So not only the tenants, but even the mice have moved out. Others call this a great disaster, but I don't even speak of it as a problem. Socrates and the Socratic school – I will never be able to thank you enough. Good gods, this stuff is the equivalent of nothing in my eyes. But all the same, we're starting to plan the rebuilding, using Vestorius as adviser and backer to turn this loss into a profit.

6.26 Fires at Rome

A constant theme in Roman literature is the high cost of rental housing in the city. Partly, this is the result of the density of the urban population (usually estimated at a million or more) crammed into a limited space, partly the high risk of investing in housing. Major fires were regular events: the fire at Rome under Nero (AD 64) is perhaps the most spectacular of these, but, as this passage indicates, much smaller blazes would damage the neighbouring buildings due to the narrow streets and the practice of building extensions out over them. The practice of constructing the upper storeys of apartment buildings with timber frames would have lightened the load on the lower floors, but increased the fire risk.

Julianus' recommendation of using alum as a fire retardant does not appear to have been adopted. Rather the passage shows his keen familiarity with authors who were generally regarded as antiquated in the second century AD (Quadrigarius wrote in the 70s BC).

Aulus Gellius, *Attic Nights* 15.1

Antonius Julianus the rhetor had delivered a public lecture and, although his speeches were always fine wherever he gave them, this one was amazingly delightful and successful. Generally those academic lectures show the same man and the same eloquence, but not the same success each day. So we friends of his were surrounding him on all sides, escorting him back home, when as we came up to the Cispian hill we saw an apartment building alight. It was constructed to a great height out of many tall storeys and already everything in the neighbourhood was burning in a great fire. Then one of Julian's companions said, 'The returns on urban property are great, but the risks are far greater. If there was any solution that would prevent houses at Rome burning so regularly, I would sell my country property and buy property in the city.' Julianus, however, amid the discussion replied with remarkable polish, as was his way, 'If you had read Book 19 of the *Annals* of Claudius Quadrigarius, a very fine author of the purest style, you would, of course, have learnt from Archelaus, king Mithridates' commander, the cunning remedy for combating fire, so none of your buildings constructed out of wood would catch fire and burn as the flames spread.'

I asked him what that wonderful thing in Quadrigarius was. He replied, 'Well, I found it written in that book that, when Lucius Sulla was besieging the Pieraeus in Attica and Archelaus, Mithridates' commander, was defending it from inside the town, a wooden tower was built for defence that would not catch light, although it was surrounded by fire on all sides, because it had been smeared with alum by Archelaus.'

These are the words of Quadrigarius in that book: 'When he had made various attempts over a long time, Sulla led out his troops in order to set alight a wooden tower of Archelaus, which he had set in their way. He came up, got to it, placed wood under it, drove the Greeks back, and applied fire. Although they tried for a long time, they could not set it alight: Archelaus had smeared all the wood with alum. Sulla and his troops were amazed at this and, when they could not set it alight, he withdrew his forces.'

6.27 Fire at Rome (AD 237), after civil conflict

There were numerous major fires at Rome because of the limited building space and the regular use of wood in construction. We know that the problems under Augustus were significant enough for the creation of a permanent night-watch (the *vigiles*: Dio 55.26). Claudius found it necessary to intervene personally to fight a fire by the Campus Martius (Suetonius, *Claudius* 18). The great fire of AD 64 is described in detail in Tacitus, *Annals* 15.38–43: despite the tales of Nero's fiddling, the emperor seems to have done all he could to assist the homeless and to promote rebuilding in an orderly fashion, which would reduce the fire risk. But major fires still occurred, such as that under Titus in AD 80, and the one described below.

Herodian, *Histories* 7.2.5–7

When the mobs were defeated in hand-to-hand fighting, they climbed onto the roofs of the houses and hit them with tiles and with volleys of rocks and broken pottery, causing casualties among the soldiers. The soldiers did not risk climbing up to them because they did not know the housing and because the buildings and workshops had their doors barred. If there were any wooden balconies (there are many of these in the city) they set fire to them from below. Because the apartment buildings were so closely packed together and there were so many wooden structures next to one another, the fire spread to most of the city. As a result, many of the rich became poor when they had lost splendid property everywhere, valued for its rich income and costly elegance. Many men were burned alive at the same time, unable to escape because the fire had got to the exits first. The entire wealth of rich individuals was looted when criminals and poor civilians joined with the soldiers in plundering. The fire destroyed an area of the city whose size could not be matched by any other great city as a whole.

6.28 Crassus as property speculator

In the late republic, the wealth of Marcus Licinius Crassus was legendary. Much of this was founded on buying the property of those proscribed under Sulla, but Crassus also exploited the demand for high-quality housing by the wealthy in this period. This is part of the competition for prestige that might prove financially ruinous for its participants (Cicero, for instance, was often heavily in debt because of his houses). Although credited with creating a 'fire brigade', Crassus was instead a pioneer in having a permanent team of purchasers and rebuilders to assist his property business.

Plutarch, *Crassus* 2

Still before the Parthian expedition, when he made an account of his personal wealth, he found that he had the amount of 7,100 talents. Most of this, if we must speak the truth even at the cost of criticism, he gained through fire and war, using public misfortunes to maximise his profit. When Sulla captured Rome and sold off the goods of those he had killed, regarding this as, and even calling it, war booty and wanting to tarnish as many of the most powerful as possible with this dishonour, Crassus did not refuse to accept or purchase this. In addition, he observed that the disasters of fire and collapse at Rome were interlinked and connected from the size and number of the buildings. So he bought up slave builders and architects. Then, when he had more than 500 of them, he bought up the burning properties and the buildings in the neighbourhood of those alight, as the owners would surrender them for a small sum of money out of fear and uncertainty. So most of Rome came into his possession. But, although he had so many workmen, he only built himself one house for personal use and used to say that those who were keen on mansions would be ruined by themselves without needing enemies.

6.29 Rebuilding of Rome after the Gallic sack
(387–386 BC) and the Neronian Fire (AD 64)

Ancient Rome was notorious for its haphazard street patterns, the result of accretion rather than planning. After the Great Fire of 64, Nero could take advantage of the damage to extend his palace, which caused considerable resentment, but also to attempt to create planned rebuilding. The effectiveness of anti-fire measures does not seem to have lasted for long, given later fires (**6.27** above). Tacitus, with some black humour, also records the complaints of those who felt that the new plan intensified the often stifling heat in the city.

(a) Livy, 5.55

The populace began to rebuild the city everywhere. Tiles were provided at public expense; everyone was granted the right to quarry stone and cut timber wherever they wanted to, so long as they offered their land as security for completing their building that same year. This haste removed any concern for making the streets straight as they built over empty land without concern for what was theirs and what belonged to others. That is the reason why the old drains that originally were built through public land now pass under private dwellings all over the place and the outline of the city looks more like the land had been squatted on rather than parcelled out to its inhabitants.

(b) Tacitus, *Annals* 15.43

But the part of the city that escaped Nero's palace was not constructed haphazardly all over the place, as after the Gallic burning of the city, but with the boundaries of the wards marked out and with roads laid out with wide dimensions. The height of buildings was to be restricted, and there were to be open courtyards and porticos around to protect the apartments' frontage. Nero promised that he would erect these porticos at his own expense and hand over the courtyards, cleared of debris, to their owners. He added rewards according to the status and financial position of each owner and set a time limit within which they would receive them if they had completed their houses and apartment buildings. He regulated that the Ostian marshes should receive the rubble and that the boats that brought the grain supply up the Tiber were to sail down it laden with debris. The buildings themselves should be built to a certain height without timbers but wholly out of Gabian or Alban stone, since that stone is impervious to fire. He appointed custodians so that the water supply that had been diverted by the abusive practices of individuals should flow in greater quantities to more places for public use. Everyone should have the means of stopping fires openly available and all buildings should have their own walls on all sides, not shared party walls. The changes brought about from reasons of utility brought some elegance as well to the new city. Still there were those who thought the old shape of the city was more healthy, since the narrow roads and high buildings were not penetrated by the sun's heat to the same extent – now it blazed more fiercely down on the wide open ground, which was unprotected by shade.

FURTHER READING

Atkins, M. and Osborne, R. (eds) (2006) *Poverty in the Roman World*, Cambridge.

Brunt, P.A. (1973) 'Aspects of the Social Thought of Dio Chrysostom', *Proceedings of the Cambridge Philological Society* 199: 9–34.

Champlin, E. (1981) 'Owners and Neighbours at Ligures Baebiani', *Chiron* 11: 239–64.

Champlin, E. (1991) *Final Judgments*, Berkeley and Los Angeles, CA.

Coleman, K. (1990) 'Fatal Charades: Roman Executions Staged as Mythological Enactments', *Journal of Roman Studies* 80: 44–73.

de Ste Croix, G. (1981) *The Class Struggle in the Ancient World*, London.

Frier, B. (1980) *Landlords and Tenants in Imperial Rome*, Princeton, NJ.

Garland, R. (1995) *The Eye of the Beholder: Deformity and Disability in the Graeco-Roman World*, London.

Gray, C. and Parkin, A. (2003) 'Controlling the Urban Mob: The *Colonatus Perpetuus* of CTh 14.18.1', *Phoenix* 57: 284–99.

Grunewald, T. (2004) *Bandits in the Roman Empire*, London.

Hamil, G. (1990) *Poverty and Charity in Roman Palestine*, Berkeley, CA.

Schofield, M. (1991) *The Stoic Idea of the City*, Cambridge.

Shaw, B.D. (1984) 'Bandits in the Roman Empire', *Past and Present* 105: 3–52.

Treggiari, S. (1980) 'Urban Labour in Rome', in Garnsey, P. (ed.) *Non-slave-labour in the Greco-Roman World*, Cambridge, pp. 48–64.

7

THE ECONOMY

In its most basic sense, economics is the study of production and consumption. While there is considerable debate over the details, it is undeniable that the basis of the Roman economy is agricultural wealth (as was true of all economies until around a century ago and as still holds good for many countries today). From production to transport to consumption, particularly by the Roman populace, the largest market in the Roman world, the agricultural process calls for careful attention and analysis.

In Italy, agriculture is predominantly based on the triad of cereals, vines, and olives. Given the semi-arid climate and unreliable rainfall, relatively small farms with a mixture of produce seem to have been the safest investment. Large quantities of grain were imported to Rome from throughout the empire (7.1), but Italian farmers were likely to look first to self-sufficiency and safety (7.2, 7.3). The country villa might be both a retreat for the large landowner and the busy centre of a working farm (7.3, 7.4). Produce might be sold and necessary equipment purchased at local markets, and, in the case of large estates, there might be competition with nearby communities for control of this exchange (7.5). In general, however, estates were small, both to reduce risk and as a result of inheritance and marriage customs. Given variable returns on items such as wheat (7.6), few would risk all on such production. The large estate (*latifundium*) appears to be rare in most of Italy, the object of moralistic attack rather than a true economic threat (7.7).

Actual farming methods varied and were the subject of considerable debate. In some cases, intensive farming through the use of skilled slave labour was a possibility. More often, land was leased to tenants who would in turn undertake the risks and decide what extra labour they would need (7.8). In a peasant economy, where too much success was frowned on (7.9), tenants were likely to be limited to traditional methods by social pressures (cf. 7.29). The landlord also had to consider how much personal intervention was possible (7.10) or look to minimise his own risks and the demands on his time required by personal inspection (7.11).

Produce also needed to be transported to market, a costly exercise if land transport was involved, but much cheaper if waterways were available

(7.12). In the case of the essential supply of grain to Rome, shared investment was encouraged (7.13) and traders might rise to positions of considerable standing in their local communities (7.14). While other goods were liable to customs duties (7.15, 7.16), the grain supply for the Roman people was exempt. The emperors also sought to ensure that grain was available all year round, but the historical records of the first century AD indicate that crises still occurred from time to time (7.17). Since Rome had priority demand on food supplies, there were also substantial price variations for staples in the provinces (perhaps even encouraged by deliberate hoarding). The result could be riots and even intervention by the Roman authorities (7.18). Under the worst conditions, the peasants might need to live off barley or wild foods until the next harvest became available (7.19). The grain trade also had other effects. Safely guarded grain stocks might be used for security on loans. The warehouses used for grain might also provide space for shops and offer secure storage for general valuables (7.20).

The existence of schemes to provide support for children at Rome and in Italy raises the question of how these recipients were selected and for what purpose (7.21). Were these the ancient equivalent of social security beneficiaries or are we simply dealing with public displays of generosity, based more on the civic standing of those receiving the benefaction? Pliny the Younger's generosity towards his hometown, supporting local children and providing baths and a library to Comum, indicate both his local patriotism and his desire that his memory live on among the worthy (7.22).

Vineyards might be an alternative or additional to growing grain. Roman authors note the promise of high returns, but it is uncertain how many understood the complexities of investment of this type (7.23). The emperor Domitian was sufficiently alarmed by a perceived linkage between increasing wine production and decreasing wheat harvests to attempt (unsuccessfully) to place a ban on vineyards in the provinces (7.24). Olive growing for oil could also be profitable – if proper presses, storage facilities, and transport were available (7.25). Alongside such crops, the wise investor might raise animals (7.26). A few might speculate on large herds, in particular, of sheep, if they had sufficient grazing areas for year-round pasturing. In Italy this would often require transhumance, moving stock from low-level pastures in winter to higher elevations in summer (7.27). Certainly some gained considerable wealth (7.28), but the details of how this occurred elude us.

The expansion of the Roman empire led not only to agricultural development throughout the Mediterranean, but also to a substantial increase in mineral exploitation through open-cast mines and tunnelling (7.30). In addition, expenditure on civic amenities at Rome and in the provinces would have provided substantial, if perhaps highly seasonal, employment of labour (7.31). The economic effects of trade, both within the empire (7.32) and outside (7.33) continue to be the subject of debate. While some see trade as an indicator of substantial economic growth, others, notably

Moses Finley, have been much more conservative in their assessments. Numerous recent articles and books indicate that the debate continues, refining our understanding of the ancient economy as it progresses.

7.1 Agriculture in the Roman empire

Columella's work on farming is a comprehensive treatment of agriculture, especially viticulture (see **7.23**), written under Nero and based on personal experience in Italy, Spain, and the eastern Mediterranean. As indicated below, Rome had long relied on imported grain as its agricultural hinterland was unable to produce enough to feed the metropolis.

Columella, *On Agriculture* 1, *praef.* 20–1

So in 'this Latium and Saturnian land', where the gods had taught their offspring about the fruits of the fields, there now we let contracts by tender so that grain may be carried to us from provinces across the sea, so that we may not labour under hunger, and we store up vintages from the Cycladic islands and from the regions of Baetica and Gaul. And it's no wonder, since common opinion is now publicly conceived and confirmed that farming is a lowly task and a business that requires no teaching or instruction. But, when I review the magnitude of the entire subject, like the hugeness of some body or the intricacy of its parts like individual members of that body, then I am afraid that my final day may overtake me before I can comprehend the entire field of rural studies.

7.2 The constituent parts of farming

In the late republic, Varro has his interlocutors criticise Greek sources (including the philosopher, Theophrastus) for excessive use of classification by division in their studies. For practical purposes, a fourfold division will do. Placing labour under the heading 'equipment' helps to explain Varro's later remark on means of cultivation that some divide this subject into three parts: 'vocal tools (such as slaves), semi-vocal tools (e.g. oxen), and mute tools (e.g. wagons)' (1.17.1).

Varro, *On Agriculture* 1.5.1–3

Gnaeus Tremelius Scrofa: Since I have now defined the origin and limits of agriculture, it remains to investigate how many parts this discipline has.

C. Agrius: They really seem to me to be infinite in number, when I read the several books by Theophrastus, those that are entitled *The History of Plants* and *The Causes of Vegetation*.

C. Licinius Stolo: But those books are more suitable for those who want to tend to the studies of the philosophers than those who want to tend fields – not that I'm saying they don't contain elements that are both useful and of general interest. So, anyway, explain to us the parts of agriculture.

Scrofa: There are in four main parts to agriculture: first, a knowledge of the soil, as to the nature of soil and its constituents; second, what equipment [including people] is necessary for the working of a farm; third, what things need to be done on an estate for the purpose of cultivation; and, fourth, when each operation should be carried out on the farm.

7.3 How a young man can start out farming

In the second century BC, Cato the Elder commends the life of the farmer as the best opportunity for a young man., since farmers are the best and most highly regarded citizens and their livelihood most assured. He then offers practical advice, particularly recommending growing olives and grapes. Note that this is large-scale agriculture, not subsistence farming, growing cash crops (including fruit, small animals, and poultry) and exploiting a permanent nucleus of slave labour, topped up seasonally with casual workers (both free rural labourers and seasonal workers from the urban centres: cf. **6.8**).

Cato, *On Agriculture* 1–3

1. When you are thinking about acquiring an estate, keep the following points in mind: don't be too keen to buy and make sure you examine things thoroughly and don't settle for going over things only once. However often you go, a good piece of land will please you more each time. Pay attention to how the neighbours look after their places. In a good region their properties should look good. Go in and look around so you can get out again. It should have a good climate, it shouldn't be prone to storm damage, the soil should be good and naturally strong. If you can, get a place that sits at the foot of a mountain and faces south, in a healthy locality with a plentiful force of labourers, a good water supply, a flourishing town nearby, or the sea or a navigable river, or a good, well-frequented road. It should be among farms that do not often see a change in owners, in an area where those who do sell their farms live to regret it. It should be well furnished with buildings. Be careful you don't rashly scorn the learning of others. It will be better to buy from an owner who is a good farmer [*colonus*] and a good builder. When you come to the *villa*, make sure there are a good number of presses for grapes or olives [*vasa torcula*] and large earthenware vessels for wine or grain [*dolia*]; if there are not, you may surmise that the yield is proportionate. There needn't be much equipment, so long as the farm is well situated. See to it that there is as little equipment as possible and that the land is not lavishly expensive. Remember that a farm is like a human being: even though it is profitable, if it is lavish, not much

will be left. If you ask me what is the best sort of estate, I would say, out of all the types of farms, one hundred iugera of land in the best area, best of all a vineyard, if it produces good and plentiful wine; second, an irrigated garden; third, a collection of willows [*salictum*]; fourth, an olive-yard; fifth, a meadow; sixth, a grain field; seventh, a timber plantation, eighth, a plantation of trees on which vines are trained [*arbustum*]; and ninth, a corn grove, for livestock feed [*glandaria silva*].

2.   When the *paterfamilias* arrives at the villa, after he has paid his respects to the household god, let him go around the farm on the same day, if he can; if not on the same day, then on the next. When he has learnt the condition of the farm, what work has been done and what is still to be done, let him call the overseer [*vilicus*] on the next day and ask him what part of the work has he done and what remains, whether what has been completed was done in good time, and whether what remains is able to be completed; and what has been the yield of wine, of grain, and of all the other produce. When he has worked out these things, he should calculate the number of workers and of days required. If the amount of work done does not appear satisfactory to him, the *vilicus* says that he has done his best, the slaves had not been well, the weather was bad, slaves have run away, he has had public work to do; when he has given these and many other excuses, draw the *vilicus'* attention back to your account of the work and the labourers. If it is the rainy season, remind him what jobs can be done on rainy days: washing and pitching the *dolia*, cleaning the villa, shifting grain, hauling out manure, making a midden, cleaning seed, mending ropes, making new ones; and that the household should have mended their cloaks [*centones*] and hoods [*cuculiones*]. On holidays, old ditches could have been cleared, the public road strengthened, the thorn-bushes cut, the garden dug up, the meadow cleared, faggots bundled, prickles weeded out, grain ground, tidying-up done. Since the slaves were sick, such generous rations should not have been served. Once this has all been dealt with calmly, instruct the work that remains be done; balance the cash account and the grain account and what has been obtained in the way of feed; also the wine and oil accounts, what has been sold, what has been collected, what is left, and what is good for sale; where security for accounts needs to be taken, order it be taken; order an inventory to be taken of what is left. If anything is lacking for the current year, order that it be obtained, and that anything that is surplus be sold off, and that what work needs to be let out be let out. Give written instructions as to what work you want to be done and what work you want to be let out. Inspect the livestock and hold an auction. Sell oil if the price is right, and sell surplus wine and grain. Sell old oxen, slightly defective cattle and sheep, wool, hides, an old cart, old tools, an aged slave, a sick slave, and whatever else is surplus. The *paterfamilias* should be a seller, not a buyer.

3. In early *adulescentia*, the *paterfamilias* should devote his attention to sowing his field. He should think a long time about building but it is not necessary to think about sowing; what he should be doing is *doing* it. When you have reached the age of 36 years then you ought to build, if you have sown your land. Make sure you build in such a way that you don't end up with a villa without a farm.

7.4 Building an appropriate villa

A major farming complex required suitably sited buildings to match (though see **7.3** above: first the farm, then the villa). This allows for storage and shelter for cattle and humans (cf. Columella's advice: **5.16**).

Varro, *On Agriculture* 1.11.2–12.1

For buildings that are too big cost too much to build and are more expensive to maintain, whereas buildings that are smaller than the farm requires typically lead to spoilt produce. There is no doubt that a bigger cellar should be built for land in which grapes are grown, and bigger granaries if the land is used to grow grain. The villa should be built so that above all it has water within its enclosure, or at least as close by as possible. The best thing is to have a spring there or, failing that, a perennial stream. If there is no running water at all, cisterns must be built under cover, and a reservoir out in the open, one for people, the other for cattle. Particular care should be taken that the villa is placed at the foot of a wooded mountain, where there are broad pastures and so that it is exposed to the healthiest winds in the area.

7.5 Local markets

Local markets (*nundinae*) were essential for the well-being of the economy of the regions they catered for. In order to maximise profits, landlords of large estates might seek to open their own markets in competition with traditional fairs. Permission was in the hands of the senate, but, as the senators were themselves owners of substantial amounts of land, it might be difficult for non-senators to register opposition, as can be seen in the case of Vicenza (North Italy).

(a) Pliny, *Letters* 5.4.1–3 (AD 105)

Gaius Plinius to Iulius Valerianus, greetings.

A small matter, but the beginning of something far from small. A praetorian named Sollers has petitioned the senate to be allowed to set up a weekly market on his estate. Representatives of the inhabitants of Vicetia opposed it; Tuscilius Nominatus [not a senator] was there on their behalf. The case was adjourned. At another meeting of the senate the Vicetians entered without an advocate and said they had been cheated – difficult to know if this was a slip of the tongue or a genuine belief. They were asked by the praetor Nepos whom they had instructed; they replied, 'The same man as before.' When asked whether he had been there on their behalf for free, they replied, 'For 6,000 sesterces.' When asked whether they had given him anything for a second appearance, they replied, '1,000 denarii.' Nepos requested that Nominatus be required to attend. So much that day. But I can see it will go a lot further.

(b) Pliny, *Letters* 5.13.1–4

Gaius Plinius to Iulius Valerianus, greetings.

I promised that if you asked I would write to you about the result of Nepos summoning Tuscilius Nominatus, and now you ask. Nominatus attended; he acted on his own behalf, and no one brought any charge. For the representatives of the Vicetians not only pressed no charge but even backed him up. His line of defence was that what had failed him in his duty as advocate was not his sense of loyalty but his resolution. He had appeared in good faith, and had even been seen in the House, but then after conversing with his friends he had withdrawn in fright. They had warned him not to be too persistent, particularly in the senate, in opposing the wishes of a senator [Sollers] who was defending not so much his right to hold weekly markets as his influence, reputation, and standing; otherwise Nominatus would make himself even more unpopular than on the previous occasion. In fact when he left on the former occasion he had been applauded, albeit only by a few. Now he offered prayers amidst much weeping; indeed throughout his speech he made a concerted effort to be seen not to be defending his actions but rather to be begging for pardon – for a man trained in public speaking that was clearly the safer course to take, and one more likely to win favour. He was acquitted.

7.6 Wheat yields

Planting grain would seem the safest form of farming, given that there was an almost unlimited market for the produce and there was less need for skilled manpower and investment in equipment compared to vines and olives. However, the final product was bulky and required considerable effort to transport over distances. It was also prone to spoilage (e.g. from vermin or water damage). Pliny the Elder cites some exceptional returns on seed, but it is unlikely that normal returns were anywhere near the levels he suggests. With variable climatic conditions (droughts, floods) and the necessity of tenants paying a return to their landlords, grain farming could be very marginal indeed.

Pliny the Elder, *Natural History* 18.94–5

Nothing is more fertile than wheat [*triticum*] – Nature has given it this attribute because it used to be her main form of nourishment for human beings – inasmuch as a modius of wheat, if planted in suitable soil such as that of the Byzacium plain in Africa, returns a yield of 150 modii. From that region the deified Augustus received from his procurator (incredible as it seems) nearly 400 shoots grown from a single grain; the letters about this are still extant. He likewise sent to Nero 360 stalks from a single grain. In any event the plains of Leontini and other places in Sicily, as well as the whole of Baetica, and especially Egypt, yield wheat at a good hundredfold.

7.7 The spread of large estates (*latifundia*)

Archaeology shows that most estates in Italy in the classical period were medium-sized villas rather than massive estates. What Pliny the Elder is really complaining about is not the size of individual estates but the amount of land, spread over a number of properties, held by a relatively small number of individuals. The largest landowner of the Roman world was, of course, the emperor himself and, on his estates, abuses could most easily occur (cf. **1.51**, **8.19**).

In the case of Apulia, it is likely that use of marginal lands for pastoralism, especially transhumance farming (moving from coastal plains in winter to upland pastures in summer) has created the impression that there has been a movement away from intensive farming.

(a) Pliny the Elder, *Natural History* 18.35

In the old days people thought it was essential to maintain moderation in the size of a farm, inasmuch as they used to believe that it was better to sow less land and plough more thoroughly; and I notice that Vergil agreed with this opinion [*Georgics* 2.412]. If the truth be told, *latifundia* have ruined Italy and are in the process of doing the same to the provinces too – six masters used to own half of Africa, until the emperor Nero executed them.

(b) Varro, *On Agriculture* 1.2.6–7

Is there any useful product that not only isn't grown in Italy but isn't also grown there to perfection? What spelt [*far*] shall I compare to the Campanian, what wheat to the Apulian, what wine to the Falernian, what oil to the Venafran? Italy is covered with trees, so that it all seems like an orchard. Is Phrygia, which Homer calls 'vine-clad' [*Iliad* 3.184], more covered in vines than Italy? Is Argos, which the same poet calls 'rich in corn' [*Iliad* 14.372], more covered in wheat than Italy? In what land does one iugerum bear 10 or 15 cullei of wine, as do some regions of Italy?

(c) Seneca, *Letters* 87.7

You call a man rich just because his gold plate follows him even on the road, because he farms lands in every province, because he unrolls an enormous account book, because he possesses so much land near the city that people would begrudge him owning even in the waste lands of Apulia.

7.8 Columella's solution

Columella suggests that, rather than excessively purchasing property, the best profit will be gained from labour-intensive methods of cultivation. This will preferably involve trained slaves (not prison slaves or debtors) where close supervision is possible: **7.8a**; if estates are distant, use of tenants (*coloni*) will be preferable as they will do less harm if unsupervised: **7.8b**.

(a) Columella, *On Agriculture* 1.3.12

As in all things, moderation shall be exercised even in the acquiring of land. Only so much should be obtained as is required, so that we may be seen to have bought only so much as we are able to control, not so much as to burden ourselves and to deprive others of its enjoyment – in the manner of those powerful men who possess entire countries so vast they can't even go round them but instead leave them to be trampled over by cattle and wasted and ravaged by wild animals, or keep them occupied by citizens enslaved for debt and by slave chain gangs [*ergastula*].

(b) Columella, *On Agriculture* 1.7.6–7

On distant estates, to which the *paterfamilias* cannot easily make excursions, with every type of land it is more acceptable to have it under free tenant farmers than under slave overseers, and this is particularly true of grain land, to which a tenant farmer can do the least harm, as he can to vines or a plantation of trees with vines [*arbustum*], whereas slaves do it the utmost harm: they hire out cattle, and keep them and all the other stock poorly fed, they do not turn the land over properly and they charge up far more seed as used than they have actually sown, nor do they tend that which they have committed to the earth to make it shoot up properly, and when they have brought it to the threshing floor, every day during the threshing they lessen the quantity either through fraud or negligence. For they themselves steal it and they do not protect it from other robbers, and even when it is in storage they do not enter it accurately into the accounts. As a result both the manager and the household slaves commit offences and the land more often than not gets a bad reputation. So I believe that an estate of this sort should be leased, if, as I have said, it must be without the presence of the master.

7.9 Profitable farming

The well-known tale of Chresimus indicates not only a belief in the virtues of hard work, but also the collective mentality of his neighbours who objected to the success of an ex-slave and attributed it to the use of nefarious methods.

Pliny the Elder, *Natural History* 18.41–3

C. Furius Chresimus, a freedman, was greatly disliked because on his quite small farm he made much larger returns than his neighbours enjoyed from enormous estates. It was believed that he had put magic spells on everyone else's crops. As a result he was indicted by the curule aedile Spurius Albinus. Fearing a guilty verdict, when the time came for the tribes to vote, he brought into the forum all his farm equipment and produced his household slaves – strong people and, according to Piso, well looked after and clothed; he showed off his beautifully made iron tools, his heavy mattocks, his ponderous ploughshares, his well-fed oxen. Then he said: 'These are my magic spells, citizens; unfortunately I can't show you or bring into the forum my nightly labours, my early starts, and the sweat I've expended.' He was acquitted by a unanimous verdict. It is certainly true that farming depends on expenditure of labour, which is why our ancestors said that the greatest fertiliser on a farm is the master's eye.

7.10 How to get the best compost

Varro's advice to provide a large farm with two farmyards (*cohorts*) not only confirms the concluding remark of Pliny the Elder (**7.9**), but also indicates the care needed to extract maximum return out of the capital invested in a farm – including human waste (cf. **5.16**).

Varro, *On Agriculture* 1.13.4.

Because the outer farmyard is regularly covered with straw and chaff that are trampled down by the hooves of the cattle, it becomes a handmaid [*ministra*] of the farm because of what may be cleaned off it. Close by the villa there should be two manure heaps, or one divided into two. One part should be made of fresh manure, and from the other the old manure should be hauled into the field; for manure that has rotted works better than fresh manure. The best type of manure heap is that which has its sides and top protected from the sun by twigs and foliage, for the sun ought not to be allowed to draw out the juice [*sucus*] that the land requires. It is for this reason that experienced farmers arrange where possible for water to flow into it (this is the best way to keep in the juice). Some people place the household slaves' latrines [*sellae familiaricae*] on it.

7.11 The supervision of estates by an absentee landlord

For various reasons, including the ownership of a number of separate properties as a result of the Roman inheritance and dowry system and necessary duties
in the capital or elsewhere in the empire, wealthy landowners would need to
make regular visits to their properties when they would make arrangements for
the period until their next visit. Pliny the Younger has estates throughout Italy: in
7.11a, his assessment of the value of a property available for sale includes
valuable comment on the cost of labour and equipment and local farming methods;
in **7.11b**, he indicates that the indebtedness of his tenants suggests that it would
be more profitable now to set up a sharecropping system to replace the simple
lease contracts that have not been fulfilled. Given the distance from Rome of
some of his property, he also needs to obtain imperial permission to be absent
(he was at the time – AD 98 or 99 – prefect of the Treasury of Saturn, the senatorial
treasury): **7.11c**. Note how he seeks the emperor's approval: he begins the letter
by stating that, in accordance with the wishes of Nerva, he had sought to transfer
statues of former emperors from his estate to the town of Tifernum, and to add
a statue of that emperor too, on a site Pliny would choose. He now wants leave
to go and arrange this. Incidentally, he can also carry out the necessary inspection
of his property at the same time.

(a) Pliny, *Letters* 3.19

Gaius Plinius to Calvisius Rufus, greetings.

As is my habit, I call on you to advise me about my property. An estate
neighbouring my own fields – in fact joined to them – is for sale. Many
factors tempt me in all this, but also some factors, no less important, make
me wary.

The primary temptation is the very beauty of having the two places joined.
Then there's the fact that it would not only be enjoyable but also useful to
be able to make only one trip to visit both places at the same time. They
could both be under the same agent and practically the same foremen; I
would only need to maintain and furnish one house, just keeping the other
one in a state of repair. In this calculation is included the cost of furniture,
and the cost of the stewards, gardeners, workmen, and also hunting
equipment. It makes a good deal of difference whether you keep these in
one place or spread them out over several different locations.

On the other hand, I'm afraid it might be rash to expose the same property
to the same storms and risks; it seems safer to face the hazards of fortune
by spreading one's resources. A change in locale and climate affords
considerable pleasure, as does the very travel from estate to estate.

But the most important point in our deliberation is that the fields are
fertile, rich, and well watered; they consist of meadows, vineyards, and

woods; the timber from the latter provides a yield that is stable if not huge. But this fertility is being weakened by ineffective methods of cultivation. The previous owner quite regularly sold off the possessions [*pignora*] of the tenant farmers [*coloni*], in the process temporarily reducing their arrears but also draining their resources for the future, the lack of which caused their debts to mount up again. So they will have to be set up with good slaves, which raises the expense. I nowhere use chain gangs, nor does anyone else there.

It remains for you to know at what price the property can apparently be bought: three million sesterces, though at one time it was going for five million. But this scarcity of tenants and the general distress of our times have meant that the returns from landed property have dropped, and thus so has the price. You ask whether I can easily raise this three million. To be sure, nearly all my assets are in land, but I have some money loaned out at interest, and it won't be difficult for me to borrow. I can get some from my mother-in-law [mother of his first or second wife, not of Calpurnia] – her capital I use as freely as my own. So don't worry about that aspect, if the other aspects don't concern you – but do please give them your full and careful attention. For, in the administration of investments, as in everything else, you have an abundance of experience and foresight. Farewell.

(b) Pliny, *Letters* 9.37.1–4

Gaius Plinius to Paulinus, greetings.

It is not in your nature to exact from your close friends the conventional formalities when it is inconvenient for them, and I love you more firmly than to fear you might take it the wrong way that I won't see you become consul right on the first of the month, especially when I have to stay here to see to the leasing-out of my farms on a long-term basis and this requires me to set up a whole new system. For over the last five years the arrears [of the tenants] have increased, even though I gave them large remissions. Consequently most of them have no interest in reducing their debt because they have given up any hope of paying off the entire balance. They even seize and consume the things they do grow in the belief now that they'll gain nothing by saving it. So these growing failings must be met head-on and remedied. One type of remedy would be for me to let the farms out not for cash but for a share of the produce, and then set some of my workmen as overseers to watch over the harvest. And there is certainly no more just return than that which is paid by the land, the climate, and the seasons. But this requires great trust, sharp eyes, and many hands. Nonetheless it must be tried out, and all aids to change must be tested against this chronic ailment, as it were.

(c) Pliny, *Letters* 10.8.4–6

Gaius Plinius to the emperor Trajan.

So I ask above all that you allow me to adorn the work that I am about to begin with your statue too; and second, so that I may do this as soon as possible, that you grant me a leave of absence. But my straightforwardness to you and your kindness to me demands that I not conceal the fact that my own personal affairs will incidentally benefit a good deal in the process. For the leasing of the farms that I own in the same region cannot possibly be postponed, particularly since the rent is over 400,000 sesterces, and the new tenant [*sic*] should attend to the pruning, which is very close at hand. Moreover, repeated bad seasons oblige me to think of reductions in rents, the accounting of which I cannot undertake except in person. I shall therefore be indebted to your indulgence, my lord, for the speedy accomplishment of my act of devotion and for the settling of my private affairs, if you grant me a leave of absence for thirty days on both these accounts. For I cannot specify a shorter time, since both the township [*municipium*] and the farms to which I refer are over 150 miles away from Rome.

7.12 Transport of goods

Production without access to a market would make no sense. While Varro sees the movement from grain and vine cultivation in Italy to pastoralism as a moral question, the mention of imports from elsewhere in the Roman world indicates that this change may often have been a response to economic pressures. Land transport was generally expensive, so if waterways could be made available there was likely to be economic growth. Hence Pliny the Younger's plan to build a canal from lake Sophon (Sabanja), 18 km south-east of Nicomedia, to a river flowing west into the Gulf of Izmid. Despite imperial assent to a survey, nothing seems to have come of this scheme. Yet, as Strabo indicates, a considerable volume of goods was transported by land to rivers over substantial distances (here, from Aquileia over the Alps to Nauportus: 75 km); in 4.1.14 he mentions regular land transport from the Rhône to the Loire (140 km).

(a) Varro, *On Agriculture* 2, *praef.* 1–4

Not without good reason did our great ancestors prefer rural Romans to urban ones. Just as in the country those who live in the villa are lazier than those who are busy in the field performing some task, so they thought those who sit in town were more idle than those who inhabited the country areas ... [Varro goes on to note the detrimental influence of the Greeks on the traditional Roman way of life, leading to a decline in traditional farming.] ... So nowadays the *patresfamilias* have almost all snuck within the walls, abandoning the sickle and the plough, and have preferred to busy their hands in the theatre and circus than in the grain fields and the vineyards; nowadays we hire a man to bring us grain to stuff our bellies from Africa and Sardinia, and we store the vintage from ships from Cos and Chios. And so, in a land where the shepherds who founded the city taught their offspring how to cultivate the land, there instead *their* offspring, through greed and against the laws, have turned grain lands into pastures, not knowing that agriculture and pasturing are two different things ... For cattle do not produce what grows on the land; instead they remove it with their teeth.

(b) Pliny, *Letters* 10.41

There is a very large lake in the territory of the Nicomedians, across which marble, farm produce, wood, and lumber are transported by boat to the road with very little expense or labour; but from there they are carried to the sea on carts, with considerable labour and greater expense.

(c) Strabo, *Geography* 4.6.10

We now come to the Iapodes, a mixed tribe of Illyrians and Celts, who dwell around these regions, close to Mount Ocra [Alpis Iulia, between Aquileia and Nauportus; now Nanos]. Now the Iapodes, although formerly they were well supplied with strong men and held as their homeland both sides of the mountain [Mt Albius, now Mt Velika, the sides towards the Pannonii and the Danube, and towards the Adriatic] and as bandits enjoyed control over the area, were brought low and totally conquered by Augustus Caesar. Their cities are Metulum, Arupini, Monetium, and Vendo [Avendo]. After these people comes the city of Segetica, on the plain past which the Saus [Save] river flows and empties into the Ister [Danube]. The city lies in a naturally fine position for making war against the Daci. The Ocra is the lowest part of the Alps in that region in which they join the country of the Carni and through which the merchandise from Aquileia is carried in wagons to the place called Nauportus, over a road of not much more than 400 stades; from here it is carried down by the rivers as far as the Ister and the regions around there. For a river [the Corcoras or Gurk] actually flows past Nauportus, a river that runs out of Illyria and is navigable; it empties into the Saus, so that the merchandise is easily conveyed down to Segestica ...

7.13 Corporations

In certain areas, the Roman government encouraged production by permitting the formation of corporate bodies to share the investment and risk of large-scale production. Worth noting are the shipping corporations that ensured the import of, among other goods, fish sauce (*garum* – a staple of the Roman diet) and grain to Rome. For regulations banning senatorial participation in such activity, see **1.13**.

Digest 3.4.1, preface

Gaius, *On the Provincial Edict*, Book 3. *Societates, collegia,* and bodies of this sort are not allowed to be formed by everyone at will; this right is restricted by laws, *senatus consulta,* and imperial constitutions. Only in a few cases are bodies of this sort permitted: for example, partners in tax farming, gold mines, silver mines, and salt works are allowed to form corporations. Likewise there are certain *collegia* at Rome whose status as corporations has been confirmed by *senatus consulta* and imperial constitutions, such as those of the bakers and of certain others, and of the shipowners, who are also in the provinces.

7.14 Tombstone of a shipowner

This is from Nicomedia (Bithynia), in the Roman imperial period.

Supplementum Epigraphicum Graecum 27 no. 828

Telephoros, councillor [*bouleutes*] and shipowner [*naukleros*] [made this] for himself, for Faustina, for their children, and for no one else....

7.15 Tax farming in Asia

The excerpts in the following inscription, a copy of an original made at Rome under Nero, list the details of a contract law (*lex censoria, leges locationum*) between the Roman government and the tax collectors (*publicani*) for the collection of import/export taxes (*portoria*). Note the development of its provisions by alterations and exceptions from the passage of the law in 75 BC to the latest addition c. AD 47, e.g. exceptions made for goods intended for use of the Romans (including presumably grain from the Black Sea) and a special provision for exemption for Augustus' friend, the freedman Vedius Pollio (cf. **4.3**).

Supplementum Epigraphicum Graecum 39 no. 1189 = *L'Annee Epigraphique* 1989 no. 681 (Ephesus, AD 62)

Law for the customs dues of Asia, both imports and exports by sea and land ... in accord with senatorial decrees or according to law or plebiscite ... [where] a customs office is leased, in these places whatever is imported or exported by sea [will be taxed]. Also whatever is carried, transported, or driven out over land is subject to a levy of two and a half per cent paid to the tax farmer [i.e. the *publicanus*, Greek: *telonês*].

For slave boys and slave girls no greater tax than 5 denarii per head is due ...

[Anyone exporting goods to the Black Sea] is to declare these and have them registered with the tax farmer or his agent . . .

On these goods there should be no tax nor is anyone liable to pay tax: whatever they transport on behalf of the Roman populace or for religious purposes or for the public activities of the Roman people . . . nor for minted gold or silver, nor for recorded money . . . One should not pay tax on books, writing tablets, letters, and inscribed materials, nor on footware or rings [for making one's seal] that one customarily uses when away . . .

For the goods of Vedius Pollio, immunity is granted by decree of the senate; if they are over the value of 10,000 denarii, [. . .] per cent will be given to the publican.

The same consuls [Gaius Furnius and Gaius Silanus in 17 BC] added: on slaves per head the publican should not receive more than set down in the contract [lex censoria]: two and a half denarii for import, 1 denarius for export.
    The publican who has contracted with the Roman people to collect these taxes shall make payment to the Treasury of Saturn on 15 October of the year following that in which he obtains the right to collect taxes and likewise, for each year after, on 15 October in each following year . . .

The consuls Publius Sulpicius Quirinius and Lucius Valgius Rufus [12 BC] added: the tax on imports and exports by land and sea in the territories and harbour of the colony of Augusta Troas are exempted so the colony itself may receive the dues. Everything else should follow the law [i.e. the contract] . . .

If a dispute occurs between the same person [i.e the contractor] [and another official, it is to be referred] to the procurator of Nero Augustus who is in charge of the province. . . .

7.16 Goods liable to taxation

As seen in **7.15**, taxable goods included, for example, slaves (who might be confiscated if undeclared, but not if runaways: *Digest* 39.4.16.1–4). The list in **7.16a** seems designed to add other items that might have been subject to dispute. The sophist Proclus of Naucratis imports a wide range of goods from Egypt, requiring a defence from Philostratus: **7.16b**.

(a) *Digest* 39.4.16.7, Marcian

Types of goods liable to import tax [*vectigal*]: cinnamon, long pepper, white pepper, pentasphaerum leaf, barbary leaf, costum, costamomum, balls of nard, Tyrian casia, casia-wood, myrrh, amomum, ginger, malabrathrum, Indic spice, galbanum, asafoetida juice, aloe, lycium, Persian gum, Arabian onyx, cardamonum, cinnamon-wood, cotton goods, Babylonian hides, Persian hides, ivory, Indian iron, linen, all sorts of gem, pearl, sardonyx, ceraunium, hyacinth stone, emerald, diamond, sapphire, turquoise, beryl, tortoise stone, Indian (real or alleged) drugs, raw silk, silk or half-silk clothing, embroidered fine linen, silk thread, Indian eunuchs, lions, lionesses, pards, leopards, panthers, purple dye; also: Moroccan wool, dye, Indian hair.

(b) Philostratus, *Lives of the Sophists* 2.21

See 1.40.

7.17 The grain supply of Rome

Wheat, consumed as bread or as broth, was a staple of the ancient diet. Yet, because of the size of Rome (conventionally set at a million people), maintaining grain supplies year-round required considerable effort. In 57 BC, the new post of *cura annonae* was created and bestowed on Pompey; those eligible for a grain handout were registered and provided with regular supplies. Under Augustus, the numbers eligible were limited to 200,000, but food shortages still occurred, often leading to riots and even leading to threats against the emperor himself. Efforts were made by Claudius to offer insurance for shippers and increase the tonnage of ships involved in the grain supply, as well as improving the harbour at Ostia, but it was only in the time of Trajan that reliable shelter was provided for Rome's supply ships.

(a) Cassius Dio, 54.1 (22 BC)

In the following year, when Marcus Marcellus and Lucius Arruntius were consuls, the city was submerged when the river flooded again and the statues in the Pantheon were struck by lightning, as were many others – the spear even fell from Augustus' hand. The Romans were suffering from pestilence and famine (there was an epidemic throughout Italy and no one was working the land, and I expect that the same thing occurred in the rest of the empire) and they thought that this had only occurred because Augustus was no longer consul. They wanted to elect him dictator and, shutting up the senators in the Senate House, forced them to vote for this by threatening to burn them alive. After this, they took the twenty-four fasces [the rods of the two consuls] and brought them to him, asking him to accept the title of dictator and commissioner of the grain supply as Pompey had once been. He undertook this task under duress, ordering that two men from those who had been praetors in the last five years be chosen each year to organise the grain supply.[1] But he wouldn't accept the dictatorship and even tore up his own robes when he could not stop then in any other way by reasoning or entreaty.

1 The post of *praefectus annonae* is established later, in AD 10.

(b) Tacitus, *Annals* 6.13 (AD 32)

The excessive price of grain led practically to an insurrection and, for several days, the theatre was the scene of many demands shouted with greater boldness than was customary towards the emperor. Aroused by this, Tiberius upbraided the magistrates and the senators for failing to restrain the populace by the authority of the state, and reminded them of the provinces from which he imported the supply of grain and of how much greater a supply it was than Augustus had provided.

(c) Tacitus, *Annals* 12.43 (AD 51)

Many prodigies occurred in that year ... A shortage of grain again and the resulting famine were regarded as a portent. And people did not merely grumble in private, but they surrounded Claudius with a mutinous clamour as he sat in judgement, drove him to the edge of the Forum, and kept jostling him about until the arrival of a band of soldiers made it possible for him to force his way through the hostile throng. It was ascertained that the city had provisions for fifteen days, no more, and the desperate situation was relieved only by the great mercy of the gods and the mildness of the winter. And yet, by heaven, in former times Italy used to export supplies for the legions into far-distant provinces, and even now it does not suffer from infertility, but it is we who prefer to cultivate Africa and Egypt and commit the life of the Roman people to ships and all their risks.

(d) Suetonius, *Claudius* 18–20

Claudius always interested himself in the proper upkeep of the city and the regular arrival of grain supplies ... Once, after a series of bad harvests had caused a scarcity of grain [AD 51], a mob stopped Claudius in the Forum and pelted him so hard with curses and stale crusts that he had difficulty in regaining the palace by a side-door; as a result he took all possible steps to import grain, even during the winter months – insuring merchants against the loss of their ships in stormy weather (which guaranteed them a good return on their ventures), and offering a large bounty for every new grain-transport ship, proportionate to its tonnage. The shipowner, if he happened to be a Roman citizen, was exempted from the Papian-Poppaean Law; if only a possessor of Latin rights, acquired full Roman citizenship; if a woman, enjoyed the privileges granted to mothers of four children. These regulations have never since been modified.

Claudius' public works, though not numerous, were important. They included, in particular, an aqueduct begun by Gaius; the draining of the Fucine Lake; and the building of the harbour at Ostia – though he knew that Augustus had turned down the Marsians' frequent requests for the emptying of the lake, and that Julius Caesar, while often at the point of excavating the harbour at Ostia, had always abandoned the project as impractical ... At Ostia, Claudius constructed a new port by throwing out curved breakwaters on either side of the harbour and built a deep-water mole by its entrance. For the base of this mole he used the ship in which Caligula had transported a great obelisk from Heliopolis; it was first sunk, then secured with piles, and finally crowned with a very tall lighthouse – like the Pharos at Alexandria – that guided ships into the harbour at night by the beams of a lamp.

(e) Cassius Dio, 60.11

On the occasion of a severe famine he considered the problem of providing an abundant food supply, not only for that particular crisis but for all future time. For practically all the grain used by the Romans was imported, and yet the region near the mouth of the Tiber had no safe landing places or suitable harbours, so that their mastery of the sea was rendered useless to them. Except for the cargoes brought in during the summer season and stored in their warehouses, they had no supplies for the winter; for, if anyone ever risked a voyage at that season, he came to grief. In view of this situation Claudius undertook to construct a harbour, and would not be deterred even when the architects, upon his enquiring how great the cost would be, answered, 'You don't want to do it!' – so confident were they that the huge expenditures necessary would shake him from his purpose if he should learn the cost beforehand. He, however, conceived an undertaking worthy of the dignity and greatness of Rome, and he brought it to accomplishment. In the first place, he excavated a very considerable area of shore, built retaining walls on every side of the excavation, and then let the sea into it; second, in the sea itself he constructed huge moles on both sides of the entrance and thus enclosed a large body of water, in the midst of which he reared an island and placed on it a tower with a beacon light.

(f) Tacitus, *Histories* 4.38 (AD 70)

Meanwhile Vespasian entered on his second consulship, Titus on his first, although both were absent from Rome. Rome was dejected and anxious from many fears, on top of which were added false alarms to the real troubles that threatened, namely the rumour that Africa was in revolt, led on by Lucius Piso. Piso, proconsul of Africa at the time, was far from being a turbulent spirit. The real problem was that the grain ships coming to Rome were held up by the severity of the winter, and the common people [*vulgus*], who were used to buying their provisions on a daily basis and whose sole interest in public life was in the food supply, in their fear believed that the harbour was closed and the supply-line cut off. The Vitellians bolstered the report – they had not yet given up their support of that faction – and in fact the rumour was not unpleasing even to the victors.

7.18 Food supply in the provinces

Although population sizes were smaller in provincial centres, poor harvests and the demands of the metropolis could result in hoarding and food shortages. Dio and another rich landowner in Prusa (Bithynia) were nearly stoned to death because the mob suspected them of manipulating the grain market. In response to the accusation that he had done nothing to alleviate the crisis, Dio emphasises the past generosity of his family and his own service in performing liturgies but makes no offer of assistance, even defending the high prices (**7.18a**). By contrast, the Roman governor might intervene in order to maintain order, as seen by the actions of Antistius (**7.18b**) and an unknown governor of Asia (**7.18c**).

(a) Dio Chrysostom, *Orations* 46.8–10

No man is more blameless than I am in regard to the food shortage we now suffer. Have I produced the most grain of all the farmers and then locked it up in storage, thus raising the price? But you yourselves know the productive capacity of my farms, that I have rarely – if ever – sold grain, even when there has been a considerable surplus in the harvest, for in these years I have hardly had enough for my own needs: my entire profit is made from wine and cattle.

What's more, though it's true that the matter about which you are so enraged does require some attention, it is nonetheless not irremediable, nor is it so extreme as to warrant acting the way you are. Yes, the price of grain is higher than it usually is among us, but it is not so high as to make you desperate. In fact, there are cities in which it is *always* this expensive, even when conditions are at their best. There you go, shouting at me again, as if I'm saying it should always be that price here for you, and never lower. But what I'm trying to say is that, yes, we need to take steps to make the price go lower, but you don't need to feel so bitterly about what has happened or to go crazy about it. The way you have acted just now is quite out of proportion to what has happened – if I'd murdered your wives and children you couldn't have behaved with greater savagery.

(b) *L'Année Epigraphique* 1925 no. 126b
(Antioch, Pisidia, AD 93)

Lucius Antistius Rusticus, legate with propraetorian power of the emperor Caesar Domitian Augustus Germanicus, declares:

'Since the duovirs and decurions of the most illustrious colony of Antioch have written to me that, as a result of the severity of the winter, the market price of grain has soared, and they have petitioned that the people be given the means to purchase.

'Therefore – may good fortune attend! – all who are either citizens [*coloni*] or residents [*incolae*] of the colony of Antioch shall declare before the duovirs of the colony of Antioch, within thirty days after this edict of mine has been posted in public, how much grain each has and in what place, and how much he deducts for seed or for the year's supply of food for his household; and he shall make all the remaining grain available to the buyers of the colony of Antioch. Furthermore, I fix next August 1 as the last day for sale. And, if anyone does not obey, let him know that I shall claim for confiscation whatever is withheld contrary to my edict, reserving a one-eighth share as a reward for informers [*delatores*].

'Since, furthermore, it is confirmed for me that before this prolonged severe winter a modius of grain in the colony cost eight or nine asses, and it is most unjust for anyone to profiteer from the hunger of his fellow citizens, I forbid the price of grain to exceed 1 denarius [sixteen asses] per modius.'

(c) *Supplementum Epigraphicum Graecum* 4.512
(Ephesus, second century AD)

And according to agreements . . . thus it happens at times that the populace is plunged into disorder and riots by the inexcusable audacity of the bakers' sedition in the market place. For these actions they should by now have been summoned into court and have paid the penalty. But, since it is necessary to prefer the welfare of the city to the punishment of these individuals, I thought it best to bring them to their senses by an edict. I therefore forbid the bakers to assemble in association and their officers to make inflammatory speeches, and I order them to give complete obedience to those in charge of general welfare and to provide the city fully with the necessary production of bread. If any of them is apprehended from this time on either meeting contrary to orders or starting any riot or agitation, he shall be summoned into court and suffer the appropriate punishment; and if anyone dares to hide and continue disrupting the city, he shall in addition be branded on the foot with the word 'decuria' [i.e. the mark of punishment by the town council], and anyone who harbours any such person shall thereby become liable to the same punishment.

7.19 Galen on famine in the countryside

Remarks by the medical expert Galen from the second century AD suggest that the peasants could suffer as much as the townspeople in times of shortage. Although they would have access to wild foods and lowly regarded grains (such as barley), the nutritional value of such substitutes was much less than that of processed wheat.

(a) Galen, *De Alimentorum Facultatibus* (The Powers of Foodstuffs) 1.7

If I had not myself at one time eaten wheat boiled in water, I would never have believed there to be anything beneficial in that type of food. For no one, even during a food shortage, would resort to such a practice, since, if there is a good supply of wheat, bread can be made from it ... I would never have expected anyone would serve wheat boiled in water for the following reason. I myself was travelling a good distance from the city [of Pergamum] with two young men the same age as me as my guides. I came upon some peasants who had just had their supper. And the peasant women were just about to make some loaves because they had run out of bread. Immediately one of them tossed some grains of wheat into the pot. Then she seasoned it with a little salt and offered it to us to eat. We had travelled a long way and were hungry, so it was natural that we should eat it. So we ate a good deal of it, and we felt a great heaviness like mud in our stomachs. And the next day we had bad indigestion and could eat nothing at all the whole day, for we had no appetite and were bloated with wind; we had headaches and blurred vision. For nothing of what we had eaten could be evacuated – and that is the only way indigestion can be relieved. So I asked the peasants if they ever ate boiled wheat, and how they coped with it. They replied that they often ate it through necessity, just as had happened to us on that occasion, and that wheat prepared in this way was a heavy and indigestible foodstuff.

(b) Galen, *De Alimentorum Facultatibus* 1.11

Some races use barley groats [meal] in place of bread, as I myself have seen peasants in Cyprus doing, even though they grow a lot of wheat. In the old days, groats were prepared for soldiers. But nowadays the Roman army does not use groats because they are recognised as being weak. For they give little nourishment to the body; they are sufficient for ordinary people who take no exercise, but they are not enough for those who exercise.

(c) Galen, *De Bonis et Malis Alimentorum Sucis*
(Wholesome and Unwholesome Juices in Food) 1

The food shortages that have occurred over a number of years in succession among many of the peoples subject to the Romans have demonstrated clearly to those not completely devoid of intelligence that the consumption of bad foods has a primary role to play in the genesis of diseases. For those who live in the cities, as it was their custom to collect up and store enough grain for the entire next year immediately after the harvest, took from the fields all the grain as well as the barley, beans, and lentils, and they left to the peasants the other fruits of the fields, what they call pulses [*ospria* and *chedropa*] – and even a good number of these they took to the city. Now in the course of the winter the peasants consumed what had been left for them and then they were forced to make use of unhealthy foods through the whole of spring, eating branches and shoots of trees and shrubs, and bulbs, and roots of indigestible plants; they filled themselves up with what are known as wild herbs, as much they could get hold of, gorging themselves until they were full; they even boiled up fresh grass and ate it – something they had never tasted before, not even as an experiment.

7.20 The grain warehouses

Storage of grain with minimum spoilage and exposure to vermin required the construction of numerous warehouses around Rome, which also allowed for multiple centres of distribution of grain, with each recipient having a tag (*tessera*) that indicated place and day of month. Grain in storage, much of which was privately owned and sold alongside public supplies, might be used as surety on loans (**7.20a**). The warehouses might also be used in part for other business activities (**7.20b-e**) and, especially, as carefully controlled storage facilities for valuables (**7.20f-g**).

(a) *L'Année Epigraphique* 1972 no. 86
(Tablet from Murecine, near Pompeii)

In the consulship of Gnaeus Acceronius Proculus and Gaius Petronius Ponticus [AD 37] on 18 June, I Gaius Novius Eunus set down that I received from Evenus Primianus, the freedman of Tiberius Caesar Augustus, in his absence through his slave Hessucus, and that I owe him 10,000 sesterces, which I will return when he asks for it ... for security for the debt of 10,000 sesterces I give specifically:
7,000 modii of Alexandrine wheat (more or less)
4,200 modii of chick-peas, emmer, and lentils in bags (more or less).
All of which I have in my name in the public warehouse, the *horrea Bassiana*, at Puteoli – this I say and declare is insured against risk at my personal expense.

(b) *Corpus Inscriptionum Latinarum* 6.4226

Calamus Pamphilianus, slave of the emperor Claudius, steward [*vilicus*] in charge of the Lollian warehouse [*horrea Lolliana*].

(c) *Corpus Inscriptionum Latinarum* 6.9973

T. Aquilius Pelorus, garment-maker [*vestiarius*] at the Agrippian warehouse [*horrea Agrippiana*].

(d) *Corpus Inscriptionum Latinarum* 6.33886

C. Tullius Crescens, marble merchant at the Galban warehouse [*horrea Galbana*].

(e) *Corpus Inscriptionum Latinarum* 6.9801

Aurelia Nais, fishmonger [*piscatrix*] at the Galban warehouse.

(f) *Digest* 19.2.55.preface

The owner of a granary shall not be held liable if the granary is broken into and robbed; but the slaves of the lessee can be summoned to interrogation because of their knowledge of the building.

The owner of a granary is not required to undertake the risk against violent attack or the breaking and entering of brigands on behalf of the lessee. But, excluding this, if anything out of the deposits is lost with the granary untouched outside, he should make good the loss to the depositor.

(g) *Codex Theodosianus* 4.65.4

There is a definite formulation from the emperors Antoninus and Marcus Aurelius that the owners of storehouses [*horrea*] that have been burgled, if anyone makes a complaint over such a matter, only need show that they employ guards and they are exempt from liability.

7.21 Alimentary schemes

Under Nerva and Trajan (and perhaps even earlier), the imperial treasury gave money to various Italian towns. This was invested in mortgages to individuals who pledged property of around 12.5 times the cash value loaned. Either annually or at six-monthly intervals, they paid the local officials interest of 5 per cent, which was used to support children in the area.

These schemes continued at least until the third century AD. Although Pseudo Aurelius Victor regards these as supporting the needy, legitimate freeborn children receive most support. It may be best to view the schemes as imperial patronage, similar to the euergetism of Pliny the Younger to Comum (**7.22**) or the generosity bestowed on children at Rome by Trajan (**7.21d**).

(a) *Inscriptiones Latinae Selectae* 6675
(Veleia, N. Italy, AD 98–113)

The repayments due on properties for 1,044,000 sesterces so that out of the generosity of the greatest and best *princeps*, the emperor Caesar Nerva Trajan Augustus Germanicus Dacicus, boys and girls may receive support [*alimenta*]:

legitimate boys to the number of 245 at 16 sesterces each [per month], making a total of 47,040 sesterces;
legitimate girls to the number of 34 at 12 sesterces each [per month], making a total of 4,896 sesterces;
one illegitimate boy, 144 sesterces [per year];
one illegitimate girl, 120 sesterces [per year].
Total 52,200 sesterces, which equals interest of 5 per cent of the principal [1,044,000] listed above.

[I], C. Volumnius Memor and Volumnia Alce have mortgaged through their freedman Volumnius Diadumenus the Quintiacan Aurelian farm, the hill of Muletas with its forests, which is in the Veleian district of Ambitrebius, having as their neighbours M. Mommeius Persicus, Satrius Severus, and their people, for 108,000 sesterces; they should receive 8,692 sesterces and mortgage their farm as listed above.

[Nearly 50 more mortgages are listed.]

(b) *Inscriptiones Latinae Selectae* 6509
(Ligures Baebiani, S. Italy, AD 101)

... [the following, in accord with the suggestion] of the finest and greatest emperor, have mortgaged their farms ... so that [from the return and out of his generosity] boys and girls in Ligures Baebiani should receive support.

... Crispia Restituta has mortgaged the Pomponian farm in the colonial land [*pertica*] of Beneventum, in the Aequanan district in the Ligures area, which has Nasidius Viatalis as neighbour, valued at 50,000 sesterces, for 3,520 sesterces [i.e. 2.5 per cent each six months or 5 per cent per year, as with Veleia].

(c) [Aurelius Victor], *Epitome de Caesaribus* 12.4

[Among his reforms, Nerva] ordered that girls and boys born of needy parents in the towns of Italy should be fed at public expense.

(d) Pliny, *Panegyric* 28

See **6.4**.

7.22 The generosity of Pliny

Pliny the Younger regularly advertises his intention of supporting his fellow citizens in Comum, for instance by paying for a local teacher so that the children of the town will not need to leave to obtain an education (**4.6**). In a letter written to Pompeius Saturninus (*Letters* 1.8.10) he describes a speech delivered at Comum at the official opening of the library he had given; he expresses hestitation due to modesty. He mentions in passing that he also promised to make 'annual contributions *in alimenta ingenuorum* (towards the maintenance of freeborn children)'. In his will he makes provision for the maintenance of baths, a library, 100 of his freedmen, a public feast at Comum, and an alimentary scheme. For the investment of money via mortgages, see **7.21** above and Pliny's advice to Caninius below.

(a) *Inscriptiones Latinae Selectae* 2927 (Comum)

Gaius Plinius Caecilius Secundus, son of Lucius, of the tribe Oufentina, consul, augur, legate with propraetorian power of the province of Pontus and Bithynia, sent with consular power to that province in accordance with the senate's decree by the emperor Caesar Nerva Traianus Augustus, victor over Germany and Dacia, father of his country, curator of the bed and banks of the Tiber and of the sewers of Rome, prefect of the Treasury of Saturn, prefect of the military treasury, praetor, tribune of the plebs, quaestor of the emperor, sevir of a squadron of the Roman equestrians, military tribune of the third Gallic legion, magistrate on the board of Ten, left by will baths at a cost of . . . and an additional 300,000 sesterces for decorating them, . . . with 200,000 for their maintenance . . . and also to his city capital of 1,866,666 sesterces to support 100 of his freedmen, and the interest on this subsequently to provide a dinner for the urban plebs . . . Likewise in his lifetime he gave 500,000 sesterces for the maintenance of boys and girls of the urban plebs [*in aliment(a) pueror(um) et puellar(um) pleb(is) urban(ae)*], and also a library, and 100,000 sesterces for the upkeep of the library.

(b) Pliny, *Letters* 7.18

See **6.5**.

7.23 High risk, high return? Vineyards

Investment in grape growing could produce much higher returns than grain or olives. Pliny the Elder states that in the first century AD Italian wine dominated the *quality* market, and some investors did make windfall gains (**7.23b**), but what that might mean in economic terms is unclear. The complexities of production (requiring suitable land and trained workers, not to mention storage facilities and transport to market) made the actual return on investment in vineyards uncertain. Columella optimistically advises that such an investment is highly desirable (**7.23c**), yet he makes no allowance for various capital expenses and does not allow for bad seasons. As Pliny the Younger shows (**7.23d**), in practice, all may not be so simple and losses are certainly possible (the vintage in AD 107 seems to have been bad for two of his properties – **7.23d**).

(a) Pliny the Elder, *Natural History* 14.87

Of the eighty noble types from practically the whole world that can rightly be thought of in the class of fine wine, two-thirds come from Italy, which stands out well above all other countries.

(b) Pliny the Elder, *Natural History* 14.48–52

48. The greatest fame was won by Acilius Sthenelus, a freedman plebeian, who intensively cultivated his vineyard of not more than 60 iugera in the region of Nomentum [in Latium, on the Sabine border] and sold it for 400,000 sesterces [i.e. over 6,666 sesterces per iugerum]. 49. Very famous too was Vetulenus Aegialus, also a freedman, in the district of Liternum in Campania [on the coast]; he enjoyed an even greater repute among people for cultivating the estate that had been the place of exile of Africanus.[1] But the greatest repute, thanks to the same Sthenelus, belonged to Remmius Palaemon,[2] otherwise famous for his work on grammar, who within the last twenty years bought a farm for 600,000 sesterces in the same region of Nomentum, at the turning leading off the main road 10 miles from Rome. 50. The cheap price of land in all areas around Rome [*suburbana*] is very well known, but it is especially true in that area, since he had acquired estates that had also been neglected and badly cared for and whose soil was rather poor even compared to the worst properties. He undertook to cultivate these lands not through any virtuous motive but first out of vanity (for which he was remarkably well known). Under Sthenelus' supervision he had the vineyards dug and levelled afresh, so that, in the process of playing the role of farmer, Palaemon brought this estate to an almost incredible state of perfection, so much so that within eight years the vintage, still hanging on the vine, was knocked down to a purchaser for the sum of

400,000 sesterces. 51. Everyone ran there to look at the heaps of grapes in these vineyards; the neighbourhood gave as an excuse for their own laziness Palaemon's rather elevated studies. Most recently Annaeus Seneca (the leader in both learning and power, power that ultimately became excessive and came crashing down around his ears; he was certainly far from being an admirer of frivolity) was so enamoured of this estate that he was not ashamed to hand over the palm for victory to one whom he otherwise hated and who would be sure to publicise the sale, and Seneca bought the vines, within hardly ten years of their being under Palaemon's management, for four times the original price. 52. This method of cultivation would be worth applying to the farms of Caecubum and Setia, since subsequently also it has on a large number of occasions produced 7 cullei of must per iugerum. Cato has also written of returns of 10 cullei per iugerum. Such examples show quite conclusively that the merchant does not make more profit by rashly crossing the oceans to the coast of the Red Sea or the Indian Ocean in search of cargoes, than is yielded by a diligently cultivated home-farm [*ruris larem*].

1   P. Cornelius Scipio Africanus Maior retired voluntarily to Liternum in 185, where he died in or about 183.

2   See 4.5 on his extravagance, the massive income from his school, and his viticultural success.

(c) Columella, *On Agriculture* 3.3

1. Now before I discuss the planting of vines, I think it appropriate to lay down, as a sort of foundation for the discussion to follow, the principle that we should have carefully weighed up and considered beforehand, whether the cultivation of vines will make the *paterfamilias* wealthy. For it is rather pointless to give instructions on the planting of vines when it has still not been determined whether vines should be kept at all. And most people are so doubtless on this point that many would avoid and dread such an arrangement of their land and would judge it more desirable to own meadows and pastures or woodland suitable for felling. 2. For, regarding the *arbustum*, there has been quite a debate even among writers, with Saserna being against this sort of agricultural practice and with Tremelius very strongly approving of it. But we shall assess this opinion in the proper place. Meanwhile, those who make a study of agriculture must be instructed on one thing first of all, namely that viticulture makes a very rich return. And to pass over the well-known ancient fertility of the soil, of which M. Cato wrote long ago and after him Terentius Varro, recording that each iugerum of vineyard yielded 600 urnae of wine, and that this tended to happen not just in a single region but also in the countryside around Faventia [Faenza] and in the Ager Gallicus [the strip of land running

along the Adriatic coast of Italy], which is now annexed to Picenum; 3. in any event, in our own time the region around Nomentum enjoys a most celebrated renown, especially the part owned by Seneca [the Younger], a man of outstanding genius and learning, on whose estates it is revealed that every iugerum of vines has yielded generally eight cullei. For the things that happened in our Ceretanum estates seem miraculous in that one of the vines on your farm produced more than 2,000 bunches of grapes, and on my farm 800 grafted stocks of less than two years produced seven cullei, or that top-class vines produced 100 amphorae to the iugerum, while fields and meadows and woods are held to do extremely well by the owner if they bring in 100 sesterces per iugerum. 4. For we can scarcely remember a time when grain crops throughout the greater part of Italy returned a yield of four for one.[1] Why then does viticulture have a bad name? The fault is not its own but that of people, according to Graecinus: in the first place, no one makes any effort to search out cuttings, and so most people plant the worst sort of vineyards; and then they do not nourish what they have planted in order that the vines grow strong and shoot out before they wither; and, even if they do happen to grow, they are lax about cultivating them. 5. Even at the very beginning they think it makes no difference what spot they choose to plant on; or rather they pick out the very worst part of their land, as if such ground alone was particularly suitable for this plant because it could bear nothing else. Either they do not understand the method even of placing them or they understand it but fail to carry it out. And they rarely have ready the 'dowry', that is, the equipment, for the vines, even though, if they don't have it, they waste many days of work and impose a constant drain on the financial resources of the *paterfamilias*. 6. In fact most people aim for the richest possible yield in the shortest time and they make no provision for the longer term; instead, as if living merely from day to day, they put such demands upon their vines and load them so heavily with multiple shoots that they show no concern at all for later generations. After making all these mistakes, or at any rate most of them, the last thing they're prepared to do is to admit that the blame is their own; they complain that the vineyard does not give them a return, vineyards that they themselves have ruined through their greed, ignorance, or neglect. 7. But those who combine careful work with scientific knowledge receive not, I believe, 40 or at least 30, but as Graecinus says, though setting the lowest estimate, 20 amphorae per iugerum, and thus they will easily outdo in the increase of their estates those who stick to their hay and vegetables. And he's right in this: for like a careful accountant he does his calculations and sees that this kind of agriculture is of the greatest advantage to the family estate. 8. For, although vines demand a very generous outlay, nevertheless seven iugera require the labour of no more than one vineyard worker, who gener-ally people think can be acquired at little cost, accepting even some criminal picked up at a slave auction. But I disagree with the majority view: I think an expensive vine worker is absolutely paramount. Let's suppose he costs 6,000 – no, 8,000 – sesterces; I estimate the 7 iugera of ground cost 7,000 sesterces, and that the vineyards with their dowry, i.e. with stakes and osier ties, are set up for 2,000 sesterces per iugerum; so still the total cost to the last coin [*as*] is 29,000 sesterces. 9. Add to this interest at 6 per cent per annum, which comes to 3,480 sesterces over the two years during which the vines are, as it were, in their infancy before they bear fruit. The sum total to the *as* for the principal and its interest is 32,480 sesterces. And, if the farmer enters this as a debt against his vines, just as a moneylender does with a debtor, so that the owner may realise the aforementioned 6 per cent interest on the total in perpetuity, he should take in 1,950 sesterces per annum. So by this reckoning the return, according to the opinion of Graecinus, is still more than the interest on 32,480 sesterces. 10. For, even if the vines are of the very worst sort, nevertheless if taken care of they will definitely yield one culleus of wine per iugerum. And even if 40 urnae sell for 300 sesterces,[2] which is the lowest market price, nevertheless seven cullei make a total of 2,100 sesterces, a total far in excess of the interest at 6 per cent.[3] 11. And this calculation we have made takes into account Graecinus' figures. But we personally believe that vines that produce a yield of less than three cullei per iugerum should be rooted out. Nevertheless, we have made our calculations up to this point as if there were no rooted cuttings [*viviradices*] that could be extracted from the prepared soil, though this factor alone, if the land is not provincial but Italian, would clear the entire cost of the land. 12. And no one should be sceptical about this when he compares my figures with those of Iulius Atticus. For we are planting between the rows 20,000 mallet-shoots to every iugerum of land, whereas he is planting 4,000 fewer; even if his figures win the day, nevertheless no patch of land is so very rough that it will not yield a return that is greater than the expense incurred. 13. As a result, even though 6,000 of the seedlings die through the vinedresser's negligence, nevertheless the remaining 10,000 will be snapped up by the contractors for 3,000 sesterces,[4] leaving a healthy profit. This sum exceeds by one-third the 2,000 sesterces that we said before was the cost calculated for planting one iugerum of vines – although our own management has progressed to such a point that farmers are quite keen to buy quicksets from me at a price of 600 sesterces per thousand. 14. But no one else will really go past that figure, for no one will readily believe us that there is such a great abundance of wine on our small pieces of land as you, Silvinus, know to be the case. That is why I have quoted the ordinary, regular price for rooted cuttings, so that those who through ignorance shun this type of agriculture may more quickly and unanimously be won over to our point of view. 15. Therefore, either the return from prepared ground or the expectation of future vintages should encourage us to plant vines.

1 Cf. Varro 1.44.1–2, who cites grain yields of 10 to 1 in some areas of Italy, 15 to 1 in some places in Eturia, and 100 to 1, apparently, around Sybaris in Italy and in Gadara in Syria and Byzacium in Africa.
2 Less than 2.5 asses per litre or 15 sesterces per amphora – but cf. the retail price of wine at Pompeii: as low as 12 sesterces; *Corpus Inscriptionum Latinarum* 4.1679.
3 Definitely an exaggeration. Finley (1999: 117) describes it as nonsense.
4 Yet he only paid 2,000 for his 20,000 or more shoots, his stores, and labour!

(d) Pliny, *Letters* 8.2 (AD 107)

Gaius Plinius to Calvisius [Rufus] greetings.

Other men go off to their estates [Pliny is referring to his Tifernum estate] to return richer, but I end up poorer. I had sold my grape harvest to the dealers who were queueing up to buy it [n.b.: on the vine]. The price was tempting: things looked good, both then and for the future. But their hopes were dashed. It would have been simple to give them all the same rebate, but that wouldn't really have been fair. To me it is one of the most important principles that one practises justice in private just as in public, in small things just as in big things, to one's own affairs just as to the affairs of others. For, if all offences are equal, so too all merits are equal. And so to everyone, so that no one 'should leave me without a gift' [*Aeneid* 5.305], I returned an eighth of the sum he had paid. Then to those who had invested very large sums in their purchases, I made separate provision, on the grounds that they had helped me more and they had suffered greater loss themselves. So, in regard to those who had paid more than 10,000 sesterces, then in addition to the common and, as it were, general grant of an eighth, I added a tenth of the sum that exceeded 10,000. I'm afraid I didn't put that very well; I'll demonstrate my calculations more clearly. If someone had happened to pay 15,000 sesterces as his purchase price, he would receive one-eighth of 15,000 plus a tenth of 5,000. What's more, since I reckoned that some had repaid a lot of what they owed, others had repaid some, and others had repaid nothing at all, I felt it was quite unfair to treat them all with the same degree of generosity in granting a rebate when they had not been equally conscientious in discharging their debt. So again I remitted one-tenth of the sum received for those who had paid. This seemed the most suitable way both to express my gratitude to each individual in accordance with his past merits, and to entice them all in the future not only to buy from me but also to pay their debts. This system of mine – or rather this act of indulgence of mine – has cost me a great deal, but it is worth it. For the novelty and nature of my rebate has won praise throughout the entire region, and those whom I have treated not with the same measuring-rod, as they say, but according to different classifications and grades, have gone away feeling more obliged to me the more they are good and honest people, having found that I am not a person who 'holds in equal honour the good man and the bad' [*Iliad* 9.319]. Farewell.

(e) Pliny, *Letters* 9.20 (AD 107)

Gaius Plinius to Venator, greetings.

Your letter was all the more welcome to me for its length, especially as it was entirely about my own little books. I'm not surprised you enjoy them, since you are as fond of all my works as you are of me. I myself at this very moment am gathering in the grape harvest [on the Tuscan estate] – which is slight, in fact, but better than I had expected – if 'gathering' is the word for occasionally plucking a grape, inspecting the press, sampling the fermenting wine from the vat, and creeping up on the urban slaves, who are now presiding over the rural ones and who have left me to my secretaries and readers. Farewell.

7.24 State intervention in the wine trade

The plan of Domitian to convert vineyards in the provinces to wheat farms, probably to be dated to AD 92, does not seem to have made much headway in practice. It does, however, give some indication of the amount of wine being imported into Italy. The embassy from the Asian cities, which included the sophist Scopelianus of Clazomenae, is also mentioned in Philostratus' *Life of Apollonius of Tyana* 6.42.

(a) Suetonius, *Domitian* 7.2, 14.2

Once, when a bumper vintage followed a poor grain harvest, Domitian thought that the fields were being neglected through excessive attention to the vineyards. He therefore issued an edict that forbade anyone to plant more vines in Italy, and ordered the vineyards in the provinces to be reduced by at least half, if they could not be got rid of altogether; yet he did not persist in implementing this measure . . .

It is believed that nothing was more instrumental in making him ignore his edict about cutting down the vines than the pamphlets that were spreading around, containing the following lines [Evenus of Ascalon, *Anthologia Palatina* 9.75]: 'You may even gnaw at my root, yet I shall still have plentiful enough wine to pour upon you, goat, when you are sacrificed.'

(b) Philostratus, *Lives of the Sophists* 1.21.520

Scopelianus went on many embassies to the emperor, and a certain good luck always accompanied him in his missions, but his most successful was the one concerning the vines. Unlike most embassies, this one was not only on behalf of Smyrna but on behalf of the whole of Asia. I will explain the purpose of the delegation. The emperor decided that there should be no vines in Asia because it appeared that people under the influence of wine were plotting revolution. Vines that were already planted were to be pulled up, and no more were to be planted from then on. So an embassy was required from the entire community, led by a man who would charm his audience like an Orpheus or a Thamyris. Accordingly they all chose Scopelianus, and he achieved far more on this embassy than anyone had dared hope for: he returned bringing not only permission to plant but even with penalties for those who *refused* to plant.

7.25 Equipment costs for an olive grove

Cato suggests combining vines and pastoralism (indicated by the presence of a swineherd in his list). Note the considerable investment required in equipment. An olive mill bought from Pompeii (120 km away) is cheaper than one from Suessa (40 km away), but transport costs make the two prices comparable.

(a) Cato, *On Agriculture* 10

This is how an olive grove of 240 iugera [c. 60 hectares] ought to be equipped: an overseer [*vilicus*], a housekeeper or overseer's wife [*vilica*], five labourers, three ploughmen, one ass-driver, one swineherd, one shepherd, in total thirteen people; three yoke of oxen, three pack-asses to carry manure, one ass [for the mill], 100 sheep; five fully equipped olive presses, a copper vessel with a capacity of 30 quadrantals [*amphorae*] and a copper lid, three iron hooks, three water pitchers, two funnels, a copper vessel with a capacity of five quadrantals and a copper lid, three hooks, one small basin, two oil amphorae, one jar with a capacity of 50 [*heminae*], three ladles, one water bucket, one shallow bowl, one small pot, one wash-basin, one small pan, one chamber-pot, one pot for scattering water, one ladle, one candlestick, one pint measure [*sextarius*]; three sizeable carts, six ploughs and plough-shares, three yokes fitted with straps, six harnesses for the oxen, one harrow, four bins for manure, three baskets for manure, three *semunciae* [something that holds one twenty-fourth of something; panniers?], three saddle-cloths for the asses; iron tools: eight forks, eight hoes, four spades, five shovels, two four-pronged rakes, eight scythes for hay, five for straw, five pruning-hooks, three axes, three wedges, one hand-mill, two sets of tongs, one poker, two braziers; 100 oil vessels, twelve pots, ten vessels for holding wine pulp, ten vessels for holding water residue from the olives [*amurca*], ten wine jars, twenty grain jars, one lupine vat, ten earthenware vessels, one wash tub, one bath tub, two water basins, separate lids for jars and basins, one donkey mill, one pushing mill, one Spanish mill, three mill rests, one side board [*abacus*], two copper discs, two tables, three large benches, one bench in the bedroom, three stools, four seats, two high-backed chairs, one bed in the bedroom, four beds on cords [*loris subtentos*] and three ordinary beds; one wooden mortar, one fuller's mortar, one loom for togas, two ordinary mortars, one pestle for beans, one for grain, one for seed, one for crushing kernels; one modius measure, one half-modius measure; eight mattresses, eight bedspreads, sixteen pillows, ten coverings, three napkins, six hoods for slaves.

(b) Cato, *On Agriculture* 22.3

An olive-mill [*trapetus*] is bought in the district of Suessa for 400 sesterces and 50 pounds of oil. The cost of assembly is 60 sesterces, and the charge for transportation by oxen, with six days' wages for six men, including drivers, is 172 sesterces. The axle complete costs 72 sesterces, and for oil 25 sesterces. Total cost: 729 sesterces. One bought complete at Pompeii is 384 sesterces, plus freight at another 280 sesterces. It is better to assemble and adjust it at home, at a cost of 60 sesterces. Total cost: 724 sesterces.

7.26 Pastoralism

In addition to wheat, vines, and olives, the agricultural investor could consider raising animals, sometimes in conjunction with other crops. Columella devotes four of his twelve books (6–9) to animal husbandry, while Cato's recommendations were long remembered (Pliny the Elder, *Natural History* 18.30 lists the first two responses only). For Columella the bare essentials in terms of animals for a peasant are an ass and some sheep (sheep for clothing, milk, and cheese, not to mention manure; an ass for transport, ploughing, and milling). Wealthy landowners could also possess large numbers of animals, as can be seen by the legacy of C. Caecilius Isidorus (**7.26d**).

(a) Columella, *On Agriculture* 6, *praef.*

I know, Publius Silvinus, that some intelligent farmers have refused to keep cattle and have absolutely and resolutely rejected the training of shepherds of flocks as an anathema to their profession. And I don't deny that they have some grounds for acting like this, inasmuch as the aim of the farmer is contrary to that of the shepherd: the farmer takes joy in land that is tilled and cleared as much as possible, whereas the shepherd rejoices in ground that is fallow and grassy. The farmer hopes for produce from his land, the shepherd for produce from his herd. So the ploughman abhors, whereas the shepherd longs for, a good growth of grass. 2. But even amidst such conflicting prayers there exists nonetheless a sort of alliance and union between them, since generally speaking it is better practice to use the food provided by one's farm to feed one's own cattle rather than someone else's, and also the fruits of the earth are abundant through plentiful manure, manure that comes from the flocks. 3. Nor indeed is there any region in which only cereals are grown and that is not cultivated as much by cattle as by people. Hence also beasts of burden [*iumenta*] and animals for drawing the plough [*armenta*] derived their names from the fact that they help us in our work, whether by carrying loads [as if *iumentum* were etymologically linked to *iuvare*] or by ploughing [*armentum* is linked to *arare*].

Therefore, just as the ancient Romans instructed, I myself also believe that we should acquire a thorough understanding of the tending of animals as well as the tilling of fields. 4. For in agriculture the system of grazing is very ancient, as well as very profitable, and it is because of this that the words for 'money' [*pecunia*] and 'personal property' [*peculium*] are apparently derived from the word for cattle [*pecus*]. For this was the only possession our ancestors had, and still among certain peoples this is the sole form of wealth generally employed, and even among our farmers [*coloni*], no other form of agriculture is more profitable. This was also the assertion of M. Cato: someone asked his advice as to what area of agriculture could make him rich quickly, and Cato replied, 'To graze herds well.' When the same person then asked him what would be the second best way to get a fairly rich return, Cato stated, 'To graze herds fairly well.' 5. But I'm sorry to have to report what such a wise man replied, according to some authors, when he was asked what was the third most lucrative activity in agriculture, 'To graze herds even badly.'

(b) Cicero, *On Duties* 2.89

Someone asked Cato what was the best way to make money for the family estate. He replied, 'To graze herds well.' What was the second best way? 'To graze herds fairly well.' What was the third? 'To graze herds badly.' Fourth? 'To plough.' And when he who had asked said, 'What about moneylending?', Cato replied, 'What about murdering someone?'

(c) Columella, *On Agriculture* 7.1–2

Since, Publius Silvinis, we are about to discuss the lesser farm animals [in the previous book Columella had dealt with oxen, cattle, horses, and mules (*mulil-ae*), and in this book will deal with the ass, sheep, goats, pigs, and dogs, in the next book birds, including poultry and ducks, and fish, in the ninth book wild animals and bees], our first example shall be the lesser ass [*minor asellus*, as compared to the mule], that cheap and common animal from the region of Arcadia. Most agricultural writers wish particular attention to be paid to this animal when buying and tending beasts of burden

– and quite rightly so. For it can even be kept in countryside that has no grazing pasture, since it is content with very little fodder of any sort of quality. It feeds even on leaves and thorns, or even a bundle of twigs if offered it. Indeed it actually thrives on chaff, which abounds in almost every region ... This animal performs very many essential tasks, and in return requires very little care; with a light plough it can cut the surface of easily worked soil, such as that in Baetica and all over Libya, and can draw loads that are far from light in a vehicle ... This animal's almost sacred duty is now that of turning the mill and grinding corn. Hence every farm [*rus*] requires an ass as the most essential tool, so to speak ...

The second most important quadruped after the ass is the sheep, although in terms of total usefulness the sheep is the most important. For it in particular guards us against violent cold and furnishes us with quite generous coverings for our bodies. Furthermore, it not only satisfies country folk [*agrestes*] with its abundant cheese and milk but it also embellishes the tables of refined people with numerous choice dishes.

(d) Pliny the Elder, *Natural History* 33.135

C. Caecilius Isidorus, freedman of Gaius, in the consulship of C. Asinius Gallus and C. Marcius Censorinus [8 BC], in a will dated 27 January, declared that, although he had lost a great deal in the civil war, he still left 4,116 slaves, 3,600 pairs of oxen, 257,000 head of other herd animals, and 60 million sesterces in cash, and he ordered that 1,100,000 be spent on his funeral.

7.27 Transhumance

Settled conditions under Roman rule encouraged transhumance – long-distance, large-scale sheep grazing between Apulia and the Abruzzi, moving from coastal plains in winter to upland pastures in the Apennines in summer.

(a) Varro, *On Agriculture* 2.2.9

Atticus: Frequently the winter pasturelands are many miles away from the summer ones.

Varro: I am well aware of that, for my flocks used to winter in Apulia and spent summer in the mountains around Reate; between these two distant areas, like a yoke between two baskets, there were public cattle-trails.

(b) Varro, *On Agriculture* 2.5.11

Cattle are most conveniently pastured on wooded land where there is plenty of undergrowth and foliage; those that spend winter along the coast are driven in summer into the leafy mountains.

7.28 A family and its hard-won wealth

The Volusii are a model family for success under the principate (Boatwright 1982). How they obtained such riches (agricultural investment or government service are likely sources of income) remains unclear.

(a) Tacitus, *Annals* 3.30.1 (AD 20)

At the end of the year two notable men died: Lucius Volusius and Sallustius Crispus [grand-nephew and adopted son of the historian]. Volusius [consul 12 BC] belonged to an old *familia*, which had, despite its age, never advanced further than the praetorship. He himself enriched it with the consulship and, as well as discharging the functions of censor in the selection for jurors of the equestrian decuries, he was the first accumulator of the immense wealth that so strengthened that *domus*.

(b) Tacitus, *Annals* 13.30.2 (AD 56)

[In contrast to Caninius Rebilus], Lucius Volusius [son of the L. Volusius in 3.30; consul AD 3] departed life in the fullness of honour, after a lifespan of 93 years and with an outstanding fortune virtuously gained and the unbroken friendship of so many emperors.

(c) Tacitus, *Annals* 14.56.1 (AD 62)

[Nero is addressing Seneca the Younger and asks a rhetorical question:] Or perhaps you happen to regard yourself yourself lower than Vitellius, thrice consul, or you regard me lower than Claudius, and that the wealth won by Volusius through long parsimony cannot be matched by my own generosity towards you?

7.29 Some religious restrictions and superstitions of agriculture

The agricultural communities of Italy retained numerous religious customs, theoretically restricting work practices, although there were considerable exceptions as Columella indicates. Presumably practices would vary in different areas and according to the level of superstition.

Columella, *On Agriculture* 2.21

But since our ancestors saw fit to render an account of their leisure [*otium*] as well as their work [*negotium*], we also believe that farmers should be advised of what they ought to do, and ought not to do, on holidays. For there are things, as the poet says [Vergil, *Georgics* 1.268–72], which:

Divine and human laws allow to be performed on festive days; no religious constraint has forbidden us to divert watercourses, to extend a hedge along arable land, to set a trap for birds, to burn thorn-bushes, and to dip the flock of bleating sheep in the healthy stream.

2. The pontiffs, however, say that a grain field should not be fenced on holidays; they also forbid sheep to be washed for the sake of the fleece except for medicinal purposes ... 3. Moreover, the rites observed by our ancestors permit these tasks too on holidays: pounding spelt [*far*], cutting torches, dipping candles in tallow, tilling a leased vineyard, clearing and cleaning fishponds, cisterns, and old ditches, going over meadows with a sickle, spreading manure, storing hay in lofts, collecting fruit from a leased olive-grove, spreading out apples, pears and figs to dry, making cheese, and carrying (either over your shoulder or on a pack-ass) trees for planting. But it is not permitted to convey them using a yoked animal nor to plant trees that have been transported, nor to open the ground nor to thin out a tree to let in light, 4. nor even to see to the sowing of seed, unless you have first sacrificed a puppy, nor to cut, bind or transport hay. And, according to the religious dictates of the pontiffs, it is not even permissible on holidays to bring in the vintage nor to shear sheep, unless you have sacrificed a puppy. It is also permissible to make a syrup from boiled grape juice and to boil wine. Likewise it is permissible to gather grapes and olives for preserving. It is not permissible to clothe sheep with skins [to protect their fleece from dirt]. Everything you do in your garden for your vegetables is permissible. On public holidays it is not permitted to bury a dead person. 5. M. Porcius Cato says that there are no holidays for mules, horses, and asses,[1] and he also permits the yoking of oxen in order to haul wood and grain. We have read in the writings of the pontiffs that only on the holidays called the *Denicales*[2] it is not permitted to have mules in harness, but on other holidays it is permitted.

1 *On Agriculture* 138; Cato adds 'unless they are family holidays'.
2 Holidays in honour of deceased members of one's *familia*.

7.30 Mining

One of the certain areas of economic expansion in the Roman world is in mining. Along with the continuing exploitation of metal resources such as tin, iron, and copper, there were virtual gold-rushes for precious metals in areas such as second-century BC Spain (**7.30a**) and Dacia (**7.30b**) in the 2nd century AD. In general, the extraction techniques were simple, relying on a large labour force of slaves and contracted free men (**7.30b**, Alburnus Maior, Dacia (modern Rohia Montanà in Romania); cf. **1.46** for Mons Claudianus, Egypt). Because of the number of workmen involved, considerable communities would often grow around the mines. Where these were imperial property, the mining leases (cf. the leases for tax farming: **7.15**) indicated the rights for mining in detail and also arranged for provision of services by contractors (**7.30c**).

(a) Strabo, *Geography* 3.2.10

Polybius mentions the silver mines at New Carthage and says that they are very large, that they are about 20 stades from the city and cover an area 400 stades in circumference, and that 40,000 workmen stay there. In his time they brought into the Roman state each day 25,000 drachmas.

(b) *Corpus Inscriptionum Latinarum*, III, p. 948, no. 10

In the consulship of Macrinus and Celsus [AD 164] on 19 May, I, Flavius Secundinus, wrote this, having been asked to do so by Memmius son of Asclepius because he said that he did not know letters. He said that he leased himself, and he leased his labour [*operae*] in the gold mine to Aurelius Adiutor from this day until next November 13, for 70 denarii, and 10 for his children. He will be entitled to receive this pay periodically, and he will be required to provide healthy and strong labour to his contractor [*conductor*], named above. If he decides to quit or to stop working against the wishes of his contractor, he will be required to pay 5 sesterces and eight asses to his contractor each day. If flooding impedes his work he will be required to calculate his pay pro rata.[1] If at the completion of the term of lease the contractor delays in paying the salary, he will be liable to the same penalty after three days' grace. Done at Immenosus Maior [a small settlement near Alburnus Maior].

[3 signatures follow:]
Titus, son of Beusan, called Bradua
Socratio, son of Socratio
Memmius, son of Asclepius

---

1 Cf. *Digest* 19.2.38.praetor, Paul: 'A man who has leased out his labour should receive wages for the entire period if he is not responsible for his labour not being provided.'

(c) *Inscriptiones Latinae Selectae* 6891 (*lex Metalli Vipascensis*: Vipasca, Portugal, 2nd century AD)

... he shall make immediate payment. If anyone does not do so and is convicted of having smelted ore before paying the price as specified above, his share as occupier shall be confiscated and the entire diggings shall be sold by the procurator of mines. Anyone who proves that the tenant has smelted ore before paying the price of the half share belonging to the *fiscus* shall receive one fourth.

Silver diggings must be worked in accordance with the details contained in these regulations. Their prices will be kept in accordance with the liberality of the most sacred emperor Hadrian Augustus, whereby the ownership of the share belonging to the *fiscus* belongs to the first person to offer the price for the diggings and pay down to the *fiscus* the sum of 4,000 sesterces.

If anyone strikes ore in one out of five diggings he shall, as stated above, carry out the work in the others without interruption. If he does not do so, another shall have a legal right to take possession. If anyone after the twenty-five days granted for raising working capital actually begins regular operations but then stops operations for ten consecutive days, another shall have the right to take possession. If a diggings sold by the *fiscus* is idle for six consecutive months, another shall have a legal right to take possession on condition that when the ore is extracted therefrom one half shall be, according to customary practice, reserved to the *fiscus*.

The occupier of diggings shall have the right to have any partners he wishes on condition that each partner contribute his proportionate share of the expenses. If anyone does not do so, then the one who covers the expenses shall have an account of the expenses covered by himself posted on three consecutive days in a most frequented place in the forum, and shall demand of his partners through the public crier that each contribute his proportionate share of the expenses. If anyone does not thus contribute or does anything with malice aforethought to avoid contributing or to deceive one or more of his partners, he shall not have his share of such diggings, and that share shall belong to the partner or partners who cover the expenses. Alternatively, tenants who cover expenses in such diggings in which there are many partners shall have a legal right to recover from their partners anything that is shown to have been expended in good faith. Tenants shall have the right to sell among themselves, at as high a price as they can, even shares of diggings purchased from the *fiscus* and paid for. Anyone who wishes to sell his share or buy shall submit a declaration for the procurator who is in charge of the mines; otherwise he shall not be allowed to buy or sell. Anyone who is a debtor of the *fiscus* shall not be allowed to give away his share.

Ore extracted and lying at the diggings must be conveyed to the smelters by those to whom it belongs between sunrise and sunset; anyone convicted of having removed ore from the diggings after sunset in the night shall have to pay to the *fiscus* the sum of 1,000 sesterces. A stealer of ore, if he is a slave, shall be whipped by the procurator and sold on this condition, that he shall be kept perpetually in chains and not tarry in any mine or mining district; the price of the slave shall belong to the owner. If the thief is a free man, the procurator shall confiscate his property and debar him forever from the mining district.

All diggings shall be carefully propped and reinforced, and the tenant of each diggings shall provide new and suitable replacements for rotten material. It shall be forbidden to touch or damage pillars or props left for reinforcement, or to do anything with malice aforethought to render the said pillars or props unsafe ... If anyone is convicted of having injured, weakened, or damaged a diggings, or of having done anything with malice aforethought to render such diggings unsafe, if he is a slave he shall be whipped at the discretion of the procurator and sold by his master on this condition, that he shall not tarry in any mine or mining district; if he is a free man, the procurator shall appropriate his property to the *fiscus* and debar him forever from the mining district.

Anyone who operates copper diggings shall avoid the ditch that drains the water from the mines and leave a space of not less than 15 feet on either side. It shall be forbidden to damage the ditch. The procurator shall permit the driving of a drift from the ditch for the purpose of discovering new mines, on condition that the drift be not more than 4 feet in width and depth. It shall be forbidden to look for or chop out ore within 15 feet on either side of the ditch. If anyone is convicted of having done anything different in the drifts, if he is a slave he shall be whipped at the discretion of the procurator and sold by his master on the condition that he shall not tarry in any mine or mining district; if he is a free man, the procurator shall appropriate his property to the *fiscus* and debar him forever from the mining district ...

OF THE MANAGEMENT OF THE BATHS. The lessee of the baths or his partner shall, in accordance with the terms of his lease running to June 30 next, be required to heat the baths and keep them open for use entirely at his own expense every day from daybreak to the seventh hour for women, and from the eighth hour to the second hour in the evening for men, at the discretion of the procurator in charge of the mines. He shall be required to provide a proper supply of running water for the heated rooms, to the bath tub up to the highest level and to the basin, for women as well as for men. The lessee shall charge men one half an *as* each. Imperial freedmen or slaves in the service of the procurator or on his payroll are admitted free; likewise minors and soldiers. At the expiration of the lease the lessee, or his partner or agent, shall be required to return in good condition all the bath equipment consigned to him, excepting any rendered unusable through age. He shall be duly required to wash, dry, and coat with fresh grease every thirty days the bronze implements that he uses. If any needed repair prevents the proper operation of the baths, the lessee shall be entitled to prorate the rental for that period; beyond this, whatever else he may do for the purpose of operating the said baths, he shall be entitled to no reduction of rental. The lessee shall not be allowed to sell wood except for branch trimmings unsuited for fuel; if he does anything in violation of this, he shall have to pay to the *fiscus* 100 sesterces for each sale. If these baths are not properly kept open for use, then the procurator of the mines shall have the right to fine the lessee up to 200 sesterces every time they are not kept open properly. The lessee shall at all times have on hand a supply of wood sufficient for . . . days.

OF THE SHOEMAKING TRADE. Anyone who makes any of the shoes or thongs that shoemakers customarily handle, or who drives or sells shoemakers' nails, or who is convicted of selling within the district anything else that shoemakers are entitled to sell, shall have to pay double to the concessionaire, or to his partner or agent. The concessionaire shall sell nails in accordance with the regulations of the iron mines. The concessionaire, or his partner or agent, shall have the right to obtain security. No one will be allowed to repair shoes, except to mend or repair his own or his master's. The concessionaire shall be required to offer all types of shoes for sale; if he does not, everyone shall have the legal right to purchase wherever he wishes.

OF THE BARBERING TRADE. The concessionaire shall be entitled to operate with the assurance that no one else in the village of the Vipasca mines or within the district thereof shall practise barbering for profit. Anyone who so practises barbering shall have to pay the concessionaire, or his partner or agent . . . denarii for each use of the razors, and the said razors shall be forfeit to the concessionaire. Slaves attending to their masters or their fellow slaves are excepted. Itinerant barbers not sent by the concessionaire shall not have the right of obtaining security; anyone who hinders his receiving security shall have to pay 5 denarii for each such act. The concessionaire shall engage one or more skilled workers in proportion to the need.

SCHOOLTEACHERS. It is decreed that schoolteachers are exempt from taxation at the hands of the procurator of the mines.

7.31 Public building

Building programmes, particularly at Rome where various emperors sought to add to their reputation by erecting grandiose public amenities (for instance, the various fora and baths) as well as their own palace complexes, offered considerable employment for slaves, freedmen, and the free labourers of Rome. The case of Vespasian, seeking to establish the credentials of the Flavian regime as protectors of the Roman populace in contrast with Nero's use of public land for his grand palace, the *Domus Aurea*, shows him avoiding possible labour savings in order to offer employment. This may be a variation of the folktale of the emperor rejecting a fabulous invention that would spell economic ruin (**7.31b**).

(a) Suetonius, *Vespasian* 8.5–9.1, 16–18

8.5. The city had become unsightly as a result of earlier fires and collapsed buildings. Vespasian permitted anyone to take over vacant sites and build on them, if the owners failed to do so. He himself began the restoration of the Capitol and was the first to set to work clearing away the debris and carried some of it off on his own shoulders ... 9.1. He also undertook new building projects: the Temple of Peace next to the forum and the temple to the Deified Claudius on the Caelian hill, the one begun, in fact, by Agrippina, but almost totally destroyed by Nero; also an amphitheatre in the middle of the city, a work that he discovered Augustus had intended ...

16. The only thing for which he deserves blame is his greed for money. For, not content with reviving the taxes repealed under Galba, he added new [including the famous tax on urine: Suetonius, *Vespasian* 23.3] and burdensome ones, increased the tribute paid by the provinces, in some cases even doubling it, and openly conducted business that even private citizens would be ashamed to do, such as buying up goods only to distribute them subsequently at a higher price ... Some say that he was very greedy by nature ... Others, on the other hand, believe that he was forced to resort to looting and robbery because of the desperate state of the senatorial treasury [*aerarium*] and *fiscus*, to which he bore witness right at the very beginning of his reign when he declared that the state needed forty billion sesterces in order to get back on its feet. This latter view seems closer to the truth, since he made excellent use of his gains, ill-gotten though they were. 17. He was extremely generous to every class of person, topping up the census for senators [at this time with either 1,000,000 or 1,200,000 sesterces], maintaining impoverished senators with annual payments of 500,000 sesterces, and restoring to a better condition many cities throughout the world that had been struck by earthquakes or fires ... 18. To a mechanical engineer who promised to convey some enormous columns to

the Capitol at minimal expense, he gave a not ungenerous reward for his invention but declined his services with the remark, 'You must let me feed my poor commons.'

(b) Petronius, *Satyricon* 51[1]

There was once a craftsman [*faber*] who made a glass cup that was unbreakable. So he was given an audience with Caesar with his gift ... then he made Caesar hand it back and threw it down on the floor. Caesar could not have been more frightened. But the fellow picked the cup up from the ground; it was dented like a bronze bowl. Then he took a little hammer out of his pocket and made the cup all nice again, no trouble. Having done this, he thought he'd hold the throne of Jove, especially when the emperor said to him, 'No one else knows how to make glass like this, do they?' Then look what happened: he said, 'No, no one else knows,' and Caesar had him beheaded – because of course, if his invention became known, we'd treat gold like mud.

1 Trimalchio is speaking; in Pliny the Elder, *Natural History* 36.195 and Dio 57.21.7, the emperor is Tiberius.

7.32 Trade

Although there were social prejudices against petty trading (cf. **1.39**), the Roman elite were in no way averse to gaining wealth (cf. **7.28**). This could occur through various investments, such as tax farming or through trade. For the senatorial aristocracy this would be done through indirect investment. Cato, for instance, could not own a large sea-going ship (**1.13**), but he could participate in maritime loans on a share basis, thus spreading the risk. By contrast, the young Trimalchio took large risks with his (and then his wife's) capital, but when he gained sufficient profit he invested this more safely in agriculture.

(a) Plutarch, *Cato the Elder* 21.5–6

When he began to devote himself more energetically to making money, he came to regard agriculture as a pastime rather than as a source of income, and he invested his capital in solid enterprises that involved the minimum of risk. He bought up ponds, hot springs, land devoted to producing fuller's earth, pitch factories, and estates that were rich in pasture-land or forest. All these undertakings brought in large profits and could not, to use his own phrase, be ruined by the whims of Jupiter. He also used to lend money in what is surely the most disreputable form of speculation, that is the

underwriting of ships. Those who wished to borrow money from him were
obliged to form a large association, and when this reached the number of
fifty, representing as many ships, he would take one share in the company.
His interests were looked after by Quintio, one of his freedmen, who used
to accompany Cato's clients on their voyages and transact their business.
In this way he drew a handsome profit, while at the same time spreading
his risk and never venturing more than a fraction of his capital.

He would also lend money to any of his slaves who wished it. They used
these sums to buy young slaves, and, after training them and teaching them
a trade for a year at Cato's expense, they would sell them again. Often
Cato would keep these boys for himself, and he would then credit to the
slave the price offered by the highest bidder. He tried to encourage his son
to imitate these methods, and told him that to diminish one's capital was
something that might be expected of a widow, but not of a man. But he
certainly went too far when he ventured once to declare that the man who
deserved the highest praise, indeed who should be honoured almost as a
god, was the one who at the end of his life was found to have added to
his property more than he had inherited.

(b) Petronius, *Satyricon* 76.3–9

I conceived a passion for business. To cut a long story short, I built five
ships, I loaded them with wine (it was worth its weight in gold at the time)
and sent them to Rome. You'd think I'd ordered it to happen: all the ships
were wrecked. Fact, not fiction. In a single day Neptune swallowed up
thirty million. Do you think I was done in? Hell no. I shrugged off the loss
as if nothing had happened. I built other ships – bigger, better, luckier, so
no one could say I wasn't a brave man. You know, a great ship brings great
bravery. I loaded them up with wine again, as well as bacon, beans, perfume,
and slaves. At this point Fortunata did her duty and sold all her gold and
all her clothes and put 100 gold pieces in my hand. This was the leaven of
my fortune. What the gods will soon happens. With one crossing I made
a cool ten million. I straightaway bought up all the estates that had been
my patron's. I built a house and bought slaves and cattle; whatever I touched
grew like honeycomb. When I began to have more than my whole country
owns, I packed it in: I withdrew from business and began to lend money
through freedmen.

7.33 International trade

Various sources indicate substantial imports from the East, either across the
border with Parthian territories (the wealth of Palmyra gives some indication of
the extent of this trade) or by ship across the Indian Ocean to the Red Sea.

Luxuries such as precious stones and silk are likely to have been paid for in precious metals (gold and silver) and may have reduced the amount of coinage in circulation.

(a) Pliny the Elder, *Natural History* 12.84

By the lowest reckoning, India and China [*Seres*] and the Arabian peninsula take from our empire 100 million sesterces every year: that is how much our luxuries and our women cost us.

(b) Strabo, *Geography* 2.5.12

Since the Romans have recently invaded Arabia Felix with an army, led by my friend and companion Aelius Gallus, and since the merchants of Alexandria are already sailing with fleets via the Nile and the Arabian Gulf as far as India, these regions have become far better known to people now than they were to people before us. In fact, when Gallus was Prefect of Egypt, we accompanied him and went up the Nile as far as Syene [Aswan] and the borders of Ethiopia; I discovered that as many as 120 ships were sailing from Myos Hormos [on the Red Sea] to India, whereas formerly in the time of the Ptolemies very few ships indeed dared to make such a voyage and to trade in Indian merchandise.

(c) Strabo, *Geography* 17.1.13

As for the public revenues of Egypt, in one of his speeches [not extant] Cicero says that a tribute of 12,500 talents [Diodorus Siculus 17.52.6 says more than 6,000] was paid each year to Auletes, father of Cleopatra. So, if someone who ruled the kingdom in the most evil and frivolous way possible was able to make so much money for the state, what should one think of the revenues now when they are managed with so much care and attention and when the commerce with the Indians and the Troglodytes has expanded to the extent that is has? Previously, at any rate, fewer than twenty ships dared cross the Arabian Gulf far enough to catch a glimpse outside the straits, but nowadays even large fleets are dispatched as far as India and the extremities of Ethiopia, from which the most valuable cargoes are transported to Egypt, and from there sent on to the other regions. As a result double duties are collected, on both imports and exports.

REFERENCES AND FURTHER READING

Andreau, J. (1999) *Banking and Business in the Roman World*, Cambridge.

Boatwright, M.T. (1982) 'The Lucii Volusii Saturnini and Tacitus', in Carandini, A. (ed.) *I Volusii Saturnini: Una famiglia romana della prima età imperiale*, Bari, pp. 7–16.

D'Arms, J.H. (1981) *Commerce and Social Standing in Ancient Rome*, Cambridge, MA.

Duncan-Jones, R.P. (1982) *The Economy of the Roman Empire*, 2nd edn, Cambridge.

Duncan-Jones, R.P. (1990) *Structure and Scale in the Roman Economy*, Cambridge.

Duncan-Jones, R.P. (1994) *Money and Government in the Roman Empire*, Cambridge.

Finley, M.I. (1999) *The Ancient Economy*, 2nd edn (updated; ed. I. Morris), Berkeley, CA.

Foxhall, L. (1990) 'The Dependent Tenant: Land Leasing and Labour in Italy and Greece', *Journal of Roman Studies* 80: 97–114.

Frayn, J.M. (1979) *Subsistence Farming in Roman Italy*, Oxford.

Garnsey, P. (1979) 'Where did Italian Peasants Live?', *Proceedings of the Cambridge Philological Society* 25: 1–25.

Garnsey, P. and Whittaker, C.R. (eds) (1983) *Trade and Famine in Classical Antiquity*, Cambridge.

Garnsey, P., Hopkins, K., and Whittaker, C.R. (eds) (1983) *Trade in the Ancient Economy*, London.

Giardina, A. (1993) 'The Merchant', in Giardina, A., *The Romans*, Chicago, IL.

Greene, K. (1986) *Archaeology of the Roman Economy*, London.

Harris, W.V. (1980) 'Roman Terracotta Lamps: The Organization of an Industry,' *Journal of Roman Studies* 70: 126–45.

Hopkins, K. (1978) 'Economic Growth and Towns in Classical Antiquity', in Abrams, P. and Wrigley, E.A. (eds) *Towns in Societies: Essays in Economic History and Historical Sociology*, Cambridge, pp. 35–77.

Hopkins, K. (1981) 'Taxes and Trade in the Roman Empire (200 BC–AD 400)', *Journal of Roman Studies* 70: 101–25.

Hordern, P. and Purcell, N. (2000) *The Corrupting Sea: A Study of Mediterranean History*, Oxford.

Howgego, C. (1992) 'The Supply and Use of Money in the Roman World 200 BC to AD 300', *Journal of Roman Studies* 82: 1–31.

Humphrey, J.W., Oleson, J.P., and Sherwood, A.N. (eds) (1998) *Greek and Roman Technology: A Sourcebook*, London.

Jongman, W. (1988) *Economy and Society of Pompeii*, Amsterdam.

Kehoe, D.P. (1988) *The Economics of Agriculture on Roman Imperial Estates in North Africa*, Göttingen.

Kolendo, J. (1993) 'The Peasant', in Giardina, A. (ed.) *The Romans*, Chicago, IL.

de Ligt, L. (1993) *Fairs and Markets in the Roman Empire*, Amsterdam.

Mattingly, D. and Salmon, J. (eds) (2001) *Economies Beyond Agriculture in the Classical World*, London.

Meijer, F. and van Nijf, O. (1992) *Trade, Transport, and Society in the Ancient World: A Sourcebook*, London.

Morel, J.-P. (1993) 'The Craftsman', in Giardina, A. (ed.) *The Romans*, Chicago, IL.

Morley, N. (1996) *Metropolis and Hinterland: The City of Rome and the Italian Economy, 200 BC–AD 200*, Cambridge.

Parkin, H. and Smith, C. (1998) *Trade, Traders, and the Ancient City*, London.

Peacock, D.P.S. and Williams, D.F. (1986) *Amphorae and the Roman Economy*, London.

Purcell, N.P. (1985) 'Wine and Wealth in Ancient Italy,' *Journal of Roman Studies* 75: 1–19.

Rich, J. and Wallace-Hadrill, A. (eds) (1991) *City and Country in the Ancient World*, London.

Rickman, G. (1980) *The Corn Supply of Ancient Rome*, Oxford.

Scheidel, W. and von Reden, S. (eds) (2002) *The Ancient Economy*, London.

White, K.D. (1984) *Greek and Roman Technology*, London.

Whittaker, C.R. (1993) *Land, City, and Trade in the Roman Empire*, Aldershot and Brookfield, VT.

8

THE LEGAL SYSTEM
AND COURTS

Given the importance of established systems of conduct and their enforcement throughout the Roman world, it is impossible to give more than an fleeting impression of Roman law. First, it must be remembered that Roman law applied to Roman citizens and so most of the inhabitants of the Roman empire enjoyed their own legal systems. Even after the Antonine Constitution of AD 212, extending citizenship to all members of the empire, in many parts of the empire (for instance, Egypt) life continued as normal, following local practice (8.1). Roman law would, however, provide a useful bridge between different forms of law, as can be seen in the regulations for Aphrodisias (8.2). In addition, the emperor could be used as the final authority for appeals (cf. the petition of the Burunitan tenants (1.51)) and was regularly consulted by governors with respect to the laws applying to their provinces (8.3).

At Rome, patronage was regarded as the basis of all relationships, providing legal protection for weaker Roman citizens (8.4). By the imperial period, patronage had changed, more often indicating the relationship between ex-master and slave, as illustrated in Chapter 3, or used as a technical term for lawyer (cf. modern French 'patron'). Yet reciprocal power relations were extremely important in the legal system. Pliny the Younger portrays his ideal emperor as impartial, while the litigants in his courts seek to win his approval for their conduct, rather than their own self-enrichment (8.5). The importance of the judge's evaluation of the moral standing of the parties in a legal process also comes through strongly in Aulus Gellius' description of his activities as mediator (8.6). In such a system, external patronage in the form of recommendations to the judge could influence the outcome of a case (8.7). Hence it is not surprising that there are frequent references in Roman literature to the risk of invoking legal procedures if you were not at least the equal of the other party in social standing and wealth (8.8).

In practice, some verdicts delivered by the courts may appear remarkably equitable, given the pressures on the judges mentioned above (8.9). But a long series of edicts by the emperors and governors of provinces indicates that the legal system might be abused. Individuals might be forced to undertake contracts against their will (almost an indirect form of taxation) or to provide services to the state, while the renewal of accusations at different assizes by officials might force a defendant to agree to a settlement contrary to his legal rights. The reassignment of debts to the state would also add further pressure to debtors, who appear to have often been imprisoned until they had paid their arrears – an illegal, but commonly mentioned practice (**8.10**, **8.31**).

In other cases, we see applicants claiming legal rights to which they have become entitled, such as privileges for having children (**8.11**). Particularly important were the legal questions surrounding the provisions of wills (**8.12**), whose details were a major concern for the Roman jurists. There could be problems not only about accepting legacies, but also over how to avoid them (**8.13**). Furthermore, the will offered the last chance to address one's relatives, friends, and enemies. It was to be expected that those of influence should acknowledge the patronage of the emperor in their wills, but there were some notable breaches of this social etiquette (**8.14**). Fronto finds himself required to excuse the conduct of a friend after his death (**8.15**), while Petronius' final assessment of Nero and his court is a remarkable display of black humour (**8.16**).

The operation of the courts depended to a considerable extent on the actions of private citizens in bringing complaints. This might lead to professional blackmailers, the sycophants and *delatores* (informers), against whom steps are repeatedly taken by the authorities (e.g. **8.21**) without any apparent effect. In one complaint from Egypt, a Roman citizen is clearly upset that a mere Egyptian is challenging his right to the land (**8.17**). In other cases, it is far from clear that the local authorities would have the power to challenge the actions of large landowners – this forms the basis of Apuleius' tale of the conflict between rich man and poor man (**8.18**), a well-known theme parodied by Trimalchio ('What's a poor man?'), but Libanius' account of the almost unlimited power of landlords who could obtain military support (**8.19**) supports the impression that corruption was endemic in the Roman empire. A further Apuleian tale of abuse of a poor farmer by a soldier (**8.20**) illustrates not only the practice of requisitioning animals, a habit that is regularly declared to be illegal and continues uninterrupted (**8.21**), but also the tensions between the army and the civilian populace, and the exercise of military and civil law. In the most desperate circumstances, the civilian population might join the marginalised who are generally referred to as 'brigands' and major disturbances might occur, which required the use of the regular army for their suppression (**8.22**).

The strong hierarchies of social status already seen in Chapter 1 were reinforced by differentiated treatment under Roman law. The *honestiores* (the senators, knights, and decurions) could expect better treatment than the *humiliores* (the rest of the free population) who were sometimes almost assimilated into the servile classes (8.23).

Indeed, the Roman penal system placed substantial emphasis on preserving the social position of victims, as can be seen in Gellius' summary of theories of punishment (8.24). Public displays of the executions of the most notorious criminals served both to entertain and to educate, and even offered the opportunity for the display of mythological learning (8.25). Some of the condemned were kept in confinement in the mines, the quarries, or the mills (8.26), but imprisonment was mainly an intermediate stage before the establishment of the guilt of the accused. All we know about ancient prisons suggests that they were highly unpleasant, with only the most basic provisions and even these subject to the whim of the guards (8.27, 8.28). Private prisons are also mentioned quite frequently in both literary and legal sources (8.29, 8.30). Although it may often have been illegal to detain debtors and tenants in such conditions (8.31), it would be difficult for the poor to exercise their legal rights against the more powerful.

8.1 Two extracts from an Egyptian legal manual

The major areas of conflict in antiquity that required external arbitration involved property and property rights. In Egypt, for instance, the following local laws regulate local nuisances (note that where sun-dried brick is used, run-off water could be a major problem and the closeness of housing is indicated by the concern for door openings).

Oxyrhynchus Papyrus 48.3285 (after AD 150)

If someone lodges a complaint against someone else, saying that the guttering of the house of the defendant is soaking his house with the run-off water, the judges should examine these matters by pouring water into the guttering. If the water soaks the house of the plaintiff, they should cut off enough of the guttering until it no longer soaks the house.

If someone lodges a complaint against someone else, saying that the door of the defendant's house opens into his property, then, unless it is found that it is the defendant's property onto which the door opens, he will be forced to block up the door that opens there.

8.2 The use of local law rather than Roman law

Relations between Rome and the cities in the empire would ultimately be decided by the emperor, who could confirm local civic rights or remove them, and receive or politely decline special offerings (particularly 'crown gold').

Letter from Hadrian to Aphrodisias (AD 119)

Claudia Paulina as chief magistrate [*stephanophoros*] for the first time.

The emperor Caesar, the son of the divine Trajan Parthenicus, the grandson of the divine Nerva, Trajan Hadrian Augustus, pontifex maximus, in the third year of his tribunician power, consul for the third time, sends his greetings to the officials of Aphrodisias, the council, and the populace.

Having received your decree and having listened to your ambassadors about legal cases involving money owed to the treasury, I agree that if a Greek of Aphrodisian birth or one who has citizen rights among you [is prosecuted] by an Aphrodisian Greek, the trial should take place under your laws at Aphrodisias. If, however, a Greek [who is not an Aphrodisias is prosecuted], the trial should occur under Roman law and in the province. [Those who are debtors to the city or standing surety] or generally involved with your treasury should stand trial at Aphrodisias.

You are offering me a [gold] crown of . . . weight: be aware that I have declined this, not wanting to burden your city on my behalf. Farewell.

8.3 The legal position of fostered children in a province

The raising of foundlings has been already been illustrated (**5.4**, **5.24**; cf. **2.26**). Their status if they later sought to claim free birth was clearly of concern to the Roman authorities. Pliny the Younger in Bithynia is reluctant to follow the precedents set for other provinces with different legal systems and so consults the emperor for a final ruling.

Pliny, *Letters* 10.65, 66 (c. AD 110)

Gaius Plinius to the emperor Trajan.

There is a major legal problem that involves the entire province: the status and costs of upbringing of those called 'fosterlings' [*threptoi*]. I have checked the imperial decisions about this, but because I have found no specific or general ruling to apply to the Bithynians I have decided to consult you as to what course of action you would want to be adopted. I did not think that, in a case that required your approval, I could fall back on precedents. However, I have had cited to me an edict attributed to the deified Augustus, applying to Andania; also cited were letters of the deified Vespasian to the Spartans and of the deified Titus to the same recipients and the Achaeans, and a letter of Domitian to Avidius Nigrinus and Armenius Brocchus, the governors, and another from him to the Spartans. I have not sent you copies because they are not properly revised and some parts seem unreliable and because I believe you have the true, revised versions in your records.

Trajan to Pliny.

That legal problem of yours, involving those who have been born free but exposed, then taken up by others and raised in slavery, has often been considered. But I cannot find anything in the minutes of the emperors who preceded me that is a ruling applying to all the provinces. Certainly there is the letter of Domitian to Avidius Nigrinus and Armenius Brocchus, which perhaps ought to be applied. But Bithynia is not one of the provinces about which he gave a decision. So I think we should not deny their claim to those who will have a claim to freedom in a case of this type and nor does their freedom need to be purchased by repaying the cost of their upbringing.

8.4 The purported origins of patronage at Rome

Dionysius of Halicarnassus, writing under Augustus, provides an antiquarian account of the patron–client relationship at Rome, an institution that was foreign to the Greek world. Under the empire, the bonds between free clients and aristocrats were considerably weakened by the rise of the emperor as patron of the plebs and the gradual extinction of the old nobility. But patronage continued in the relationship between ex-masters and freed slaves (see Chapter 3) and in the law courts.

The need to explain legal rights can be seen against a background where customary rights were generally only known to and enforced by the elite. It might be queried whether this situation substantially improved in the empire, although it was possible to appeal to the emperor (see **1.51**). Looking after the affairs of clients was also important, as the males would often have spent considerable periods of time on campaign. In general, the system is one of paternalism in a society where the rights of the *paterfamilias* were considerable and so produced an unbalanced set of obligations that favoured the patron.

Dionysius of Halicarnassus 2.10

These were the customary rules then defined by Romulus that remained in force for a long time afterwards among the Romans. The patricians were required to explain to their clients their rights of which they had no knowledge, and to take care of them in looking after their money and their monetary arrangements whether they were present or not, acting just as fathers do for their children. They were required to obtain justice for clients who had been wronged if someone caused them loss in a contract and to support them against those who brought a lawsuit against them. To be brief, they were to offer the peace of mind in personal and public affairs that they most needed. The clients, in return, ought to assist in providing a dowry for the daughters of their patrons when they were getting married, if the father lacked the funds, and to hand over the ransom to the enemy if any of them or their children was taken prisoner. They were required to pay from their own funds the monetary cost if their patrons lost a lawsuit or owed a fine to the public treasury, not charging interest but doing this as a favour. They had to share in the costs of their magistracies and privileges and other expenses on behalf of the state as if they were blood relatives. For both parties it was impious and unlawful to bring lawsuits against one another or to give evidence or vote against the other or to join with their enemies. If anyone was charged with having done any of these things, he was subject to the treason law that Romulus has established, and if he was convicted it was legal for anyone to kill him as a sacrifice to the Jupiter of the Underworld [i.e. Dis/Pluto]. This is because it was the custom among the Romans to dedicate the bodies of those who they wished to kill without legal penalty to one of the gods, but especially to those of the underworld. So then in many families the bonds between patron and client continued as if there were ties of kinship fixed from one generation to the next and it was the greatest source of praise for those of noble houses to have the most clients, both preserving those who had been inherited from their ancestors and adding on others gained through their personal merit. It was amazing how great a contest there was between each of them in earning goodwill by not allowing the other to surpass them in services, the clients thinking that they should provide services to their patrons as much as they could, the patrons wanting to put the least burden on their clients and accepting no monetary gifts. In this way their lifestyle was in control of every pleasure and they measured their happiness by virtue, not by good fortune.

8.5 Trajan as judge

As the emperor was the wellspring of judicial wisdom in the Roman empire, Pliny the Younger seeks to portray Trajan as an exemplar in this area, as 'firm but fair' in contrast to the avaricious and cruel Domitian. In contrast to modern judicial conduct that is seen as resolving legal problems, there is a strong emphasis on the censorial role of the emperor, judging the personal characteristics of those who appear before him.

Pliny, *Panegyric* 80

What about your gentle sternness, your restrained mercy in every inquiry? You do not take your place at the bench worried about enriching the treasury, and there is no other reward for your verdict than to have reached a fair decision. The litigants stand in front of you, concerned not about their wealth, but about your opinion of them; they are not so much afraid about what you are deciding about their case as about what you are deciding about their characters.

8.6 The duties of a judge – to return a verdict according to the evidence or according to his personal evaluation of the parties involved?

Gellius' account of his practices in a 'private' lawsuit (that is, a civil case, as opposed to a public prosecution) indicates that there was a considerable amount of written legal material available, but also highlights its limitations. Legal procedure was set by the appropriate statute. Legal 'authorities' would also recommend appropriate procedure (although which authorities took precedence and methods of decision when they differed in their opinions was not settled until Justinian's codification of Roman law in the sixth century). But, on matters of evidence, considerable weight was clearly to be given to the assessment of the moral and social worth of the litigants. Some matters were open to philosophical debate, as shown by the consultation of Favorinus, but it should be noted that considerable weight is given to the conservative opinions of Cato the Elder (second century BC), in line with the archaising tendencies of the Roman Second Sophistic.

Aulus Gellius, *Attic Nights* 14.2.1–25
(second century AD)

At the time when I was first selected by the praetors as a judge to undertake the cases that are called private, I assembled a collection of books written in both Latin and Greek on the duties of a judge. Thus, as a young man called from the study of the poet's myths and the closing comments of orators to decide on personal disputes, as there was a paucity of 'live' voices, I would learn the task of the judge from the 'silent' masters. We were advised and assisted on postponements and adjournments and other legal procedures by the Julian law itself and by the textbooks of Sabinus Masurius and various other legal authorities. However, when there was uncertainty about what went on and ambiguous cases with differing explanations, books of this type were of no help to us at all. For, although judges should form their opinions from the facts of the cases presented, there are some general principles and rules that act to prepare a judge before a case and to ready him for the uncertainty of the problems he will face. So I was at once faced with that unresolvable puzzle of how to determine my verdict.

When I was judge, there was an application for a sum of money, which, it was said, had been handed over and counted out. Yet the plaintiff could not show that this had happened by receipts or witnesses and was depending on quite flimsy evidence. But it was agreed that he was a truly decent man of known and tested honesty and had lived a life utterly without reproach, and many shining examples of his integrity and probity were presented. The fellow, however, who was being sued, was barely solvent, with a disreputable low-class lifestyle, and was shown to have been discovered to be a liar in daily life and to be stocked with tricks and devices. Still he repeatedly demanded, along with his many lawyers, that it ought to be proven in front of me that the money had changed hands in the usual manner: by an entry under payments, by a bank slip, by the production of a receipt, by a signed account, or by the presenting of witnesses. If the case wasn't supported in any respect by any of these, he ought to be discharged right away and his opponent found guilty of malicious prosecution. As to what had been said about the lives and deeds of both, that had no bearing on the case and was irrelevant evidence. It was a case of an application for a sum of money before a private judge, not one concerning character in front of the censors.

Right away my friends, whom I'd asked along in an advisory capacity, men well practised and renowned in legal advising and the workings of the courts and always hurrying along with cases demanding their attention on all sides, declared that the session should not last any longer and that there was no doubt that the defendant should be acquitted since it had not been shown by any official form of proof that he had received the money. But, when I contemplated the two men, one totally honest, the other totally dishonest and with a completely vile and ill-famed lifestyle, I could hardly be persuaded to record an acquittal. So I ordered a day's postponement and set off from the bench to go to Favorinus the philosopher, to whom I was most attached at Rome at that time. I told him everything that had been said before me about the case and the men, just as matters stood, and I asked him to make me the wiser in these matters, both with respect to the case, where I was stuck, and in all other matters to which I had to pay attention in my role as judge.

Then Favorinus congratulated me for my scruples as shown by my hesitation and concern and said: 'What you are now pondering over may seem to be small and insignificant in appearance. But, if you want me to guide you over all the duties of a judge as well, this is hardly the time and place. For your dispute involves interlinked and intertwining issues and needs a long, careful examination and cogitation. So, to touch on a few points of the issue, first of all now this is a question about the duties of a judge. If a judge happened to know something about the matter that was being tried before him and that matter was known and understood, as clear as daylight, to him alone, prior to the case starting or being brought into court, through some other matter or some chance occurrence, but not proved in the passage of the trial – ought he to make his judgement according to what he knew when he undertook the case or according to the evidence presented? The question should also be whether it is becoming and fitting for a judge, once the case has been presented, if there seems to be a chance of coming to a settlement in the matter, to put aside the duties of a judge for the moment and undertake the role of a shared friend or almost that of a peacemaker? And I am aware that this is even more uncertain and doubtful: should a judge in the course of a trial make such statements and ask such questions as need to be stated and asked, even if the person in whose interest it is that they be stated and asked neither states them nor asks them? For they say that this is surely being an advocate, not being a judge.

'Apart from that, there is also argument about this as well: is the practice and duty of a judge to express and indicate the facts and the action he is judging in his remarks in such a way that before the verdict is given, from his reaction to what has been at the time spoken in jumbled and confused form, he gives clues and indications, just as occurs at all times and places, of his inclinations and feelings. For those who seem to be sharp-witted and quick-thinking judges believe that the matter that is being litigated can only be investigated and understood if the person who is judging the case makes his own thoughts clear and discovers those of the litigants by frequent questioning and relevant interruptions. On the other hand, however, those who are considered more composed and thoughtful judges say that, while the case is proceeding on both sides and before his verdict, a judge ought not to indicate what he thinks whenever he is struck by some claim that has been brought forward. For they say that the result would be that, because different emotions are felt according to the types of allegation and evidence, they would seem to think and interject in contradictory fashion in the same case and at the same time.

'But we will attempt to say what we think about these and the other aspects of judicial duties of this type, when we have free time, and we will review the advice of Aelius Tubero on the duties of the judge, which we have recently read. However, as to the money, which you say has been claimed in court, I definitely advise you to make use of the advice of Marcus Cato, a truly shrewd individual, which he expressed in his speech "On Behalf of Lucius Turius" opposing Gnaeus Gellius. It was a custom handed down from our ancestors and still observed that, if the dispute between two litigants could not be clarified by written accounts or evidence, then the question for the judge who was investigating the case was which of them was the better man and if they seemed equally good or equally bad, then the person against whom the claim was laid should be believed and judgement should be made in his favour. Still, in this case, where you are undecided, the claimant is the best of men, the respondent the worst, and the matter has concluded between them without witnesses. So go ahead and believe the plaintiff and bring in a judgement against the defendant, since, according to you, the two are not equal and the plaintiff is the better man.'

This was the advice that Favorinus gave me at that time, as befitted a philosopher. But I thought it too much and going too far for a man of my age and modest status to seem to be forming a verdict and bringing in a judgement based on character, not on the evidence about the events. All the same, I could not bring my mind to acquit the defendant and so I swore that I could not make a decision and so avoided that decision.

8.7 Two letters of recommendation

Letters of commendation are an essential part of the system of patronage at Rome. Cicero, for instance, assisted his friends to win the ear of provincial governors when in dispute with local authorities (e.g. *Letters to Friends* 13.55) and when they had cases before the praetor (*Letters to Friends* 13.58–9). Here Fronto recommends Cornelianus, both for his own accomplishments, and because he has observed the duties of respecting his patron and has thus shown himself to be likely to be a useful connection in the future. Notable is Fronto's emphasis on their shared literary interests (a sign of upper-class breeding) and the opportunity taken by one interested in oratory (an appropriate skill for the ruling class) to snipe at philosophy. Cf. the final words on Trimalchio's tombstone: 'He never listened to philosophers' (Petronius, *Satyricon* 71).

(a) Fronto, *Letters to Friends* 1.1

Fronto to Claudius Severus, greetings.

It is said that the custom of recommendation initially began from good will, when everyone wanted to indicate and introduce a friend to another friend of theirs. Then gradually the custom developed to the extent that it did not seem disreputable to recommend those who were involved in public or private lawsuits to the judges themselves or those who were members of the court – not, so I believe, to undermine the justice of the judge or to divert him from his real decision. But there was a long-established custom in court cases themselves of producing character witnesses once the arguments had been presented. They would truthfully declare what they thought about the defendant following their own opinion. Similarly, those letters of recommendation seem to have performed the function of a character reference.

Where is this lengthy introduction heading? In case you think I have paid insufficient attention to your dignity and prestige by recommending Sulpicius Cornelianus my close companion, who is going to plead his case before you in the near future, I have taken the chance of giving a character reference for my friend, following the precedent of the ancient custom, as I mentioned. He is a hard-working individual, energetic with a free and generous spirit, a great patriot, relying on his innocence but hardly confident about it, dear to my heart because of his love of literature and the polish of his well-bred attainments . . .

. . . nor was it by chance or fortune that we became joined in friendship, and I admit that I did not seek Cornelianus' friendship on my own account. For the praise of his intellect had already reached me – this I discovered from experience and proof on numerous occasions had been a true report. We lived together, studied together, shared jokes and serious discussion, tested our loyalty to one another and our counsel – in all respects our friendship was a source of pleasure and assistance. Hence, as much as I possibly can, I ask and beg of you, to [assist?] the man dearest of all to me in this [unfair?] case . . . [I do not know?] what would cause a man of our order to mount a prosecution, but when you have read the minutes of the court . . . he has attempted to repel . . . The concern I feel in my mind leads me to recommend him at length, but he replies that your love for me can be relied on that, whatever I request, one word from me will seem like an entire speech to you.

(b) Fronto, *Letters to Friends* 1.1

Fronto to Appius Apollonides.

I began to treat Sulpicius Cornelianus as a friend, having taken a liking to the man's manners and literacy: he has an outstanding talent for literature. I would not deny that our friendship first began from my side based on education. I mean education in rhetoric – this seems to me to be a man's education. Forget the display of the philosophers. So please, as much as you can, help Cornelianus, who is a decent man, and me, his friend, an orator and not a philosopher.

8.8 Is it worthwhile having recourse to the courts?

The depiction of the picaresque quarrel over the cloaks in Petronius' novel shows the recourse to self-help (by summoning the neighbourhood) and only then, with reluctance, any recourse to state-sanctioned law courts. The standard argument put by Ascyltos, that he and Encolpius (the narrator) are not locally known and the court system is corrupt, should be balanced by recollecting just how disreputable the heroes of the novel really are. The passage suggests quite a high level of knowledge of the legal system (the interdict that might be used against someone holding another's goods is the judgement of the praetor as to ownership) and even the traders have their part-time bush lawyers among them.

Petronius, *Satyricon* 12–15

We were entering the market as the sun was setting. There we observed a heap of items for sale, not ones of any value, but ones whose dubious quality was easily hidden by the darkness at that time of day. So, since we also brought along the cloak that we had stolen in our robbery, we started to use this fine opportunity and, in a corner, to flap its fringe to see if the beauty of the garment might attract a buyer. Before long a country bumpkin, whom I seemed to recognise, accompanied by his girlfriend came up and began to examine the cloak carefully. Ascyltos for his part fixed his gaze on the shoulders of the bumpkin buyer and suddenly fell silent as if

302

thunderstruck. I too could not look at the fellow without a start, as he seemed to me to be the man who had found the garment in the deserted spot. Yes, it was him, for sure. But, while Ascyltos was wondering whether his eyes were deceiving him, in case he was making a rash move, he first came up close like a buyer and pulled the hem from his shoulders and examined it carefully.

What a wonderful joke from Fortune! The bumpkin had still not laid his prying hands on the stitching and was even looking down his nose at it and trying to sell it as something he had taken off a beggar. After Ascyltos saw that our stake had not been harmed and the low status of the seller, he pulled me a little aside from the crowd and said, 'You know, bro' – the treasure trove I was griping about has come back to us? That's the tunic, still full with the gold pieces untouched, so it looks. So what are we going to do or what's the law for us to reclaim our goods?'

Overjoyed, not only because I was looking at our property, but also because fortune had freed me from being suspected of a thoroughly shameful deed, I said we should not take a roundabout path, but go head to head under public law, so if he didn't want to return someone else's property to its owner, he would come under the provisions of the interdict.

For his part, Ascyltos was scared of the law and replied, 'Who knows us here and who will put any trust in our word? I'd really prefer to buy it, even if what we've recognised is ours, and for small change recover our treasure rather than descend to the uncertainties of law.'

> What power has the law, where money rules alone,
> Or where the poor can never win?
> Those who pass the time with their Cynic's wallets
> Regularly sell the truth for cash.
> So legal judgement is nothing more than goods for public sale.
> And the knight who sits in judgement ratifies what has been paid
>   for.

But, apart from a tuppenny coin, which we had intended to use to buy chickpeas and lentils, we had nothing at hand. So then, in case our property took off in the meantime, we agreed to hand over the cloak for a lower price so that the value of the greater gain would reduce the loss. So the moment we laid out the object for sale, the woman with her head covered who was standing by the bumpkin, after checking out the marks, carefully grabbed the collar with both hands and with a loud roar called out that she had caught some bandits. For our part, flustered by the possibility that we'd achieved nothing, we also started to grab the torn and dirty tunic and with the same antagonism call out that what they had was our booty. But the cases were completely mismatched and the traders who flocked to the shouting, of course, sensibly laughed at our hostility, when on one side they were claiming back a particularly valuable piece of clothing, while on the other we were claiming a collection of rags not worth making into good patches. Then Ascyltos put a thorough stop to their laughter by declaring, when he had got silence:

'We all observe that everyone likes their own most; so let them return our tunic to us and take their own cloak back.' Although the exchange was satisfactory to the bumpkin and his woman, some lawyers or rather burglars, who wanted to make a profit out of the cloak, demanded that the two objects should be entrusted to them and that a judge should consider the dispute the next day. For it wasn't only the property that seemed to be in contention, but there was in addition another reason for investigation because there was certainly a suspicion of brigandage on both sides. They were now coming to favour the idea of someone holding the cloaks in trust, when one of the traders, a bald man with forehead covered in lumps, who sometimes pleaded cases, fell on the cloak and said he would produce it the next day. But it seemed that this was all they were looking for: once it had been deposited among these villains, they would strangle it, and we would not come to the arranged deposition from fear of being charged.

... Clearly we wanted the same thing. So chance assisted both sides' wishes. For the bumpkin, outraged that we had demanded that he make a display of the patchwork garment, hurled the tunic at Ascyltus' face and told us, now that there was no longer a complaint against us, to let go of the cloak that was the only cause of the quarrel.

8.9 A trial in Egypt

The practice of baby farming has already been discussed (5.4 above). In the following case, the well-documented evidence of Saraeus' acts in accepting payment would give a prima facie case that the child she was rearing was a foundling, but the local administrative governor, the strategos, chooses to accept Saraeus and her husband's account that it is indeed their own child.

Oxyrhynchus Papyrus 1.37 (AD 49)

From the records of the strategos Tiberius Claudius Pasion, in the ninth year of the reign of the emperor Tiberius Claudius Caesar Augustus Germanicus [AD 49], third day of Pharmouthi [29 March], court proceedings.

Persouris vs. Saraeus.

Aristocles representing Pesouris: Pesouris, for whom I'm speaking, in the seventh year of Tiberius Claudius Caesar, our reigning emperor, took from a rubbish heap a male slave-child named Heraclas. He entrusted him to the defendant. At that time a contract for child-rearing for the son of Pesouris was entered into. She took the payment of upkeep for the first year. When payday came for the second year's amount, she took it once again. To prove that I'm telling the truth, there are receipts from her agreeing that she received this. Since the slave-child was starving, Pesouris took him away. Afterwards, taking an opportunity, Saraeus rushed into our home and snatched away the child and wanted to claim ownership on the grounds that he was free. I have first the contract for child-rearing, then the receipt for payment of upkeep. I ask that the terms of the contract be enforced.

Saraeus: I had weaned my own son, when these folks' slave was entrusted to me. I received from them the full amount of eight staters. Later the slave-child died, but I still had [some of] the money. Now they want to tear away my own child from me.

Theon: We have the documentation regarding the slave-child.

The strategos: Since in appearance the child seems to be Saraeus', if she and her husband swear an oath that the child entrusted to them by Pesouris has died, I will pass the judgement in accord with the decisions of our reigning emperor that, if she gives back the payment that she received, she should keep her own son.

8.10 Edict of the governor of Egypt against forced tax farming, the reassignment of debts to imperial officials, and repeated accusations

The establishment of Roman control over Egypt also opened up opportunities for corrupt practices. The assignment of tax collection contracts might be seen as a form of fixed euergetism, but might also be used to blackmail potential candidates. In other cases, officials might assist the affluent to reclaim their debts by assigning these to the treasury, thus increasing the likelihood of collection. It may be assumed that some percentage of this debt collection would also flow to the officials. Another scam was to wear defendants out by repeating claims in different courts. The Roman governor of Egypt here specifically outlaws many such abuses, but is also forced to refer other practices back to the imperial government at Rome for a future ruling. The edict was widely distributed, as can be seen by its posting by the local governor at the Temple of Hibis. Its efficacy, given similar decrees at later dates, is more problematic.

Orientis Graeci Inscriptiones Selectae 669, AD 68
(Egypt, the Oasis: Temple of Hibis, inscription 4)

I, Iulius Demetrius, administrator [*strategos*] of the Thebaid Oasis, have set out below for your benefit a copy of the edict sent to me by the imperial governor, Tiberius Iulius Alexander, so you may know about it and enjoy his benefactions. In the second year of the emperor Lucius Livius Augustus Sulpicius Galba, Phaophi 1, the day of Julius Augustus.

Tiberius Iulius Alexander says: I am taking every care that the city of Alexandria should keep its appropriate status and enjoy the benefits that it has received from the emperors and that Egypt, enjoying tranquillity, should gladly provide for abundant food and the prosperity of the present times, unburdened by new and unjust impositions. Practically ever since I arrived from Rome I have been petitioned by those I meet, a few at a time or in crowds, both the noblest men here and the farmers of the land, complaining about the most recent abuses, and I have not failed as far as I can to remedy the most urgent of these matters. So expect in good spirits everything to be done for your salvation and enjoyment by your benefactor, the emperor Galba Augustus, who shines down for the salvation of the whole race of mankind, and know that I have considered what is involved in assisting you. I have set forth as I must what I could decide and do about each of your requests and I will report with all truthfulness on weightier matters needing the power and majesty of the emperor, since the gods have preserved the security of the world for this most sacred time.

I recognise that your request is the most reasonable of all – that men should not be enrolled by force in tax collecting or in any other public contracts contrary to the general custom in the provinces and that, as most have no experience in such business but are enrolled by force and the collection of taxes is imposed on them, this causes no little harm to our affairs. Consequently I myself have never forced anyone into tax collecting or public contracts, nor do I approve of this, knowing that it is of advantage for the imperial accounts that men who are willing and eager should undertake these duties to the best of their ability. I have decided that in the future no one should force people against their will into tax collecting or public contracts, but will arrange contracts with those willing to come forward of their own accord, following the continuous practice of previous governors rather than repeating anyone's opportunistic abuse of power.

Some, using the excuse of public revenues, have accepted other people's debts and have transferred some to the debtors' prison and to other confinement, which I know have been abolished for this very reason: that the execution of the collection of debts should be against possessions and not against persons. So, following the wishes of the deified Augustus, I command that no one using public revenues as an excuse should accept other people's debts that he has not loaned himself as part of his duties nor should he in any way confine any free persons in confinement, unless they are criminals, nor in a debtors' prison, unless they owe money to the public treasury . . .

In accord with the grants of the emperors, also native Alexandrians living in the country for business purposes are not to be made to undertake any rural duties. You have often petitioned for this and I will uphold your claim: that no native Alexandrian will be forced to undertake any rural duties . . .

In general I am ordering that, whenever a prefect has already decided that a plaintiff brought before him should be acquitted, the plaintiff cannot in the future be brought before a court. If in addition two prefects have come to the same decision, the accountant who brings these same matters before the courts should be punished as he is doing nothing other than giving himself and other officials an excuse to make money. So many have thought it better to hand over their private property as they have spent more than it is worth because the same matters are brought to court at each sitting. There is the same determination as well about matters brought to court under the Private Account [*idios logos*]: if something has been judged with an acquittal or there would be an acquittal by the assessor acting for the Private Account, then the accuser will never again be able to lay a charge or bring someone before the court, or else if he does this without special permission he will be fined. There is nothing worse than malicious prosecutions, when what has earned an acquittal is brought back into court until someone provides a conviction. Now the city has become almost uninhabitable because of the horde of malicious accusers and every household has ended up in disorder – so I am forced to order that, if any of the accusers for the Private Account acting as a joint prosecutor brings a charge acting on behalf of another, he should have to provide the informer, so he too can run the same risks. If on his own account he brings three cases and fails to prove them, he will no longer be allowed to prosecute and half his estate will be confiscated. For it would be most unjust for someone who endangers the property and reputation of others to be himself totally free from legal scrutiny. . . .

8.11 Application for the *ius trium liberorum*

Special rights were set up under Augustus' marriage laws for those who had three or more children (see **3.57**). For women, the right to act as their own guardian gave them independence if they also were sufficiently literate to be able to create their own business contracts. Aurelia here asks that her claim to this right be placed in the public archives so that she can if necessary refer to it at a later date.

Oxyrhynchus Papyrus 12.1467 (AD 263)

There are long-established laws, illustrious prefect, which give to women who have been honoured with the privilege for having three children [*ius trium liberorum*] the right to be able to be their own guardians and to make contracts in the legal transactions they enter into without a guardian, particularly if they are literate. And I myself having been blessed with many children and being literate and able to write without hesitation to a considerable degree, I am asking your highness in full confidence through this my petition to allow me to make contracts without hindrance in the business deals that I make hereafter. I request that you keep my claim in your register at your office without verifying the claim, so that I can rely on this and be forever grateful to you. Farewell.

I, Aurelia Thaisous, also known as Lolliane, have dispatched this petition for deposit.
Year 10, 2x of Epeith [mid-July].

Your petition will be placed in the register.

8.12 A Roman will and codicil

As already seen from the inscriptions on funerary monuments (Chapter 1) and the provisions for the testamentary freeing of slaves and the sealing of wills (Chapter 3), the transfer of property at death was a major concern in the Roman world. The following will from Egypt is that of a Roman veteran and so follows Roman legal protocol. It was originally written in Latin, probably at Karanis. When the will was opened at Arsinoe after Longinus' death, this account of the reading of the will was lodged (in Greek) at the office of death duties.

The will is of the old Roman form, whereby the testator would 'sell' his property to an executor for a nominal sum, with a 'scales-holder' to ensure the validity of the sale, and is duly witnessed.

Note the specification that Marcella is over 30 years old, and so exempt from the provisions of the *lex Aelia Sentia* (**5.21**).

In the process of translation (the original will was probably in Latin, the surviving copy in Greek) and in transferring dates from the Roman to the Egyptian calendar errors could easily creep in. The date of actioning of the will was most probably Phaothi (= 18 October), rather than, as written, Athur (17 November), which would require the Roman month given to be amended.

Aegyptische Urkunden aus den Staalichen Museen zu Berlin, Griechische Urkunden (BGU) 1.326 (AD 191–4)

Translation of the will. Gaius Longinus Castor, veteran, having been honourably discharged from the praetorian fleet at Misenum, has made his will. I set free Marcella, my slave, who is older than 30, and Cleopatra, my slave, who is older than 30. They are to be my heirs with an equal share. All others are disinherited. Each may enter into their share of their inheritance whenever they are informed and are able to provide witnesses that they are my heirs. They are not permitted to sell or set aside this inheritance. But, if Marcella the aforementioned suffers anything such as happens to mortals, then I wish her share of the inheritance to pass to Serapion, Socrates, and Longus. Likewise in the case of Cleopatra, I wish her share of the inheritance to pass to Nilus. If he becomes my heir, he shall be obliged to go, do, and provide all those things that are listed in this will, which I commit to him on trust.

Serapis my slave, the daughter of my freedwoman Cleopatra, is to be freed, to whom I also give and leave: five arouras of wheatland, which I have at the village of Karanis in the place called 'Sparrow'; likewise an aroura and a quarter of wadi; likewise a third of my house and a third part of the house there that I bought previously from Prapetheutes the mother of Thaseutes; likewise a third of the date-grove, which I have near the canal called 'the Old Canal'. I wish to be given a funeral and embalmed under the pious care of my heirs. If I leave anything written in my hand after this in any manner at all, I wish it to be valid. Let there be no malice or fraud in this will. Iulius Petronianus has bought the household and property of this will for one sestertius, with Gaius Lucretius Saturnilus as the scales-holder (acknowledged) and Marcus Sempronius Heraclianus as witness (acknowledged).

The will was made at the village of Karanis, in the Arisinoite nome, 18 October, when the two Silani were consuls, thirtieth year of the reign of the emperor Caesar Marcus Aurelius Commodus Antoninus Pius Felix Augustus Armeniacus Medicus Parthicus Sarmaticus Germanicus, 21 Athur [AD 191]. If I leave further instructions written in my hand, I wish them to be valid.

Opened and read aloud in the Arsionoite metropolis in the Augustan agora in the office of the collector of the 5 per cent tax for inheritances and manumissions, February 21, when the consuls were ——, in the second year of the reign of the emperor Caesar Lucius Septimius Severus Pertinax Augustus, Mecheir 27 [AD 194]. The other signatories: Gaius Longinus Acilas (acknowledged), Iulius Volusius, Marcus Antistius Petronianus, Iulius Gemellus veteran.

Translation of the diptych will. I, Gaius Longinus Castor, the veteran honourably discharged from the praetorian fleet at Miseum, have written these codicils. I have made Marcus Sempronius Heraclianus, my friend and man of good repute, the executor, acting on his own good faith. I am giving and leaving to my relative Iulius Serenus 4,000 sesterces. I have written this in my own hand, 7 February. Longinus Acilas and Valerius Priscus have signed this. Signatories: Gaius Longinus Acilas; witnessed: Iulius Philoxenus, Gaius Lucretius Gemellus, veteran. This has been opened and read aloud on the same day as the will was opened.

I, Gaius Lucius Geminianus, Roman notary, have translated the above-mentioned copy and certify that it is in accord with the original will.

[On the outside: 'the will of Gaius Longinus Castor'.]

8.13 Avoiding an inheritance

Wills might impose considerable burdens on the heirs and so there was provision under Roman law that the heir must receive at least a quarter of the estate (lex Falcidia) and some heirs could refuse to accept an inheritance. The following also serves as a prospective death notice (important, given the poll tax in Egypt).

Oxyrhynchus Papyrus 1.76 (AD 179)

Apia, daughter of Horus, informs the strategos Theon that her father who owned a room in her house is near death – she does not wish to inherit and asks how 'to free myself from responsibility after his death'.

8.14 Failure to mention the emperor as patron in one's will

It was expected that a testator should mention his patrons and friends in his will, usually by offering some legacy. The emperor, as supreme patron of the Roman world, might well expect to be included – Augustus is described as 'moodily weighing up the final verdict of his friends and unable to hide his grief if he was mentioned in too restrained language and only in words, nor his joy if he was mentioned in due tones of gratitude' (Suetonius, Augustus 66.4).

Valerius Maximus, Memorable Doings and Sayings 7.8.6

Titus Marius Urbinas deserved the same treatment [as Q. Caecilius, whose body was dragged along at the end of a rope by an outraged mob]. He was promoted from the lowest rank in the army to the highest military offices by the support of the deified Augustus and became rich from the valuable earnings associated with these posts. Not only had he declared at other times of his life that he would leave his wealth to the person who had given it to him, but he had said that very thing to Augustus himself the day before he died.

8.15 A spiteful will

While wills could be used to bestow benefits, they could also be used to settle old scores as well. After the reading of Niger's will, Fronto was forced to write two letters, one to Antoninus Pius (*Letters to Antoninus Pius* 3) and another to Marcus Aurelius, excusing his friend's conduct.

Fronto, *Letters to Antoninus Pius* 4

To Caesar, my lord [i.e. Marcus Aurelius].

Censorius Niger has passed away. He left us a fifth of his estate in his will, which was respectable, except as concerns the language, which was ill-judged – here he paid more attention to his wrath than to decorum. He attacked Gavius Maximus without mercy, a man who is a senator and to whom we must show respect. Because of this it seemed necessary for me to write to the emperor, your father, and to Gavius Maximus a thoroughly difficult letter, in which I could not criticise the action of my friend Niger, of which I disapproved, but still wished to maintain the role of a friend and heir, as was fair. I wanted you to know about this, as with all my affairs, having tried to write a longer letter about the matter to you. But when I recalled the whole matter it seemed better to me not to trouble you or to distract you from more important concerns.

8.16 Using one's will to praise and blame

The ex-consul Petronius was forced to commit suicide in the aftermath of the Pisonian Conspiracy. The debate continues as to whether he was the author of the *Satyricon*, but there can be no doubt that as described by Tacitus he was a typical figure of the Neronian age, a man with considerable cultural interests matched by a striking sense for public statements, as particularly shown by his ironic attitude to his death.

Tacitus, *Annals* 16.18–19 (AD 66)

A few extra comments should be made about Petronius. He passed his days in sleep, his nights at his duties and in the pleasures of life. Just as hard work promoted others, sloth gained him his reputation. He maintained his position not by gambling and wasting his money, unlike the many who used up their wealth this way, but by learned extravagance. And, as his words and actions were unstudied and indicated an unconcern about appearances, they were more readily welcomed as showing a type of ingenuousness. As proconsul of Bithynia and then consul he showed himself equally diligent and capable of his tasks. Then returning to his vices, or perhaps by feigning vice, he was included as one of the few intimates of Nero. He became the master of ceremonies and Nero considered that nothing was fine and dandy amid the abundance of his pleasures unless Petronius had given it the stamp of his approval. As a result, he gained the jealousy of Tigellinus, who viewed him as a rival and his superior in the science of pleasure. So Tigellinus headed for the emperor's cruelty, which overruled his other lusts, and raised an accusation against Petronius of being friends with Scaevinus ...

It so happened that at that time the emperor had set out for Campania and Petronius, who had made his way as far as Cumae, was put under arrest there. He did not put things off out of hope or fear, but neither did he rush headlong to end his life. He opened his veins, had them bound up again, and reopened them as he felt like it. He conversed with his friends, not on weighty topics nor looking for a future reputation for steadfastness, and he didn't listen to them reciting any of the stuff about the immortality of the soul and the theories of philosophers, but rather to trivial verse and light poetry. He rewarded some slaves with his generosity and others with a whipping. He attended dinner, then enjoyed a sleep, so his forced death seemed like a natural occurrence. And he did not even flatter Nero and Tigellinus or anyone else in power in his will, unlike most of those who perished, but he described the misdeeds of the emperor, listing them under the names of the catamites and women involved and the inventiveness of each sexual act. He sent this off under seal to Nero and then broke his signet ring in case it should be used to imperil others in the future.

8.17 A complaint from a Roman veteran regarding an Egyptian

In most cases, the Roman legal system would not intervene unless a complaint was made and even then there was no guarantee that the complainant would be able to ensure enforcement of any court decision. The following petition shows conflict between a Roman ex-soldier and a local minor official over the purchase of land. The petition has been duly lodged and an investigation ordered by the *epistrategus* (provincial chief), as shown by the last two additions to the papyrus.

Michigan Papyri 2848, 3000 (15 Feb., AD 163)

To Vedius Faustus, the *epistrategus* [i.e. of notable standing, equivalent to equestrian rank (*vir egregius*)], from Gaius Iulius Niger, veteran of Osirantinoian tribe and Hermeian deme.

Having received an honourable discharge, my lord, and having caused no trouble [in the past], I have been driven to this point where I need a remedy from you. I have suffered wrong undeservedly from an Egyptian fellow, Isidorus, son of Achillas, a scribe of the superintendent of sequestered property of the village of Karanis of the Heracleite part of the Arsinoite nome, with his slave Didymus helping him in this affair. This is the matter: I have bought from the treasury in [. . .] year of the divine Aelius Antoninus from the sequestered property one aroura of olive grove in the Psenarpsenesite area in the same division previously belonging to Castor, son of Pekysis, and, having paid [. . .] drachmas in price for ownership, then I gained possession and pay taxes on it. The aforesaid Isidorus wanting to hurt us . . .

First he threw away the pledges and again I complained about this. Since the actions against me are clear, I ask as a Roman who has suffered such a thing from an Egyptian, if it seems right to you to order a message to be sent to the strategus of the Heracleite part of the Arsinoite deme that he be sent there for judgement and that I should be given a hearing so I can obtain redress from you and accept your service.

I, Gaius Iulius Niger, have submitted this.
Year 3, Mechir 21.

[If the strategus ascertains that an offence has occurred, he will let me know.]

Return petition to the petitioner.

8.18 The difficulty of enforcing lawful conduct when the litigants are of unequal power

In the countryside, it might be difficult to control a large landowner with a force of armed henchmen – such events are well attested, for instance, in modern Sicily where mafiosi provided the muscle for the owners of the large estates. Access to the law was theoretically open to all free men and in the passage below it is clear that the three brothers are seeking to act as patrons of the poor farmer. But, if appeals to normal decency were to fall on deaf ears, disputes would be solved by more violent means, as occurs in Apuleius' novel. In the conclusion of the passage (not given here), two of the brothers are killed by the shepherds and their dogs, but the third brother kills the landowner and himself.

Apuleius, *Metamorphoses* 9.35–6

While everyone was still transfixed by foreboding and dreadful fear, a slave ran up to announce the last great disaster to befall the owner of the farms.

He lived priding himself in three sons who had now reached manhood, who had gained an education and possessed a sense of decency as well. The young men were old friends with a poor man who owned a modest cottage. But a powerful, rich, young neighbour owned large, prosperous lands next to the tiny little cottage. He misused the fame of being descended from his ancestors, gained his power from gangsterism and readily achieved anything he wanted in the state. He raided the poor farm of his impoverished neighbour like an enemy, killing the sheep, driving off the cattle, and crushing the crop before it was ready to harvest. Now having pillaged all his careful work, he was eager to exile him from the soil itself and by starting a court case that was completely without merit over their boundaries, he was claiming the whole land as his own. The countryman, who was normally respectful, but had already been plundered by the greedy rich man, then in total alarm called on all the friends he had to indicate the boundaries so he could retain enough ancestral soil for his tomb. Among the rest there were the three brothers bringing whatever little assistance they could for their friend's sufferings. But that madman was not in the least worried or concerned by the presence of numerous citizens at least to draw back from his legal claims, if not from his robbery. When they asked him without reproach and tried to soothe his hot-headedness with compliments, he suddenly swore the most sacred oath on his own fate and that of his kin and declared that he would take no notice of so many mediators present and that he would have the neighbour grabbed by the ears by his slaves, pulled out of his cottage, and immediately turfed out as far away as he could. When he said this a remarkable rage struck the hearts of all those listening. One of the three brothers without hesitation and rather too frankly replied that he was wrong to rely on his riches and threaten like an arrogant tyrant, since on other occasions poor men had enjoyed the generous defence of the law and had maintained their claims against the insolence of a tyrant. Like oil on flames, sulphur on a fire, a whip to a Fury, these words of his were fuel for the man's spleen. Now completely out of his mind and utterly mad, he shouted out that all of them and their laws should go hang themselves and ordered that the huge, wild hounds used by the shepherds on his estates, used to eating abandoned carcasses on his lands and also brought up by being set on passing travellers to bite them, should be set loose and encouraged to attack to kill them.

8.19 Landowners, with the help of the military, raid subsistence farmers

There are constant references in our sources to clashes between the rich and powerful (*potentes*) and the general populace, as the government could not be relied on to intervene to uphold the legal rights of the weaker. In many cases, local governmental officials are seen to be providing assistance for the wealthy. Libanius here calls on the emperor, as the source of justice in the Roman world, to curb abuses, such as the encroaching on peasant property and deliberate disregard for tax collection (cf. **8.10** above on the hard lot of those forced to guarantee tax collection). It may be that there was another side to this, as landlords might find their tenants invading estate lands and be subject to attempted shakedowns by minor officials.

Libanius, *Oration* 47.4–8

4. There are large villages, each with numerous landowners. They have taken refuge with the soldiers stationed there not in order not to suffer harm, but to have the chance of inflicting it. The wages come from what the land gives, wheat and barley and the fruit of the trees, rather than gold or pay in gold coin. So, under the protection of the soldiers' muscle, those who have hired them have bought the opportunity to do anything they want. Even now they are bringing harm and trouble to their neighbours, encroaching on their lands, chopping down their trees, seizing, sacrificing, butchering, and eating their animals. Then the owners cry out at the sight, but they laugh as they feast. So far are they from being afraid that anyone may find out about this that they add threats to their actions and do everything else as well. 5. This may seem dreadful to you, emperor, but you have not heard the worst, given that the peasants' daughters are more important than their goats and sheep and yet they don't keep away from them either. Why then do I need to mention the blows and insults and how their women drag away the wives, grabbing them by the hair, how they make the wells unusable to the inhabitants by throwing things in to them, how they deprive them of the river water and so of their gardens? How some maintain large numbers of soldiers, others fewer mainly stationed in the middle of their villages, placated with plenty of food and meat, so, if any of those who have been wronged should fight back in his pain, the blow will also fall on the soldiers and this will be ruinous to the man who strikes the blow, while he will have no chance of speaking out. He will have to promise himself to the soldier who is totally drunk and allow anything, while there is no law and order at all there. 6. This is what makes farmers into brigands, this puts the steel in their hands, not the steel that loves the land, but one that kills. While their boldness is increased by the soldiers who are stationed with them, their temerity is also enhanced by the local administrators coming to an agreement to look after them and overlook their activities, as they know they will have greater security for their property because of their protection. Yes indeed, this is the name they give to this terrible evil, one that I think applies to those asked for honourable assistance to achieve safety when they are weak and having suffered injustice. 7. But this protection is totally the opposite. It offers strength to those harming others – including the tax collectors, whom I wanted to be with me here to complain about what they have suffered. For this would be a very tearful event facing men who have become impoverished when they were once prosperous. Do you want to know how this occurred, my emperor? Those who have to take care of the taxes, having this task as a liturgy, approach these villages that have been fortified by the soldiers. First they ask nicely and in a normal tone, but they are despised and mocked when they speak angrily and louder as you would expect from people who have missed out

on their rights. Then they threaten the rulers, but this has no effect for they are weaker than those who take the village's harvests. If they seize and drag away property, they have shown that they have stones at hand. 8. So the collectors receive wounds, not the harvest, and return to the city, showing by the blood on their tunics what they have suffered and that they do not have the taxes that they were hoping for, as the power of the hired hands has not allowed it. And they earn a reputation as unfortunates because they must either contribute the taxes themselves or refuse to do so under a whipping. Because they are forced to do this, forgetting the returns from the countryside and afraid of further wounds, but having no gold or silver to pay, they wail while selling off their female slaves, while selling off their male slaves, the children of those who reared them, even though they are grasping the knees of the sellers.

8.20 The requisitioning of Lucius after he was changed into an ass

Apuleius continues his tales of the suffering of the weak with this account of how Lucius lost his owner, the market gardener. Where animals were being led unloaded, it was common practice to require that they instead provide services for the civic or military authorities (cf. Libanius, *Oration 50* on Antioch). Here the soldier begins his advances in Latin, the language of the military (especially those from the West or the Balkans), which would not generally be understood in Greece, the setting of the novel. The peasant shows his own resourcefulness in first trying to invoke the soldier's sense of pity and then taking drastic action. That he chooses to try to hide in the town (rather than flee to become an outlaw) suggests that he could count on considerable local sympathy, while the soldier has to be careful not to reveal his own responsibility for his injuries. In the end, local enmity (the informer) and the stupidity of Lucius himself are the gardener's undoing, but the tale might easily have turned out differently.

Apuleius, *Metamorphoses* 9.39–42

[After hearing the tale of the rich man and poor man (**8.18** above)], the gardener straightaway jumped on my back and took the route back the way we had come. But the return journey was not trouble free – for him, at least. A tall fellow and, as his deportment and clothing indicated, a soldier from the legion, running into us, asked him imperiously and scornfully, 'Where are you taking that ass unloaded?' But my master, still overcome with grief and, anyway, not knowing any Latin, continued on his way in silence. The soldier could not contain his habitual arrogance; regarding silence as an insult, he struck him with the staff he was holding and knocked him off my back. Then the gardener humbly answered that, as he did not understand his language, he didn't know what he was saying. So then the soldier added in Greek, 'Where are you riding that ass?' The gardener replied that he was going to the nearby town. 'But I've a job for you,' he said. 'I've got to bring the bags of our commander along with the rest of the pack animals from the nearby camp.' He immediately grabbed in his hand the rope that was being used to lead me and began to drag me off. But the gardener, wiping off the blood that was flowing from his head after the wound from the first blow, asked the soldier to act more respectfully and decently, swearing that this would bring him luck. 'And this fellow here is a lazy ass, and also a vicious beast and prone to awful epileptic fits, and he can hardly carry a few handfuls of vegetables from the nearby garden without becoming exhausted with the huffing and puffing, let alone give the impression of being capable of bearing up under weightier stuff.' When he noticed that the soldier would not be softened by any pleas and was getting angrier and likely to take it out on him, that he had now switched the end of his staff and was going to split his head with the huge knob at its end, he took refuge in desperate measures. He pretended that he wanted to touch his knees to gain his pity, bent down low, grabbed his feet, lifted him up, thumped him down hard on the ground, and immediately pummelled his face, arms, and body with his fists, his elbows, his teeth, and even with a rock he picked up from the road. The soldier, once flat on his back, couldn't fight back or defend himself in any way, but loudly and repeatedly threatened that, once he had got up, he would chop him into little bits with his sword. Taking the hint from his words, the gardener grabbed the sword, threw it as far away as he could, and attacked him again with even more savage blows. Lying flat on his back and kept down by his wounds, unable to find any other way of rescuing himself, the soldier took the only path open to him and pretended that he was dead. Then the gardener took the sword with him, mounted me, and at full speed hastened to the town and, without even taking a look in at his garden, went to the house of a friend. He told him everything and asked him to help him in his hour of danger and conceal him with his ass for a little while – just until after hiding for one or two days so he would escape this capital offence. The other fellow did not forget their old friendship and readily agreed to help, and, after dragging me with my feet tied up a ladder to the upper floor, the gardener crept down into a box in the shop and, after putting the lid back on, hid there.

The soldier, however, as I learnt afterwards, at last made his way to the town, as if recovering from a terrible hangover, tottering along and suffering from the pain of the many blows he had suffered, only just holding himself up with his staff. Ashamed to say anything about his greed and laziness to any of the civilians, he nursed his resentment in silence until he found some fellow soldiers and told them only about his ordeal. They came to a decision: he should hide himself in the barracks for a while (apart from his own disgrace, he was also afraid of punishment under his military oath for the loss of his sword), while they would locate our tracks and take good care of discovering and taking vengeance on us. And there just had to be a treacherous neighbour to declare that we were being hidden at that spot. Then the soldier's mates summoned the magistrates and lied that they had lost a silver chalice of great value on the way, that a gardener had found it and did not want to hand it back, but was hiding with a friend. The magistrates, after hearing about the loss and the commander's name, came to the doors of our guest-house and shouted out to our host that he should surrender us, who were beyond all doubt hiding with him, rather than risk his own neck. He wasn't in the least alarmed. Wanting to save the fellow who had put his trust in him, he wouldn't admit anything about us, but asserted that he hadn't seen the gardener for several days. The soldiers responded by swearing an oath on the genius of the emperor, asserting that he was there and not hiding anywhere else. Finally the magistrates decided to investigate what he was doggedly denying by making a search. So they ordered their attendants and other public employees to check everything carefully inch by inch, but they reported back that they could not find any person, let alone an ass inside the premises. Then the argument grew even more heated on both sides: the soldiers insisting that what they were saying about us was a known fact and constantly calling on the honour of the emperor, he denying this and repeatedly calling on the power of the gods. When I heard this uproar, shouting, and abuse, being an ass with a sense of curiosity and displaying a restless lack of self-control at the best of times, I pushed my neck out of a window, keen to see what the uproar meant, and one of the soldiers who just happened to catch a glance of my shadow called on everyone to acknowledge publicly what he had seen. Then there was immediately an enormous shout, a ladder was immediately pulled up, and some people grabbed me and dragged me out like a prisoner. All hesitation was now set aside and they painstakingly checked everything. The box was uncovered, the poor gardener found, brought out and presented before the magistrates. They led him off to the public prison, sure to pay with his life for his deed, while continually making jokes about my poking my head out and laughing uproariously. And that is the origin of the common proverb about the outlook and shadow of an ass.

8.21 Instructions on avoiding requisitioning and billeting

Requisitioning of transport (animals and boats), the seizing of supplies by passing officials, and demands for billeting are constant problems referred to in decrees throughout the empire. In reality, the requisitioning of labour (cf. the demands for *operae* from tenants and ex-slaves) seems to have been an essential part of the ancient economy and official attempts to reduce this could only be partially effective, especially as complaints would first be lodged with those local authorities who had the most to gain from such activities.

Supplementum Epigraphicum Graecum 17.755
(Syria; c. AD 90)

From the instructions [*mandata*] of the emperor Domitian Caesar Augustus, son of Augustus, to Claudius Athenodorus the procurator. Among the most important matters that require the greatest diligence, which I know received the attention of my father the deified Vespasian Caesar, were the privileges [*ta philanthropa*] of the cities. In pursuit of this, he ordered that the provinces should not be burdened with the hire of pack animals nor with the encumbrance of providing billets. Nevertheless, by negligence or from a lack of direction, this rule has not been kept. For there continues to this day the old and entrenched habit, which will gradually become the norm unless it is forcibly stopped from occurring. I am instructing you to give some thought to preventing anyone from taking pack animals, unless he has a diploma from me. For it is totally illegal for permits to exist, whether out of gratitude or respect for someone, which only I have the power to issue. So nothing should occur that would contravene my instructions and damage my most beneficial concern for the cities: for it is right to help the exhausted provinces that hardly have the resources for essential tasks. No one should suffer violence contrary to my desire, and no one should take a guide unless he has my diploma. For, when the country dwellers are dragged off, the lands remain unfarmed. You will do best to use your own pack animals or hire them.

8.22 Bandit activity in North Africa and the Pisidian Taurus

'Banditry', either small-scale or major outbreaks of violence, was endemic in the Roman world, as the first inscription from North Africa (AD 151–2) illustrates. M. Valerius Etruscus, military commander in the Tunisian area, had been petitioned to complete an irrigation tunnel at Saldae, but was attacked and robbed on the way.

In particular, conflict between the inhabitants of mountainous areas, who would need to move into lowland areas for pasturage in the winter, and their neighbours was common. Usually policing was left to the local villages, who might be expected to wish to reach some workable accommodation with the pastoralists, but when large-scale raiding occurred, the Roman army might intervene. The second inscription (c. AD 280) seems to have occurred in the aftermath of the suppression of a major uprising (AD 278), at a time when policing could be left again to the locals.

(a) *Inscriptiones Latinae Selectae* 5795
(Lambaesis, N. Africa)

'Both the citizens of the notable town of Saldae and I myself along with the Salditanans ask you, sir, to recommend that Nonius Datus, veteran of Legio III Augusta, come as a surveyor to Saldae, to finish off whatever is left of the work.' I set out and on the way ran into brigands. I escaped along with my men, stripped of everything and beaten up. I came to Saldae and met Clemens the procurator.

(b) *Supplementum Epigraphicum Graecum* 41.1389

Valerius Euethios, prefect, to Kiliortes, headman of the village of [Akaleis?]. Since I have learnt that out of the band of brigands roaming about the territory of Termessus, none are left around the colony.

8.23 Differing penalties for differing classes

The Roman legal system always tended to inflict harsher punishment on lower-status defendants because of the importance of upholding social distinctions (cf. **1.1**, **1.2**). As the imperial system developed, this system became more and more codified and the punishments also increased in their cruelty, perhaps in correlation to a decline in actual state power.

Codex Theodosianus 9.18.1

The emperor Constantine Augustus to Domitius Celsus, Vicar of Africa.

Kidnappers who inflict the pitiful loss of their living children on parents were previously liable to be sentenced to the mines, along with other recognised punishments. If however someone is brought forward as accused of such a crime, after his guilt is clearly established with respect to the charge, if he is a slave or a freed man, he is to be thrown to the beasts at the first available games; if he is a free man, however, he is to be put into the gladiatorial games, with this provision, that he should perish by the sword before he can do anything to defend himself. Besides, we have decided that those who have been sent to the mines because of this charge are never to be recalled.

Delivered 1 August, when Constantine Augustus for the fourth time, Licinius for the fourth time were consuls [AD 315].

8.24 Theories of penology in antiquity

Gellius here offers a summary of philosophical views of the purpose of punishment current in his day. The constant reference to Greek terms is because most philosophical effort had occurred in a Greek cultural setting and, in particular, because the work of Plato was the general starting point for later discussion of philosophical topics, including the penology.

Aulus Gellius, *Attic Nights* 7.14.1–4

It is believed that there are three reasons for punishing misdeeds. One reason, which is called in Greek either correction [*kolasis*] or admonition [*nouthesia*], is when punishment is applied for the sake of correcting or reproving, so the person who makes an accidental mistake will become more careful and precise. Another reason is what those who have defined these words with due care term retribution [*timôria*]. The reason for punishment there is when the prestige and dignity of the person against whom the offence has occurred needs defending, in case the omission of punishment should lead to him being despised and reduce his reputation. That is the reason why they believe that the word derives from the preservation of reputation [i.e. *timôria*, 'retribution', is derived from *timê*, 'reputation']. The third reason for chastisement is what is called *paradeigma* [example] by the Greeks, when punishment is necessary to set an example, so others through the fear of the punishment that they know about will be deterred from similar misdeeds, which it is in the public interest to prevent occurring. So, when there is either a considerable hope that he who has acted wrongly will, of his own accord, correct his behaviour before being punished, or, quite the opposite, there is no hope that he can be corrected or set on the right path, or if there is no need to worry about loss of prestige for the person who has been wronged, or if the misdeed is not such that an example should be made of it with due fear, then such an error has seemed not worth the effort of punishment.

8.25 Some spectacular punishments in the arena

Punishment under Roman law was often designed to humiliate the condemned (e.g. by the public degradation of crucifixion, a punishment reserved for non-citizens) and to offer a shocking warning to those who observed their fates. In particular, this might be associated with the general spectacle of the games, as can be seen in Martial's description of the fates of brigands forced to play the roles of Prometheus, Orpheus, and Daedalus in bizarre mythological charades.

(a) Martial, *On the Spectacles* 7

Just as Prometheus, bound to the Scythian rock,
    Fed the bird unceasingly with his over-bold breast,
So Laureolus, hanging on the cross, offered
    His real innards to a Caledonian boar.
His torn limbs quivered while his body dripped blood
    And there was no bodily shape anywhere in his body.
At last he suffered the punishment that someone who is guilty

[Of killing his patron] or of cutting the throat of his master
Deserves, or one who has insanely robbed temples of their ancient
> gold
Or has set savage fire to you, Rome.
But that criminal had surpassed the crimes of ancient tales
> Whose punishment was what had previously been a legend.

(b) Martial, *On the Spectacles* 8

Daedalus, when you are being so torn by the Lucanian bear,
> How you would like to have had your wings!

(c) Martial, *On the Spectacles* 21

Whatever Rhodope is said to have seen in the drama of Orpheus
> Your arena has displayed to you, Caesar.
The rocks crept up and a wood hurried in, as marvellous
> As the grove of the Hesperides is believed to have been.
Every type of wild animal was mixed in a herd
> And numerous birds flew over the bard.
But he fell, torn by an ungrateful bear.
> This is the only part that happened contrary to the tale.

8.26 Lucius as an ass discovers himself in a slave prison grinding flour

Among the harshest non-capital sentences were imprisonment in the stone quarries (*lautumiae*), the mines (*metalla*), and the flour mills. The last was particularly unpleasant not only because of the labour of turning the mills, but also from the constant inhalation of flour dust. When labour became scarce in late antiquity, there are tales of unfortunates enticed into brothels, only to be imprisoned in the mills! On the tattooing of slaves regarded as felons, see **5.12**.

Apuleius, *Metamorphoses* 9.12

Now when most of the day had passed and I was exhausted as well, the twine rope around me was untied. But, although I was dreadfully tired and thoroughly in need of restoration of my strength, still I was struck by my habitual inquisitiveness and, quite carefully, having put off my meal although it was ready in plenty, considered the team at my undesired workplace with a certain pleasure. Ye gods! What kind of men were there, their entire bodies marked with purple welts, their flogged backs shaded rather than covered with a torn collection of rags, some only cloaking their genitals with a tiny covering, but all so dressed that their skin could be seen through the scraps of cloth. Their foreheads had been tattooed, their hair mostly shaved off, and there were manacles around their ankles. They were hideously wan, their eyelids ulcerated by the smoky darkness and clouds of steam and so they could hardly see at all, and they were all over a dirty grey from floury grime, like boxers who fight after powdering themselves with dust.

8.27 Conditions in a provincial gaol (second century AD)

Imprisonment was not generally a punishment in the ancient world, but merely a holding process until a case was judged or sentence carried out. But it might be a considerable time before a trial could be arranged (for instance, the Roman governor might be holding his assizes elsewhere in a province). In the meantime, prisoners were held in shackles, dependent on their relatives or on acts of generosity for food and shelter. For a member of the upper classes, such imprisonment would be both humiliating and painful.

Lucian, *Toxaris* 29

So poor Toxaris was chained up for a long time afterwards, believed to be the most villainous of all the criminals in the jail. The gaoler, a superstitious fellow, thought that he would win points with the god and assist him in taking vengeance by coming down hard on Toxaris. If he ever tried to defend himself by saying that he had done none of this, he appeared to be unrepentant and was hated all the more because of it. So he developed an illness and was in a bad way, as you might expect when he slept on the ground and was unable to stretch his legs at night, since they were fixed in the stocks. During the day a wooden collar and one hand shackled was enough, but at night he had to be completely restrained. Furthermore, the stench and lack of air in the gaol, due to so many being imprisoned in a confined space and hardly able to breathe, the clank of iron, and deprivation of sleep – all were cruel and difficult to endure for a man unused to this and unprepared for such harsh living conditions.

8.28 Regulations for the state prisons

These fourth-century regulations providing for less painful restraints and a healthier environment in the prisons also suggest that conditions were often extremely unpleasant and not infrequently fatal. Endemic corruption could lead to extra-judicial punishment (and also the possibility of arranged escapes) and the diversion to the prison authorities of funds to be used for feeding the prisoners. The separation of male and female prisoners seems to have occurred only as a result of Christian scruples. Conditions are likely to have been thoroughly unsanitary, with the opportunity to bathe only guaranteed in the fourth century AD.

Codex Theodosianus 9.3

On the Custody of Defendants.

1. The Emperor Constantine Augustus to Florentius, Receiver of the Revenues [*Rationalis*].

In every case, once a defendant has been produced, whether there is an accuser or the efforts of those in charge of public order have produced him, a trial should be held straightaway, so that the guilty can be punished and the innocent acquitted. But, if the accuser will be away at the time or if it should appear necessary that his co-defendants be present, the trial ought to be arranged as soon as possible. Meanwhile, the defendant ought not to suffer iron manacles fastened tight around the bones, but looser bonds, which will avoid torture but maintain effective custody. When he is shut up, he ought not to suffer the darkness of the inside of the building, but to be invigorated by the enjoyment of the light. When night requires the watch to be doubled, he should be taken into the prison cells under healthy conditions and, when day returns once more, at first sunrise he should immediately be brought out to the daylight enjoyed by all, so he does not perish by the punishment of imprisonment, which has been found to be cruel for the innocent and insufficiently severe for the guilty. This practice will also be followed: it is not allowed for those who act as custodians or their servants to market their cruelty to the accusers and put to death the innocent within the confines of the prison or cause them to waste away by slow suffering by depriving them of a hearing. A judge will face the threat not only of losing his reputation, but even of his own imprisonment, if any of the attendants cripples someone by withholding food past the due time or in any other manner whatsoever and the judge has not immediately inflicted capital punishment on the gaoler and his servants.

(Delivered, 30 July, at Serdica, when Constantine Augustus, for the sixth time, and Constantius Caesar were the consuls [AD 320].) . . .

3. The Emperor Constantius Augustus to Acidynus the Praetorian Prefect.

Since the single enclosed space of the prison holds all types of criminals, we have fixed by this law, that, although the form of punishment should be increased by this mingling, the different sexes should be guarded in different parts of the gaol.

(Delivered on 5 April, when Acindynus and Proculus were consuls [AD 340].) . . .

7. The emperors Honorius and Theodosius, the Augusti, to Caecilianus, Praetorian Prefect.

324

[After other matters.]

On every Lord's Day, the judges should examine the defendants who have been produced from prison custody and ask them whether they have been denied basic needs [*humanitas*] while in prison by the corrupt prison guards. If they do not have food to eat, the judges should ensure that it is provided, either 2 or 3 pounds [*libellae*] each day, or what the registrars consider in their pronouncements a suitable expenditure for the nourishment of the poor. The prisoners should also be brought to bathe under secure guard. A fine of 20 pounds of gold is set for the judges and an equal amount for their bureaus, if they ignore these highly beneficial regulations. There will also be the praiseworthy care of the priests of the Christian faith to raise this caution to the judge that he should observe this decree.

(Delivered 25 January, at Ravenna, when the Augusti, Honorius for the eighth time and Theodosius for the third time were the consuls [AD 409].)

8.29 Private imprisonment

There are a number of references to private imprisonment in our sources, including debtor prisons (**5.16** above) and slave prisons (*ergastula*: **5.16**). Although these were unlikely to be legal, they were sufficiently well known to appear in popular sources, such as Artemidorus' dream book, and in the legal sources (**8.30**). Maia, as mother of Hermes, symbolises pregnancy and hence various metaphorical possibilities.

Artemidorus, *The Interpretation of Dreams* 3.32

The appearance of Maia in a dream exposes what is hidden through seeking out what is secret and concealed and also signals harm and, for the sick, death. For she extracts from what encloses that which is enclosed and gives it to the earth. She rescues those held by force by anyone. This is because she rescues the enclosed body from what is enclosing it and so makes it less heavy. Often the appearance of Maia to a woman who is not pregnant portends illness; but to pregnant women, she portends nothing significant because of their expectations of giving birth.

8.30 Legal assistance for those held by *force majeure*

Note the reference here not only to illegal confinement by brigands, but also to arrest, including the use of restraints, by the rich and powerful, either in *ergastula* or in debtor prisons.

Digest 4.6.9

Callistratus, *Monitory Edict*, Book 2. Assistance will also be given to someone who was in chains. This not only applies to someone who is confined in public imprisonment, but to someone who has been violently overpowered by brigands or bandits or one of the powerful and confined in chains. The definition of 'chains' is taken in a broad sense: it has been decided that those shut up, for instance, in the stone quarries should be included in the 'chained', because it makes no difference whether someone is imprisoned by walls or fetters. But Labeo thinks that only public imprisonment counts as imprisonment.

8.31 Private prisons are declared to be illegal

Although private prisons are clearly declared to be illegal by this fifth-century decree of Zeno (echoing the ruling of Tiberius Alexander in the first century: **8.10**), the repeated mention that they are unlawful suggests that, as with requisitioning, they were a constant abuse.

Codex Iustinianus 9.5.1 (AD 486)

We order that no one at all in the most glorious city of Alexandria or the diocese of Egypt or in any province of our empire may maintain confinement in a private prison on his land or anywhere in his house. We order the illustrious imperial prefect and the glorious governors of all the provinces to make every effort and to be always on the lookout so that this often mentioned arrogance of the most criminal of men be repressed in every manner.

1. For, after this most salutary decision, the illustrious imperial prefect and any governor of a province will undoubtedly incur the charge of treason if they are aware of a crime of this type and do not avenge our injured majesty. The heads of the bureaus as well are to be ensnared in the net of this same charge when, as soon as they know what has been indicated to be an illegal act has been committed somewhere, they do not immediately take care to set up their own judges to stamp out this most infamous crime.

2. For it is clear that those who have committed this type of crime should, in accord with the ancient laws and imperial decisions, undergo the ultimate punishment as violators of the emperor's majesty.

(Zeno Augustus to Basilius, the Praetorian Prefect. 1 July, at Constantinople, when Longinus was consul [AD 486].)

FURTHER READING

Champlin, E. (1991) *Final Judgments*, Berkeley, CA.
Coleman, K. (1990) 'Fatal Charades: Roman Executions Staged as Mythological Enactments', *Journal of Roman Studies* 80: 44–73.

de Ste Croix, G. (1981) *The Class Struggle in the Ancient World*, London.

Gardner, J. (1998) *Family and Familia in Roman Law and Life*, Oxford.

Garnsey, P. (1970) *Social Status and Legal Privilege in the Roman Empire*, Oxford.

Grünewald, T. (1999) *Bandits in the Roman Empire*, London.

Holford-Strevens, L. (2005) *Aulus Gellius: An Antonine Author and his Achievement*, 2nd edn, Oxford.

Johnston, D. (1999) *Roman Law in Context*, Cambridge.

MacMullen, R. (1988) *Corruption and the Decline of Rome*, New Haven, CT.

Millar, F. (1981) 'The World of the *Golden Ass*', *Journal of Roman Studies* 71: 63–75.

Millar, F. (1984) 'Condemnation to Hard Labour in the Roman Empire', *Papers of the British School at Rome* 52: 124–47.

Millar, F. (1992) *The Emperor in the Roman World*, 2nd edn, London.

Mitchell, S. (1999) 'Native Rebellion in the Pisidian Taurus', in Hopwood, K. (ed.) *Organised Crime in Antiquity*, London, pp. 155–75.

Nippel, W. (1995) *Public Order in Ancient Rome*, Cambridge.

Reynolds, J. (2000) 'New Letters from Hadrian to Aphrodisias', *Journal of Roman Archaeology* 13: 5–20.

Saller, R. (1982) *Personal Patronage under the Early Empire*, Cambridge.

Shaw, B. (1993) 'The Bandit', in Giardina, A. (ed.) *The Romans*, Chicago, IL.

9

LEISURE AND GAMES

The citizens . . . might perhaps insinuate, that the last remains of a martial spirit were preserved in this school of fortitude, which accustomed the Romans to the sight of blood, and to the contempt of death: a vain and cruel prejudice, so nobly confuted by the valour of ancient Greece, and of modern Europe.

Edward Gibbon, *Decline and Fall of the Roman Empire*, ch. 30

Romans liked to be entertained, and the physical evidence that remains attests both to the quantity and to the sophistication of the entertainment. Theatres and arenas litter the empire; it has been well said that amphitheatres like the Colosseum, the great arena built under the Flavians, serve as the ancient equivalent of cathedrals in cities of the empire. Entertainment ranged from drama on the stage and elite poetry readings, to chariot-racing, beast hunts, staged sea battles, and gladiatorial sport, not to mention public executions. The latter types of events increasingly come to dominate our written sources. As time passed, the desire of audiences and therefore producers for novelty and enhanced spectacle led to greater sophistication and heightened levels of bloodthirsty violence.

Literary and epigraphical evidence reinforces the archaeological testimony (cf. **9.11**) and adds greater nuance to it. This is the aim of the passages in this chapter. Rather than provide details of, for example, the types of gladiators who fought or the number of laps in a chariot race, information readily available in secondary literature, these passages will focus more on the alleged reasons the more violent entertainments were held, and the reactions to them, in order to attempt to make the 'cultural leap' required to comprehend this aspect of Roman society and culture.

At one level, the games catered to a taste for violent spectacle, and passages make it clear how popular such entertainment was (**9.1**). It was also something of a cliché to suppose that the games kept the idle mob busy and diverted. But, at another level, the games could be seen to act as both a training ground for a martial people, and a 'safety valve' for people's more violent urges (**9.2**).

While gladiatorial combat seems to have originated as part of funeral games, the shows increasingly become a means by which individuals could make themselves better known and more prominent, and putting on shows became a requisite for election to high office: whereas original combat displayed an individual's valour, public shows emphasised the giver's generosity (**9.3**, **9.4**). The displays from Julius Caesar (**9.7**) and Pompey the Great (**9.8**) in the late republic clearly illustrate the competitive nature of such events, as capturing the public imagination could also lead to political success (cf. **9.17c**). Under the emperors, circumstances were different: the imperial family tended to usurp the right to put on popular shows, particularly at Rome (**9.9**). The audience, carefully arranged according to social status, is a very public expression of the social structure of the Roman world, and reinforced this message of stratification to all present. While watching the power that Rome exerted over both animals and 'barbarians' or criminals, an audience member also participated in the ranking of Roman society itself. The behaviour of the emperor at the games soon became a stock topic. Augustus was the model against which Tiberius (too stingy), Gaius (too popularist), Claudius (too cruel), and Nero (too vain) were evaluated (**9.10**). The Flavian dynasty sought to emphasise the contrast in their reign by constructing the Colosseum on land that had belonged to Nero's grand palace and using it to display their power and generosity (**9.11**), a practice followed by Trajan and others (**9.1b**). Commodus was notorious for appearing in public as a gladiator (**9.12**); by contrast, the young Caracalla is portrayed in the *Historia Augusta* as sensitive and merciful (**9.13**). The mass of spectators could also be expected to take to heart the lessons of ordered violence (**9.14**).

Not all entertainment at Rome was so socially structured, however. The less violent races in the Circus Maximus allowed for much greater social mingling and were much more frequent in the capital and urban centres of the empire than blood sports (cf. **9.5**).

One further aspect is worth stressing: it is not so much that the people are kept quiet and happy with the entertainment provided by their social superiors (**9.15**), but that the games also provided an almost unique forum for the people to assemble en masse and express both their pleasure and gratitude for the spectacle provided, but also their displeasure over some contemporary event – the price of grain, the corruption of a particular official, or the confiscation of a particularly popular statue (**9.16**).

Another aspect of the games that is of interest to the Roman social and cultural historian concerns the averred attitudes of individuals to the games, and below are presented a range of views, from that of the enthusiastic freedman (**9.2**) and addicted student (**9.21f**) to that of the ambitious politician and refined aristocrat who is above such dehumanising passions (**9.17–21**).

9.1 *Panem et circenses*

The poet Juvenal, writing under Trajan and Hadrian, dismissively termed the grain distribution programme (*annona*) and the regular horse races at Rome 'bread and circuses'. As Fronto indicates, when discussing the actions of the emperor Trajan, this was a common upper-class attitude, regarding both food and money handouts and public entertainment as the preserve of the lower classes.

(a) Juvenal, *Satires* 10.77–81

Now that there's no one to sell your votes to, the public has long since cast off its cares. They who once upon a time bestowed commands, offices, legions, the lot – now rein themselves in and long eagerly for just two things: bread and the games.

(b) Fronto, *Principia Historiae* 20 (van den Hout, AD 165–6)

It was clearly the height of political wisdom for the *princeps* not to neglect even mime artists and other performers of the stage, the circus, and the arena, since he knew that the Roman people is captivated by two things in particular, the grain supply and the shows [*annona et spectacula*], and that the success of his reign depends on amusements as much as on serious things. Neglect of serious matters entails the greater detriment, of amusements the greater unpopularity. The money largesses [*congiaria*] are less keenly desired than the shows; the largesses appease only the plebs on the grain register singly and individually, while the shows regularly satisfy the whole population.

9.2 A magnificent spectacle

Echion, the mat seller (*centonarius*), is looking forward to a good new, expensive show; his rough and ready Latin highlights his enthusiasm, both for games and for gossip.

Petronius, *Satyricon* 45.4–8, 10–13

And look, we're about to have a first-class show within three days at the festival, and not a professional band of gladiators but freedmen mostly. My mate Titus [a local magistrate, with whom Echion claims a very close relationship, hence the use of the *praenomen*] has a big heart and a hot head; it may be one thing, may be another, but it'll certainly be something. I'm an intimate friend of his, you see, and he does nothing by halves. He'll give us the best sword fight, with no quarter; there'll be a slaughterhouse

330

right in the middle so the amphitheatre gets a good view. And he's got the wherewithal: he was left 30 million sesterces when his father died. Even if he wastes 400,000, his inheritance won't feel it, and his name will go down in history. He's already got some dwarfs, as well as a woman to fight from a chariot, plus Glyco's steward, the one who was caught pleasuring his master's wife. You'll see a mob-riot between jealous husbands and Casanovas. But Glyco, that cheap bastard, turned over his steward to the wild animals. And that's just giving himself away. How's the slave to blame when he's forced to do it? His piss-pot of a wife's the one who really deserved to be tossed by a bull. But if you can't get at the ass, you thrash the saddle ... Anyway, I can almost smell the feast that Mammea [presumably he and Norbanus are competing for a magistracy in the *colonia*; Mammea is elsewhere a woman's name] is going to give us – 2 denarii each for me and my lot [probably fellow-members of a *collegium*]. If he does that, he'll snatch away all support for Norbanus. It's obvious – he should beat him hollow. And, after all, what good's the other guy done us? He gave us some cheap gladiators who were already so passed it that, if you so much as blew at them, they'd fall over. I've seen better animal-fighters [i.e. relatively untrained individuals sent in to be killed by animals]. As for the horsemen he killed, they were straight off a lamp, they were so small; you'd think they were poultry-cocks; one was a mule-driver [*burdubasta*; perhaps 'thin as a rake'], another was bandy-legged, and the reserve was as dead as the corpse he replaced – in fact he was hamstrung. One of them showed a bit of spirit; he was armed like a Thracian, but even he fought by the book. In fact, they were all flogged afterwards, they got so many shouts of 'Sock it to 'em' from the huge crowd. It was an absolute rout. 'Nonetheless,' he said, 'I have put on a show for you.' And I applaud you. Add it all up, and I'm giving you more than I received. One good turn deserves another.

9.3 Winning popular support

The walls of Pompeii offer a treasure trove of graffiti, including political notices and announcements of future entertainments.

(a) *Corpus Inscriptionum Latinarum* 4.4999 (Pompeii)

Marcus Casellius Marcellus, a good aedile and a great sponsor of gladiatorial games [*munerarium magnum*].

(b) *Corpus Inscriptionum Latinarum* 4.1189 (Pompeii)

The *familia* of gladiators of the aedile A. Suettius Certus will fight at Pompeii on 31 May. There will be a hunt, and the awnings will be used.

9.4 Social mobility and the games

Umbricius is bewailing the fact that good old-fashioned honest Romans like himself no longer have a place in the city; those who had once travelled around with gladiatorial troupes, providing musical accompaniment, now put on the shows themselves.

Juvenal, *Satires* 3.34–40

These former horn-blowers and perpetual attendants of the provincial arena, their puffed-out cheeks a well-known feature in every town, now put on their own shows and kill democratically, when the crowd commands it with a turn of the thumb. From there they turn back to contracting for latrines, and why shouldn't they do the lot? For these are the sort whom Fortune, whenever she feels like a joke, raises from lowliness to the great heights of state.

9.5 Career of a charioteer

The inscription is the epitaph of Scirtus (Greek *skirtos* = 'leaper'), charioteer of the Whites, and of Carisia Nesis, his wife (presumably), a freedwoman. It lists all Scirtus' 106 races from AD 13–25. It is noteworthy that he remains with the Whites all his career; but, as Cameron (1976: 202 n. 4), points out, seven wins in an entire career is not stunning. Cf. Friedländer (1908–13, vol. 2: 23): 'from 13–25 AD, a period meagre in spectacles'.

Corpus Inscriptionum Latinarum 6.10051 = *Inscriptiones Latinae Selectae* 5283 (Rome, AD 25)

Carisia Nesis, freedwoman of Gaia [i.e. of a woman].

Scirtus, charioteer of the Whites, in the consulship of L. Munatius and C. Silius [AD 13], in a four-horse chariot won once, came second once, and third once.

In the consulship of S. Pompeius and S. Appuleius [AD 14], he won once, came second once, and came third twice.

In the consulship of Drusus Caesar and C. Norbanus [AD 15], he won once, came second twice, and came third five times.

In the consulship of Sisenna Statilius and L. Scribonius [AD 16], he won twice, was recalled [*revocatus*: called back to repeat a race; the more usual term is *remissus*, but perhaps this was for a tie, rather than for an infraction] once, came second five times, and came third five times.

In the consulship of C. Caelius and L. Pomponius [AD 17], he won twice, was recalled once, came second eight times, and third six times.

In the third consulship of Tiberius Caesar and the second of Germanicus Caesar [AD 18], he came second seven times and third twelve times.

In the consulship of M. Silanus and L. Norbanus [AD 19], he was recalled once, came second five times, and third five times.

In the consulship of M. Valerius and M. Aurelius [AD 20], he came second three times and third four times.

In the fourth consulship of Tiberius Caesar and the second of Drusus Caesar [AD 21], he came second twice and third five times.

In the consulship of D. Haterius Agrippa and C. Sulpicius [Galba] [AD 22], he came second three times and third four times.

In the consulship of C. Asinius and C. Antistius Vetus [AD 23], he was recalled once, came second once, and third five times.

In the consulship of Ser. Cornelius Cethegus and L. Visellius [AD 24], he came second once and third four times.

In the consulship of Cossus Cornelius Lentulus and M. Asinius [AD 25], he came third twice.

Grand total: in a four-horse chariot, won seven times, called back four times, second thirty-nine times, third sixty times; he once raced in a contest held during an official cessation of public business and he twice raced in a six-horse chariot.

9.6 The business of hiring gladiators

This is part of a legal discussion of the rules of hire, *locatio*. The rule seems to be 'if you break it, you have bought it.'

Gaius, *Institutes* 3.146

If I supply you with gladiators upon the terms that for each man who comes out unscathed, I shall be paid 20 denarii for his exertions, but for each one who is killed or disabled 1,000 denarii, the question arises whether it is a contract of buying and selling or of letting and hiring. The prevailing opinion is that it is a contract of letting and hiring in the case of those who come out unscathed but a contract of buying and selling in the case of those who are killed or disabled.

9.7 Julius Caesar's games of 65 BC: boosting one's visibility and popularity

The first recorded gladiatorial show at Rome occurred in 264 BC, when two brothers put on a show of three pairs of gladiators at the funeral of their father. Two hundred years later Julius Caesar put on a show as curule aedile, at a memorial service for his father, who had died twenty years earlier.

(a) Plutarch, *Julius Caesar* 5

As aedile, he put on a show involving 320 pairs of gladiators ... The result of all this was to make the populace so favourably disposed towards him that every man among them was trying to find new offices and new honours to bestow upon him in return for what he had done.

(b) Pliny the Elder, *Natural History* 33.53

Caesar, who subsequently was dictator, was the first man holding the aedileship, at the funeral games for his father, to use nothing but silver for the equipment in the arena; this was also the first time that criminals were made to fight wild animals with weapons made of silver – a practice nowadays matched even by municipal towns.

(c) Suetonius, *Julius* 10

As aedile Caesar also put on a gladiatorial show, but with rather fewer pairs than he had planned; for he had collected from all parts such a great *familia* that he terrified his enemies, and a bill was passed restricting the number of gladiators that anyone was allowed to retain at Rome.

9.8 Pompey's games of 55 BC: overdoing it

Pompey the Great held magnificent games at Rome in mid-August, following the dedication of his theatre (the first at Rome to be built of stone) and the temple of Venus Genetrix. They were still remembered a century later, but not necessarily as Pompey would have wished – for instance, Pliny the Elder includes this event in a lengthy section on elephants, stressing their intelligence and gentleness.

(a) Cicero, *Letters to his Friends* 7.1
(to M. Marius, August, 55 BC)

If some physical ailment or the poorness of your health kept you from coming to the games [*ludi*], I give credit more to your good fortune than to your good sense. But, if it was because you thought these shows, which everyone else admires, contemptible and, although as far as your health was concerned you could have come, you nonetheless didn't want to, then I am doubly delighted, both at your freedom from physical distress and at your strength of mind, in disregarding what others admire without reason. I just hope you made the most of your leisure! ... Yes, the games (in case you're wondering) were most elaborate, but not to your taste (I judge your taste by my own). First off, the actors [in the pantomime show] came back on stage by way of compliment, whereas I thought they'd left the stage by way of saving their reputations. In fact your favourite, our friend Aesopus, was in such a state that everyone was only too willing to let him retire. When he began the oath, his voice failed him just as he got to 'if I deliberately make a mistake . . .'. What else need I tell you? For you know what the other shows are like. They did not even have that element of charm that the ordinary shows usually have. For the sight of the décor took away all the fun – I don't doubt you're very happy to have missed that. For what pleasure can there be in 600 mules in the *Clytemnestra*, or 3,000 mixing-bowls in the *Trojan Horse*, or a multi coloured display of infantry and cavalry equipment in some battle or other? These excited public admiration, but would have brought you no pleasure at all . . . You have shown in the past that you despise gladiators. Pompey himself admits that he wasted his time and effort on them. That leaves the hunts: twice daily for five days; very lavish, no one denies that. But what pleasure can a man of refinement get out of seeing a powerless human being being torn to pieces by the mightiest beast, or a splendid beast being transfixed by a hunting spear? Anyway, if such things are worth seeing, you have seen them often, nor did we who watched them see anything new. The last day was devoted to the elephants. The sight caused much astonishment among the common crowd, but no pleasure. Indeed there was a certain feeling of pity, and a general belief that these wild animals had something human about them.

(b) Pliny the Elder, *Natural History* 8.21

Pompey's elephants, having lost all hope of escape, tried to gain the compassion of the crowd, entreating them with indescribable gestures and deploring their fate with a sort of wailing. The crowd became so upset that they quite forgot about the imperator and his munificence, carefully devised for their honour; instead they burst into tears, rose as a body, and heaped curses on the head of Pompey, for which he soon afterwards paid the penalty.

(c) Seneca, *On the Shortness of Life* 13.6–7

What possible use is there in knowing that Pompey was the first to show the slaughter of eighteen elephants in the circus, pitting convicted criminals against them in a mock battle? He, a *princeps* of the state and one who by tradition stood out among the leaders of old for his outstanding good-ness, thought it a noteworthy kind of spectacle to destroy human beings in a novel fashion. Do they fight to the death? That is not enough! Are they torn to pieces? That is not enough! Let them be crushed by animals of enormous bulk! It would be better for such things to pass into oblivion so that no powerful man afterwards might learn them and be jealous of an act that was in no way human.

9.9 The right way to do it

As ever, Augustus provides the model of the beneficent emperor at Rome.

(a) Augustus, *Res Gestae* 22

On three occasions, I put on gladiatorial games [*munus gladiatorium*] in my own name, and on five occasions in the name of my sons or grandsons. At these games [*munera*], around 10,000 men took part in the fighting. Twice in my own name and on a third occasion in the name of my grandson I provided for the people shows [*spectaculum*] involving athletes assembled from all over the world. I produced [theatrical and circus] shows [*ludi*] in my own name four times, and in place of other magistrates twenty-three times ... On twenty-six occasions, I gave for the people hunts of beasts [*venationes bestiarum*] from Africa, in my own name or in the name of my sons or grandsons, in the circus or in the forum or in the amphitheatres; in these hunts around 3,500 wild animals were destroyed.

(b) Suetonius, *Augustus* 43

Augustus surpassed all before him in the frequency, the variety, and the magnificence of his shows [*spectacula*]. He says that on four occasions he provided games on his own account, and twenty-three times for the benefit of other magistrates who either were away from Rome or could not afford the expense themselves.

(c) Suetonius, *Augustus* 45

Augustus himself usually watched the circus games from the upper storeys of the houses of friends and freedmen, though sometimes he would sit in the imperial box [in full view of the spectators] and with his wife and offspring. He would absent himself from a show for several hours, sometimes even for whole days, but he would excuse himself and appoint substitutes to preside in his stead. Whenever he was present, however, he would pay full attention to the proceedings – either to avoid the bad reputation earned by his father Caesar for reading or answering letters and petitions while watching the shows, or because of his keenness for and pleasure in watching, something that he never tried to disguise; indeed, he often frankly admitted the fact.

9.10 The wrong way to do it: other Julio-Claudians

Various members of the imperial family fail to live up to Augustus' example.

(a) Tacitus, *Annals* 1.76 (on AD 15)

Drusus presided over the gladiatorial games that he presented in his own name and in that of his brother Germanicus, and, although it was a cheap show, he gloated excessively over the bloodshed. This caused alarm among the populace, and his father was said to have rebuked him for it. As to why Tiberius himself did not attend the show, accounts vary: some said that it was through his loathing of a crowd, while according to others it was his gloomy temperament and a fear of contrast with the cheerful presence of Augustus. I cannot believe that he allowed his son this opportunity of displaying his cruelty and of arousing the dislike of the people, though this too has been stated.

(b) Suetonius, *Caligula* 35

One day during the games, a gladiator [*essedarius*, who fights from a war chariot] by the name of Porius manumitted his slave after a successful fight; for this the crowd applauded him with some enthusiasm. The emperor rushed from the games with such haste that he trod on the hem of his own toga and fell head first down the steps, shouting in a fury that the most powerful people in the world gave more honour to a gladiator for the most trifling of deeds than to their deified emperors or to himself, their present emperor.

(c) Suetonius, *Claudius* 34

Claudius' cruel and bloodthirsty nature was exhibited equally in great and small matters ... At gladiatorial shows, whether they were presented by himself or by others, he ruled that all combatants who fell accidentally should have their throats cut – above all net-fighters [*retiarii*], so that he could see their faces as they died ... Claudius so greatly enjoyed wild-beast shows and the fights that took place at midday that, after he had spent the whole morning in the amphitheatre from daybreak, at noon he would dismiss the audience to lunch, keep his seat, and not only watch the regular combats but match others on any slight and sudden occasion, for example from among the stage carpenters and their assistants, and similar members of the theatre staff, as a punishment for the failure of any machine or apparatus to work as it should. He even forced one of his ushers [*nomen-culatores*] to enter the arena and fight in his toga.

(d) Suetonius, *Nero* 53

What Nero wanted more than anything else was to be popular. He was jealous of all those who in any way inspired the enthusiasm of the common people. The general belief was that, after the crowns he had won from his performances on the stage, at the next set of games he would take his place among the athletes at the Olympics. For he was a keen wrestler and he watched the athletic contests all over Greece in the same way as the umpires, sitting down at ground level in the stadium, and if pairs of combatants withdrew too far from the middle he would push them back into place with his own hands. Because he was believed to emulate Apollo in song and the Sun in chariot-racing, he was determined also to imitate the deeds of Hercules. They say a lion was got ready so that a naked Nero could slaughter it in the arena with a club or by squeezing it in his arms, while the people looked on.

9.11 Flavian innovation: getting it right again

Since their dynasty had only begun in AD 69, the Flavians sought to enhance their popularity by stressing their differences from the Julio-Claudian emperors, especially Nero. The Flavian Amphitheatre (nicknamed the Colosseum from the converted statue of Nero nearby) turned what had been part of Nero's palace complex into a permanent and striking public monument.

In particular, the Flavian poets Martial and Statius laud the behaviour of Titus and Domitian at these games. In *Silvae* 1.6 (**9.11g**), Statius celebrates the people's jubilation at one particularly extravagant spectacle in the time of Domitian, the Saturnalian games (held in December); cf. Suetonius, *Domitian* 4, and Newlands (2002: ch. 7).

(a) Martial, *On the Spectacles* 2

Where the starry Colossus [i.e. the colossal statue of Nero, transformed by Vespasian into a statue of the sun] views the stars from nearby, and in the middle of the road tall scaffolds [*pegmata*] rise, once gleamed the odious palace of a savage king, and a single house stood in all the City. Here, where the far-seen amphitheatre lifts its mass august, was once Nero's lake. Here, where we admire the warm baths [of Titus] (a gift swiftly wrought), a haughty domain had before robbed the poor of their dwellings . . . Rome has been restored to herself, and under your rule, Caesar, that is now the delight of the people that was once a master's.

(b) Suetonius, *Titus* 7

Titus was no less generous than any of his predecessors. At the dedication of the amphitheatre, and of the baths that had been quickly built beside it,

Titus provided a most lavish and generous gladiatorial show; he also staged a sea-fight on the old artificial lake, and a gladiatorial display there too, in a single day showing 5,000 wild beasts of every sort.

(c) Martial, *On the Spectacles* 1

Let barbarous Memphis be silent about the wonder of the pyramids, let Assyrian toil not boast of Babylon; nor let the soft Ionians be praised for Trivia's temple [the temple of Diana at Ephesus], nor let the altar [of Apollo] packed with horns cease to boast of Delos, nor let the Carians exalt to the skies with excessive praises the Mausoleum [the tomb of Mausolus, king of Caria] poised in empty air. All labour yields to Caesar's [Titus'] amphitheatre. Fame shall speak of one work in place of all.

(d) Martial, *On the Spectacles* 3

What race is so secluded, what race so barbarous, Caesar [Titus], that no spectator from it is in your city? . . . Diverse sounds the speech of the peoples, and yet it is one, when you are declared true father of the fatherland.

(e) Martial, *On the Spectacles* 10

A treacherous lion had with ungrateful mouth wounded his master, daring to violate hands so familiar; but he paid a penalty fitted to so great a crime, and he that had not suffered stripes suffered the steel. What manners befit men under such a *princeps*, who commands the nature of wild beasts to grow more mild?

(f) Martial, *On the Spectacles* 20

When this faction called for Myrinus, that faction for Triumphus, Caesar, with either hand uplifted, promised both. There could have been no better way to end the friendly debate. O splendid device of our unconquered *princeps*!

(g) Statius, *Silvae* 1.6, lines 1–8, 35–50, 81–4, 93–102

Father Phoebus and stern Pallas, and you Muses too, go far away, take a holiday! We'll call you back in the New Year. Saturn, slip your fetters and come here to me, and December loaded with much wine, and you too, laughing Fun and wanton Wit, while I recount the happy day of our joyful Caesar and the evening's drunken banquet and rich revels . . . Oh generous one, you foster the whole circle the better and more serious as well as the toga-clad folk, and, since you feed so many peoples, arrogant *Annona* [the food supply] knows nothing of this day [i.e. everything is free]. Go on, Antiquity, compare our times now with those of ancient Jupiter and the golden age; not so freely then did the wine flow, nor did the harvest so anticipate the tardy year. One table serves every class: the little ones, the women, the plebs, the equites, the senators. Freedom has set loose reverence. And even you yourself, Jove – which god could so be summoned or make such promises? – you have come and joined our party. And now everyone, whoever he is, rich or poor, boasts himself our leader's fellow guest ... Countless voices are raised to the stars, acclaiming the *princeps*' Saturnalian festival; with sweet favour they acclaim their lord [*dominus*] – this one licence did Caesar forbid [cf. Suetonius, *Domitian* 13] ... Who can sing of the spectacles, the unrestrained merriment, the banquets and priceless feasts, the generous rivers of Bacchus' gift? Ah but now I faint and, drunk with your wine, I drag myself off at last to sleep. Through how many years shall this day live on! Never shall the passage of time destroy so holy a day! While the hills of Latium remain, while Father Tiber flows, while your Rome and the Capitol that you restore to the world still stand, so shall this day remain.

9.12 A gladiator emperor

Other sources, such as Cassius Dio, indicate that Commodus was immensely proud of his gladiatorial prowess. The *Historia Augusta* draws on such material, but may also deliberately exaggerate or even invent.

Historia Augusta Commodus 15.3–8

At gladiatorial shows, Commodus the spectator would take up arms, covering his bare shoulders with a purple cloth. What is more, it was his custom to order the insertion in the city's official gazette [*acta urbis*] of everything he did that was disgusting or filthy or cruel, or the sort of thing a gladiator or a pimp would do ... He even called the Roman people the 'People of Commodus', so very frequently had he fought as a gladiator in their presence. And, although the people regularly applauded him in his frequent combats as though he were a god, he became convinced that he was being mocked and gave orders that the Roman people should be slaughtered in the amphitheatre by the marines who spread the awnings ... Among other triumphal titles, he was also given the name 'Leader [*Palus Primus*] of the Light-armed Pursuers [*Secutores*]' 620 times.

9.13 A gentle youth

Caracalla became emperor at around the age of 10 years (AD 198; he reigned until 217).

Historia Augusta Caracalla 1.5

If ever [as a child] he saw condemned criminals pitted against wild beasts, he wept or averted his eyes, and this was more than pleasing to the people.

9.14 A training ground for the martial arts?

Although the games were clearly sought for their entertainment value, there is also a desire to defend them as offering practical value as well. This may be from observing the punishment of the guilty or in watching even the lowest ranks of society perform bravely against wild animals or each other. Needless to say, it was also possible to take the opposite philosophical view and condemn the needless cruelty of such spectacles.

(a) Historia Augusta Maximinus and Balbinus 8.5–7

As to how the custom arose of emperors setting out to war staging gladiatorial games and hunts, a brief word needs to be said. Many say that among the ancients this was a solemn ritual [devotio] performed against enemies, so that, with the blood of citizens being offered in this way under the guise of fighting, Nemesis [i.e. a certain avenging power of Fortune] might be appeased. Others have recorded in books – and this I believe is nearer the truth – that when, about to go to war, the Romans felt it necessary to behold battles and wounds and steel and naked men contending among themselves, so that in war they might not be afraid of armed enemies or shudder at wounds and blood.

(b) Plutarch, *Whether Land or Sea Animals are Smarter* 959c–d

Soklaros: ... I was especially pleased with his mention of gladiators and his argument that hunting warrants praise not least because, after diverting to itself much of our innate or acquired pleasure in watching men fight with weapons, it provides an innocent spectacle of skill and intelligent daring pitted against mindless force and violence ...

Autoboulos: Yet that is the very source, my dear Soklaros, from which they say insensibility spread among people and the sort of savagery that has learned the taste of slaughter on its hunting trips and has grown accustomed to feel no repugnance at the blood and wounds of animals, but takes pleasure in their violent death.

(c) Plutarch, *On the Eating of Flesh* 997b–c

We have become dissolute and debauched, and now conceive a passion for shameful caresses and effeminate titillations. Such things have taught the sight not to take pleasure in war-dances or gesticulations or refined dancing or statues and pictures, but to regard the slaughter and death of human beings, their wounds and fights, as the finest spectacle. Just so . . . insensitivity and cruelty towards people follow savage spectacles.

(d) Seneca, *On Clemency* 1.25.1

Cruelty is an evil befitting least of all a human being, and it is unworthy of his spirit that is so mild; for one to take delight in blood and wounds and, throwing off the human, to change into an animal of the woods, is the madness of a wild beast. For what difference does it make, I ask you, Alexander, whether you throw Lysimachus [one of Alexander the Great's generals] to a lion, or you tear him to pieces yourself with your own teeth? That lion's mouth is yours, and yours its savagery.

9.15 Power to the people?

The provision of games came to be seen as an essential part of the euergetism (public service) required of the aristocracy of the Graeco-Roman world. Although Plutarch rails against the ruinous expense of such generosity and the incessant demands from the populace for entertainment, few would dare to invite public odium by refusing to conform to expectations (cf. Veyne 1990). Pliny the Elder (discussing the work of the fourth-century BC Greek sculptor Lysippus) and Macrobius (recalling an anecdote from the late republic) illustrate how the games might be used as one of the few opportunities for the population to voice their views to those who governed.

(a) Plutarch, *Precepts of Statecraft* 821f–822c

Those falsely named and falsely attested honours that come from giving theatrical shows, handouts, or gladiatorial games, are like the flatteries of a harlot. The masses always smile upon those who give them things and do them favours – a fleeting and shaky reputation. He who first said that the people were ruined by the first man who bribed it was well aware that the multitude becomes weaker and loses its strength when it takes bribes. But those too who give such bribes should bear in mind that they are destroying themselves whenever they buy a reputation at great expense, thereby making the multitude strong and daring in the thought that they have the power to give and take away something important ... So you must try to drive out of the state all those ambitious displays that excite and nourish the murderous and savage or the obscene and debauched, or, failing that, avoid them and oppose the multitude when they demand such spectacles.

(b) Plutarch, *Precepts of Statecraft* 802d–e

Now they say that you cannot hold the wolf by its ears, but one must lead a people or a city chiefly by the ears, not, as some do who are untrained in speaking and seek uncultured and inartistic holds upon the people, dragging them by the belly by offering banquets or giving away purses of money or providing strange dances or gladiatorial shows, by which they always lead the common people or rather curry their favour. For leadership of a people is over those who are persuaded by speech, whereas enticing the mob by such means as have just been mentioned is no different from catching and herding irrational animals.

(c) Pliny the Elder, *Natural History* 34.62

[One of Lysippus' sculptures was of] the man scraping himself [with a strigil: the *Apoxyomenos*], which Marcus Agrippa dedicated in front of his Hot Baths [*Thermae*]. Tiberius was remarkably impressed by this statue. Although he exercised some control over his own passions in the beginning of his reign, in this case he could not restrain himself and removed the statue to his own bedroom, having another one set up in its place. But the Roman people were so incensed by this that they staged a rowdy protest in the theatre and demanded the *Apoxyomenos* back. The *princeps*, although he was very much in love with the statue, had to restore it.

(d) Macrobius, *Saturnalia* 2.6.1

The lawyer Cascellius was regarded as a man of remarkable wit and frankness. The following is his best-known joke. Vatinius had been stoned by the people when he had put on a gladiatorial show. As a result he prevailed on the aediles to pass an edict forbidding anyone to throw anything except fruit into the arena. It so happened at the same time that Cascellius was asked by a client whether a pine cone is a fruit. His reply: 'If you plan to throw it at Vatinius, then it's a fruit.'

9.16 A vulgar pastime or murder pure and simple?

Since the amphitheatre was used for the punishment of criminals (Coleman 1990), as well as contests of skill between relatively evenly matched gladiators or hunters and animals, it was possible to despise not only the vulgarity of the show, but also the tediousness of watching amateurs be killed.

(a) Seneca, *Letters* 7.2–5

Associating with large crowds of people is harmful: every one of them makes some vice attractive to us, or stamps it on us, or befouls us with it unawares.

Certainly the greater the crowd with whom we mingle, the greater is the danger of this. But nothing is more ruinous to sound morals than hanging around at some show [*spectaculum*]. For then vices creep in more easily through decadence. What do you think I am saying? 'I go home more greedy, more competitive, more self-indulgent'? Yes – in fact crueller and less humane as well, because I was among human beings.

By chance I happened to go into the midday show, expecting games and witty performances and some sort of respite by which people's eyes might have a break from human bloodshed. Far from it. Whatever fighting took place earlier was merciful by comparison. Now the trifles are put aside and there is plain and simple murder. They have nothing with which to protect themselves. With their entire bodies exposed to each blow, they never strike without success. Most people prefer this to the regular matches and requested performances, and why shouldn't they prefer it? The sword is driven off by no helmet, no shield. What use is defensive armour? What use is skill? All such things are delays for death. In the morning, men are thrown to the lions and bears, at midday they are thrown to their own audience. They order those who have killed their opponents to be thrown to others who will kill them, and they keep the victor for some other kind of slaughter. The way out for the fighters is death. The slaughter is kept going with fire and steel. These things go on while the arena is empty.

'But one of them was a highway robber.' So what? Did he kill a man? 'Yes, he *did* kill a man.' Because he committed murder, he deserved this punishment. But what have *you* done, you wretch, to deserve to watch this? 'Kill him, whip him, burn him! Why does he run at the sword so timidly? Why does he kill with so little boldness? Why isn't he a bit more enthusiastic about dying and being driven by blows to get him wounded? Let them offer each other bare breasts and exchange blow for blow on them. There is an interval in the show: let some men have their throats cut while we're waiting, so that something's happening.'

Come now, surely you people realise this at least, that bad examples redound upon those who set them? Give thanks to the immortal gods that the man you are teaching to be cruel is not able to learn.

(b) Seneca, *On Clemency* 1.25.1–2

We call it now *clementia* if to kill a friend, the butcher is chosen from among humankind. The reason why brutality is most of all abhorred is because it transgresses first all normal, and second all human, bounds, searches out new kinds of torture, calls ingenuity into play to invent devices by which pain may be varied and prolonged, and takes delight in the afflictions of humankind; then indeed the dire disease of that man's mind has reached the furthest depths of insanity, when cruelty has been turned into pleasure and to kill a human being now becomes a joy.

(c) Seneca, *Letters* 95.33

Human beings, objects of reverence in the eyes of human beings, are now slaughtered as a joke, for fun; and those whom it used to be unholy to train for the purpose of inflicting and enduring wounds, are now thrust forward naked and unarmed, and it is a satisfying spectacle to see a human made a corpse.

(d) Tacitus, *Dialogue on Oratory* 29.3–4

I really think that the characteristic and peculiar vices of this city, a fondness for actors and a passion for gladiators and horses, are all but conceived in the mother's womb. When these occupy and possess the mind, how little room has it left for cultural pursuits! You'll find precious few who talk of any other topic at home, and, whenever we enter a classroom, what else is the conversation of the young? Even with the instructors, these are the more frequent topics of talk with their audience.

(e) Marcus Aurelius, *Meditations* 6.46

Just as the shows in the amphitheatre and such places irk you, being as they are an everlasting repetition of the same sights, and the similarity makes you sick of the spectacle, such must be the effect of life as a whole.

9.17 'Refined' attitudes in Cicero

Cicero's attitudes are influenced by the Greek philosophical tradition's hostility to public display and demagoguery and his own experiences in Roman politics. It is interesting to note that Curio (**9.17b**) rejected Cicero's advice and provided a remarkable (and financially ruinous) display of games. Cicero himself elsewhere accepts that politicians may be required by the populace to put on such spectacles. In a speech defending Lucius Licinius Murena (63 BC), he even urges Servius Sulpicius Rufus (who failed to gain the consulship for 62 BC and was now accusing the successful Murena of resorting to bribery) not to resent the fact his opponent had gained popular favour by putting on games.

(a) Cicero, *On Duties* 2.16.55–6

In general there are two kinds of large-scale givers, the extravagant and the generous. The extravagant ones are those who squander money on public banquets, free distributions of meat, gladiatorial shows, expensive games, and wild-beast hunts – things that are remembered for a short time, if at all. The generous ones are those who, out of their own resources, ransom prisoners from bandits or take on the debts of friends or help finance their daughters' weddings, or offer help in the acquisition and augmentation of property.

(b) Cicero, *Letters to his Friends* 2.3
(to C. Scribonius Curio, 53 BC)

The gifts that your nature and application, as well as good fortune, have granted you, will count for more in winning you the highest political prizes than will games [*munera*]. No one admires the capacity to put on games (it is a matter of means, not of personal qualities), and everyone is sick and tired of them.

(c) Cicero, *Tusculan Disputations* 2.17.41 (45 BC)

Gladiatorial shows are apt to seem cruel and inhuman to some, and I tend to agree, as they are now conducted. But in the days when it was criminals who crossed swords, there could be no better schooling against pain and death – at least for the eye; for the ear perhaps there might be many.

(d) Cicero, *On Duties* 2.57–8

And Aristotle goes on, quite rightly, to reach the following conclusion: 'Entertainment of this kind amuses boys and mere women and slaves and free men who are as good as slaves. But a serious man, capable of weighing things up sensibly, could not possibly approve of such shows.' I do realise, however, that in our city, even in the good old days, it had become a tradition to require the best men as aediles to provide something splendid. Hence Publius Crassus, 'Rich' [*Dives*] in both name and resources, carried out his duties as aedile in a most exemplary fashion, and shortly thereafter Lucius Crassus, together with the most moderate of all men, Quintus Mucius, carried out the aedileship most magnificently; they were followed by Quintus Claudius, the son of Appius, and many others too, the Luculli, Hortensius, and Silanus. In my consulship [63 BC], however, Publius Lentulus outdid all his predecessors, and Scaurus followed his example. My friend Pompey's second consulship [55 BC] saw truly magnificent games. You can see from all these examples what sort of thing I approve of. 58. On the other hand, any suspicion of avarice must be avoided. Mamercus, an extremely rich man, bypassed the aedileship and was rejected for the consulship as a result. So, if something is demanded by the people, and if good men, even if they do not want it, also do not disapprove of it, then it must be done, so long as it is in proportion to one's resources, as we ourselves have done.

(e) Cicero, *Speech in Defence of Murena* 19.38–40
(63 BC)

Do not be too scornful of the splendour of the games or the magnificence of the spectacles Murena gave. These helped him considerably. For why should I speak of the great delight that the people and the uneducated masses take in games? It is not to be wondered at; it is enough for my case to point out that they are occasions when the people get together in huge numbers. So, if the magnificence of the games pleases the people, it is no wonder that this helped Murena with the people. 39. But if we ourselves, who are kept from the public entertainments by pressure of business and who can find many other pleasures in our work itself, if we nevertheless are delighted by the games and fascinated by them, why should you be surprised at the ignorant crowd? 40. . . . Believe me, people do find pleasure in such spectacles, not only those who admit it, but those as well who pretend they do not.

9.18 'Refined' attitudes: Pliny the Younger

Once again, Pliny indicates that it is not the entertainment itself, but the spirit in which it is presented that is important. Hence, he can contrast the games of Trajan with those of the now discredited Domitian and praise Maximus for putting on games to honour his deceased wife in the face of public pressure.

(a) Pliny, *Letters* 9.6 (to Calvisius Rufus)

I have been spending all my time of late occupied with my notes and books in a most welcome period of peace. How could that be, at Rome? The circus games were on, a type of spectacle in which I have never been even slightly interested. It can provide nothing new, nothing different, nothing that is worth seeing twice. This makes me wonder all the more that so many thousands of grown men should long so childishly to see again and again horses galloping and people standing in chariots. Now, if they were attracted by the speed of the horses or the skill of the drivers, that would be some sort of a reason. But in actual fact they applaud and support the colours, and, if on the course itself in the middle of a race, the colours were to be interchanged, their enthusiasm and support will be transferred and suddenly they would desert the famous drivers and horses whom they recognise from a distance and whose names they shout. Such is the popularity, such is the influence in one totally worthless tunic – and I'm not talking about the crowd, who are more worthless than the tunic, but about certain respectable individuals. When I recall how in this empty, dull, and endless affair they sit so idly and never grow bored, I take some pleasure in the fact that I am not taken by that pleasure. So during the past few days I have filled my leisure time most gladly with literary work – time that others have wasted in the most idle of occupations.

(b) Pliny, *Panegyric* 33–34

Citizens and allies alike had their needs supplied. Next a *spectaculum* was put on – nothing lax or dissolute to soften and shatter men's spirits, but one to inspire them to face fine wounds and show scorn for death, by exhibiting love of glory and desire for victory even in the persons of slaves and convicted criminals. What generosity in producing such a show, what justice the emperor showed, unaffected by or superior to every personal feeling. Requests were granted, what was not requested was anticipated . . . Spectators could express their enthusiasm freely and show whom they supported without worry. No one risked the old charge of impiety if he loathed a particular gladiator, no spectator was turned into a spectacle, dragged down by the hook or cast to the flames to satisfy an emperor's wretched pleasures . . . What a wonderful spectacle *you* provided for us, Caesar.

(c) Pliny, *Letters* 6.34

You acted correctly in putting on a gladiatorial show for our people of Verona; they have long loved, respected, and honoured you. And Verona was also the place whence your most beloved and excellent wife came; to her memory you owed some public work or show, and this kind of show in particular, most suitable for a funerary tribute. And, what's more, so many people asked you for it that it would have appeared churlish rather than strong-minded to have refused the request. You have also performed outstandingly by putting on the show so readily and so generously; this shows how magnanimous you are. I only wish the African beasts you had bought in such great number had turned up on the appointed day. But, even though the weather meant they arrived late, you nonetheless deserved the credit for them – it wasn't your fault you couldn't show them.

9.19 'Refined' attitudes: Dio Chrysostom

Dio Cocceianus (nicknamed 'Chrysostom' because of his golden voice) was a Greek orator and popular philosopher who lived from *c.* AD 40/50 to after AD 110 and travelled widely. His attitude is generally that of philosophic rejection of a vulgar entertainment.

(a) Dio Chrysostom, *Orations* 31 (*To the People of Rhodes*) 121

There is no practice current in Athens that would not cause anyone to feel ashamed. For instance, regarding gladiatorial shows, the Athenians have so zealously followed the example of the Corinthians, or, rather, have so outdone both them and all the others in their raving madness, that, whereas the Corinthians watch the games outside the city in a gully, a spot that can contain a crowd but otherwise is filthy and such that no one would even bury a free person there, the Athenians look on at this fine spectacle in their theatre under the very walls of the Acropolis, in the place at the orchestra where they set up their statue of the god Dionysus, so that often someone is slaughtered among the very seats in which the high priest and the other priests must sit.

(b) Dio Chrysostom, *Orations 32 (To the People of Alexandria)* 45, on public entertainments

Now don't think that I'm saying that all such spectacles should not take place in cities; for perhaps they should, and it may be necessary, because the masses are weak and idle. And perhaps they should even take place among the better people too, since some of them need some diversion and amusement in life. But they should view them in an orderly manner, in a fashion befitting free men.

9.20 'Refined' attitudes: Philostratus

L. Flavius Philostratus, who lived from *c.* AD 170 to *c.* AD 245, wrote a life of Apollonius of Tyana, a Neopythagorean holy man and miracle worker of the first century AD around whom a large number of tales had grown up.

Philostratus, *Life of Apollonius* 4.22

The Athenians were in the habit of going as a body to the theatre beneath the Acropolis to watch the slaughter of human beings. The passion for this spectator sport was greater there at that time than it is in Corinth today. They would pay huge sums for adulterers, fornicators [*pornoi*], burglars, kidnappers, and all such types, then they gave them weapons and made them fight one another. Apollonius took them to task over this. When the Athenians invited him to attend their assembly, he declared that he would not enter a place 'so polluted and defiled with gore'. He wrote this in a letter to them. He added that he was surprised that 'the goddess had not already deserted the Acropolis, when you shed such blood in her presence. Going on as you are, I imagine that when you hold the Panathenaic procession you'll no longer sacrifice bulls to the goddess, but hecatombs of humans. And you, Dionysus, do you still visit the theatre after such bloodshed? And do the wise Athenians pour libations to you there? You leave too, Dionysus. Cithaeron is less polluted.'

9.21 Christianity and the Roman games

Both Tertullian (c. AD 160–240) and St Augustine (AD 354–430) were Christian writers from North Africa. While Tertullian adopts a haranguing and satirical tone in condemning the games, Augustine uses his personal reminiscence of Alypius to warn his audience of the attractions of popular entertainment.

Although the Christian emperors of the fourth century put restrictions on who might perform as gladiators (so removing condemned prisoners from those who would be eligible and stressing that soldiers could not take on such employment), it is likely that economic factors were the main reason for the end of gladiatorial games (but not other blood sports) in late antiquity.

(a) Tertullian, *On the Spectacles* 4

So, once we have established that everything to do with the *spectacula* is idolatrous, there is absolutely no doubt what conclusion we must reach: the profession of renunciation we made in baptism relates to the spectacles too, since they, being idolatrous, belong to the devil, his pomp and his angels.

(b) Tertullian, *On the Spectacles* 12

The most famous and the most popular spectacle of all is the gladiatorial show [*munus*], so-called from its being rendered as a service, and *munus* means 'service'. The ancients thought that, by putting on this kind of show, they were performing a service to the dead, after they had tempered it with a more humane form of cruelty. For in the past, since it was believed that the spirits of the deceased are propitiated with human blood, they used to sacrifice at funerals prisoners or poor-quality slaves they had bought. Later they decided to disguise their impiety with pleasure. So those they obtained they trained to use the arms that they then had as best they could, or more specifically they taught them how to be killed, and then on the decreed day of the funeral they set them to die among the tombs. Thus they found comfort for death in murders. This is the origin of the *munus*. But gradually they progressed to the same level of refinement as of cruelty, for the pleasure of the holiday was no longer quite enough unless human bodies were torn to shreds by wild animals ... This type of show has passed from serving to honour the dead to serving to honour the living ... The amphitheatre is the temple of all demons. As many unclean spirits reside there as it contains people.

(c) Tertullian, *On the Spectacles* 15

Every spectacle brings with it some violence to the spirit. For where there is pleasure, there is eagerness, which certainly gives pleasure its flavour.

Where there is eagerness, there too is rivalry, which gives eagerness its flavour. And of course, where there is rivalry, there too are madness, bile, anger, pain, and all the things that proceed from them and that, like them, are incompatible with discipline. For, even if someone enjoys the spectacles in a modest and upright fashion, in accordance with his rank, his age, and even his natural character, still his mind is not unstirred and his spirit does not but suffer some unspoken agitation.

(d) Tertullian, *On the Spectacles* 16

So, since madness is forbidden to us, we keep away from every spectacle, even from the circus, where madness of its own right rules. Look at the crowd coming to this show – already mad, disorderly, blind, and excited about its bets! The praetor is too slow for them, always their eyes are rolling about in his urn along with the lots. They are all in suspense for the signal, anxious suspense, one voice of a single madness. You can recognise their insanity from their emptiness. 'He's let the hankie go,' they scream, and report to one another straightaway what all of them can see: this to me is proof of their blindness.

(e) Tertullian, *On the Spectacles* 19

Are we now to wait and seek a scriptural condemnation of the amphitheatre? If we can maintain that cruelty, impiety, and savagery are permitted to us, then let's go into the amphitheatre. And, if we are the sort of people we are said to be, then let's take pleasure in human blood. 'It's good when the guilty are punished.' Who will disagree, unless he is himself guilty? And yet the innocent ought not to derive pleasure from the punishment of another. And who will vouch to me that it is always the guilty who are condemned to the beasts, or whatever the punishment, and that it is never inflicted on the innocent as well, whether through the vindictiveness of one judge, or the weakness of the defence, or the brutality of the inquisition? How much better it is, therefore, *not* to know when the bad are punished, if then I may not know when the good also perish ... Certainly some innocent men are sold as gladiators for the games, to become victims of public pleasure ... As for the Christian, I would certainly hope *he* should need no further teaching to detest the shows! Though no one can more fully lay out all the details unless he is still a spectator; I prefer to leave it incomplete rather than recall the details.

(f) St Augustine, *Confessions* 6.8.13

Alypius went ahead of me to Rome to study law, and there became absolutely obsessed with gladiatorial shows. He began by hating such things and refused to attend. But one day he happened to meet a group of friends and fellow-students coming back from dinner and, being friends, they brushed aside his vehement protests and resistance and carried him off to the arena (this was during some days of cruel and bloody games). 'Even if you drag my body to that place and make it stay there,' he said, 'you can't force me to turn my eyes or my mind to those shows. I'll be there in body, but in fact I will be absent – so shall I defeat both you and the games!' ... So they arrived and found what seats they could; the whole place was seething with bloodlust and cruelty. Alypius shut his eyes tight, determined that his mind would have nothing to do with such atrocities. If only he had shut his ears as well! Something happened in one of the fights to make the whole crowd let out a great roar, and this so startled him that his curiosity overcame him; at the same time he was confident that, whatever it was that was happening, he would be able to conquer the sight and treat it with the disdain it deserved. So he opened his eyes. At once he was stabbed in his soul, and with a far more deadly wound than that which the gladiator he was so anxious to see had received in his body. He fell, and fell more miserably than the man whose fall had caused the crowd to roar in the first place ... For the moment he saw that blood, it was as though he had drunk a full dose of savage passion. Rather than turn away, he riveted his gaze on the scene and drew in all its frenzied madness, not knowing what he was doing. The cruelty of the fighting delighted him, the thrill of seeing blood shed intoxicated him. He was no longer the man who had come to the arena, he was now part of the crowd to which he had come, a fit companion indeed for those who had brought him. What more needs to be said? He watched, he cheered, he burned with excitement. He left the arena that day with a mind so crazed that it gave him no peace till he went again – and he went not only with those who had taken him the first time, but even preceded them, and drags others along himself.

But with your most mighty and merciful hand, Lord, you rescued him from his madness, and taught him to trust in you rather than in himself. But that was much later.

(g) *Codex Theodosianus* 15.12

1. The emperor Constantine to the Praetorian Prefect Maximus [AD 325].

Bloody spectacles do not please Us amid civil peace and domestic tranquillity. Therefore, We wholly forbid to be gladiators those persons who, by chance, on account of some crime, customarily sustained that condition and sentence; you shall cause them to serve rather in the mines, so that they will assume the penalty for their crimes without shedding their blood.

2. The emperor Constantius and the Caesar Julian to the Urban Prefect Orfitus [AD 357].

All those who exhibit gladiatorial shows in the city of Rome shall know that it is forbidden to solicit soldiers, or those endowed with any palatine rank, to hire themselves out as gladiators. If any person should attempt to violate this regulation, he shall be subject to the threat of a fine of six pounds of gold. If any such soldiers should voluntarily approach a producer of gladiatorial games, the office staff of Your Sublimity shall send them, loaded with iron chains, to the masters of the horse and foot, or to those who govern the palatine offices, so that, pursuant to the provisions of this law, the dignity of the palace may be vindicated from the detested gladiatorial name.

REFERENCES AND FURTHER READING

Auguet, R. (1972) *Cruelty and Civilisation: The Roman Games*, London.

Barton, C.A. (1993) *The Sorrows of the Ancient Romans: The Gladiator and the Monster*, Princeton, NJ.

Bomgardner, D.L. (2000) *The Story of the Roman Amphitheatre*, London.

Cameron, A. (1976) *Circus Factions: Blues and Greens at Rome and Byzantium*, Oxford.

Carter, M.J.D. (2003) 'Gladiatorial Ranking and the *SC de pretiis gladiatorum minuendis*: (*CIL* II 6278 = *ILS* 5163)', *Phoenix* 57: 83–114.

Coleman, K.M. (1990) 'Fatal Charades: Roman Executions Staged as Mythological Enactments', *Journal of Roman Studies* 80: 44–73.

Coleman, K.M. (2000a) 'Entertaining Rome', in Coulston, J. and Dodge, H. (eds) *Ancient Rome: The Archaeology of the Eternal City* , Oxford, pp. 210–58.

Coleman, K.M. (2000b) '*Missio* at Halicarnassus', *Harvard Studies in Classical Philology* 100: 487–500.

Friedländer, L. (1908–13) *Roman Life and Manners*, 4 vols, London.

Gunderson, E. (1996) 'The Ideology of the Arena', *Classical Antiquity* 15: 113–15.

Hope, V. (2000) 'Fighting for Identity: The Funerary Commemoration of Italian Gladiators', in Cooley, A. (ed.) *The Epigraphic Landscape*, London, pp. 93–113.

Hopkins, K. (1983) *Death and Renewal*, Cambridge.

Hopkins, K. and Beard, M. (2005) *The Colosseum*, Cambridge, MA.

Jacobelli, L. (2003) *Gladiators at Pompeii*, Los Angeles, CA.

Kyle, D.G. (1998) *Spectacles of Death in Ancient Rome*, London.

Lintott, A.W. (1968) *Violence in Republican Rome*, London.

Newlands, C. (2002) *Statius' Silvae and the Poetics of Empire*, Cambridge.

Plass, P. (1995) *The Game of Death in Ancient Rome*, Madison, WI.

Robert, L. (1971) *Les Gladiateurs dans l'Orient grec*, Amsterdam.

Scobie, A. (1998) 'Spectator Security and Comfort at Gladiatorial Games', *Nikephoros* 1: 191–243.

Veyne, P. (1990) *Bread and Circuses*, Harmondsworth.

Ville, G. (1981) *La Gladiature en Occident des origines à la mort de Domitien*, Rome.

Wiedemann, T. (1992) *Emperors and Gladiators*, London.

Wistrand, M. (1992) *Entertainment and Violence in Ancient Rome*, Göteborg.

Appendix A

LIFE EXPECTANCY

Coale-Demeny 2, Model West, Level 3, Female

x	q_x	d_x	l_x	e_x	C_x
(age)	(probability of dying in next period)	(no. of original group dying in period)	(cohort)	(life expectancy from age x)	(% of population in each age group)
0	0.3056	30,556	100,000	25.000	3.21
1	0.2158	14,988	69,444	34.846	9.53
5	0.0606	3,300	54,456	40.062	10.53
10	0.0474	2,424	51,156	37.502	10.00
15	0.0615	2,998	48,732	34.237	9.46
20	0.0766	3,503	45,734	31.312	8.81
25	0.0857	3,617	42,231	28.693	8.10
30	0.0965	3,728	38,614	26.138	7.36
35	0.1054	3,677	34,886	23.134	6.62
40	0.1123	3,504	31,208	21.134	5.91
45	0.1197	3,315	27,705	18.477	5.22
50	0.1529	3,728	24,389	15.636	4.52
55	0.1912	3,950	20,661	12.988	3.75
60	0.2715	4,537	16,712	10.443	2.91
65	0.3484	4,241	12,175	8.366	2.03
70	0.4713	3,739	7,934	6.448	1.23
75	0.6081	2,551	4,194	4.878	0.58
80	0.7349	1,208	1,644	3.567	0.19
85	0.8650	377	436	2.544	0.04
90	0.9513	56	59	1.784	0.00
95	1.0000	3	3	1.234	0.00

Some basic demographic functions (see further Parkin, 1992)

BR   Crude Birth Rate; the number of births in a year for every 1,000 members of the population.

C_x In a stationary population, the percentage of persons between x and $x+n$ years.

d_x The number of persons dying between x and $x+n$ years.

DR   Crude Death Rate; the number of deaths in a year for every 1,000 members of the population.

e_x Average life expectancy at age x years.

GRR   Gross Reproduction Rate; in effect, the number of female births that on average each mother in a population has in her reproductive career.

IMR   Infant Mortality Rate; the number of deaths under age 1 in a year for every 1,000 members of the population.

l_x Number of survivors at age x from an original cohort; 10 is conventionally set at 100,000 in the life table.

q_x Probability of dying between age x and age $x+n$ years.

r Rate of Growth; the difference between the BR and DR, i.e. natural increase or decrease in population numbers. Usually expressed as a percentage per annum.

SR   Sex Ratio; the number of males for every 100 females in a population. SR_x is the sex ratio at age x years.

For the early Roman empire, it is likely that the population was essentially stable (that is, there was no marked rate of increase in population nor any substantial decrease). Assuming similar mortality to the Model West, Level 3, Female (taken from pre-Second World War Mauritius), although life expectancy at birth is low, this is mainly due to high infant death rates. Of those who lived to age 5, 50 per cent would live for more than 40 more years (e_x where $x = 5$).

The table can be used to suggest various possibilities. For instance, if a male is aged 25, there is only a 1 in 3 chance of his father being alive (assuming the father's age = 50).

Another example would be considering how likely it would be for a consul to be alive to assist his son in election to the consulship. Taking an intermediate figure between 40 and 45 for election as consul and assuming that the son was born 20 years earlier, we will find that only about a quarter of the cohort at age 40–45 is alive 20 years later and that only half the people aged 25 lived to be 45. This reduces the chances to around 1 in 8.

Note, however, that these figures work *in general*. That is, they will help to see what happens in a large sample, but cannot be used to predict individual outcomes. Some people will die within the year, others will live to be 100. Caesar's life expectancy on the morning of 15 March, 44 BC, appeared much higher than it was at the end of that day!

Appendix B

THE ROMAN
STATUS HIERARCHY

These figures for the early imperial period are taken from Walter Scheidel, 'Human Mobility in Roman Italy', *Journal of Roman Studies* 94 (2004: 1–26) and 95 (2005: 64–79), and 'Stratification, Deprivation, and Quality of Life in the Ancient World' in M. Atkins and R. Osborne (eds), *Poverty in the Roman World* (Cambridge, 2006), pp. 40–59.

Italy 5–6 million
Slave population in Italy 1–1.5 million

Senators: 600
Equites: 10,000
First-class Citizens: 40,000
Second-class Citizens: 60,000
Third-class Citizens: 90,000
Fourth-class Citizens: 135,000
Fifth-class Citizens: 200,000
Sixth-class Citizens: 615,000 (propertyless)

(Note: multiply all groups by approximately 5 to give the inhabitants in the household.)

This produces an extremely steep status pyramid:

In terms of wealth, it is likely that the pyramid would generally be reversed, with the emperor (easily the wealthiest man in the Roman world), the senate, and the equestrians possessing the lion's share of resources. Similarly, a chart of slaves according to ownership would show the majority attached to the top of the pyramid, with the lowest classes possessing few of the 1–1.5 million slaves in Italy.

Appendix C

GREEK AND ROMAN WEIGHTS, MEASURES, AND COINAGE

Weights and measures

1 *modius*	=	approx. 8.7 litres
		(the principal Roman dry measure)
1 *medimnus*	=	approx. 53 litres
	=	6 Roman modii
		(the principal Greek dry measure)
1 *artaba*	=	varied in size from approx. 39 litres in the early empire to 29 litres in the later empire
		(the principal Egyptian dry measure)
1 *mation*	=	an Egyptian dry measure (size uncertain)

Weights per modius of wheat after threshing (Pliny the Elder, *Natural History* 18.66ff.):

Light:	20 librae	=	14.4 lb	=	6.55 kg
Medium:	20¾ librae	=	15.03 lb	=	6.82 kg
Heavy:	21½ librae	=	15.7 lb	=	7.12 kg

Therefore

1 ton of wheat on average = approx. 150 modii or 25 medimnoi

cotyla	=	½ pint
chous	=	12 *cotylae*
	=	3 litres (local variation occurs)
sextarius	=	2 *heminae*
	=	1 pint (approx. ½ litre)
congius	=	6 sextarii
	=	⅛ of an amphora
amphora	=	5.7 imperial gallons (approx.)
		(equivalent to 7 US gallons, approx.)
	=	26 litres (approx.)

urna	=	½ amphora
	=	2.85 imperial gallons (approx.)
		(3½ American gallons, approx.)
	=	13 litres
culleus	=	20 amphorae
	=	40 urnae
	=	114 imperial gallons (approx.)
	=	520 litres (approx.)
1 *iugerum*	=	2,518 square metres
		(so 4 iugera = 1 hectare, approx.)
	=	⅝ of an acre (approx.)
1 *aroura*	=	2,767 square metres,
		i.e. ¾ of an acre (approx.)
		(the principal Egyptian measure of area)

Coinage

Greek (Attic)

drachma	=	6 *obols*
mina	=	100 *drachmae*
talent	=	60 *minae*

Roman

as (plural *asses*) the smallest copper coin, often of nominal value

sestertius	=	4 *asses*
denarius	=	4 *sesterces* = Attic *drachma*
aureus	=	25 *denarii*
libra	=	72 *denarii*

INDEX LOCORUM

*Aegyptische Urkunden aus den
    Staatlichen Museen zu Berlin,
    Griechische Urkunden (BGU)*
    1.326   308

Alciphron, *Letters*
    3.24   225
    3.40   227

Ammianus Marcellinus 27.4.14
    54

L'Année Epigraphique
    1925 no. 126b   264
    1945 no. 136   96
    1946 no. 211   174
    1958 no. 177   27
    1971 no. 88   174
    1972 no. 86   266
    1985 no. 355   69
    1989 no. 681   258
    1995 no. 665   191
    1998 no. 1322   199

Apuleius
Apologia 89   65
Metamorphoses
    1.5–7   213
    4.13–14   224
    6.7–8   173
    9.12   322
    9.31–2   233
    9.35–6   313
    9.39–42   316

Artemidorus, *On the Interpretation
    of Dreams*
    1.35   38
    1.53   149

2.9   207
2.26   207
2.54   208
3.32   325

Athenaeus, *Deipnosophistae*
    6.272c–273a   156

Augustine
City of God 15.9   65
Confessions 6.8.13   351

Augustus, *Res Gestae*
    8.5   100
    15   49
    22   336

Aulus Gellius, *Attic Nights*
    1.6   82
    2.15.4–7   117
    5.19   120
    7.14.1–4   321
    11.7   147
    14.2.1–25   298
    15.1   239

[Aurelius Victor], *Epitome de
    Caesaribus*
    1.6   50
    12.4   269

Carmina Latina Epigraphica
    (ed. Bücheler)
    237   92
    368   92
    422   67
    423   89
    516   94
    1532   68

Cassiodorus, *Variae* 11.39.1–2
  52

Cassius Dio
  53.33 53
  54.1 260
  54.16 109
  56.1–10 110
  60.11 262
  72.14.3–4 54
  76.10.1–7 214

Cato, *On Agriculture*
  1–3 247
  10 277
  22.3 277

Catullus
  61.209–13 104
  68.119–24 104

Cicero
Letters to Atticus
  5.1.3–4 98
  14.9 239
  14.13.5 99
Letters to his Friends
  2.3 346
  7.1 334
On Duties
  1.53–8 77
  1.150–1 33
  2.16.55–6 345
  2.57–8 346
  2.89 279
On His Own Home 109 77
On the Republic
  1.43 6
  1.67 6
  5.3.5 151
Speech in Defence of Murena
  19.38–40 347
Tusculan Disputations 2.17.41
  346
Verrines 2.2.163 47

Codex Iustinianus
  5.4.27 116
  5.24.1 103
  5.25.2 127
  8.47(48).5 122
  8.58.1 119
  9.5.1 326

Codex Theodosianus
  4.65.4 267
  8.17.3 119
  9.3 323
  9.18.1 320
  15.12 352

Columella, *On Agriculture*
  1 *praef.* 20–1 246
  1.3.12 252
  1.6 188
  1.7.6–7 252
  1.8.1–4, 12–13 151
  2.21 281
  3.3 272
  6, *praef.* 278
  7.1–2 279

Corpus Inscriptionum Latinarum
  (CIL)
  2.5477 68
  3, p. 948, no. 1 283
  3.3572 52
  3.6687 47
  3.6759 69
  4.1189 331
  4.4999 331
  5.2108 94
  6.4226 267
  6.6835 56
  6.7578 67
  6.9326 90
  6.9454 146
  6.9801 267
  6.9973 267
  6.10051 332
  6.11602 92
  6.13738 90
  6.14094 68
  6.18817 91
  6.19128 68
  6.20427 69
  6.23324 91
  6.23942 70
  6.26192 92
  6.27109 91
  6.27856 91
  6.28790 92
  6.28965 91
  6.29460 95
  6.29580 94
  6.33886 267
  6.35887 68

8.152   94
8.5798   93
8.11294   93
9.3215   93
10.4273   95
10.5920   89
11.1491   95
12.832   93
13.2182   99
15.7192   174

Corpus Papyrorum Graecarum
   1.11   158

Cyprian, *To Demetrianus* 3   63

Digest
   1.9.1   21
   1.9.12   21
   3.4.1, *praef.*   258
   4.6.9   325
   7.8.5–6   128
   11.3–4   169
   19.2.55, *praef.*   267
   21.1   161
   23.2.6   81
   23.2.19   113
   23.2.20   113
   23.2.21   114
   23.2.22   114
   23.2.23   114
   23.2.24   114
   23.2.25   114
   23.2.26   102
   23.2.27   114
   23.2.28–29   114
   23.2.35   114
   23.2.41   115
   23.2.42   115
   23.3.1–2   81
   23.3.7.3   82
   23.3.69.8   82
   23.3.75   82
   24.1.60.1   102
   24.1.61   103
   24.2.1   102
   24.2.3   102
   24.3.1   82
   24.3.2   82
   25.4.1   108
   27.1.6.1–2   143
   29.5   177
   33.8.19   203

35.2.68   65
38.1   201
39.4.16.7   259
40.1.4–5   203
40.2.5–9, 23   198
40.16.1   200
43.30.1.1, 5   103
48.5.6.1   100
48.5.13   101
48.5.25   101
48.5.30   101
48.5.30.3   101
50.5.3   17
50.16.46.1   124
50.16.195–6   79, 123

Dio Chrysostom, *Orations*
   7.103–51   216
   31.121   348
   32.45   349
   46.8–10   263

Diodorus Siculus
   1.31.6–8   48
   17.52.5–6   47

Dionysius of Halicarnassus
   2.10   296
   2.26.4   122

Eusebius, *History of the Church*
   7.21.9–10   63

Flavian Municipal Law 56   117

Fronto
Letters to Antoninus Pius 4   311
Letters to Friends 1.1   301–2
Principia Historiae 20   330

Gaius, *Institutes*
   1.9–54   192
   1.48–55   79
   1.111   80
   1.142–5   131
   1.171   132
   1.189–91   132
   3.146   333

Galen
De Alimentorum Facultatibus
   1.7   265
   1.11   265

De Bonis et Malis Alimentorum
  Sucis 1   266
De Propriorum Animi Dignotione
  et Curatione 9   48

Gnomon of the Idios Logos 24–7
  116

Gospel of Luke 2.1   64

Gospel of Matthew 20.1–16   215

Herodian, *Histories* 7.2.5–7   240

Historia Augusta
Caracalla 1.5   341
Commodus 15.3–8   340
Elagabalus 26.6   52
Maximinus and Balbinus 8.5–7
  341
Septimius Severus 8, 23   50

Horace
Carmen Saeculare 17–20   110
Epistles 1.7.46–97   31
Satires 2.5.45–50   106

Inscriptiones Latinae Selectae (ILS)
  932   14
  939   14
  950   13
  986   15
  1166   20
  1319   25
  1374   26
  1396   27
  1886   30
  1901   30
  1914   69
  2683   47
  2927   269
  5283   332
  5795   319
  6140   27
  6256   31
  6261   89
  6271   28
  6509   268
  6675   268
  6870   40
  6881   29
  6891   283
  7293   36
  7457   39
  7519   34
  7542   35
  7545   36
  7695   37
  7750   151
  7864   90
  7906   91
  7965   91
  8006   91
  8041   92
  8157   190
  8160   70
  8168   68
  8398   92
  8402   92
  8439   93
  8443   93
  8444   93
  8447   93
  8450   94
  8451   68
  8453   94
  8459   95
  8461   95
  8466   95
  8480   69
  8483   68
  8496   68
  8512   99
  8781   9
  8794   10
  9454   174
  9455   174

Isidorus, *Origines* 5.15.1   112

Jerome, *Chronicle* (ed. Helm)
  188h   54
  233e   54

John Chrysostom
Homilies on First Letter to
  Corinthians
  11.5   225
  21.5–6   230
  34.4–5   210
Homilies on First Letter to
  Thessalonians 11.3   228
On Lazarus 3.2   37
To Stagirus 3.13   226

Josephus, *Jewish War* 2.385   48

Justinian, *Institutes*
  1.11.4   120
  4.18.4   101

Juvenal, *Satires*
  3.34–40   332
  6.21–8   81
  10.77–81   330

Libanius, *Oration* 47.4–8   315

Livy
  5.55   242
  21.63.3–4   16
  27.37   60

Lucian, *Toxaris* 29   323

Macrobius, *Saturnalia* 2.6.1   343

Marcus Aurelius, *Meditations* 6.46
  345

Martial
On the Spectacles
  1   339
  2   338
  3   339
  7   321
  8   322
  10   339
  20   339
  21   322
Epigrams
  2.26   106
  2.56   88
  2.91   117
  2.92   118
  4.53   208
  9.68   138
  11.32   209
  11.39   137
  11.53   117
  11.56   209
  12.57   235

*Mosaicarum et Romanarum Legum
  Collatio* 4.2.3   101

Musonius Rufus
  13a   83
  13b   83
  15   125

*Orientis Graeci Inscriptiones Selectae
  (OGIS)* 669   306

Ostraca Claudiana 4751   36

Ovid, *Art of Love* 3.81–2   58

P. Bod. (*Bodleian Papyri*) 1.44   159

Papyri Graecae Magicae 36.321–32
  60

Papiri greci e latini (*PSI*) 9.1040
  191

P. Mich. (*Michigan Papyri*)
  176   128
  177   129
  178   129
  2848   312
  3000   312

P. Osl. (*Papyri Osloenses*) 1.1.321–32
  60

P. Oxy. (*Oxyrhynchus Papyri*)
  1.37   304
  1.76   310
  1.95   159
  4.722   197
  12.1467   308
  18.2190   140
  48.3285   294
  51.3617   169

Paul, *Sententiae*
  2.26.14   102
  4.9   119
Leiden fragment 2   17

Pausanias, *Guide to Greece* 10.4.1
  234

Petronius, *Satyricon*
  12–15   302
  45.4–8, 10–13   330
  51   287
  58   148
  76.3–9   288

Philo
Against Flaccus 43   48
On Special Laws 3.114–15   61

Philogelos 9, 12, 13, 16, 18, 25, 32, 54, 57, 61 146–7

Philostratus
Life of Apollonius 4.22 349
Lives of the Sophists
  1.21.520 276
  2.21.2 33, 260

Pliny the Elder, *Natural History*
  7.37–8, 41, 42 58
  7.45 58
  7.48–9 59
  7.58–60 104
  7.121 127
  7.156 56
  7.158 56
  7.162–4 57
  7.168 52
  8.21 335
  9.77 139
  10.171–2 59
  12.84 289
  14.48–52 271
  14.87 271
  18.35 251
  18.41–3 253
  18.94–5 251
  26.3 55
  29.19 157
  33.32 24
  33.53 334
  33.135 280
  34.62 343

Pliny, *Letters*
  2.12.2–3, 6 18
  3.19 254
  4.13 142
  4.19 85
  4.21.1–3 59
  5.4.1–3 249
  5.6.5–6 55
  5.13.1–4 250
  6.24.2–5 89
  6.26 84
  6.33 123
  6.34 348
  7.5 86
  7.18 212, 270
  8.2 275
  8.10 87
  8.11 87

8.16 190
8.18 106
9.5 7
9.6 347
9.15 152
9.20 275
9.37.1–4 255
10.2.1 118
10.8.4–6 256
10.41 257
10.65, 66 295
10.94–5 118
Panegyric
  2, 3 8
  11 11
  23 8
  28 211, 269
  33–34 348
  59 8
  77 8
  80 297
  83, 84 12

Plutarch
Aemilius Paullus
  5.1–2 103
  5.4–5 128
Cato the Elder 21.5–6 288
Crassus
  1.1 127
  2 241
Julius Caesar 5 334
Moralia
  8f 139
  508a 105
  802d-e 343
  821f-822c 342
  959c-d 341
  997b-c 341

Polybius 36.17.5–10 61

Quintilian, *The Education of the Orator* 1.3.14–17 139

Sallust, *Jugurthine War* 17.6 54

Sammelbuch Griechischer Urkunden aus Aegypten (SB) 5.7573 160

Seneca the Elder
Controversiae

4 *praef.* 10   201
10.4 *praef.* 17–18   229

Seneca the Younger
Letters
7.2–5   343
27.5–8   156
56.1–5   236
87.7   252
95.33   345
104.1   55
123.7   23
On Anger 1.2   60
On Benefits 3.16.2–3   99
On Clemency
1.25.1   342, 344
1.25.2   344
On the Shortness of Life 13.6–7   335

Statius, *Silvae* 1.6   339

Strabo, *Geography*
2.5.12   289
3.2.10   282
4.6.10   257
5.3.7   234
17.1.13   289

Suda, *Epaphroditus,* e 2004   145

Suetonius
Augustus
34   110
38.3   24
40.1–2   24
43   336
44.1   18
45   336
Claudius
2.2   138
18–20   261
23   116
35   337
Domitian
7.2   276
14.2   276
Gaius Caligula
34   337
Julius Caesar 5   334
Nero
39.1   53
53   338
Titus 7   338

Vespasian
8.5   153
8.5–9.1, 16–18   286
9.2   25
On Teachers of Grammar and
    Rhetoric 23   144

Supplementum Epigraphicum Graecum
    (SEG)
4.512   264
17.755   319
27.828   258
39.1189   258
41.1389   320
46.745   201

Tabula Heracleensis 89–97   29

Tabula Larinas   19

Tacitus
Agricola 4.2–4   124
Annals
1.76   337
2.33   17
2.85   21
3.25.1   113
3.30.1   280
3.36   22
4.62–3   34
6.13   261
12.43   261
13.30.2   281
14.42–5   175
14.56.1   281
15.20–22.1   22
15.43   242
16.13   53
16.18–19   311
Dialogue on Oratory
28.2–29.2   124
29.3–4   345
Histories
1.12   12
4.38   262
5.5   61
Germania
18   97
19   61, 97
20   125

Tertullian
Apologeticum 4.8   113

On the Soul 30.3   62
On the Spectacles
   4   350
   12   350
   15   350
   16   351
   19   351

[Ulpian], *Epitome*
   11.1   132
   11.27   132
   16   115

Valerius Maximus, *Memorable Doings and Sayings*
   5.4.7   126
   5.10.2   121
   7.8.6   310

Varro, *On Agriculture*
   1.2.6–7   251
   1.5.1–3   246
   1.11.2–12.1   249
   2.2.9   280
   2.5.11   280

Vegetius, *Handbook of Military Matters* 1.2.6, 19, 20
   150

Vitruvius
On Architecture
   1.13.4   253
   2, *praef.* 1–4   256
   2.1.3–6   232
   2.8.17–20   237

GENERAL INDEX

Individuals included in the *Index Locorum* (e.g. Cicero or Pliny the Younger) are only indexed here for their other references in the text.

abortion 45, 58, 60, 76, 126
absentee landlords 252, 254–5
Achaea (province) 10, 295
Acilius Sthenelus (freedman) 270
Acraephiae (Boeotia) 10
acrostich 35, 94
actors 19–20; age restrictions on 20; may not marry senatorial females 115; unsuitable occupation 219
Acutius Nerva (senator) 18
address: as sign of status 25
adoptatio: defined 120
adoption: age of adopter 121; exception for consolation 122; of emperor (*see also* succession) 12; legal forms 76; rules of 119–21; *SC Silianum* 178; Tiberius by Augustus 76; women may not adopt 122
adrogatio: defined 119, 120
adultery: Augustan laws 76; definition of 76, 100; divorce mandated 101; father's rights 101; husband's rights 101; killing of adulterers 101; low status participants 101; penalty if not divorce wife 101; punishment by Germans 97; punishment for males 102; punishment for wife 102
advisers of emperor 3, 12
Aelii Tuberones (senatorial family): fraternal lifestyle 128

Aelius Agathoclianus, P. (*apparitor*) 30
Aelius Lamia (cos. AD 3) 15
Aemilia Pudentilla (wife of Apuleius) 66
Aemilius Paulus Macedonicus, L. (conqueror of Perseus): adoption out of two sons 121; divorce of Papiria 103
Aeneas (mythological founder of Rome) 14–15
Aeturnia Zotica (wife of lictor) 69
affectio maritalis: defined 73–4
Africa (North) 5, 18, 27, 40, 44, 50, 54, 66, 88, 94, 174, 198, 251, 257, 261, 263, 274, 319–20, 336, 348, 350
age: birth records 66–7; errors in recording 66; personal knowledge of 46
Ager Gallicus (wine-growing area) 271
agnates (relatives in male line) 72, 79, 80, 132
agriculture *see* farming
Agrippa, M. (Vipsanius – general of Augustus) 50, 58, 343;
Agrippina (Older and Younger) 12
Agrippina (Younger) 286
Alexander the Great 342
Alexandria 43, 46, 48, 63, 141, 145, 158, 262, 289, 306, 326, 349; population 46–7

alieni iuris: defined 79

alimenta (annuity) 65

alimenta (child support): begun by
Nerva? 269; at Comum 212, 269;
forms of investment 267–8; at
Ligures Baebiani 268; purposes
268; through rent on land 212;
at Veleia 211, 268

Allius Maximus (procurator of
Burunitan estate) 40

alms-giving 229, 231

amicitia 77

amphitheatre (Flavian) 50, 138, 287,
328–9, 338–9, 345

amphitheatres 34, 234, 287, 331,
336–7, 343, 350–1; engineering
requirements 34

Ampliata (sister of Tutilia Supera)
91

Amymone (wife of Marcus) 92

androgyny 61

animal husbandry 245

animal liberation 6

Annius Flavianus (lictor) 69

annona (grain supply) 205, 260–1,
330, 340; *see also* food supply,
grain

Antioch (Syria) 46–7, 226, 229, 316

Antioch (in Pisidia) 264

Antoninus Pius (emperor) 21, 67, 143,
172, 178, 267, 311

Antonius Julianus (rhetor) 239

Apamea (Syria): census figures 43,
47

Apollo Ptoios: cult in Boeotia 10, 11

Apollonius of Tyana (miracle worker)
276, 349

apparitores (minor officials) 4, 30,
172

appeals: to governor or emperor 292

Apronius Caesinus, L. (father of
L. Apronius Caesinus) 15

Apronius Caesinus, L. (victor in
Africa, AD 20) 14

Apuleius of Madaura: as itinerant
lecturer 66

Aquileia 26, 256–7

Aquincum (Pannonia) 52

Aquinum (Italy) 98

Aquitaine (province) 26

Arabia 27

arbustum (trees for vines) 248, 252,
271

Arcanum (estate of Q. Cicero) 98

archaisms 148

Archelaus (Mithridates' general) 240

Arelate (Narbonese Gaul) 93

Arganthonius (king of Tartessians) 56

Armenia 16

Arpinum (Cicero's estate) 98

Arria (wife of Paetus) 88–9

Asculum (Italy) 20

Asia (province) 15, 26–7, 55, 143,
153, 199, 263, 276

Asinius Gallus 17

ataraxia (freedom from concern):
as Stoic ideal 236

Athens 6, 147, 216, 233, 348

Atia (mother of Augustus) 125

Atilius (freedman) 34

Attia Viriola (upper-class Roman
woman) 123

auctioneers 31, 219

Augusta (title for imperial women) 11,
13

Augustan marriage legislation 1, 45,
76, 100–2, 109–19; amended by
Tiberius 116; attempts to thwart
21; benefits 45; consular privileges
for three children 117; informers
113; opposition to 110; penalties
45, 109, 112, 116; penalties as
revenue-raising device 113;
permission to marry freedwomen
109, 112; preference in elections
117; privileges for three children
(*see also ius iii liberorum*) 117–19;
repeal of age restrictions by
Justinian 116; revision under
Septimius Severus 113; rewards
109, 112

Augustus (emperor) 3, 9, 18, 24, 45,
49, 53, 64, 76, 82, 85, 100, 104–5,
109–13, 116, 139, 192, 234, 240,
251, 258, 260–2, 286, 295, 307,
310, 329, 336–7; attempts to

restore traditional morality 76;
behaviour at games 336; building
restrictions at Rome 234–5;
establishes fire brigade 234;
extramarital affairs 109; family
problems 105; games of 336–7; and
grain supply 260; love life 100;
marriage laws (see also Augustan
marriage legislation); moral reforms
100; morality legislation 110;
renounces friendship with Fulvius
105; restores public procession of
knights 24
Augustus, deified (divus Augustus) 11,
14, 20, 27, 44, 47, 56
Aurelia Violentilla, Maria (woman of
consular status) 20
Aurelis Procopton (freed slave)
199–200
Ausonius (fourth-century writer) 46
Autarcius (father-in-law of Iulia
Tyrrania) 93

baby-farming 304; see also foundlings
Baetica (Spain) 7
banditry 313–14, 319–20
bandits 38, 205, 241, 257, 293;
capture Remmius Palaemon 145;
exemplary punishment of 321–2,
343–4; Robin Hood types 214
bankers 38
Bastarnae (barbarian tribe) 16
baths: endowments for heating 227,
245, 269; established as benefaction
30; noise in 236; regulations for
operation at Vipasca 284–5;
segregation by opening hours 285;
as shelter for poor 226–7; of Titus
338
beast hunts 19, 206, 224, 331, 335–6,
339, 342, 345, 348, 350; see also
damnatio ad bestias
bed-wetting 164
beggars: abuse of non-donors 228; at
baths 213; compliment rich 227;
deliberately maimed 228; as
entertainers 206, 228; Jewish 235;
at market-places 225; in rags 213;

rejection by rich 231; self-
mutilation 231; supported by
Church 229
benefactions 28, 30–1, 205, 229–30,
245; from Augustus 49; for
education 136; of emperor 10;
for heating baths 227, 245, 269;
matched contributions 142; Pliny to
Comum 245, 269; presenting games
329, 342; Quinctilius Priscus to
Ferentinum 28; safeguarding of
142–3
bequests: method of calculation 65
bestiarii (animal hunters) 19, 224, 343
bilingualism 149–50
birth: cases of dispute over 108–9;
miscarriage 87
birthday celebration 28
birth rate 109, 111
Bithynia (province) 27, 212, 269,
295–6, 311
branding 154, 173–4, 192, 264, 322
bread and circuses 330
bricks 237–8, 294
Britain (province) 15, 37, 124, 214
brothel keepers 115, 221; brothels
151, 322
building programmes: as employment
for poor 286; as philanthropy 10;
at Rome 286; of Vespasian 286
building regulations: height restrictions
242; under Augustus 234; wall
thickness 237
buildings: appropriate for working
farm 249; clay roofing 233;
construction at top of walls 238;
earth and straw 233; hillocks in
Phrygia 232; multi-level 234, 237;
qualities of fired brick 238; reed
huts 232–3; risks 239; speculation
in 234, 238; thatch 233;
wattlework construction 238; wood
in Colchis 232
bulla (amulet) 67
Bulla Felix (brigand) 214–15
Burunitan estate (Tunisia) 40, 292
Byzacena (Byzacium, N. Africa) 93,
251

Caecilia Epigone (mother of Sex. Caecilius Felix) 90
Caecilia Festiva (wife of Pomponius Antiochus) 93
Caecilius Felix, Sex. (son of Caecilia Epigone and Thallus) 90
Caecilius Frugi, Sex. (brother of Sex. Caecilius Felix) 90
Caecilius Isidorus, C. (freedman of Augustus): wealth, including animals 279
Caecilius Metellus, L. (cos. 251, 247 BC) 104
Caecilius Metellus Macedonicus, Q. (censor 131–0 BC) speech on marriage 82, 104
Caecilius Metellus Numidicus (censor 102–1 BC) 82
Caecilius Thallus, Sex. (freedman, father of Sex. Caecilius Frugi) 90
Caecina Paetus, A. (cos. suff. AD 37) 88
Caecina Severus, A. (cos. suff. 1 BC) 88
Caecubum: Italian wine-growing area 271
Caelius Donatus, C. (magistrate in N. Africa) 29
Caelius Sedatus, C. (son of C. Caelius Donatus) 29
Caligula (Gaius) (emperor) 58, 262, 329, 337
Calistinus (child) 68
Calpurnia (wife of Pliny) 75, 85–7, 255
Calpurnia Hispulla (aunt of Pliny's wife) 85, 87
Calpurnius Fabatus (grandfather of Pliny's wife) 86
Calpurnius Macer (senator) 89
Calvisius Sabinus (freedman) 156
Campania Felicissima (wife of L. Papinius Verus) 95
canals 256–7
Canuleius Zosimus, M. (freedman engraver) 37
capital punishment: body dragged off by hook 175; see also games

captatio see will-hunting
Capua (Italy) 95
Caracalla (emperor) 46, 329; behaviour at games 340–1
Carennas Verecundus, C. (husband of Herennia Cervilla) 69
Carinae (Italy) 31
Carsulae (Umbria) 30
Carthage 46, 94
Cassius, C. (senator) 175–6
castration: limited by Domitian 229
Cato the Elder: as authority 298, 300; and lending 278, 287–8; opinion on grazing 278; on returns from vineyards 271
Censorius Niger (equestrian) 311
census: Egyptian data 44, 64, 128–31; in Judaea 64; records longevity 57; -takers 47; for taxation 46; value of data 46
Centuripae (W. Sicily) population 47
Cestius, C. (senator) 22
charioteers: career of Scirtus 332–3
Chersonese, Borysthenic (Crimea) 16
child abuse 140
childbirth: confirmation of paternity 107–9; difference between male and female children 58; effects of multiple 58; maternal mortality 58–9
childlessness: advantages 76, 105
children: blessings of 104, 111; differential support according to legitimacy 212; disadvantage of too many 105; exposure 126, 229; German practices 76; husband's rights to 108; inspection of 109; legally required to support parents 127; legitimacy 76; preference for males 117; premature death 28–29; privileges to mothers of four 262; as providing rights for sposal inheritance 115; raising of 125–6; reliable paternity 107–9; slave nurses of 76
Christians 62, 93, 152, 323–5; and games 350–3; on poor 209–11

chronology: Roman emperors, first two centuries AD vii
Chrysippus (Cicero's architect) 239
Chrysippus (Stoic philosopher) 236
Cicero: as translator of Plato 5
circus 30, 151, 173, 257, 329–30, 335–6, 347, 351; Augustus at 336; social mingling at 329
Circus Maximus 329
citizenship: grant of 38; indicated by three names (*tria nomina*) 39
city gazette (*acta urbis*) 340
City Prefect 16
civic records: access to 137
Claudius 11, 15, 26, 60, 116, 138, 144, 240, 260–2, 280, 286; behaviour at games 337; offers rewards to shipowners 261; pelted by mob 261
Claudius Quadrigarius (historian) 239–40
Claudius Secundus, Tib. (imperial freedman) 190
Claudius Timarchus (Cretan grandee) 22
Clemens (decurion of Carsulae) 30
clients: services to patrons 297; *see also* patrons, *operae*
Clodia (wife of Ofilius) 56
Clodius Pulcher, P. (senator) 77
coemptio: defined 73
coinage 360
collapse 34, 165, 234, 241, 237, 238–9, 241, 286
collegia (associations): to assure burial 36, 213; legally permitted 258; *see also* corporations
colonus (farmer) 5, 247, 252, 255, 278; *see also* tenants
Colosseum *see* amphitheatre (Flavian)
Colossus (of Nero) 338
Cominius Firmus, L. (senator) 89
comitia curiata: for adoption 120
commissions of inspection 23
Commodus (emperor) 40, 329, 340

Comum (Italy) 89, 142–3, 212, 245, 268–9
conception: multiple 59; *see also* childbirth
concubinage 114–15, 220–1
confarreatio: defined 73
congiarium (gifts of food) 211, 330
Constantinople 46
contraception 45, 60, 126
contracts: for child-rearing 304–5; empire-wide pay rates 36; *see also locatio conductio*
conubium: defined 73
Corinth 10, 225, 349
Cornelii Scipiones: as exemplars 17
Cornelius Drosus, L. (child) 68
Cornelius Scipio Aemilianus, P. 5–6, 103, 151
Cornelius Scipio Africanus, P. 270–1
Cornelius Sulla, L. (dictator) 240–1
corporal punishment: as part of education 136, 138, 140, 149; use of eelskins 139
corporations: of bakers at Antioch 264; of bakers at Rome 258; for *garum* imports 257; for mining 258; of muleteers and ass-drivers 36; for salt works 258; of shipowners 27, 258; of tax-farmers 258
corruption 121, 293, 306, 323
country estates: healthiness compared to towns 55; *see also* villas
countryside: as refuge from Rome 236
Crete 22
Crispinius Hilarus, C. (plebeian from Faesulae) 105
crown gold 294–5
Cupid and Psyche 173
Curator: of bed and banks of Tiber 267; for preservation of sacred temples and public monuments 14; of public buildings 13–14
curator (guardian) 113, 143; *see also* guardianship
customs duties 33, 245, 258
Cynics 208–9, 303

Dacians 16
damnatio ad bestias (condemned to the beasts) 161, 172, 209, 214–15, 224, 320, 341, 351
Danube 16
death: after childbirth 69; premature 46, 67–8
death records 310
debt 37–8, 178, 203, 241, 295, 345; imprisonment for 293–4, 305–7, 325; reason to become gladiator 19; rural 252, 254–5, 274
declamations (imaginary cases) 229
decurions 20, 27, 30, 39, 264, 293; as civic benefactors 28; definition 4; eligibility 29; regulations 4
demography: definition 43; functions 355
demonstrations: against Augustan marriage legislation 110; against execution of Pedanius' household 176; *see also* games, public demonstrations
depopulation of Greece 61
diatribes (as popular sermons) 209
dinner invitations 31–2
dinners: display of literary knowledge at 157
Dionysius (bishop of Alexandria) 63
disabled: not required to parade with horse 24
disease: Antonine plague 54; bad foods as cause of 266; cancer 227; elephantiasis 227; epidemics 53; seasonal 53; smallpox 54; spread by kissing 55; venereal? 89; as work of poisoners? 54
display: of costly cups 23; through entourage 23
divinisation: as imperial strategy 11
divorce: for adultery 101; Cicero and Terentia 99; custody of children 103; formula 74; frequency of 99; from incompatibility 104; limitations on 110; because of military service 103; pregnancy after 108; rates 45, 76, 89, 99–100; reasons for 102–3; in Roman law 102–4

doctors 55, 66, 184; exemption from liturgies 143–4; as outsiders 157
domestic violence 76, 99
dominica potestas 73–4, 197; defined 73
Domitian (emperor) 7–8, 11, 118, 200, 211, 229, 245, 275, 295, 297, 319, 338–40, 347
Domitius Tullus, Cn. (senator) 106
domus (free-standing house): 50–1, 206, 235; defined 72; as family 59, 72, 77–80, 84, 97, 113, 121, 123, 125, 280; sanctity of 77; supersedes *familia* 72
dowry 74, 81–2, 97, 99, 102, 113, 116, 254, 296; husband's rights to 81–2; may be compelled 113; repayment 82, 99
dreams: different for poor and rich 207; of fighting beasts 208; fire in 207; of head 38; human excrement in 207–8; interpretation of 38–9; lightning in 207; of literacy 149–50; of Maia 325; meaning for slaves 207; sickness predicted in 207
Drusus (son of Tiberius) 22, 337
dwarfs 228, 331

economic development: mineral exploitation 245; of Roman empire 245
economics: consolidating holdings vs. spreading risk 254; defined 244
education as social cachet 136; away from home 136, 142; better in olden times 149; from books 32; by encouragement 139–40; of Germans 125; in home 136; imperial benefactions 142; knowledge of Greek literature 156; by mothers in past 124–5; by nurse and *paedagogus* 124–5; philanthropic endowments 136, 142; practical 137, 149; for public service 137; school hours 138; self-educated mocked 147–8; under school teacher 136
egeni (needy) 205, 208, 229, 268

Egnatius Proculus, Q. (consul) 20
Egypt 26, 33, 43–8, 50, 63–4, 66, 77,
    116, 128, 130, 145, 154, 158–60,
    169, 251, 259–61, 282, 289,
    292–4, 304–8, 310, 312–13, 326;
    contracts for raising slaves in 158;
    law in 294; population 48–9
elephants: in animal hunts 334–5
elite: difficulties in ensuring succession
    59
embassies: from provinces 23
emperor (optimus princeps) 3; censor
    297; citizen 8; divinisation 3;
    intervention of 40–41; judge 297;
    mediator 3; monarch 3; use of
    image of as protection 22, 197;
    women in family of 12
employment: fixed term 5; seasonal
    245; see also inscriptions
engraving: styles of 37
Epaminondas (chief priest of divine
    Augustus) 10
Epaphroditus (grammaticus) 145–6
Epaphroditus (steward of the Volusii)
    90
Ephesus 258, 264, 339
epidemics 44, 53, 61, 260
epitaphs: attitude to life 70; for
    children 68; common motifs 75;
    as evidence 75; posthumous
    manumission on 199–200; praising
    hedonism 190; for wives 68–9
equality: as inequitable 6, 7
equites (knights): careers 25–6; femina
    stolata as female equivalent 4, 27;
    imperial service 4; legal
    qualifications for status defined
    24–5; need three generations of free
    birth 25; obligations on 4; origin 4;
    privileges 4; procession with public
    horses 4, 24; qualifications for
    reserved seating (14 rows) 24–5;
    status as legal protection 25; status
    marked by gold rings 24; vir
    egregius 312; vir eminentissimus 27;
    vir splendissimus 26
ergastula (slave gangs, slave prisons)
    154, 188–9, 245, 252, 341

Eryx (Sicily) 14
eunuchs 163, 245, 260
ex-slaves see freedmen

Fabius Maximus Aemilianus, Q.
    (son of Aemilius Paulus) 103
Fabricius (Republican Roman
    exemplar) 17
Fadia Maxima (wife) 96
Faesulae (Italy) 104
familia: as agnate family 72–3, 75,
    79–80, 89, 96, 119–20, 123, 125,
    280–12; as group of slaves 80, 158,
    175, 190, 331, 334; legally defined
    79; women in 80
family: adoption 76; evidence from
    inscriptions 89; extended 77,
    127–8; extended in Egypt 128–131;
    fraternal (frérèche) 131; as ideal
    72; imperial, in oath 9; large
    families (polypaidia) 126; as legal
    definition 72; multigenerational
    130; non-nuclear examples 77;
    nuclear 74; obligations 75; patterns
    of commemoration 74–5; as
    revealed by epitaphs 74; shared
    ancestral monuments 78; shared
    rites 78; slave 200; as social unit 72
famine 44, 53–4, 62, 225, 260–2,
    265–6
farming: absentee landowning 244;
    carrying capacity 43; commended
    by Cato 247; constituent parts
    according to Varro 246–7; festival
    day work 248; inspection of 248;
    in Italy 244; labour intensive 244,
    252; methods 251; productivity 33;
    rainy day work 248; as respectable
    investment 32–33; as respectable
    occupation 217; returns from 255;
    slaves or tenants? 244; social
    conservatism of farmers 253; wealth
    from 244
farms: appropriate features 254;
    equipment and storage 247; need
    owner's attention 252–3; size of
    244; things to look for in 247;
    types rated 248

Faventia (wine-growing area in Italy) 271

Favorinus (eunuch sophist) 298–300

females: may not be adopted 120; see also women

Ferentinum (Italy) 28

fertiliser 253

fertility: lack of 45; limitation of 45; maternal mortality 87

Fidenae (Italy) 34

fire brigade 172, 194, 234, 240–1

fire exits 241

fires: 206; at Rome 53, 153, 165, 213, 234, 237–42, 286; prevention 206, 239

Flaminius, C. (cos. 223, 220, 217 BC) 16

floods 53, 206, 237–8, 250, 260

flour mills 52, 195, 235, 294, 322–3

food: of poor 205–6, 233

food supply at Rome 260–3; in country 265; hoarding 245, 263; intervention of Roman government 263–4; price variations 245; in provinces 263–6

Fortuna Primigeneia (temple of) 31

Fortunata (wife of Trimalchio) 94

Forum Clodii (Italy) 30

Forum Iulii (Fréjus) 13

foundlings 155, 158, 160, 304; legal status 295; may claim freedom 296

freedmen: duties of 155; in education 136; eligibility for adoption in dispute 120; exempt from SC Silianum 177; half goods to patron 195; honoured by patrons 91; honour patrons 96; imperial 189; imperial, assisting bandits 214; may not marry senatorial females 115; Pliny's provision for his 269; as public benefactors 31; share tomb 96; social aspirations 149; stereotyped (as grasping, promiscuous, extravagant) 34, 137–8, 144, 156–7

freedwomen: can marry all except senatorial class 109, 114

freeholders 5

funeral funds: in the army 150

Furia Spes (wife of L. Sempronius Firmus) 91

Furius Chresimus, C. (industrious freedman) 253

Gaetulians (African tribe) 15

Galatia (province) 27, 69

Galba 286, 306; behaviour of court 12; brings charges against fast-food shops 25

Galeria Copiola (actress) 56

Galli (castrated priests of Cybele) 235

gambling 151; not a fault in a slave 162

games: Apollonius intervenes at 349; apparitor puts on 30; athletics 39; attitudes of Christians 350; boring 335; cause undue excitement 351; costs 331; cruel 343–5, 350; demeaning to participants 19; demons at 350; desensitising 342; disorder at 349; display imperial generosity 329–30; display imperial power 329; display social stratification 329; expense 342; extravagant 334–5, 345–6; grandstands 224; in Greece 349; harenarius 202; as idolatry 350; imperial prerogative 329; individual attitudes toward 329; martial training 329; origins 341, 350; pandering to the mob 342–3; peer pressure at 351–2; pleasure in punishment bad 351; Pliny feigns boredom at 347–8; for political support 331; for profit 34; public demonstrations 329, 343; purpose 341; reason for demise 350; required generosity 342, 345–8; in Roman Republic 346; seductive for Christians 351–2; site of punishment 343; slaughter at 330–1; slaves at 168, 256; slaves signing up for 172–3; throwing of fruit at 343; topic of conversation 335; trained animals 338–9; Trajan's behaviour at 347–8;

unusual combatants 331; on water
(*naumachiae*) 339; *see also* bandits;
bread and circuses; circus;
gladiators
Gangra (Paphlagonia) 9
Gargilius Venator, L. (husband of Iulia
Rogata) 94
garum (fish sauce) 257
gender: age restrictions according to
20; differentiation in child support
212; imbalances 44; male vs. female
duties 210
Germans 61, 76, 97, 125
Geta (emperor) 46
gifts: between husband and wife
102–3
gladiatorial trainers 20
gladiators 19, 20, 31, 38, 224; age
restrictions on 20; ban on soldiers'
participation 352–3; drawn contest
339; production restricted to upper
classes 34; restrictions on use of
criminals 352
Gordian (emperor) 46
gradus dignitatis (social hierarchies) 5
grain: as surety on loan 266; barley
groats 265; consumption in late
Republican Rome 50; effects of
boiled wheat 265; imports 257;
pros and cons of growing wheat
250; shortages 260–3; storage 266;
transport of 17, 260; wheat yields
251; yields 272, 274
grain distribution: at Alexandria 64;
Augustus' distributions 49;
eligibility 49; at Rome 49–50
grain imports 49; from Africa 50;
under Augustus 50; from Egypt 50;
under Septimius Severus 50
grain shipping: Claudian edict 195,
260–2
grain supply: construction of
warehouses 245; imperial
intervention in 245; prefect of 14;
Rome as net importer 246; selection
of recipients 245; tax-exempt 245
grammaticus (teacher) 136, 144
grapes *see* vines

Graxia Alexandria (wife of Pudens) 68
Greece: freedom from taxation 11
guardianship: adult women, only
apparent for 132; age of
emancipation for males 77; of
agnates removed by Claudius 132;
cura (defined) 131–2; of lunatics
(*furiosi*) 131; of minors 131–3;
reasons why given to women 133;
of spendthrifts (*prodigi*) 131; *tutela*
(defined) 131–2; when women need
approval of guardian 132
guilds *see collegia*, corporations

Hadrian (emperor) 84, 180, 194, 235,
283, 295
halitosis 164
Haterius, Q. 17
health: avoidance of hot foods 54;
healthy localities 54; unhealthy
localities 54–5
Helios (sun-god) 11
Hell 231
Hellenistic philosophies 208–9
Hellespont 26
Helvidiae (daughters of Helvidius
Priscus the Younger) 59
Helvidius Priscus (the Younger,
consular) 59
Hercules: companions of (youth club?)
27
Herennia Cervilia (wife of C. Carrenas
Verecundus) 69
heres extraneus: defined 184
heres institutus: defined 183
heres necessarius: defined 184
heres suus: defined 177, 184, 194
Hermeros (freedman) 148
Hesiod 60, 156, 217–18
hierarchies 2, 3, 5
hierarchy: social need to preserve 7
historical evidence: satirical and
moralising content 76; types of 2
holidays: rural work permitted on 248,
281
Homer 145, 156, 217, 219, 223, 251,
275
honestiores (respectable) 293

honorary statue 31
horrea see warehouses
horti (pleasure gardens) 235
hospices 226
hostages 16
Hostilius Firmus (deputy of Marius
   Priscus) 18
House of Romulus 233
housing: building collapse 206;
   building techniques 206; *domus* 50;
   insula 50; party walls 237, 243; for
   poor 206; problems with 206; rents
   206, 239; speculation in 206; for
   status at Rome 241
humiliores (common folk) 294
huts: of poor 233
hygiene 44

idios logos (private account, i.e.
   Roman government of Egypt) 116,
   307
imperial cult 11, 15; participation of
   Roman citizens and provincials 9;
   sign of provincial loyalty 9
imperial family: female members 3;
   prestige 3
imperial privileges: non-citizens given
   right of patronage 26
imprisonment for debt 293–4; in mines
   294
indigent *see egeni*
infanticide 45; drowning 61; exposure
   61; German ban on 61; Jewish ban
   on 61; of malformed 60; of
   portentous births 61; suffocation
   61
infant mortality 52; twins 58
informers (*delatores*) 67, 113, 230,
   264, 293, 316; rewards for 187–8
Ingenuinius Ianuarius (son of Iulia
   Maiana) 99
ingratitude: clients attack patrons 22;
   slaves attack owners 22
inheritance: between spouses 115;
   dependent on punishment of
   household if master killed 177;
   incapacity for inheritance 115; to
   Treasury if heir 'ungrateful' 186–8

inscriptions: citation of 153; as
   evidence for employment/careers 36,
   151, 258; restoration of tablets
   under Vespasian 153; as urban
   wall-paper 152–3; about women
   68–70, 93
insulae (apartment buildings) 50–1,
   206, 217, 235
inventions: suppressed by emperor
   287
investment: in land 288; in shipping
   287–8; in slaves 288
Iulia Donata (freedwoman of Gaius)
   69
Iulia Maiana: murdered by husband
   99
Iulia Mammaea (cousin of Antoninus)
   21
Iulia Procilla (mother of Agricola)
   124
Iulia Rogata (wife of L. Gargilius
   Venator) 93
Iulia Tyrannis (wife of Laurentius)
   93
Iulius Agricola, Cn. (father-in-law of
   Tacitus) 124
Iulius Alexander, Tib. 306
Iulius Caesar, C.: gladiatorial shows
   333–4
Iulius Demetrius (administrator of
   Thebaid Oasis) 306
Iulius Donatus (mortally wounded by
   brigands) 181
Iulius Fortunatus, Ti. (husband of
   Veturia) 52
Iulius Maius (brother of Iulia Maiana)
   99
Iulius Niger, C. (Roman veteran)
   312–13
Iulius Romanus, C. (purchaser of slave
   in Egypt) 159
Iulius Ursus Servianus, L. (cos. AD 90,
   102, 134) 84, 118
Iunius Faustus, M. 27
ius anulorum 24–5, 177, 185, 200
ius iii liberorum 84, 117, 307–8;
   abolished in 410 119; granted to
   Martial 118; granted to Pliny 118;

granted to Suetonius 118–19; patronage in acquiring 118; privilege granted without children 118; rules for women 119
iustum matrimonium: defined 73

jesters 228
Jews: beggars 235; not kill children 61; population in Egypt 48
jokes: about doctors 157; against freedmen 157; from Pompeii 25; *scholastikoi*: 137, 145–7
judges: evaluate character vs. evidence 298–300; legal knowledge 298; using advisers 299
Julia/Julius *see* Iulia/Iulius
Julian law: on bribery 22; on extortion 17
Junian Latins 75, 90, 155; legal disabilities 193; ways to become Roman citizens 194–5

kidnapping 320
kissing: as means of greeting 8; edict against 55; spreads plague 55

Labienus, T. (orator) 229
labour: casual 215; forced 40; for harvests 215; for hire 33; paid by full day's work 215; recruited at market place 215
labourers: tied 5
Lactora (province of Gaul) 26
Laelius (friend of Scipio Aemilianus) 6
land: best in Italy 251; concentrated in hands of few 251–2; as safe investment 238; types of 248
landowners: ability to intimidate locals 249–50; law unto themselves 313–16; required to hear petitions of locals 152
language: use of archaisms 147–8
Laodamia (mythological heroine) 89
latifundia (large estates) 251; frequency 244; as subject of moralizing 244
Latin: as language of military 316
Laurentes Lavinates (priesthood): praetor of 30

Laurentius (husband of Iulia Tyrannia) 93
Laureolus (bandit) 321
law: character witnesses 301; of dependency 79; exploitation of loopholes 19; lack of respect for 7; local vs. Roman 294–5; non-Roman 292; of persons 79; praetor's interdict 302–3; problems with powerful 313; scrupulousness in administration 8; self-help 302; as unsuitable occupation 219; used for blackmail 305, 307; use of imperial precedents 295; *see also* entries under Julian laws, *lex, SC*
lawyers: intimidated by higher status opponents 250; mocked 147, 303
left-handedness: not a fault in itself 164
legal rights 5, 6
legal system: abuses of 293; patronage within 292
lex Aelia Sentia (slaves not to be manumitted under age 30) 192–6, 308
lex Aquilia: for remedial damages 171
lex Calpurnia: on corruption 23
lex Cincia: on lawyers' fees 22
lex de sicariis (homicide) 187
lex Falcidia 65, 310
lex Fufia Caninia: number of slaves permitted to be freed in will 192, 196
lex Iulia de adulteriis see Augustan marriage legislation
lex Iulia de maritandis ordinibus see Augustan marriage legislation
lex Metalli Vipascensis 283–5
lex Oppia 88
lex Pappia Poppaea 109, 112, 113; *see also* Augustan marriage legislation
lex Visellia 194
Libitina 53, 154, 174
Licinius Crassus, M. (triumvir): fire brigade 241; fraternal lifestyle 127–8; property speculation 241; slave *familia* of 241; wealth 206, 241

Licinius Nepos, L. 34
life expectancy 44–5, 354–6
lifestyle: appropriate 220
life tables: ancient 46; modern 354
lineage: as assuring public office 87
literacy 191, 308; in army 137, 150;
    of overseers 137, 151; rates of 137;
    significance in dreams 149; use of
    scribes 137
Liternum 270–1
liturgies: in Egypt 306; exemptions
    from 17, 144
Livia (wife of Augustus) 53, 85, 105,
    110
Livia (wife of Rutilius) 56
living conditions 44
locatio conductio: labour contracts
    282, 333
longevity: of Africans 54; evidence for
    45; long-lived men 56; long-lived
    women 56; in North Italy under
    Vespasian 57
Longinius Castor, C. 308
looting 241
Lucceia (mime actress) 56
ludi magister (schoolmaster) 138
Lyons (Lugdunum) 26, 76, 99

Mactar (Tunisia) 5, 39
Maecenas 102
magic 45, 66, 253
Maglianum (Italy) 35
maiestas (treason) trials under Tiberius
    22
Maionia (Asia) 199
makrobioi (long-lived individuals) 56
malaria 162
Malthus, T. 44, 62
mancipium: defined 79, 131–2, 175
Manlius Torquatus (Republican
    exemplar): executed by father 122
manual labour: dignity of 35
manumission: cannot create free status
    200; disputes over 155, 175, 203–4;
    5 per cent tax 148, 198, 309; by
    fulfilling conditions (statuliber) 178;
    of gladiator 337; Junian Latins 155;
    legitimate causes for freeing slaves

under 30 193–4; for marriage 114;
    paramone contract 200–1; places
    for freeing slaves 193, 198–9;
    predicted by dream 38; record of
    197; requirements for legality 193;
    restrictions on 195–6; stigma of
    155; on verge of death 190–1; by
    will 177, 191, 309
manus: defined 73, 79–80, 101,
    131
Marcia (recipient of Seneca's
    consolation) 106
Marciana (sister of Trajan) 12–13
Marcianus (child poetaster) 67
Marcus Aurelius (emperor) 127, 172,
    181, 267, 311
Marius Maximus Perpetuus
    Aurelianus, L. (cos. II, AD 222)
    20
Marius Priscus (ex-governor of
    N. Africa) 18
Marius Urbinas, T. (disloyal friend of
    Augustus) 310
markets: on estates vs. traditional fairs
    225, 244, 249
marriage: age at 45, 116; age
    difference in 66, 107; among
    Germans 97; appropriate
    characteristics in partners 75;
    benefits of 84; betrothal to children
    110; cannot be forced by father
    114; cannot be forced by patron
    on freedwoman 114; contracts 81;
    cum manu companionship in 85–6;
    customs of Germans 97; death of
    spouse 89; defined vs. concubinage
    114; desirable physical qualities 84;
    devotion of wife 85; divorce 89;
    dowry 81, 97; engagement 81;
    expectation of children 104; females
    of senatorial class restricted 115;
    harmony (concordia) in 75, 83, 86,
    103; illegal to prevent 113; in
    absentia 81; legislation to promote
    111; maintaining family line 111;
    as medical remedy 66; minimum
    age for female 110; not duty of
    guardian 113; outside Roman

empire 75; polygamy 97; to produce children 86–7, 110; remarriage 20–21; reputation of wife 88; requirements for legitimacy 73; rights of ward 113; rings 81; romantic 75; single (*uniiuga*) 52, 93, 95; social expectations 85; of soldiers 114; Stoic view of 83; time limit on betrothal 110, 112; as total union 83; by *usus* 80

Marseilles 6

Martina (wife erects memorial) 95

master of ceremonies 29

materfamilias 79; defined 124

Mattucius Entimus, T. (weaver) 96

Mattucius Pallas, T. (patron of weavers) 96

Mattucius Zmaragdus, T. (weaver) 96

mead 28

measures 359–60

Mediterranean world: custom disparities 1; geographical disparities 1

memorial feasts 28

memorial statuary: to curry imperial favour 254, 256

mental illness: not a fault in a slave 162

Messalina: sexual appetite of 60

metals: sources of xiv–xv

midwives 108–9

migration 44, 45

Milan 36, 142, 191

military awards 26

military service 29

milites stationarii (soldiers on police duty) 172

mills 52, 294, 322; *see also* flour mills; olives

mines (*metalla*) 227, 322; *see also* mining

Minicius Italus, C. (equestrian) 26

mining 281–5; in Dacia 282; duty to work leased land 283; in Egypt 282; leases at Vipasca, Portugal 283–5; penalties for stealing ore 284; right to sell lease 283; in Spain 282

mint 15

Minucia 27

modelling: as historical technique 1

Moesia 15–16

money lending 33, 54, 216, 278, 287–8

monna (term of endearment) 93

monopolies 2, 5; at mines 285

Mons Claudianus (Egypt) 36, 282

monuments: size of site listed 34

mortality: infant 44, 45, 57, 67, 190, 355; maternal 44–6, 57; of twins 58

munus see games

murder: investigation of 177; on journey 180

Mus (as name of child) 68

Nauportus (Slovenia) 256–7

Nero (emperor) 10–11, 53, 211, 240, 242, 251, 280, 286, 293, 311–12, 329, 338; as performer 338

Nerusius Mithres, L. (merchant) 35–6

Nerva (emperor) 11, 211, 254, 267, 269

New Carthage 282

night watch *see* fire brigade

Nile: cataracts 237

noise: in Rome 138, 206, 236–7

nomenclator (reminder of names) 8, 156, 337

Nomentum (Latium): 55, 235; as grape-growing area 270, 272

Novellus Atticus, Torquatus (governor of Narbonese Gaul) 13

Novia Trophime (heir of C. Popilius Heracla) 96

nutrition 44, 49, 265

oath: of allegiance to emperor 3, 9

Octavia (wife of Nero) 11

Octavius Fronto (senator) 17

Octavius Trypho, C. (freedman) 91

Oea (Tunisia) 66

ointment: to maintain complexion 24

old: as burden 6; not required to parade with horse 24; respect for 6; supported by slaves 200 old age: debilitating effects 52, 107; of emperor 12; as humiliating 107; limits claims of operae 202; not a fault in itself 164; as reason for divorce 103

olives: cost of mill and transportation 277; equipment for olive grove 245, 276; limits of cultivation xvi

operae: as full day's work 201; hired hands 201, 218; limited by status 202; sexual favours 201–2; in trade learnt as slave 202; work owed by ex-slaves 155

Oppia Eunoea (freedwoman) 89

Oppidum Novum (Algeria) 29

Ostia: development of harbour 260, 262

Pachoumis (mine superintendent) 36

paedagogus (child minder) 137–8, 218

Paelignians (central Italian ethnic group) 14

Panopeus (Greece): as example of impoverished town 234

Paphlagonia (province) 9, 27

Papinius Verus, L. (husband of Campania Felicissima) 95

Papiria (wife of Aemilius Paulus) 103

Papirius Maso, C. (cos. 231 BC) 103

parasitos (witty dinner guest) 156

pastoralism 277–9

paterfamilias 72–3, 75–6, 79–80, 103, 119, 122–3, 155, 177, 248–9, 252, 271–2, 296; defined 73; legal powers of 79, 122

Paternus (husband of Urbana) 94

patria potestas 72–3, 79, 101, 103, 113–14, 119–20, 122–3, 131, 133; cannot be used alone for divorce 103; cannot force marriage 114; defined 73, 123; restricted by social convention 123

patronage 3, 31, 301; across generations 297; cannot restrict competition 202; in legal system

292; of municipium 30; origins 296; as paternalism 296; shown in monuments 37

patrons: as lawyers 296–7; fides with clients 297

pauperes see poor

peculium ('pocket-money') 155, 166–7, 169–70, 190, 192; belongs to slave if freed 203; defined 203; origin 278; used to 'buy' liberty 203

peculium castrense 177–8, 184

Pedanius Fuscus Salinator, Cn. (cos. AD 118) 84

Pedanius Secundus (city prefect) 175

penal system: to preserve social status 294

peregrini dediticii (surrendered foreigners): legal disabilities 193–4

Pergamum: 265; population 47–8

Perpenna Firmus, Sex. (nihilistic epitaph) 70

petitions: from tenants 40

Petronius (cos. suff. AD 62): suicide 311–12

Phazimon (Paphlagonia) 9

philanthropy see benefactions

philhellenism 10

Philippus (cos. 91 BC) 31–2

philosophy: mocked 211, 301–2

Phlegon of Tralles (writer) 57

pietas 14, 76, 85, 92, 107; aetiology for temple of 126–7; defined 74

pimps 20, 101, 221, 340

Pisa (Italy) 95

Piso Licinianus (adopted successor of Galba) 12

Plataea (Greece) 224

Plautius Silvanus Aelianus, Tib. (victor in Balkans under Nero) 15

Plautus 148

Pliny the Elder: on Alexandria 46

Pliny the Younger: benefactions for Comum 269; childlessness 118; estates throughout Italy 254

Plotina (wife of Trajan): moderation of 12–13

poison: not covered by SC *Silianum* 179

poll-tax: as evidence for Egyptian population 48

Pompeius Magnus, Cn. (Pompey the Great): games 334–5; grain supply 260

Pomponia (wife of Quintus Cicero) 75, 98–9

Pomponius Antiochus (husband of Caecilia Festiva) 93

poor: appearance of 209; as butt of jokes 208; defined vs. rich 205; exploited by wealthy 293; foodstuffs of 224–5; forced to sell tools 37; lifestyle of 209, 233; necessary for rich 209–10; occupations for 205, 210, 216–23; rise in status 39; underemployment of 5, 217; vs. indigent 209; work created for 287

Popilius Heracla, C. (codicil to will of) 96

Poppaea Sabina (wife of Nero) 11

population: decline at Alexandria 63–4; estimates 43; estimates for Italy 357; levels of 45; over-population and effects 62; problems with evidence 43; rates of growth/ decline 355; structures 44

Porcius Cato, M. (the Elder) 138, 157, 247, 271, 277–8, 281, 287–8

Postumia Matronilla (model mother) 93

potentes (rich and powerful) 40, 293, 313–16

Potentia (Italy) 36

Potestas see dominica potestas, patria potestas

poverty: praise of 205; *see also egeni, poor*

praefectus annonae 261

praefectus fabrorum 28

Praeneste (Italy) 31

praetor ad hastam 13

praetors: legal duties 9

pregnancy: confirmation of 108

priesthoods 10, 14–15, 27–8, 102

princeps see emperor

prisons: conditions in 226, 294, 323–5; food within 324–5; private 325–6; segregation of prisoners 323–4; for slaves 229

Proclus (of Naucratis, sophist and trader) 33, 259

Procula (wife of M. Vinicius Secundus) 91

procurator: guardian 108; imperial agent 27, 40–1, 251, 259, 283–5; imperial governor 26–27; steward 59

professions: at baths 236; demeaning 19; engraver 37; goatskin seller 35; harvester 39; lower-class 235; quarryman 36; respectable 33; sandal cobbler 36; smiths 37; tools of 37; unsuitable 115, 216; work-gang leader 39

prostitution 114–15, 202; as adultery 222; banned for women of higher status 21; laws regulating 221; leads to seduction of respectable males 223; registration with aediles 21; of slaves 221; as slippery moral slope 216; threatens respectable families

provinces: allotment of governorships 18

provincial assemblies: votes of thanks from 23

provincial government 7; abuses 22

Psenamounis Harpocrates (will of) 191

puberty: defined 180

public burial 31

publicani (tax farmers) 258–9

punishment: according to status 320; crushes the spirit of children 140; differentiated for slaves and free 284; as entertainment 294; exemplary 321; mythological spectacles 321–2; public service 174

Puteoli (Italy) 18, 174; Guild of Funeral Directors 161

quarries (*lautumiae*) 234, 242, 322
Quinctilius Priscus, Au. (benefactor of Feretinum) 28

recitations 86
recommendation: letters of 301
religious fanaticism: as fault in slave 162
Remmius Palaemon, Q. (freedman) 136, 270; as entrepreneur 144–5; jokes about 144–5; literary judgements 144–5; as teacher 144–5; as typical freedman 144–5
reputation (*gloria*) 86
requisitioning: of animals 40, 293, 316, 318–19; of billets 318–19; of labour 248, 293, 317–19
rhetor (teacher of rhetoric) 136
Rhoxolani (barbarian tribe) 16
Roman empire: map x–xi
Rome: baths 52; *Breviarium* lists 51; building projects 234, 237, 242; calculation by cobwebs 52; *Curiosum* lists 50; districts 51; entertainment venues 52; food supply 52; geographical advantages 234; haphazard development 242; imports 52; map xii–xiii; natural disasters in 234; noise in 235; *Notitia* lists 50; number of *domus* 51; number of *insulae* 51; number of private baths 51; planned rebuilding after AD 65 fire 242; population 260; rebuilding after Gallic sack 242; regions 50–1; requirements for open space 242; size (area) 51; size of population 52; as subject of emulation 1
Romulus (founder of Rome) 122, 233, 296–7
Rufilla, Annia (opponent of C. Cestius) 22
ruina (building collapse) *see* collapse
runaways 230, 248; action for ruining a slave 169; announced by town crier 173; branding of 173–4; collars 173–4; damages for harbouring 169–70; defined 165;

excused if avoiding harsh treatment 165; heralds announce rewards for 219; Paul on Philemon 169; public notices of rewards 169, 173; rights to search for 169–72; slaves 154, 161, 165–9

sanitation 44
Sarmatians (barbarian tribe) 16
Saserna (writer on agriculture) 271
Saturnalia: under Domitian 338, 340
Saturninus (jurist) 21
SC Calvisianum 116
SC Claudianum 116
SC Persicianum 116
SC Silianum 177–88; defining 'under the same roof' 179–80; extra time to fulfil conditions of will 183; rewards for informers 187
scholastikos (absent-minded student/professor) 137, 146–7
Scopelianus (sophist): leads embassy over vineyard reduction in Asia 275–6
scribes: for drafting wills 151; use in drafting contracts 159–60
Scribonia Hedon (wife of Q. Tampius Hermeros) 95
Scythians (barbarians) 16
searches: by legal authorities 171–2, 317
secretaries 30; *see also apparitores*
self-education/late-learning (*opsimathia*) 147–8
self-sufficiency 157, 208, 210, 216–17
Sempronia (wife of Moschis) 92
Sempronius Atratinus, L. (cos. suff. 34 BC) 56
Sempronius Firmus, L. (husband of Furia Spes) 91
Sempronius Lathaeus, L. (freedman of Sempronius Atratinus) 56
senate: as court 22; composition 3; expansion 3; privileges 4; public service 3
senators: as administrators 3; allotted special seats in theatre 18–19;

banned from providing racehorses 17; banned from shipping 16–17; banned from tax collection 17; defend reputation 22; preservation of dignity 7, 21; privileges 8, 9; public service 17; required to uphold dignity of order 17; restrictions on public appearances 4, 19

senatus consultum see SC

Seneca the Elder 14

Seneca the Younger 76, 206, 280; as vine cultivator 271–2

Septicia Maura (wife of L. Trebius Divus) 190

Septimius Severus (emperor) 50, 58, 113, 214

Seriphos: island for exile 21

servus vicarius (underslave) 166

Setia (wine-growing area) 271

sexual deviancy 60

sexual intercourse: humans have no mating season 59; humans insatiable 60

sexual practices 145

shipowners 38, 217, 258

shipping: size of vessels 16; Trimalchio's investment 288

Sicinius Aemilianus (uncle of Sicinius Pontianus) 66

Sicinius Clarus (uncle of Sicinius Pontianus) 66

Sicinius Pontianus (friend of Apuleius) 66

Sigus (N. Africa) 93

Silanus, M. (cos. AD 46) 104

skeletons as evidence 44, 46, 65

slaves: admiring art 168; age at sale 159–60; agrarian 5; at the Athenian silver mines 156; aware of actions within familia 176; baby-farming contracts 158; best treatment of household 190; black arts 170; can damage farms 252; chosen for appearance 24; collars on 173–4; compared to animals 154, 163; compensation for slaves manumitted as reward 186; custom-made 156; defects in 161–9; definition of truant 166; diseases vs. faults 162; domestic slaves 155; education of 288; embezzlement 170–3; estimates of population 158; 'experienced' vs. 'newcomer' 169; family groups should not be broken 168; fans at games 170; fear of 175–6; female: still births not a fault 164; fighting in arena 161; for display 154, 156; fraudulent sales 161; freedom *see* manumission; full restoration of free status 199–200; guarantees against legal claims 161; guarantees on sale 154, 158; identifying marks 159–60; jointly owned 195, 198 Junian Latins 192; keeping mistresses 170–1; knowledge of Latin 169; latrines for 253; murder of master: acquittal by disability 182, acquitted by mortally wounded master 181, acquitted if could not bring help 181–2, execution of household 154, not covered by SC *Silianum* if underage 185; need of close supervision 252; not tortured if underage 180; of husband and wife as one group 179; over-reliance on 157–8; *peculium* 169; positions of responsibility 38; prices 159–60; prisons *see ergastula*; protection against 177–8; punishment 154; punishment for passing as free 172–3; purchasing other slaves 168–9; reliability of evidence 168; in Republican Rome 156; resold if masters treat cruelly 197; rights of asylum 166; rights of return 161–8; runaways *see* runaways; sale contracts: modelled on animal sales 160; sale of 146, 154, 158–68, 248, 316; sale of infants 160–1; sales recorded in public archives 158–60; as security 178, 182; seller's guarantees enforceable 166–7; source of 154; stereotypes of 175; suicide 161, 165, 167; surrendered foreigners' as status 192–3; tax on sales 158; unjustified homicide punished 197; urban vs. rural 152; watching games 168; wills permitted in *familia* 190; working to support students 140–1

sneeze: as abortifacient 58

social advancement 5, 34, 39

social disabilities 4

soldiers: aid landowners 40–1, 315–16; mistreat civilians 316; punishment for losing sword 317

sponsalia: defined 73

stammering 162

standard bearers: in charge of military burial accounts 150

Statilia (long-lived senatorial woman) 56

status: believed to offer protection 176; as grounds for variable rebate 274; importance in legal system 292–3, 298–300; levels of distinction 6; loss of (*infamia*) 19–20; no right to attack person of superior status 25; preservation of differentiation 7; preserved by punishment 321; as protection 4; pyramid 357; reverse pyramid for slaves 358; right to defend one's own status 25; Roman vs. Egyptian 313; social rise of theatrical types 332

sterility: as reason for divorce 102

stewards 38, 59, 106, 171, 188–9, 215, 254, 267, 331

storms 53, 146, 227, 232, 247, 261

Strabo (geographer) 46

students: accommodation 141; away from home 140–2; bad behaviour of 140–1; food parcels to 140–2

stuprum 170, 175; legally defined 100–1

suburbana (country around Rome) 270

succession: emperors 12, 105; difficulties for elite 59; within a *familia* 79

sui iuris: defined 73, 79, 123

suicide: of children 140; political 88–9, 105, 312; from poverty 231; responsibility of slaves 179; of slaves 161, 165,167

Sulpicius Quirinius, P. (governor of Syria) 47

sumptuary laws 17

Superaequum (central Italy) 14

superstitions: of the countryside 281

suus heres 178, 194

Tampius Hermeros, Q. (husband of Scribonia Hedon) 95

Tarquitia Eutycha (mother of L. Tarquitius Marcianus) 91

Tarquitius Marcianus, L. (son of Tarquitia Eutycha and Tarquitius Trophimus) 91

Tarquitius Trophimus, L. (father of L. Tarquitius Marcianus) 91

tax collection 315–16; arbitration of disputes 259; in Asia 258; forced 305, 315–16; payment to Treasury 259

taxation: immunity from 10

taxes: dutiable items 259–60; 5 per cent on manumission 27; non-dutiable items 259; on slaves 258–9

teachers 6, 76, 122, 136, 140–5, 147, 149, 269, 245; competition for 141, 143; enrolling with 141; exemption from liturgies 143–4; fees 138; freedmen as 136; need for discipline 6; public performances 141; in secondary employment 136; selection of 143

temples: use as refuge 22

tenancy: sharecropping vs. lease 254–5

tenants 238–9, 252; imperial intervention 5; social pressures on 244; terms of lease 40

Terentia (wife of Cicero) 56, 85, 99

Terentius Varro, M. (polymath) 144, 271

tessera (tag): for grain distribution 266

theatre: as demeaning to participants
19; 'fourteen rows' 18; public
demonstrations at 110, 261; seating
arrangements 18; *see also* games
Theophrastus (Greek philosopher)
246
Thrace: as healthy locality 54
Thrasea Paetus (senator) 22
threptoi (fosterlings) 295
Tiber (river) 53, 81, 165, 234, 242,
262, 269
Tiberius (emperor) 11, 20, 22, 24, 76,
105, 116, 144, 153, 261, 287, 329,
337, 343; behaviour at games 337;
edict against kissing 55; few games
under 34
Tibur (Tivoli) 13
Tigellinus (Praetorian Prefect under
Nero) 312
Tiro (governor of Baetica) 7
Titidius Labeo (husband of Vistilia) 21
Titus (emperor) 11, 57, 240, 338–9
Titus Vinius (adviser of Galba) 12
toga praetexta 14, 28, 29
toilets: tax on urine 286
tombstones: as evidence for lifespan
44
town councillors 3, 26, 28, 34; *see
also* decurions
town crier 29
trade: in antiquarian products 33;
disapproval of small businesses 32;
drain on precious metals by
international trade 289; duties on
trade outside empire 289; economic
growth model 245–6; Indian 289;
international 288–9; map of trade
routes xiv–xv; prejudice against
petty trade 287; in Roman empire
245; senatorial participation 32
Trajan (emperor) 7, 11–12, 26,
118–19, 195, 205, 211–12, 256,
267–8, 295–6, 329–30, 347;
alimentary scheme 211; openness
of 13
transhumance: Apulia to the Abruzzi
245, 279; conflicts with locals 319;
public cattle-trails 279–80

transport: costs of 244–5, 256
travel: as procession 4; dangers of 146;
times xiv–xv
treason: informants 9
treasury: exempt from guarantees on
slaves 162; quaestors of 27; receives
confiscated property 184–5
Trebius Divus, L. (husband of Septicia
Maura) 191
tribal chiefs 3
tribunician power 11
Trimalchio 94, 148, 287–8, 293,
301
triumphal decorations 16
Tullius Cicero, M. (cos. 63 BC) 4, 56,
75, 81, 85, 121, 156, 237, 241,
289, 301
Tullius Cicero, Q. (brother of Marcus)
75, 98–9
Tuscilius Nominatus (equestrian
patron) 250
Tusculum (Italy) 98
Tutilia Supera (sister of Ampliata) 91
twins: by different fathers 59

Ulpian: 'life table' of 65
Ulpius Narcissus (tomb of, in Rome)
96
underemployment 205
undertakers: disbarred from public
office 29; *see also* Libitina
unemployment 149–50
Urbana (wife of Paternus) 94
Urbanilla (wife of Lucius) 94
Urvineius Philomusus, L. (freedman
benefactor of Praeneste) 31
usus defined 73

Valerius Etruscus, M. (soldier and
engineer) 319
Valerius Messala, M. (cos. 3 BC)
88
Varius Geminus, Q. (Paelignian
senator) 14
Vedius Pollio (wealthy freedman):
cruelty of 139; friend of Augustus
258–9
venationes see beast hunts

vernae (houseborn slaves) 144, 158, 160

Verres (governor of Sicily) 47

Vespasian (emperor) 15–16, 153, 295, 319, 338; defines difference between senators and equestrians 25; generosity of 286; reform of senate and equestrian order 25

Vetulenus Aegialus (freedman) 270

Vibius Cerinthus, Q. (patron of Vibius Crescens) 92

Vibius Crescens, Q. (freedman of Vibius Cerinthus) 92

Vicetia (North Italy) 249

vilicus (overseer) 151–2, 248, 267, 277

villa: appropriate features 188, 244, 249 *fructuaria* (storage) 188; kitchen 189; orientation 188–9; *rustica* (work quarters) 188; stables 189; *urbana* (living quarters) 188

vindicta (assertion of liberty) 196–9

vines: limits of cultivation xvi

vineyards: buying crop on vine 274; Domitian's edict 245, 275; equipment and staff 272–3; harvesting 275; investing in 32, 245, 270–5; Italy makes finest wine 270; need good stock 272; need supervision 252; rebate for lost crop 274; require quality land 272; returns in wine per acre 271–3

Vinicius Secundus, M. (husband of Procula) 91

vir clarissimus (senator) 26, 174

vir egregius (equestrian) 312

vir eminentissimus (equestrian) 27

vir splendidissimus (equestrian) 26

Vistilia (senatorial woman registered as prostitute) 21

Volcia Chreste (wife of Volcius Euhemerus) 95

Volcius Cerdo, M. (son of Volcius Euhemerus) 95

Volcius Euhemerus, M. (husband of Volcia Chreste) 95

Volusia Olympias (freedwoman) 90

Volusia Prima (freedwoman) 90

Volusii: tomb of 90; wealth of 280

Volusius Saturninus, Q. (cos. AD 92) 90

Volusius, L. (cos. 12 BC) 280

Volusius, L. (cos. AD 3): longevity 280

voting: as inequitable system 18

Vulteius Mena (auctioneer) 31

warehouses: burglary of 267; as business premises 266–7; for grain storage 266; as strongrooms 266–7; uses 245

wealth: public display of 17; as reward for public service 18; as sign of social distinction 18

wealthy: above the law 293; group solidarity of 205, 213; restore fire losses 213

weapons: dedication of 15

wedding hymns 104

weights 359

wet-nurses 158, 218

widows 66, 89, 100–1, 107, 122, 124, 128, 130, 288; supported by Church 229

will-hunting (*captatio*) 105–7

wills: as final judgement 293; intestate inheritance 183; legal concerns 293; mention of emperor 310; as mirror of character 107; not to be opened until investigation into death 182; provision for burial 309; by scales-holder 308–9; unduteous 123, 186; used for spite 311

wine: imports into Italy 275; *see also* vineyards

wives: accompanying governors 88; appropriate behaviour and dress 12, 52, 92, 110

women: in business 132, 308; of consular status 20; as host for embryo 161; insults to 315; menstruation 165; as patrons 20, 27; rights of 6; status derived from husbands 20